THE REIGN OF GOD

"How beautiful upon the mountains are the feet of him . . .
who says to Zion, 'Your God reigns'" (Isa 52:7).

THE REIGN OF GOD

AN INTRODUCTION TO CHRISTIAN THEOLOGY
FROM A SEVENTH-DAY ADVENTIST PERSPECTIVE

BY RICHARD RICE

ANDREWS UNIVERSITY PRESS, BERRIEN SPRINGS, MICHIGAN

Andrews University Press
Berrien Springs, MI 49104

© 1985 by Andrews University Press
All rights reserved. Published August 1985
Printed in the United States of America

92 91 90 89 88 87 86 85   9 8 7 6 5 4 3 2 1

ISBN 0-943872-90-1
Library of Congress catalog card number 85-70344

For my children,
Alison and Jonathan

ABOUT
THE AUTHOR

Richard Rice is Professor of Theology at Loma Linda University, Loma Linda and Riverside, California. He holds a Master of Divinity from the Seventh-day Adventist Theological Seminary at Andrews University, and an M.A. and Ph.D. in Christian Theology from the University of Chicago Divinity School. He has served in pastoral work and has taught religion on the college level for the past eleven years.

Among Dr. Rice's published writings are two other books, *The Openness of God: The Relationship of Divine Foreknowledge and Human Free Will* (Washington, D.C.: Review and Herald Publishing Association, 1980), and *When Bad Things Happen to God's People* (Boise, Idaho: Pacific Press Publishing Association, 1985). He has also contributed articles and book reviews to both scholarly and Seventh-day Adventist journals, including the *Journal of Religion, Religious Studies Review, Andrews University Seminary Studies, Ministry, Insight,* and *Spectrum.*

CONTENTS

3 / THE DOCTRINE OF GOD: BASIC CONSIDERATIONS / 47

4 / THE DOCTRINE OF GOD: A CONSTRUCTIVE PROPOSAL / 67

5 / THE DOCTRINE OF MAN: ESSENTIAL HUMANITY / 96

6 / THE DOCTRINE OF MAN: THE HUMAN CONDITION / 123

7 / THE DOCTRINE OF CHRIST: WHO JESUS WAS / 142

8 / THE DOCTRINE OF CHRIST: WHAT JESUS DID / 165

9 / THE NATURE AND PURPOSE OF THE CHRISTIAN CHURCH / 181

10 / THE MISSION OF THE CHRISTIAN CHURCH / 209

**11 / MEMBERS OF THE CHRISTIAN CHURCH:
THEIR SPIRITUAL STATUS / 237**

**12 / MEMBERS OF THE CHRISTIAN CHURCH:
THEIR WAY OF LIFE / 259**

13 / THE MEANING OF CHRISTIAN WORSHIP / 288

**14 / THE DOCTRINE OF LAST THINGS:
THE ROOTS OF ADVENTIST ESCHATOLOGY / 310**

15 / THE DOCTRINE OF LAST THINGS: THE CONTENT AND MEANING OF HUMAN DESTINY / 329

16 / THE DOCTRINE OF THE SABBATH / 354

INDEX OF BIBLICAL REFERENCES / 382

INDEX OF PERSONS / 397

INDEX OF SUBJECTS / 401

PREFACE

This book, like many others, arises from the needs of the classroom. For the past ten years I have taught courses at Loma Linda University in the areas of Christian theology and Seventh-day Adventist beliefs. One thing this task calls for is a college-level discussion of the major doctrines of the church along with the distinctive concerns of Seventh-day Adventists. I have found nothing that quite meets this need.

There are various surveys of Adventist doctrine, but most of them are written on a rather elementary level and rely heavily on a proof-text approach. In addition, of course, there are many introductions to Christian theology, but their usefulness is limited by the omission of many topics of vital interest to Seventh-day Adventists. In recent years, Adventist theologians have produced a number of stimulating works, but most of them deal with one or two aspects of Christian faith, and in general they are less interested in reviewing traditional positions than in urging our thought to take new directions.

The present work is an attempt to provide, in one volume, an introduction to the major Christian doctrines that includes the distinctive concerns of Seventh-day Adventists. It has four major objectives.

The first is a degree of comprehensiveness. "In constructing a ship or a philosophy," Bernard Lonergan remarks, "one has to go the whole way."[1] The same is true of theology. Any significant doctrinal position reaches far beyond itself. We can understand the Christian faith only by taking into account all its facets. This work is not a full-fledged theological system, but it seeks to explore enough of what

1. Bernard Lonergan, *Insight: A Study of Human Understanding* (3d ed.; New York: Philosophical Library, 1970), p. xiii.

Christians believe to communicate a reliable sense of what the faith is all about.

This is particularly important at the present time. For various reasons, Seventh-day Adventists have lately become acutely aware of the doctrinal concerns that distinguish them from other religious groups.[2] Among some, there is a tendency to think of these Adventist distinctives as the most important of our beliefs, if not the only reason for our existence. The distinctive beliefs of Adventism deserve the most serious consideration, of course, but we need to view them within the larger framework of Christian thought. This is not just to prevent us from exaggerating their importance. The fact is that their full significance emerges only when they are related to other aspects of Christian faith.

This brings us to the second objective of this work. It intends to be an exercise in theology. As the first chapter explains more fully, this involves more than just describing various beliefs. It involves reflecting carefully on the meaning of these beliefs. It means looking for their connections with each other. And most basically, it means providing reasons for our conclusions. This often leads to a discussion of different positions and sometimes requires us to take one side or the other of a disputed question. This book seeks to encourage students to begin a careful consideration of their own religious beliefs, so they will be thinkers in their own right and not mere reflectors of others' thoughts.

Because this work is directed to general students, not necessarily those majoring in religious studies, I have tried to make it readable and understandable. Its sentences are short. It eliminates technical terminology as much as possible and attempts to explain unfamiliar terms when their use is unavoidable.

Finally, this work is also traditional in its approach. It proceeds on the conservative assumption that the Bible is the inspired Word of God and provides us with reliable knowledge in matters of ultimate importance. It seeks to present the various elements of a biblical faith in an organized and integrated way. And it follows the standard outline of traditional works in systematic theology.

The present approach is further defined by several limitations, and it will be helpful to describe them here. For one thing, this work

2. One reason may be the insistence by a prominent critic of Adventism that Seventh-day Adventists must give up their distinctive beliefs in order to become fully Christian. See Robert D. Brinsmead, *Judged by the Gospel: A Review of Adventism* (Fallbrook, Calif.: Verdict Publiations, 1980), for a brief reaction to this proposal, see my review of Brinsmead's book, "Evangelical Essentials and Adventist Distinctives" (*Spectrum,* vol. 13, no. 1, pp. 55–57).

does not, strictly speaking, qualify as contemporary theology, for it does not address some of the most important issues confronting Christian faith today. A truly contemporary theology, for example, must take into account the results of critical biblical scholarship. In the thinking of many people, it is no longer possible to regard the Bible as a uniform sourcebook for religious belief. The differences, contrasts, and tensions among its various parts must be reckoned with, along with questions about its historical backgrounds. Theology must also address the secular world view of Western culture. One can no longer simply assume the reality of God, or the religious interpretation of human existence. Such convictions must be argued for today. Third, Christian theology cannot ignore the religious pluralism in which we live. Our society is no longer overwhelmingly Christian. Other faiths are gaining adherents, and their claims deserve careful consideration.

Even though it sets aside these important issues, the present work may be valuable in the contemporary context, nonetheless. Surely the first step toward meeting the challenges of the day is to have a clear understanding of one's own beliefs. My hope is that this book may contribute to that end.

The subtitle of this volume requires some explanation. "An Introduction to Christian Theology from a Seventh-day Adventist Perspective" may suggest a thoroughgoing interpretation of Christian faith in light of a distinctive Seventh-day Adventist theme. Such a project would be of immense value, I believe, not only to Seventh-day Adventists as they attempt to understand and appropriate their religious heritage, but also to other people as an introduction to the essence of Seventh-day Adventist life and thought.

The present work may provide the basis for a constructive effort of this nature at some future time, but its specific objective is less ambitious. It is primarily an introduction to theology for Seventh-day Adventists. It incorporates a discussion of distinctive Seventh-day Adventist concerns within a review of major Christian doctrines, and its primary emphasis is on the great truths that Seventh-day Adventists share with other members of the Christian community.

This discussion is introductory in another sense as well. It takes as its guiding theme "the reign of God," for reasons described in the first chapter. In a more rigorously systematic work, such a theme would dominate the discussion of each topic. Conceivably, it could alter the traditional sequence of doctrinal discussion, or even modify its contents. As a major biblical theme, "the reign of God" certainly has that potential. In the following chapters, however, it serves more as a leitmotiv, or a familiar reference point. As our discussion moves through the major doctrines of the Christian faith, this theme provides us with a means of focusing and integrating our reflections, but it remains clearly subordinate to the various doctrines we examine, rather than the other way around.

An important question that arises in connection with works of this type is the relation between theological reflection and the study of the Bible. Seventh-day Adventists are clearly committed to the Bible as the authoritative source of religious truth. They have always insisted that their beliefs are based directly on the Scriptures, rather than on human reason or ecclesiastical tradition. Among Christians in general, Adventists are widely regarded as careful students of the Bible, and the denomination's scholars have contributed more to the field of biblical studies than to any other area of religious scholarship. So it is understandable that Adventists should regard this question with particular concern.

Chapter 1 deals at some length with the nature and purpose of Christian theology, but it may be helpful to emphasize here that Christian theologians have never intended their work to eclipse the authority of the Bible for the church. Nor do they regard the study of theological writings as a substitute for the direct study of the Scriptures. On the positive side, theology relates to the Bible in several different ways.

Theology may be described as subsequent to the study of the Bible. One may wonder just how the various themes of Scripture are best related to each other. Or, after a careful analysis of the biblical passages bearing on a certain topic, the question may remain as to what the specific meaning of the Bible is for us, or how it applies to our situation. Such questions arising from the study of Scripture are theological in nature.

It is also possible to view theology as introductory to the study of the Bible. This is how many theologians regard their work. John Calvin, for example, described his greatest writing, *Institutes of the Christian Religion,* as a summary of the basic teachings of Christian faith. He intended it to prepare students for the more advanced task of investigating the Scriptures directly.[3]

---

3. "It has been my purpose in this labor to prepare and instruct candidates in sacred theology for the reading of the divine Word, in order that they may be able both to have easy access to it and to advance in it without stumbling" ("John Calvin to the Reader," 1559, *Institutes of the Christian Religion,* ed. John T. McNeill, trans. Ford Lewis Battles [Philadelphia: The Westminster Press, 1960], p. 4). "Although Holy Scripture contains a perfect doctrine, to which one can add nothing, since in it our Lord has meant to display the infinite treasures of his wisdom, yet a person who has not much practice in it has good reason for some guidance and direction, to know what he ought

Perhaps theological reflection is best understood as an aspect of Bible study itself. In its quest for logical arrangement and present significance of biblical themes, theology is an integral part of the Christian community's attempt to understand and respond appropriately to the Word of God.

At any rate, it should be clear that reading a book like this is by no means a substitute for the direct study of the Bible itself, nor should any other source replace the authority of God's Word. Ideally, works like this will motivate their readers to examine the Bible for themselves with increased interest and intensity.

Another point that deserves mention here is the personal nature of theological work. Although, as I argue in chapter 1, theology seeks to express the faith of a religious community, rather than someone's private opinions, it inevitably reflects the viewpoint of its author. To some, this appears to be the universal weakness of theology: it never seems to break out of the author's intellectual cocoon. From another perspective, however, this personal quality is something positive.

Just as one person's statement of faith may encourage others to formulate theirs, one theological proposal may promote the development of others. Perhaps this volume will stimulate other attempts to interpret the beliefs of the Seventh-day Adventist Church. At its best, theology is a conversation, not a soliloquy. The personal nature of theology also prevents any one work from acquiring "authoritative" status. One individual's reflections are never entirely adequate. The church needs a variety of interpretations to display the rich texture of its faith.

Because this book is intended for classroom use, each chapter concludes with several items designed to help the reader master its content and give further study to the topics covered. Students will find the "questions for review" helpful in preparing for quizzes and tests. The "questions for discussion" may provide the basis for personal reflection, classroom discussion, or even written assignments. The various "suggestions for Bible study" present ways of involving the reader directly in examining passages of Scripture related to the topics of the chapter. They too may generate classroom discussions or written assignments.

In all likelihood, the "suggestions for further reading" will interest primarily the teacher and the advanced or highly motivated student.

---

to look for in it, in order not to wander hither and thither, but to hold to a sure path, that he may always be pressing toward the end to which the Holy Spirit calls him" ("Subject Matter of the Present Work," from the French Edition of 1560, *Institutes of the Christian Religion* [Philadelphia: The Westminster Press, 1960], p. 6).

The selections from Adventist writers seek to give a representative account of how members of the Seventh-day Adventist Church have dealt with the topics of the chapter. The various selections by writers outside the Seventh-day Adventist community should give the beginning student a general idea of the concerns of other Christian thinkers and the more advanced student a place to begin further theological investigation.

Unless otherwise indicated, all biblical quotations are from the Revised Standard Version (Old Testament section, © 1952, New Testament section, © 1946, 1971). There are few direct references to the writings of Ellen G. White, but the influence of her thought will be evident throughout the discussion.

Even modest efforts like this place one in debt to others. I want to express my appreciation to my colleagues at Loma Linda University, especially in the Division of Religion, for freeing me from classroom responsibilities during the latter part of 1982. Their cooperation enabled me to put this material in writing. A faculty research grant in 1983 from the College of Arts and Sciences, Loma Linda University, made it possible to have the manuscript reviewed by a number of different readers.

For their careful analysis of the manuscript and many helpful suggestions, I am indebted to Dalton Baldwin, Roy Branson, Barry Casey, Richard Coffen, Steve Daily, Norman Gulley, Fritz Guy, Jack Provonsha, and Charles Scriven. None of them, of course, bears responsibility for any of its shortcomings. I owe special thanks to Helen F. Little, Emeritus Professor of English, Loma Linda University. She read the manuscript with great care and suggested numerous stylistic improvements. I want to thank George Knight, of Andrews University, for his ideas about the study aids that accompany the chapters. And I must thank the staff of Andrews University Press—Robert E. Firth, Director, for his encouragement and for his extensive efforts in seeing this project to completion, and Sue Schwab, his assistant, for her long hours of work editing the manuscript and reducing it to printed form, her many suggestions for its improvement, and her unfailing graciousness in accepting changes and additions to the text. I am also grateful to Karen Knutsen for typing much of the material that concludes each chapter and for faithfully checking the biblical references throughout, and I appreciate the last-minute help of Alexander Lian and Stephan Mitchell in preparing the indexes.

Finally, I am grateful for the contributions that family, friends, former teachers, and students have made to my thinking in ways far too numerous and diffuse to detail here. I dedicate this book to my children, who have taught me a great deal of theology.

ABBREVIATIONS

OLD TESTAMENT

Genesis	Gen	Ecclesiastes	Ecc
Exodus	Ex	Song of Solomon	Sg
Leviticus	Lev	Isaiah	Isa
Numbers	Num	Jeremiah	Jer
Deuteronomy	Dt	Lamentations	Lam
Joshua	Josh	Ezekiel	Ezek
Judges	Jdg	Daniel	Dan
Ruth	Ru	Hosea	Hos
1 Samuel	1 Sam	Joel	Jl
2 Samuel	2 Sam	Amos	Am
1 Kings	1 Kgs	Obadiah	Ob
2 Kings	2 Kgs	Jonah	Jon
1 Chronicles	1 Chr	Micah	Mic
2 Chronicles	2 Chr	Nahum	Na
Ezra	Ezr	Habakkuk	Hab
Nehemiah	Neh	Zephaniah	Zep
Esther	Est	Haggai	Hag
Job	Jb	Zechariah	Zec
Psalms	Ps	Malachi	Mal
Proverbs	Prov		

NEW TESTAMENT

Matthew	Mt	1 Timothy	1 Tim
Mark	Mk	2 Timothy	2 Tim
Luke	Lk	Titus	Ti
John	Jn	Philemon	Phlm
Acts	Ac	Hebrews	Heb
Romans	Rom	James	Jas
1 Corinthians	1 Cor	1 Peter	1 Pet
2 Corinthians	2 Cor	2 Peter	2 Pet
Galatians	Gal	1 John	1 Jn
Ephesians	Eph	2 John	2 Jn
Philippians	Phil	3 John	3 Jn
Colossians	Col	Jude	Jude
1 Thessalonians	1 Thess	Revelation	Rev
2 Thessalonians	2 Thess		

1

THE TASK
OF CHRISTIAN THEOLOGY

**Biblical
basis**

"You shall love the Lord your God . . . with all your mind" (Matthew
22:37).

"I want them . . . to come to the full wealth of conviction which
understanding brings" (Colossians 2:2, NEB).

"Always be prepared to make a defense to anyone who calls you to
account for the hope that is in you" (1 Peter 3:15).

Deuteronomy 32:2	Ephesians 3:14–19
Psalm 1:1–2	Ephesians 4:13–14
Psalm 19:7–10	1 Timothy 4:6
Matthew 28:19–20	Titus 2:1
John 7:16–17	Hebrews 5:11–6:2
John 8:31–32	Hebrews 13:9
Acts 2:42	2 Peter 1:5–7
Romans 10:14–15	2 John 9
Romans 16:17	

THE IMPORTANCE OF THEOLOGY

The most important thing about a religious community is what it believes. This is not the only thing that matters, of course. The way it worships and the kind of life it leads are important, too. But what it believes
is basic to everything else. This is particularly true of Christianity.

This book is an introduction to Christian beliefs from a Seventh-day Adventist perspective. It seeks to express the faith of the Seventh-day Adventist church. Since this is an exercise in theology, it will be helpful to begin by explaining what theology is and why it is important.

The meaning of "theology"

The Greek roots for "theology" are *theos,* meaning "God," and *logos,* meaning "speech" or "word," among other things. Literally, then, theology is "God-talk," or "language about God." Any use of the word "God," or any reference to divine beings, would then qualify as theology. But "theology" usually has a more specific meaning.

In one sense, "theology" refers to the beliefs of a religious community. We use the word in this way when we speak of "Roman Catholic theology," or "Protestant theology," or perhaps of "Jewish theology" or "Buddhist theology." We may use the expression "Seventh-day Adventist theology," therefore, to designate the beliefs of this particular religious group.

In another sense, "theology" refers to the activity of reflecting on our religious beliefs. Broadly speaking, we all do theology when we think or talk about what we believe. More specifically, theology is the activity in which we examine our religious beliefs and seek to express them in a clear and logical way.

As used in the subtitle of this book the word "theology" incorporates both senses of the term, because the purpose of the book is twofold. It summarizes what Seventh-day Adventists believe, and it also attempts to examine these beliefs in a careful and methodical way.

Objections to theology

Many people have a negative attitude toward religious beliefs, or "doctrines," as they are often called, so they approach the study of theology with misgivings. One reason for this suspicion is the widespread conviction that religion is largely a matter of practice rather than belief. In the view of some, what's really important is how you live. What you think is strictly secondary.

Other people object to theology on the grounds that religion is primarily emotional in nature. They find that intellectual activity often fails to produce the kind of feelings they are looking for. In fact, sometimes it interferes with those feelings.

Theology and religious experience

It is true that behavior and emotions are part of religious experience. Religion includes ethical and affective dimensions, we might say. But it also includes a cognitive dimension; it involves believing something. This is why theology is important: it gives these beliefs a careful examination.

It is clear from the history of Christianity that beliefs are central to the life of the church. Its earliest advocates, the apostles, presented Christianity by making certain claims about Jesus and arguing for their truth. In his sermon on the day of Pentecost, for example—the first Christian sermon ever preached—Peter asserted that Jesus was the Messiah. He appealed to his resurrection from the dead to prove it (Ac 2:14–36). So from the beginning, being a Christian involved believing that certain things were true.

Beliefs are not only essential to Christianity; they are also closely related to the other dimensions of religious experience just referred to. Seventh-day Adventists are probably best known by the general public for some of their distinctive practices. Many people identify Adventists by the things they don't do, such as their abstinence from tobacco and alcoholic drinks. Sometimes Adventists are remembered for sabbath observance, or for their medical or educational work. But whatever the distinctive practice is, behind it lies some specific religious belief, or doctrine. The commitment to healthful living, for example, arises from the belief that our physical condition affects our spiritual condition. This belief follows from the Adventist doctrine of human being, with its view of man as a physical, mental, and spiritual unity. What we believe, therefore, determines to a large extent how we live. Our doctrines affect our practice.

Turning to the other aspect of religious experience mentioned above, we find a similar relationship to belief. We identified this aspect as "emotional" or "affective." A better word might be "relational." It involves a person's attitude toward God and his perception of God's attitude toward him.

This dimension of experience will have an important influence on belief. On an individual level your experience of God will affect your beliefs about him. If God seems especially close to you during difficult circumstances, then you will find it natural to believe that he is loving and compassionate. On the other hand, if you feel utterly alone when you need help, then you may find it difficult to attribute these qualities to God.

On the corporate, or community, level, this relation between belief and experience is even more significant. The doctrines of the church express the experience of its members on the grand scale. This was certainly true of the earliest Christians. The claims they made for Jesus expressed the impact his life had made on them. Their doctrines expressed their experience. Similarly, the great doctrines of Christianity are those which express the experience of believers in every age.

This interchange between doctrines and experience flows in the other direction, too. Doctrines not only express experience, they also influence and shape it. To a great extent, what you believe about God will determine the quality of your relationship to him. An inadequate doctrine of God will have a negative effect on your experience of him. If you have always thought of God as a stern judge, preoccupied with your mistakes, then you will find it difficult to love and trust him.

Happily, the converse is true as well. Good doctrine can have a positive effect on religious experience. A friend of mine once said that she had the happiest sabbath of her life shortly after she studied the meaning of the sabbath in one of her religion classes. A more adequate doctrine of the sabath made possible a richer sabbath experience. So religious beliefs and religious experience are closely related.

FAITH AND REASON

Theology involves the application of reason to the contents of faith. Therefore, we need to examine the relationship between faith and reason, too.

Faith and reason in tension

Many people feel that faith, in the sense of personal trust in God, and reason, or serious intellectual activity, stand in conflict with each other. They fear that the close application of reason to our religious beliefs will weaken our convictions, so they are suspicious of theology.

We can illustrate this view of faith and reason with the graph below. Here faith and reason stand at opposite ends of a line, in tension with each other. And, as mathematicians would say, they are "inversely proportional." That is, the more you have of one quality, the less you have of the other. As the diagram shows, the closer you come to one end of the line, the farther you move from the other. According to this view, the best religious experience is one in which there is a good deal of faith, and consequently very little intellectual activity.

FAITH————————————————REASON

This view of faith and reason forces us to make a choice between the two. We have to decide between trusting in God and thinking carefully about our beliefs, because we cannot do both effectively. But we have just seen that understanding plays a very important role in religious experience. We observed that inadequate doctrine has a negative effect on religious experience, while good doctrine has a positive effect. So we cannot accept the idea that faith and reason are opposed to each other. We must find another way of expressing their relationship.

Faith and reason in balance

Let's exchange the line graph for one that's a bit more complicated. Instead of placing faith and reason at opposite ends of a single line, make them the coordinates of a graph like the ones we study in algebra. Let's put "faith" at the side of the graph and "reason" along the bottom, like this:

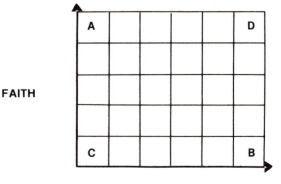

FAITH

REASON

With this graph, we can describe a number of ways in which faith and reason may be related in a person's life. It *is* possible to have a great deal of faith and relatively little understanding (Position A). This is typically the case in the early stages of religious experience. Just as a young child has great affection for its parents, although it understands very little about them, a person may have enormous confidence in God even though he knows relatively little about God.

On the other hand, a person can know a great deal about God and not have much of a relationship with him (Position B). Someone with a Ph.D. in nutrition may have poor eating habits. An avid sports fan may be in terrible physical condition. Similarly, someone could know a great deal about the Bible, theology, and church history, and still have very little trust in God. Knowledge alone certainly doesn't guarantee faith.

As this graph illustrates, the options are not limited to faith without reason, or reason without faith, or to some unattractive compromise between them, like Position C, where a person has very little of either faith or understanding. Ideally, a person's experience should be somewhere in the vicinity of Position D, where both faith and reason abound.

In a healthy religious experience, faith and reason complement, rather than compete with, each other, just as knowledge and affection reinforce each other in important human relationships. People in love naturally want to find out more about each other—where they grew up, what they like to eat, and so on. If the relationship has real possibilities, the more they learn, the stronger their feelings for each other grow.

In a similar way, someone who trusts God will want to keep learning about him. And the more he learns, the more his trust and love for God will grow. In one of his letters, Paul expresses the desire for his readers to "come to the full wealth of conviction which understanding brings" (Col 2:2, NEB). Serious intellectual activity has an important role to play in religious experience. Good theology will strengthen our confidence in God.

Solving theological problems

But haven't people lost their faith as a result of asking questions about it? Isn't there a danger in thinking too much about religion? Won't you kill a religious experience by over-analyzing it?

It is true that there is a risk in thinking carefully about what you believe. Doing so, people occasionally discover that what they always believed lacks adequate evidence or no longer makes sense. There is no guarantee that our ideas will never change if we think about them carefully.

The solution, however, is not to avoid thinking, nor to give up as soon as we run into difficulties. The solution is to keep on thinking, to work our way through the problems that arise. Typically, people who become disillusioned when they examine their faith have not thought enough about it. The proper response to theological difficulties is more theology. We cannot eliminate problems by ignoring them, by pretending they do not exist. Careful reflection will help us to answer many of our questions.

Furthermore, if it is risky to think about what you believe, not to do so can be fatal. It is not only that an unexamined faith is not worth having, to paraphrase Socrates' famous maxim. An unexamined faith can be downright dangerous. It can give us a false sense of security, and it can lead us to be intolerant of people whose views differ from ours.

Although careful thinking can help to solve many of our questions, it is unlikely to answer all of them. In the event that certain questions persist, it is helpful to remember this. In the final analysis, our faith is not in a doctrine, but in a Person. It is Christ who saves, not our understanding of him. In the last letter he wrote, Paul declared to Timothy, "I know whom I have believed" (2 Tim 1:12). The great apostle never claimed that his behavior was perfect (cf. Phil 3:12), nor that his knowledge was perfect (cf. 1 Cor 13:9). He wasn't looking to these things for salvation. He was looking to Christ. With our confidence firmly rooted in Jesus, we can face the questions that arise in our attempt to understand what he has done for us, without being afraid that they will unsettle our faith.

We have examined the general importance of intellectual activity for religious experience. Now we need to take a closer look at the theological task itself.

THE NATURE AND PURPOSE OF THEOLOGY

During the centuries of Christian history, people have described theology in many different ways. One of the happiest definitions is that of Anselm, the eleventh-century bishop of Canterbury. He identified theology as "faith seeking understanding."[1] In his view, theology is a Christian's attempt to make sense out of what he believes. This fits nicely with what we have said about the relation of theology and religious experience.

We could list other definitions of theology, or formulate one ourselves and then comment on its parts. Instead, let us work toward a definition by considering some of the essential characteristics of the enterprise.

Theology is biblical

Without question, the most important feature of theology is its biblical character. Christians universally associate the Bible with divine revelation. Some regard it primarily as a source of supernaturally imparted information, others as an expression of authentic human existence. But however the Bible is viewed, Christians accept it as authoritative. The basic purpose of theology is to express the

1. "For I do not seek to understand that I may believe, but I believe in order to understand. For this also I believe,—that unless I believed, I should not understand" (Anselm, *St. Anselm: Basic Writings,* trans. S. N. Deane [2d ed.; LaSalle, Ill.: Open Court Publishing Company, 1966], p. 7).

contents, or the message, of the Bible reliably. Faithfulness to the Scriptures is the most important criterion for evaluating any theological work. The mere intention to be faithful to the Bible, of course, does not guarantee that a theologian's work will be. But the intention is indispensable nonetheless.

Theology is rational

A second feature of theology is its attempt to be rational, or intelligible. Theology seeks to make sense of what the Bible says. This is not a departure from its biblical character, although people sometimes think so. It is really an extension, or a corollary, of it. As expressed in Scripture, the message of salvation is addressed to the whole person, the mind as well as the heart. From the beginning, Christians have maintained that there are good reasons for believing the gospel. So in accepting the authority of the Bible, theology presupposes that the Bible makes sense.

As it seeks to express the message of the Bible, theology searches for the most adequate concepts available. It strives for clarity and coherence; it seeks to avoid confusion and contradiction.

Theology is historical

Good theology must also be historically sensitive. We are fortunate—in fact, we are blessed—to have ready access to the Bible. It must always be the principal source of our religious knowledge. But our understanding of the Bible is shaped by long centuries of biblical interpretation, whether we realize it or not. Just think, for example, of the way the Protestant Reformation has influenced the interpretation of Paul's writings. This isn't something negative. To the contrary, we can learn a lot from previous attempts to understand the Bible. It would be foolish to ignore the help they can give. At the same time, we must be critical of views that depart from the Bible. We can never be content to accept something simply because it has a long tradition behind it.

Theology is contemporary

As an outgrowth of its historical character, good theology is also contemporary. This means, first of all, that it arises out of the present experience of the Christian community. Every generation faces the task of theology anew, because its experience is unique in certain ways.

The notion of ''present truth'' played an important role in the thinking of early Adventists. They accepted much of what earlier Christians believed. But they emphasized other doctrines, such as the sabbath, because they were convinced that God was uniquely active in their experience and that they had something new and important to share.

Accordingly, good theology is creative and constructive. It brings to the task of interpreting the biblical message the conviction that our present experience may enable us to see things that have never been as fully appreciated before.

Because the faith of a religious community is dynamic, the work of theology is never completed. The 1980 statement of Seventh-day Adventist beliefs includes this important sentence: "Revision of these statements may be expected at a General Conference session when the church is led by the Holy Spirit to a fuller understanding of Bible truths or finds better language in which to express the teachings of God's Holy Word."[2]

Truth doesn't change, but our perception of it does. So does the situation in which we are called on to express it, as we noticed above. For these reasons, the work of theology is never done once and for all.

Problems with creeds

This is one reason why Seventh-day Adventists have always avoided the formulation of a creed to express their beliefs. On a purely linguistic level, a "creed" is simply a statement of beliefs. Historically, creeds were intended simply to summarize the teachings of the Bible. But the word "creed" has certain connotations which have made Adventists wary.

One is finality. Once a creed is formulated, people tend to regard it as definitive. They become reluctant to consider revising it. Another is comprehensiveness. For people in certain religious groups, the official creed states all that is worth discussing. If a topic isn't mentioned in the creed, they are unwilling to give it any consideration. A third connotation of the word "creed" is authority. People often hold certain things to be true simply because they are formally stated in a creed, not because they have examined the issues for themselves.

This brings us to some other reasons why Seventh-day Adventists have avoided developing a creed. They insist that nothing replace the Bible as the supreme authority in the church. "The Bible is our creed," early Adventists were fond of saying. They believed that every person should examine for himself what the Bible teaches.

Theology must be contemporary because the challenges it faces are new in every age. The problems confronting the church today are not the same as the ones it met before. Theology must speak to these problems, if the Christian message is to be heard.

This means that Christians must be willing to revise their terminology in order for their message to be understood. The task of theology

2. "Fundamental Beliefs of Seventh-day Adventists," *Seventh-day Adventist Yearbook 1984* (Hagerstown, Md.: Review and Herald Publishing Association, 1984), p. 5.

is to communicate the gospel, and communication requires translation, not mere repetition. As Francis Schaeffer says, "You have to preach the simple gospel so that it is simple to the person to whom you are talking, or it is no longer simple."[3] This is why we have sermons as well as Scripture reading in our worship services. We need to hear the Word, to be sure, but we also need to hear the Word interpreted for us by someone who is familiar with our spiritual needs.

Theology is for the church

From what we have just said, it is apparent that theology is the task of the whole church, not merely of the individual Christian, theologically trained or otherwise. Theology attempts to express the faith of a religious community. It speaks out of the experience of the community and it intends to enrich the life of the community.

As an exercise in Seventh-day Adventist theology, this book seeks to express the faith of the Seventh-day Adventist church. I hope that any Adventist reader would recognize it as a statement of his or her own faith. At the same time, it is not just a summary of traditional Adventist doctrines. It contains occasional suggestions for rethinking our beliefs in ways that may enrich our corporate experience, recover overlooked biblical themes, and increase the effectiveness of our witness to the world.

Theology is systematic

Finally, good theology is systematic. In fact, the discipline as a whole is often called "systematic theology." It seeks to organize the various Christian doctrines in a logical way, so the discussion of one topic leads naturally to the consideration of the next.

There is a traditional sequence of doctrines that appears in theological works. Most systematic theologies either follow it or explain why they don't. Here is a brief outline of this scheme:

1. Doctrine of Revelation
2. Doctrine of God (Theology)
3. Doctrine of Man (Anthropology)
4. Doctrine of Salvation (Soteriology)
5. Doctrine of the Church (Ecclesiology)
6. Doctrine of Last Things (Eschatology)

Along with a traditional arrangement of the central Christian doctrines, theology also has its own terminology. The words in parentheses above are some of the most common theological terms. Most of them come from Greek roots, such as *eschatos,* meaning "last,"

3. Francis A. Schaeffer, *He Is There and He Is Not Silent* (Wheaton, Ill.: Tyndale House Publishers, 1972), p. 11.

and *ekklēsia,* meaning "church." Since the doctrinal discussions in this book follow this general outline, it will be helpful for you to be familiar with it as we proceed.

The systematic character of theology involves more than arranging the different Christian doctrines. Theology also seeks to show how the different aspects of Christian faith are related to each other. Everything we believe has an influence on everything else we believe. What a person thinks about God, for example, will affect his view of the end of history, and vice versa.

The interrelation of Christian doctrine

The different Christian doctrines are not like building blocks, having exactly the same size and shape, capable of any sort of arrangement. They are more like the pieces of a puzzle. They fit together one way better than another, and it is only in relation to the others that the value of each piece emerges. This analogy breaks down, however, because the pieces of a puzzle have only one way of going together, and there is no one pattern to which Christian theology conforms. At least, no theologian claims to have found the perfect pattern yet.

As it interrelates the different Christian doctrines, theology also shows the relative importance of each aspect of faith. All the doctrines are important, and each of them has an effect on the others, but they are not of equal importance. Certain beliefs are absolutely central to faith. There would be no Christian experience if they were absent. Other beliefs are peripheral; they are not quite so important. This does not mean that they are inconsequential, or that our experience would be just the same without them. But their importance is derivative, rather than fundamental.

Take the doctrine of God, for example. Belief in God is clearly basic to Christian experience. Remove it, as certain people suggested several years ago, and Christianity drastically changes. In contrast, consider something like infant dedication. For many Christians the practice is very important. It has theological and psychological significance. But it is not central to Christianity. People can, and do, disagree as to what it means and whether it should be observed, while still regarding each other as Christians. So here we have a practice that is "Christian," but not a fundamental aspect of our faith.

There are two pitfalls we need to avoid. Either does violence to the nature of Christian faith and leads to theological distortion. One is to insist that each item of belief is just as important as every other. The second is to maintain that anything not absolutely central to faith is inconsequential, and we might as well throw it out. Strange as it may seem, these errors tend to go together.

I once heard a mother argue against a minor change in the dress code of the church school her daughter attended. She feared that it would undermine the girl's confidence in all that Christians believe. The daughter attached equal importance to everything she had been taught, her mother indicated, so if one item changed, she might easily conclude that all the others could slide away, too.

String-of-beads model for theology

We might call this a "string-of-beads" concept of doctrine for three reasons. First, just as beads in a string have the same size and shape, this view gives all the doctrines equal value. None of them is any more or less important than another. Second, each bead is essentially independent of the rest. It would be what it is regardless of the other beads around it. Similarly, in this view of theology each doctrine is an independent unit with no integral relation to other doctrines. Third, all the beads on a string could slip away just as easily as one of them could. In the same way, any doctrinal change renders all the doctrines vulnerable.

Organic model for theology

To do justice to the nature of Christian faith we need to exchange this model for one that recognizes that the doctrines are interrelated, yet some of them are more basic than others. We might call this an "organic" model of Christian doctrine. All the parts of a living organism are connected together, and each has an important role in its activities. But not every one is equally vital to its existence. A theology conceived along such lines can do justice to the true nature of the Christian faith, without either exaggerating or slighting the importance of each element.

Doctrinal summaries sometimes convey a string-of-beads concept of theology. This is true of the "Statement of Fundamental Beliefs of Seventh-day Adventists," officially voted by the General Conference in 1980. It contains a list of twenty-seven items, beginning with "The Holy Scriptures" and ending with "The New Earth." There is a certain logic to the progression of themes presented. But there is no attempt in the document itself to call attention to this progression or to show how the different ideas are related to each other. In contrast, theology takes the various beliefs of the religious community and explores their interconnection. It seeks to determine the underlying unity, as well as the complexity, of Christian faith.

In the attempt to be systematic, theology not only relates different Christian beliefs to each other. It also seeks to draw the individual beliefs together by means of a comprehensive theme, or a central idea. There may be more than a single unifying concept, and many themes and ideas may emerge along the way. But good theology—

certainly great theology—exhibits a dominant theme, or motif, that permeates its various parts. The best indication of a theologian's importance is the grandeur of the themes which characterize his or her work. The highest test of theological skill is the task of drawing the different aspects of Christian faith together to form a unity.

In view of such a formidable challenge, it is not surprising that few people have attempted theological systems in recent years. The present work reflects this reluctance. This is not a full-fledged theological system, but an "introduction" to theology. Nonetheless, because it has theological aspirations, it seeks to meet the criteria of theological work conceived on a grander scale. Before turning to the different Christian doctrines, therefore, we need to select a theme that will guide us in our work.

"THE REIGN OF GOD"

Our theme must be sufficiently comprehensive, or fundamental, to help us pull together all the major Christian doctrines. Because this is a Seventh-day Adventist theology, it should also reflect some of the distinctive concerns of the Seventh-day Adventist church. Among several ideas that could serve these purposes, I have selected the "reign of God" as the guiding theme for this introduction to Adventist thought. Several factors make this an appropriate choice.

One is the significance of this theme in the Bible. The idea of the "kingdom of God" dominated the ministry of Jesus. It was the central topic of his preaching, and his various miracles were object lessons intended to demonstrate its reality and its character. Scholars tell us that the biblical expression "kingdom of God" is more accurately translated "kingship of God," or "reign of God." It refers not so much to the territory over which God rules, as to his ruling activity itself.[4]

In the Bible

4. C. H. Dodd makes this point in his famous book, *The Parables of the Kingdom* (New York: Charles Scribner's Sons, 1961), p. 21. The precise meaning of "the kingdom of God" is a matter of ongoing scholarly debate. In contrast to Dodd's "realized eschatology," which interprets the kingdom as a present reality, others maintain that the kingdom is not only present, but future as well. According to Norman Perrin, for example, the kingdom of God as proclaimed by Jesus involves the anticipation of dramatic divine activity intervening in the course of history in the future (*The Kingdom of God in the Teaching of Jesus* [Philadelphia: The Westminster Press, 1963], p. 167). George Eldon Ladd argues for a twofold interpretation of the expression. In his article "The Kingdom of God—Reign or Realm?" Ladd analyzes several interpretations and proposes this

The theme of divine rule or lordship is equally prominent in other portions of the Bible. Israel's deliverance from Egypt and miraculous conquest of Canaan demonstrated Yahweh's supremacy over the gods worshiped by other peoples.

In church history

In the history of the church, the theme of God's reign figures prominently, too. The sovereignty of God, especially in the work of salvation, was central to the concerns of the Protestant Reformers. It is the dominant idea in John Calvin's great work, *Institutes of the Christian Religion.*

The reign of God has been of great interest to Seventh-day Adventists throughout their history. The Advent Movement originated with the expectation of Christ's soon return to establish his kingdom in the mid-nineteenth century. From their beginning, Seventh-day Adventists have found their principal reason for existing in the prophecies of Daniel and Revelation. These books describe the coming of God's reign as a cataclysmic event. The sovereignty of God establishing itself against the opposition of evil powers permeates the thought of Ellen G. White, by far the most influential of Adventist writers. Her most important book is *The Great Controversy.* It is the fifth and final volume in the "Conflict of the Ages Series," which has probably contributed more to the thinking of Seventh-day Adventists than any other source outside the Bible.

So the reign of God is a reasonable choice to guide our review of Christian doctrine from a Seventh-day Adventist perspective. To set the stage for what follows, let us summarize a few of the elements in this important concept.

How God reigns

As the Bible describes the reign of God, its most impressive feature is the quality, or content, of God's rule. The Bible affirms the unrivaled superiority of God's power. But it is more interested in the

---

answer to his question: "*Malkuth* [the Aramaic word behind "kingdom"] can be either a monarch's kingship, his reign, or it can be the realm over which he reigns. It is our thesis that both meanings are to be recognized in the teachings of Jesus, and that the primary meaning is the abstract or dynamic one, for it is God's kingly act establishing his rule in the world which brings into being the realm in which his rule is enjoyed" (*Journal of Biblical Literature* 81 [1962]:236). Ladd interprets the meaning of the phrase as Jesus used it this way: "Jesus taught that the rule of God, which would manifest itself to all men at the end of the age, was also manifesting itself in his person, mission, and message, to those who would hear and respond. Before the eschatological manifestation was a manifestation of a different sort. God, who would act at the end of history to transform history, had invaded history in the person and mission of Jesus to bring his reign and rule to men" (ibid., p. 237).

kind of person God is. It is his love and concern for his creatures, his commitment to their best interests, and his willingness to sacrifice for their well-being that dominate the biblical portrayal of the divine reality.

Because God's relations to his creatures are motivated by love, he does not establish his reign by the imposition of sheer power. His reign depends upon the willing acceptance of his subjects. The situation which God seeks—in fact, the only situation which will satisfy him—is the glad acceptance of his lordship that arises from an appreciation of his loving character. Consequently, God gives his creatures the choice of serving him or not. He allows them time to examine the alternatives and make an intelligent decision.

When God reigns

From the present situation of our world, it is apparent that the reign of God is not fully realized; its arrival still lies in the future. God is now working in the world to overcome the forces that oppose his reign and to restore human beings to his kingdom. The idea of God's reign emphasizes God's initiative in the work of human salvation.

But even though the full realization of his reign is yet to come, God is still sovereign of the world right now. This has two implications for the various structures of human authority. On the one hand, the reality of God's reign legitimizes the structures of human power. Governments ultimately derive their authority from him, and he exercises his sovereignty through them. On the other hand, however, the reign of God relativizes the significance of these same structures. They have no right to claim our ultimate allegiance. That belongs to God alone. They must be resisted when they overreach their bounds and fail to serve the interests of their people.

On another level, the reign of God reminds us that God's lordship is universal. Every aspect of life is subject to his sovereignty. This justifies the attention that Seventh-day Adventists have given over the years to such matters as physical health and religious education, and it calls us to extend the sovereignty of God into other areas as well.

The concept of God's reign effectively draws together some of the characteristic interests of Seventh-day Adventists. It encourages us to give our attention to some issues we have neglected in the past. And perhaps most important, it relates Adventist theology to some of the historic concerns of the Christian faith.

We have described the task of theology, and we have found a reference point to guide us in our study. We will begin our work by considering the doctrine of revelation.

STUDY HELPS

Questions for review

1. What meanings does the word "theology" have?

2. What is the relation between religious beliefs and religious practices and feelings?

3. How are faith and reason related in a mature religious experience?

4. What are the characteristics of good Christian theology?

5. What are the major Christian doctrines and how are they related to each other?

Questions for further study

1. How should a Christian congregation respond to someone who enjoys the social life of the church but has no interest in its doctrines?

2. What doctrinal beliefs lie behind things Seventh-day Adventists are often known for, such as a vegetarian diet, not wearing jewelry, sabbath keeping, operating a private school system, and not bearing arms in military service?

3. Under what circumstances should a denomination change its "statement of fundamental beliefs"? Who should make such a change and what steps should they follow?

4. The text suggests "the reign of God" as a theme that unifies the various beliefs of Seventh-day Adventists. What other theme(s) would serve this purpose?

5. Which are more important to Seventh-day Adventists—their distinctive beliefs, or the beliefs they hold in common with other Christian groups?

Suggestions for Bible study

1. John 3 and 4 record Jesus' conversations with Nicodemus and the Samaritan woman. Among other things, these important chapters illuminate the relation between religious ideas and personal religious experience. Read these two passages and answer the following questions: What erroneous religious ideas did these two individuals have? What effect did their inadequate theology have on their experience with God? What new ideas did Jesus suggest and how did he apply them to their experience?

2. According to the Bible, sound doctrine is important for a number of

reasons. What are some of the reasons suggested by the following passages?

1 Peter 3:15	1 Corinthians 3:1–3
Colossians 2:2	2 Timothy 2:15
Hebrews 5:12	Ephesians 4:11–14

3. According to the Bible, sound doctrine will exhibit certain characteristics. What characteristics of sound doctrine do the following passages indicate?

1 Timothy 4:1–2
Galatians 1:6–9
John 8:32

4. The preaching of the apostles gives us insight into what is central to Christian faith. What theological concepts figure prominently in the following apostolic sermons, or summaries of apostolic preaching?

Acts 2:17–36	Acts 13:16–41
Acts 3:12–26	Acts 17:22–31
Acts 4:8–12	1 Corinthians 15:1–11
Acts 10:34–43	

5. Traditionally, Seventh-day Adventists have regarded Revelation 14:6–12 as the prophetic mandate for their existence and the description of their specific mission. What themes or concerns characteristic of Seventh-day Adventism does this passage summarize?

SUGGESTIONS FOR FURTHER READING

Two standard doctrinal summaries are *Bible Readings for the Home* (rev. ed.; Washington, D.C.: Review and Herald Publishing Association, 1963), which employs a question-answer format, and T. Housel Jemison, *Christian Beliefs* (Mountain View, Calif.: Pacific Press Publishing Association, 1959), for years a textbook in college religion classes.

From Adventist writers

Recent statements of Christian faith from a Seventh-day Adventist perspective are Jack Provonsha, *God Is With Us* (Washington, D.C.: Review and Herald Publishing Association, 1974), and Charles Scriven, *The Demons Have Had It: A Theological ABC* (Nashville, Tenn.: Southern Publishing Association, 1976).

Each year, major Adventist publishing houses present a book designed to communicate the church's beliefs to a contemporary audience. Two noteworthy books to appear on this basis are William Henry Branson, *Drama of the Ages* (Washington, D.C.: Review and Herald Publishing Association, 1950), and Arthur E. Lickey, *God Speaks to Modern Man* (Washington, D.C.: Review and Herald Publishing Association, 1952).

The book *Seventh-day Adventists Answer Questions on Doctrine* (Washington, D.C.: Review and Herald Publishing Association, 1957), generally referred to simply as *Questions on Doctrine,* contains answers formulated by certain Adventist thinkers in the 1950s to questions concerning specific Adventist beliefs posed by a group of non-Adventist scholars. Some Adventists consider the positions expressed there to be controversial.

Discussions of various aspects of Seventh-day Adventist beliefs regularly appear in the following periodicals: *Adventist Review,* the general and more-or-less official paper of the Seventh-day Adventist Church; *Ministry,* the church's publication for clergy; *Signs of the Times,* the church's primary missionary or evangelistic journal; *Insight,* directed to the senior youth of the church; and *Spectrum,* published quarterly by the Association of Adventist Forums.

For further reading on the topic of faith and reason, see Richard Rice, "The Knowledge of Faith" (*Spectrum,* vol. 5, no. 2, pp. 19–32), James Londis' reply (ibid., pp. 32–37), and further discussions of the article by Larry M. Lewis, Dalton Baldwin, and Eric D. Syme (*Spectrum,* vol. 6, nos. 1, 2, 3, pp. 77–86). Herbert Douglass provides an analysis of faith in his book *Faith: Saying Yes to God* (Nashville, Tenn.: Southern Publishing Association, 1978). Edward W. H. Vick discusses the theological method and related topics in *Theological Essays* (Berrien Springs, Mich.: The Theological Seminary, Andrews University, 1965).

For Ellen G. White's views on the relation of faith and reason in general, and theological reflection in particular, see the following passages: *Steps to Christ,* pp. 105–113; *Counsels to Writers and Editors,* pp. 33–51; *Ministry of Healing,* pp. 409–466; *Testimonies for the Church,* vol. 5, pp. 580–586; *Christ's Object Lessons,* pp. 333–335.

From other writers

There are literally thousands of theological texts and treatises available, ranging from the very elementary to the highly advanced. Space permits us to list only a few relatively recent offerings.

On the elementary end of the scale are books like James W. Sire's *Beginning With God: A Basic Introduction to the Christian Faith* (Downers Grove, Ill.: Inter-Varsity Press, 1981), which developed from the author's experience teaching confirmation classes. Another readable introduction to fundamental Christian beliefs is John R. W. Stott's *Basic Christianity* (rev. ed.; Grand Rapids, Mich.: William B. Eerdmans Publishing Co., 1978).

More challenging books directed to the general reader include *The Common Catechism: A Book of Christian Faith* (New York: The Seabury Press, 1975), prepared as an ecumenical endeavor by Protestant and Roman

Catholic scholars, and Wolfhart Pannenberg's *The Apostles' Creed in the Light of Today's Questions,* trans. Margaret Kohl (Philadelphia: The Westminster Press, 1972).

Serious students will learn a great deal from one-volume works such as Dale Moody, *The Word of Truth* (Grand Rapids, Mich.: William B. Eerdmans, Publishing Co., 1981), which takes a conservative theological position, and John Macquarrie, *Principles of Christian Theology* (2d ed.; New York: Charles Scribner's Sons, 1977), written from a liberal perspective. Though old, Augustus Hopkins Strong, *Systematic Theology: A Compendium Designed for the Use of Theological Students* (Valley Forge, Pa.: The Judson Press, 1907), contains a wealth of material.

On a larger scale, the three volumes of Emil Brunner's "Dogmatics," *The Christian Doctrine of God,* trans. Olive Wyon; *The Christian Doctrine of Creation and Redemption,* trans. David Cairns; and *The Christian Doctrine of the Church, Faith and the Consummation,* trans. David Cairns (Philadelphia: The Westminster Press, 1974–1982), are richly rewarding. A recent evangelical effort is also noteworthy, namely, Donald G. Bloesch, *Essentials of Evangelical Theology* (2 vols.; New York: Harper & Row, Publishers, 1978–1979).

Specialists will appreciate works such as Karl Barth's massive *Church Dogmatics,* ed. G. W. Bromiley and T. F. Torrance (4 vols.; Edinburgh: T. & T. Clark, 1936–1977); Paul Tillich, *Systematic Theology* (3 vols.; Chicago: University of Chicago Press, 1951–1963); and Roman Catholic theologian Karl Rahner, *Foundations of Christian Faith: An Introduction to the Idea of Christianity,* trans. William V. Dych (New York: The Seabury Press, 1978).

2

THE DOCTRINE
OF REVELATION

**Biblical
basis**

"Man does not live on bread alone but on every word that proceeds from the mouth of the Lord" (Deuteronomy 8:3, NIV).

"All scripture is inspired by God and profitable for teaching, for reproof, for correction, and for training in righteousness, that the man of God may be complete, equipped for every good work" (2 Timothy 3:16).

"No prophecy of scripture is a matter of one's own interpretation, because no prophecy ever came by the impulse of man, but men moved by the Holy Spirit spoke from God" (2 Peter 1:21).

Exodus 20:18–19	Luke 24:27
Numbers 12:6	John 5:39
Deuteronomy 6:6–9	John 6:68
Psalm 19	Acts 1:22
Psalm 119:97–105	Romans 3:2
Isaiah 40:8	Hebrews 1:1–2
Amos 3:7	2 Peter 3:15–16
Matthew 5:17–18	1 John 1:1, 3

It makes sense to begin a study of Christian beliefs by discussing the doctrine of revelation, for in talking of God at all we assume that we know something about him and his will for us. Is this assumption valid? Are there good reasons for believing that we know anything about

God? Where do we get such knowledge? What does it include? How can we tell when we find it? What purpose does it serve?

The doctrine of revelation attempts to answer such questions. It discusses the source(s), the means, the contents, and the purpose of revelation.

THE NEED FOR REVELATION

At first glance, it seems presumptuous to speak of "knowing God." One thing we learn from the enormous proliferation of information today is that we know hardly anything about anything. The more we study something, the more complicated and mysterious it becomes. We even find our own behavior baffling. How, then, can we know anything about God—the greatest thing imaginable? What makes us think we could possibly understand him?

The answer is simple. We *can't* know anything about God— unless he reveals it to us. Our knowledge of God is entirely dependent upon divine revelation. Without it, we would be in total ignorance.

There are several reasons for this. We just mentioned one of them: the fact that God is infinitely greater than we are. For us to know anything about him he has to come down to our level of understanding. There is no way we can raise ourselves to his.

Divine revelation is also necessary because God is a person. You can't say that you know a person unless he communicates with you. If someone asks, "Do you know the President of the United States?," you might say, "I know who he is," or "I know of him," or "I've heard about him." But you cannot say, "I know him," unless he has communicated with you in a personal way—unless he has *revealed* himself to you.

As we shall see, Christian faith affirms that God is a person. Consequently, we can say that we know God only if he communicates with us.

There is a third reason that revelation is so important. The great distance between us and God is due not only to our creaturely limitations. It is also due to the fact that we are sinners. Whatever our original capacity to know and comprehend God, it has been seriously damaged by sin. This makes it utterly impossible for us to learn anything about God on our own.

The fact that God is a person has other consequences for revelation. For one thing, it has a bearing on its content. The most important

The content of revelation

things we know about other people are the things they reveal to us about themselves—not just abstract information like height, weight, hair color, birth date, and so on, but important things like attitudes, feelings, values, hopes, and fears. These are the sort of things that you can never know unless someone reveals them to you by significant words and gestures. Strong personal relationships depend on communication of this kind.

There is much discussion among theologians today about the real content of revelation. Conservative Christians typically insist that revelation consists of information. They maintain that this information is completely reliable, whether it deals with history, astronomy, and geology, or with religious and spiritual matters. In contrast, many theologians emphasize the personal nature of revelation. In their view, God himself is the content of revelation, not mere information about him.

There is a difference in terminology, too. For conservatives, "revelation" is the means to a relationship with God; for many others, "revelation" typically refers to the relationship itself.

Both viewpoints contain elements of truth. Revelation does contain information—information about God and information about other things, too. But its most important part, its essence, is God's self-communication, and the basis it provides us for responding to him.

Revelation as address

Because divine revelation originates in a Person, it has the character of address. When he reveals himself, God speaks to us, and when we are spoken to, we have to reply. If you are reading a book, or watching television, or listening to a lecture, you don't have to respond. You can put the book down, unplug the TV, or doze off. But when someone greets you by name or asks you a question, you must respond. It is insulting not to answer. When God reveals himself to human beings, he speaks to them; he addresses them personally. It is the height of disrespect not to respond. Revelation confronts us with God's claim on our lives, and we must give an answer.

Revelation and grace

Revelation is also a manifestation of divine love and grace. It involves an enormous condescension on God's part to stoop to the level where finite, rebellious human beings can hear his message. We might say that God lisps when he talks to us, just as an affectionate parent uses baby-talk to communicate with a very young child. To reveal himself, God must accommodate himself to our level of understanding.[1]

1. John Calvin describes the condescension God manifests in revelation in his comments on Matthew 23:37: "Whenever the word of God is exhibited to us, he opens

We have identified God as the source of revelation and have touched briefly on its content and purpose. All of these have an important bearing on the means of revelation, or the different ways God reveals himself.

THE MEANS OF REVELATION

It is customary to say that God reveals himself in nature and in history. The word "history" can refer either to past events, or to the record of such events. The idea of "historical revelation" encompasses both senses of the term. Christians believe that God has been uniquely active in certain portions of history. These include the experiences of ancient Israel, the life of Jesus, and the early Christian church. They regard these events as revelatory. They also believe that God reveals himself in the record of these events—that is, in the Bible.

But has God revealed himself in other ways, too? Is there "natural" as well as "historical" revelation? Or, is there "general" as well as "special" revelation, as the question is sometimes phrased? If so, what is the relation between the two?

This is one of the most extensively discussed issues in Christian theology. The Bible apparently supports the idea that God is revealed in nature. A famous psalm begins with the words, "The heavens are telling the glory of God; and the firmament proclaims his handiwork" (Ps 19:1). The apostle Paul declares, "Ever since the creation of the world his [God's] invisible nature, namely, his eternal power and deity, has been clearly perceived in the things that have been made" (Rom 1:20).

So it is clear that there is a revelation of God in nature. But just what this revelation accomplishes is not so clear, and there is considerable disagreement over the issue. On the one hand, there are those who admit that God has revealed himself in nature, but deny

The question of natural theology

his bosom to us with maternal kindness, and, not satisfied with this, condescends to the humble affection of *a hen* watching over her *chickens.* . . . And, indeed, if we consider, on the one hand, the dreadful majesty of God, and, on the other, our mean and low condition, we cannot but be ashamed and astonished at such amazing goodness. For what object can God have in view in abasing himself so low on our account? When he compares himself to a mother, he descends very far below his glory; how much more when he takes the form of *a hen,* and deigns to treat us as his *chickens?*" (*Commentary on a Harmony of the Evangelists, Matthew, Mark, and Luke,* trans. William Pringle [Edinburgh: The Calvin Translation Society, 1846], 3:107).

that this revelation can give us reliable knowledge of God. Because of sin's effect on the environment, they argue, nature speaks of God with a muted voice. The picture it provides of God is blurred and ambiguous. We not only see beauty and tenderness, we also see suffering and cruelty. Moreover, sin has a negative effect on the human mind. We do not have the ability to perceive the evidence in nature clearly. So, even though there may be "natural revelation," there is no such thing as "natural knowledge of God," or "natural theology."

Opponents of natural theology also call attention to the actual effects of natural revelation. As described in Romans, natural revelation renders human beings inexcusable in their sin (Rom 1:20b). It doesn't lead them to a saving knowledge of God.

Finally, opponents argue that a natural knowledge of God would compete with special revelation and compromise the significance of Christ. It would provide human beings with the basis for a relationship with God outside his revelation in Jesus Christ.

On the other side, there is evidence to support the idea that nature provides us with reliable knowledge of God. One evidence is God's desire for the salvation of all men (1 Tim 2:4; cf. 2 Pet 3:9). If God desires the salvation of all men, then his purpose in revealing himself in nature must be to save human beings, not to condemn them.

We also find evidence for natural theology in Paul's sermon in Athens. On that occasion, Paul introduced his proclamation of the gospel by referring to the religious practices of his listeners and analyzing what they already knew about God: that God made the world and everything in it, that he gives to all men life and breath and all things, that human beings have an inclination to seek God (Ac 17:24–26). From such passages it appears that people can know something of God outside his special revelation in Jesus Christ.

Something else that supports the idea of natural theology is God's universal influence in human life. The fourth Gospel describes Jesus as "the true light that enlightens every man" (Jn 1:9). In one way or another, it seems, God is active in the life of every human being.

But what about the suspicion that natural theology competes with special revelation? Is the idea incompatible with the conviction that we are saved only through Jesus Christ?

General revelation and special revelation

To believe that human beings can know something about God through his revelation in nature does not require the conclusion that anyone can be saved apart from God's work in Jesus Christ. It isn't knowledge that saves us anyway, as we shall see when we talk about salvation.

In the second place, whatever people learn about God from nature will always be less vivid and complete than God's special revelation in Christ. General revelation is like a faint sketch in comparison with the full-color portrait of God in the person of Jesus.

Without special revelation, then, our knowledge of God would be vague and indistinct. We could never have the assurance of his love that the message of the Bible provides. The Bible and the events it records are irreplaceable as a source of our knowledge of God.

Special revelation, then, doesn't invalidate general revelation. It clarifies and completes it. It corrects the inadequate understanding of God that people may have whose only knowledge of him is through nature. John Calvin compared Scripture to the glasses of a weak-sighted person.[2] With the aid of corrective lenses, what before was blurred and indistinct becomes clear and vivid. With the aid of special revelation, the additional light of God's Word, we can see his revelation in nature in its full splendor.

The Bible, then, is the primary source of our knowledge of God. Christians believe that it records the saving acts of God in human history, and that God was directly involved in its production. As everyone knows who is familiar with it, the Bible is a complicated book. In order to understand it, we need to examine the nature of its contents. And we need to consider its appropriate interpretation.

THE NATURE OF BIBLICAL REVELATION

We find the Christian view of the Bible in two important verses in the New Testament. The writers were speaking specifically of the writings of the Old Testament, but their description applies to the New Testament as well. "All Scripture is inspired by God" (2 Tim 3:16). "No prophecy came by the impulse of man, but men moved by the Holy Spirit spoke from God" (2 Pet 1:21).

As expressed in these verses, the biblical doctrine of "inspiration" contains two important ideas. One is the divine authority of Scripture. The prophets, the writers of the Bible, did not speak or write on their own initiative; their messages originated with God. Moreover, God guides in the transmission of these messages to ensure that what is heard and read is the reliable expression of his will.

---

2. *Institutes of the Christian Religion,* Bk. I, ch. iv, par. 1, trans. Ford Lewis Battles (Philadelphia: The Westminster Press, 1960), p. 70. Vols. 20 and 21 of The Library of Christian Classics, ed. John T. McNeill.

Scripture as divine and human

A second implication of inspiration is the divine-human character of Scripture. The message comes from God, but it is expressed in human terms and concepts, and the different writings clearly reflect the personalities of the authors. It is important to emphasize both aspects of biblical revelation—divine and human. Properly understood, they rule out three inaccurate concepts of the Bible.

One is the idea that God is the real "author" of the Bible and the writers were merely his secretaries. He dictated the messages, and they transcribed them. This view exalts the divine aspect of Scripture, but slights the human. It presents us with a Bible that only appears to be the work of human beings, but is really divine in its entirety.

The twofold character of Scripture also excludes the notion that the biblical writings express nothing more than human ideas and aspirations. They are the products of religious geniuses, according to this theory, and they stand among the greatest literary masterpieces. But in the final analysis they are human documents and nothing more. The Bible supports the view that its writers were men who thought and wrote in human terms, but it claims they were moved, or inspired, to do so by God. He is ultimately responsible for their messages.

Third, the divine-human character of Scripture is incompatible with the idea that the Bible is a mixture of the human and the divine. The Bible has a variegated texture. Some parts seem to be more important, and more valuable, than others. The Gospel of John, for example, means more to most people than the book of Obadiah. The Sermon on the Mount expresses loftier ideals than Ecclesiastes. Such differences have led people to conclude that certain parts of the Bible are divinely inspired, while others are merely human, so we can get the pure Word of God by separating the two.

But the two aspects of Scripture, the divine and the human, are inseparable. The Bible is not a combination of the words of God *and* the words of men. It expresses the word of God *in* the words of men. Eliminate the human and you will also eliminate the divine.

The union of divine and human in the Bible is a little like the genetic combination of two parents in a child. Some things about a child will remind you of its mother. In other ways, it resembles its father. But there is no way to separate the two without doing violence to the person involved.

The humanity of the Bible

Several things about the Bible underline its human character. For one, it is written in the language of human beings. Its writers employed the language of their times. The Old Testament is written largely in Hebrew. The New Testament is written in Greek—not the classical

Greek of poets and philosophers, but Koinē Greek, as it is called, the language of the playground and marketplace.

Literary styles also vary in the Bible from one writer to another. Some books, like Hebrews, show a fine command of the language, with a rich vocabulary and well-developed sentences. Others, such as Revelation, are rather poorly written, with grammatical errors and a limited vocabulary.

Many of the biblical writers used other documents as they wrote. The authors of Kings and Chronicles, for example, relied on previous works. The evidence indicates that Matthew and Luke copied extensively from the Gospel of Mark, as well as from a written collection of Jesus' sayings.

A further indication of the human character of the Bible is the frequent expression of human emotions we find in its pages. There is no better example of this than Psalm 137, which describes the feelings of the Hebrew captives in Babylon. ''O daughter of Babylon, you devastator! Happy shall he be who requites you with what you have done to us! Happy shall he be who takes your little ones and dashes them against the rock!''

It is clear, then, that the Scriptures are definitely human documents, written by different men, in different circumstances, with different personalities, different concerns, and different abilities.

The divinity of the Bible

There is a divine as well as a human aspect to the Bible, although this element is far more difficult to identify. Christians often appeal to two sorts of evidence to support the claim that the Bible is more than a collection of merely human writings. One is the thematic harmony of the writings, numerous and widely different as they are. Christians find a common theme running through the biblical documents, uniting them into a coherent whole, and they believe that only God could ensure such unity over the centuries of the Bible's composition. The love of God, the plan of salvation, and the covenants are popular candidates for such a theme.

The biblical studies of recent years tend to emphasize the enormous diversity among the writings of the Bible, and some scholars are now convinced that there is no unifying theme in Scripture. They point out that some of the documents seem to have little in common other than the fact that they belong to the same collection.

Another sort of evidence for the divine character of the Bible is its impact on human lives. For centuries, millions of people in widely differing circumstances have found the Bible speaking directly to them. It exposes their faults, it guides their lives, it comforts them in difficulty, it gives them courage and inspires them with hope. Certainly no other book has meant so much to so many. How could a book have such power, the argument goes, unless it originated from a higher than human source?

The miraculous preservation of the Bible through history further emphasizes its remarkable character. The biblical documents variously suffered deliberate destruction and uncomprehending neglect. Yet manuscript discoveries indicate that the Bible has remained substantially unchanged for thousands of years. In some cases, the oldest biblical documents we have take us very close to the composition of the originals. We can be confident that our Bibles are trustworthy versions of the original writers' messages.

In the final analysis, there are two basic tests of the Bible's validity. One is conceptual and the other is existential. The conceptual test asks, Does the Bible make sense? Does it describe our human situation accurately? Does it propose a reasonable solution to our problems? As a whole, do its teachings make sense? And do they agree with each other? The existential test concerns the personal reliability of the Bible. Can I trust its claims and commit my life to its promises? To a certain extent, we can discuss the first test publicly. But the second is intensely private. We can apply it only within the realm of our own lives.

All the available evidence falls short of conclusively proving that God is ultimately responsible for the Bible. In the end, deciding whether the Bible is the Word of God is a highly personal matter. It depends on our ability to comprehend its teachings and our willingness to hear its message for our own lives.

THE NATURE OF PROPHETIC INSPIRATION

The writings of the Bible not only claim that God was responsible for their origin, but a number of them describe his involvement in their production rather specifically. The most vivid descriptions recount the experiences of the prophets who spoke on God's behalf with remarkable directness.

A brief look at the phenomenon of prophetic inspiration, or "prophetism," will help us to understand how the divine and human elements combine to give Scripture its twofold character. It also shows that the question of the divine origin of the Bible cannot be avoided.

The prophetic experience   The biblical prophets were divine spokespersons. They communicated to people the messages they received, or claimed to have received, from God. Each aspect of their experience deserves careful consideration. The first is the prophets' reception of their messages.

According to various biblical accounts, the message came to a prophet in experiences variously identified as "visions" and "dreams." "If there is a prophet among you, I the Lord make myself known to him in a vision, I speak with him in a dream" (Num 12:6). The essential characteristics of these experiences emerge from the different accounts provided by prophets like Isaiah, Jeremiah, Ezekiel, and Daniel.

In every case, the prophet received the message in discrete, or definite, experiences. The vision or dream was a specific event. Its occurrence could be located in time and place. Ezekiel's first vision, for example, occurred "in the thirtieth year, in the fourth month, on the fifth day of the month, as I was among the exiles by the river Chebar" (Ezek 1:1–2). Other prophets similarly describe the circumstances of their visions.

The content of the message was equally specific. It did not represent a growing conviction on the prophet's part; it did not arise gradually over a long period of time. Nor was it a vague impression in the prophet's mind; rather, the content was vivid and precise. The prophets did not always understand the meaning of what they saw or heard (cf. Dan 8:27), but they were always very clear about the experience itself.

Another important feature of the prophetic experience is the fact that it involved an encounter with divine power. The prophets were absolutely certain as to the source of their messages. They never attributed them to an unknown origin. There was no question in their minds that God was communicating with them. And they condemned others who "prophesy out of their own minds" (Ezek 13:17).

Since we, or certainly most of us, do not have prophetic experiences, it is impossible for us to know exactly what they consisted of. They apparently involved the reception of sensory impressions. The very word "vision," of course, refers to one of our senses. The prophets spoke of seeing and hearing things—often highly dramatic and sometimes very disturbing. Daniel, for example, was deeply perplexed by the beasts he saw coming out of the sea in one of his visions.

It is important to notice that the prophets did not lose self-awareness during these experiences. If anything, they became even more aware of who and what they were. Habakkuk asked God questions during one of his visions (1:13), and Isaiah felt woefully unworthy when he saw the glory of God (6:5). So the personalities of the prophets were not suppressed when the word of the Lord came to them.

**Prophecy
versus ecstasy**

These characteristics prevent us from regarding the prophets' experiences as forms of mysticism or ecstasy. In the history of every religion there are accounts of people who have felt extremely close to God. They deeply desire his presence. From time to time they feel so near to him that they lose their sense of personal identity. They seem to become one with his reality. People who have these experiences typically find it impossible to describe them, they are so completely unlike anything else. They also tend to regard them as the most wonderful, the most profoundly meaningful, part of their lives.

But notice how different the experiences of the prophets were. Their visions came whether they desired them or not. They did not physically or mentally prepare for them. Far from being indescribable, the prophets related the contents of their visions at great length. In addition, the experience of having a vision was never an end in itself. It was always the means to an end. Its purpose was fulfilled only when the prophet communicated the message that had been received to its intended audience.

**The prophet's
personality**

Before we turn to the communication of the prophetic message, there is one more thing we need to notice about the prophets' visions. This is the fact that each prophet perceived and responded to what he saw and heard in vision in a way that reflected his individual personality. This is true of all experience, of course. No two people experience anything exactly the same way. Our background, our education, our interests, our prejudices, our hopes and fears—all these things influence our perception. The same thing was true of the prophets in vision. Their personalities and their overall view of reality had an inevitable effect on the way they saw and heard.

The prophets' personalities also played an important role in the communication of the messages they received in vision. The language, the words, the concepts, and perhaps the literary form with which the messages were expressed depended upon the individual abilities and inclinations of the prophets, along with the situations to which they spoke.

**The purpose
of prophecy**

In a sense, the reception of the vision was merely preliminary to the central work of the prophets. By definition, their task consisted of speaking, or communicating, to the people on God's behalf. The prophets themselves were more concerned with communicating the message than they were with receiving it.

It is important to emphasize this fact in order to avoid reducing the doctrine of revelation to the phenomenon of inspiration. When this happens, people become preoccupied with the production of the Bible and less concerned with its function, which is to communicate the message of salvation to human beings. How the Bible came into existence is important, of course. It calls attention to the divine origin of its contents. But it must be subsumed within the larger dynamic of God's communication to human beings, and this communication has not occurred until the prophets articulate the message and the people receive and respond to it. Inspiration, therefore, is but one aspect of revelation, and we must not lose sight of the larger whole.

Although the prophets expressed their messages in their own words, we should not conclude that God's role in the process of revelation ended with the prophetic visions. In fact, he is involved in the entire process, including the people's reception of the message. The language of 2 Peter 1:21, "men moved by the Holy Spirit," suggests that they were borne along by the Holy Spirit as they spoke. The activity of the Spirit ensures that their expressions communicate the intended message.

As a result, the prophetic message, spoken and written, represents divinely imparted truth expressed in human words. It is reliable as the expression of God's will, even as it bears the individual characteristics of the authors. Its divine and human aspects form an integral, indivisible whole, as we have seen.

Prophetic inspiration of the type we have just examined does not account for the production of all the books of the Bible. By no means do all of them attribute their contents to what was received in vision. Some of the writers are quite direct in acknowledging their use of other writings. Luke, for example, begins his Gospel by citing other attempts to compile a narrative of Jesus' life, and he indicates that a careful investigation lies behind his writing (1:1–3).

Before his death, Jesus promised his disciples that the Holy Spirit would help them remember what he had said to them (Jn 14:26), so divinely aided memory also accounts for the origin of certain biblical writings. Viewed as a whole, in fact, this is just what the New Testament represents. It is the divinely authorized memory of Jesus.

THE QUESTION OF BIBLICAL INERRANCY

Conservative Christians all agree that the Bible is a reliable source of knowledge about God and his will for human life. They accept it as divinely authoritative. But there is a sharp disagreement among contemporary evangelicals as to what this belief involves. Some insist that the divine source of revelation guarantees that the final product, the Bible, is entirely free of errors. Others, equally committed to the authority of the Bible, disagree. They accept the Bible as the supreme authority of Christian faith and practice, but they do not believe that the Bible is totally without error.

**The case
for inerrancy**

The supporters of inerrancy include some of the best-known evangelicals in the world, such as Carl F. H. Henry and Francis Schaeffer.[3] They are motivated by a strong desire to preserve the uniqueness of the Bible and to affirm its reliability as a source of truth. We can summarize their basic argument in three statements: (1) God is the author of the Bible; (2) God is never the author of error; (3) therefore the Bible is free of error.

This does not mean that the Bible contains no mistakes in grammar or spelling. Nor does it mean that God dictated its contents on a word-by-word basis. What it means is that God guided the minds of the biblical writers in such a way that they were prevented from making any erroneous statements. Whatever they assert is true—when they speak of geography, chronology, and history, as well as when they speak of religion and theology. If the Bible is reliable at all, they argue, it must be reliable in all.

It is also important to notice that supporters of inerrancy typically apply this quality only to the original documents produced by the biblical writers—that is, to the "autographs," as they are called. God was not as directly involved in the process of copying the biblical manuscripts as he was in their original production. So whatever errors appear in the available biblical manuscripts are due to the copying process. They were not in the original documents. Consequently, as important as the quality of inerrancy is, it applies only to documents which no longer exist! The Bible as we have it is not inerrant, but only infallible.

What probably motivates supporters of inerrancy more than anything else is the fear that the Bible will lose its authority for people unless they believe it is entirely free from errors. Once we compromise the uniqueness of the Bible as a source of truth, they seem to think, nothing prevents us from concluding that it is just another book, and that we can pick and choose from among its contents what to believe.

3. Carl F. H. Henry provides an extended argument for biblical inerrancy in his recent series of books, *God, Revelation, and Authority* (6 vols.; Waco, Tx.: Word Books, 1976–1983), 4:129–255. His discussion contains the points made in this and the following three paragraphs.

There are several reasons why other conservative Christians object to the concept of biblical inerrancy.[4] For one thing, it seems to overlook the human dimension of Scripture. If we believe that human beings were genuinely involved in the production of the Bible, that they were God's spokesmen and not merely his secretaries, then it is unrealistic to insist on an error-free Bible. No human product is entirely free of errors.

Another objection to biblical inerrancy is that it sometimes leads to distorted and unconvincing interpretations of the Bible. Different biblical descriptions of the same item or event often disagree in certain respects. In one famous case, the Gospels give divergent accounts of Peter's denial of Jesus in relation to the crowing of the cock. Instead of regarding this as a minor discrepancy in the Gospel narratives, supporters of inerrancy try to reconcile all the accounts, so each one can be literally true. One proposed solution is that Peter denied Jesus a total of six times on the morning of the crucifixion.[5]

A third objection to the concept of inerrancy is that it miscasts the fundamental purpose of Scripture. It focuses attention on the form of revelation, when the truly important thing about the Scriptures is their saving function. Their real purpose is to lead human beings to a saving relationship with God. Inerrancy distracts people from the Bible's basic purpose, emphasizing its formal characteristics at the expense of its content.

Closely related to this is the observation that the concept of inerrancy is itself unbiblical. Nowhere do the writers of the Bible assert that all their statements are inerrant. Those who adhere to this idea have deduced it from their concept of divine inspiration and imposed it on the Bible. Opponents of inerrancy call for an inductive, rather than a deductive, approach to the nature of Scripture. They want us to consider the data provided by the Bible itself, rather than drawing out rational inferences from certain premises.

Seventh-day Adventists have never advocated biblical inerrancy, although they support the divine authority and complete reliability of the Scriptures. One reason is the fct that Ellen G. White allowed for minor discrepancies in the production of the Bible.[6] Another is the

4. Stephen T. Davis carefully analyzes the arguments for inerrancy and rejects this view of Scripture in favor of infallibility in *The Debate About the Bible: Inerrancy Versus Infallibility* (Philadelphia: The Westminster Press, 1977).

5. Harold Lindsell, *The Battle for the Bible* (Grand Rapids, Mich.: Zondervan Publishing House, 1976), pp. 174–76; cited in Davis, *The Debate About the Bible*.

6. "Some look to us gravely and say, 'Don't you think there might have been some mistake in the copyist or in the translators?' This is all probable . . ." (*Selected Messages,* bk. 1, p. 16). "There is not always perfect order or apparent unity in the

example of her own writings. Although she insisted on the divine origin of her messages, she never claimed that her writings were infallible.[7]

THE CONTENTS OF THE BIBLE

Appreciating the origin and nature of the Scriptures is only one aspect of the doctrine of revelation. Understanding the message of the Bible is equally important, and responding to the message in our personal lives is no doubt the most important part of all. But before turning to the question of how to interpret the Bible, let's take a quick look at its contents.

The Christian Scriptures as accepted by Protestants contain sixty-six documents in two major divisions: the Old and New Testaments. The documents included in the Old Testament were written before the time of Christ by some thirty different people over a period of about a thousand years. All of them were originally in Hebrew, except for parts of Daniel and Ezra, which were written in Aramaic.

The Old Testament

The Old Testament contains a variety of literature, including a good deal of history; considerable legal material, especially in the first few books; a lot of poetry; a number of prophetic writings; and a few examples of a distinctive type of literature called "apocalyptic," which describes the dramatic triumph of God and his people over the forces of evil at the end of time.

The overall theme of the Old Testament is God's dealings with the people of Israel. He rescued them from Egypt. He made them a nation. After their apostasy and captivity in Babylon, he restored their fortunes in Palestine. From a Christian perspective, which the expression "Old Testament" reflects, these writings anticipate the climax of divine revelation in the ministry of Jesus. In light of that revelation the significance of the Old Testament becomes clear.

The Apocrypha

Catholic versions of the Old Testament contain several documents which Protestants refer to collectively as the "apocrypha," a

---

Scriptures. The miracles of Christ are not given in exact order, but are given just as the circumstances occurred, which called for this divine revealing of the power of Christ" (ibid., p. 20).

7. "In regard to infallibility, I never claimed it; God alone is infallible. His word is true, and in Him is no variableness, or shadow of turning" (*Selected Messages*, bk. 1, p. 37).

Greek word which means "hidden" or "doubtful." These fourteen or fifteen documents, or parts of documents, were written during the last two hundred years before Christ. They reflect some of the popular beliefs of the time. They were included in the Septuagint, the earliest Greek translation of the Hebrew Scriptures, which was the "Bible" of the early Christian church. But the New Testament never quotes directly from the Apocrypha. From the beginning, these writings have been controversial in the church. Jerome, who translated the Bible into Latin, did not accept them as authoritative, nor did the Reformers, such as Martin Luther. But Augustine, the greatest thinker of the early church, did, and Roman Catholics follow his precedent.

The New Testament

The New Testament contains twenty-seven documents and is less than a third as long as the Old. It was written entirely in Greek by about eight writers over a period of fifty or sixty years, according to conservative estimates. The overall theme of the New Testament is the origin of the Christian church. This theme is developed in two parts. The first four books, the Gospels, describe the mission of Jesus, the founder of the church. The rest all pertain to the ministry of the apostles, Jesus' appointed leaders of the church. Most of them are apostolic letters to different individuals and groups in the church.

Biblical scholarship

An enormous range of questions confronts us in the study of the Bible. We may wonder about the original composition of the documents. Who wrote them? When? To whom and for what purpose? Under what circumstances? In what form? With what literary assistance? Questions of this type are the concern of a discipline called "biblical criticism." The purpose of the discipline is not to destroy our confidence in the Bible, as people sometimes suspect; rather, it is to help us understand the history of its contents. The fact that it was written by human beings justifies a critical study of the Bible.

The text of the Bible also poses questions. None of the original manuscripts of the biblical documents are known to exist. There are hundreds of variations among the handwritten copies we have. So how do we know if our Bibles read as the original documents did? The science of "textual criticism" explores the history of the transmission of the Bible and seeks to determine the most accurate biblical text. For the most part, there is little question about the reading of the originals, because the documents of the Bible were transcribed with such painstaking care.

We may also ask about the formation of the biblical canon. The Bible is a collection of some sixty-six documents. How did this collection come about? Who decided what books to include? When? On what basis?

THE BIBLICAL CANON

The story of how the Bible reached its present form is far too long and complicated to recount here. But we can review a few of its high points, especially if we confine our attention to the Christian canon.

The word "canon," not to be confused with "cannon," a large gun, comes from a Sumerian word for "reed," and originally referred to something made of reeds or straight like reeds. It now refers to a body of sacred writings that carry the highest authority for some religious community. The Jewish canon consists of the Hebrew Scriptures. The canon of Islam is the Koran. The Christian canon contains the Hebrew Scriptures (Old Testament) and an additional collection of documents originally written in Greek (New Testament).

By the time of Christ, there were three collections of documents that carried authority in the Jewish community. They were the "law," the "prophets," and the "writings." Jesus accepted all three as divinely authoritative, as did the Pharisees of his day. (The Sadducees accepted only the Law.) These works formed the original Scriptures of the early Christian church. When the writers of the New Testmaent spoke of the "scriptures," it was these documents they had in mind (cf. Jn 5:38–39; Lk 24:27; Ac 18:24; 2 Tim 3:16).

The Christian church added the writings of the New Testament to form our present canon in a gradual process that was not complete until the fourth century after Christ. Several factors led early Christians to formulate an additional list of writings to which they attached the highest religious authority.

The most important factor was the death of the apostles. The apostles occupied a position of great significance in the early church. Paul described them as the foundation of the church, along with the prophets (Eph 2:20), and as the most important of the gifts of the Holy Spirit (1 Cor 12:28). The reason was their unique relation to Jesus. The apostles were the official witnesses of Jesus' ministry. They bore the authentic, authoritative testimony to his life, death, and resurrection. Indeed, in their work and words, the ministry Jesus began was continued in the world.

The apostles all met two qualifications: personal contact with Jesus and divine ordination for their work. For the most part, of course, the original apostles had been among Jesus' twelve disciples.

After Judas' death, the eleven, with divine guidance, selected Matthias to take his place from among several men who had contact with Jesus during his earthly life (Ac 1:21–26). The apostles often appealed to their personal contact with Jesus to authorize their message (cf. 2 Pet 1:16; 1 Jn 1:1–3).

Among the apostles, Paul was a special case, as he himself was acutely aware. He did not know Jesus during his life on earth. But he claimed to be the recipient of a resurrection appearance (1 Cor 15:8), and he was adamant that his apostolic call came from God (Gal 1:1).

Because the apostles provided a "living link" to Jesus, their preaching was essential to the church. As they died one by one over the years, their writings became the only form in which their witness was available. So it was natural for the church to invest these writings with authority, just as they had the preaching of the apostles.

This, then, is what the New Testament represents. It is the written record of the apostolic witness to Jesus. Early Christians accepted as authoritative only documents written either by an apostle himself or by someone closely associated with an apostle. Mark, for example, was a close friend of Peter; Luke was Paul's companion. In this way, the testimony of the apostles continues to guide the church and proclaim Christ in the world.

Canonical authority

The authority of the New Testament arises from the authority of the apostles,[8] but the authority of the apostles comes from Jesus. So Christians base their attitude toward the New Testament on their belief in Jesus Christ. They believe that the life of Jesus was utterly unique. In him God was personally present to human beings in a way he has never been before or since. As a result, the testimony of those who witnessed the history of Jesus is likewise unique and unrepeatable. This fact has three important consequences.

First, it means that the canon is closed. No post-apostolic writing can have the same significance, because no later writer can have the same contact with Jesus. Second, the authority of the apostles cannot be passed on from one generation to another. The apostolic office was not an institutional function. It was an activity for which only the first generation of Christians could qualify, because of their personal acquaintance with Jesus on earth. Early Christians formulated the canon

8. Oscar Cullman establishes the relationship between apostolicity and canonicity presented here in his essay, "The Tradition," in *The Early Church: Studies in Early Christian History and Theology*, ed. A. J. B. Higgins (abridged ed.; Philadelphia: The Westminster Press, 1966), pp. 59–99.

because they recognized the unrepeatable character of the apostles' work.

Third, it means that the Bible has authority over the Christian church. It is true that the canon is the creation of the church. During the first four hundred years after Christ, Christians selected from among a large number of different writings which ones should be accepted as authoritative. The New Testament as we now have it reflects the universal consensus the church had achieved by the late fourth century. There was no question about most of the New Testament documents. The four Gospels, Acts, Paul's letters, 1 John, and 1 Peter were accepted everywhere from the beginning. There were several writings accepted by some Christians for a time but not by all. Some of them eventually gained universal acceptance and are included in the canon. Others never did and were finally left out.

A letter written by Athanasius of Alexandria, a bishop in Egypt, in A.D. 367 lists the "books that are canonized and handed down to us and believed to be divine." Included are the Old Testament and the twenty-seven books of the New Testament.[9]

But the fact that the church created the canon does not mean that the church has authority over the Bible. In creating a canon, the church did not confer authority upon certain writings. It recognized the authority within these writings.[10] In fact, the recognition that these writings have authority over the church is what led it to form a canon to begin with.[11]

Versions of the Bible

People often ask which version of the Bible is best. There is no simple answer to this question. For years the venerable King James Version was the Bible of English-speaking Protestants. But the past thirty years have seen an enormous number of new translations. Of these, the Revised Standard Version probably enjoys the widest use. It remains in the tradition of the King James Version and is the standard

9. F. W. Beare, "Canon of the NT," in *The Interpreter's Dictionary of the Bible,* ed. George Arthur Buttrick (4 vols.; New York: Abingdon Press, 1962), 1: 531.

10. In the words of biblical scholar F. F. Bruce, "The New Testament books did not become authoritative for the Church because they were formally included in a canonical list; on the contrary, the Church included them in her canon because she already regarded them as divinely inspired" (*The New Testament Documents: Are They Reliable?* [5th ed. rev.; Grand Rapids, Mich.: William B. Eerdmans Publishing Co., 1960], p. 27).

11. As Oscar Cullman observes, "The fixing of the Christian canon of scripture means that *the Church itself,* at a given time, traced a clear and definite line of demarcation between the period of the apostles and that of the Church, between the time of foundation and that of construction, between the apostolic community and the Church of the bishops, in other words, between apostolic tradition and ecclesiastical tradition. Otherwise the formation of the canon would be meaningless" ("The Tradition," p. 59; italics his).

translation used by scholars. The New English Bible is an entirely new translation based on the best Greek text available. Today's English Version, or the Good News Bible, was prepared for people with a limited understanding of English and is easy to read. The New International Version is popular among conservative Christians.

Which Bible you should read depends upon personal preference and intended use. For personal devotions, any version will do as long as it makes sense to you. For doctrinal study, it is better to rely on translations prepared by groups rather than individuals, and more-recent translations are generally based on better editions of the original texts. This limits the value of The Living Bible, for example, which is a one-man paraphrase of the American Standard Bible and not a true translation.

BIBLICAL INTERPRETATION

We said above that the dynamic of revelation is not complete until the people of God hear and respond to his message. Consequently, none of the questions the Bible raises is more important than what it means for us today. This is the general concern of theology. In fact, it is the fundamental task of the church as a whole. More specifically, the task of interpreting the Bible is identified as the science of "hermeneutics." To interpret the Bible accurately we need to follow several hermeneutical principles.

The most important requirement for effective Bible study is a proper attitude. To learn what God has to say to us in the Bible, we must approach it in the right frame of mind. This includes recognizing the authority of the Bible as the Word of God. We must be willing to submit our preferences and desires to the teachings of the Word. We must be willing to learn, and not just look for ways of reinforcing our preconceptions. We must also seek the guidance of the Holy Spirit. The Bible not only records what God has said in the past; it is also the primary means through which God speaks to us today. We need the assistance of the Spirit in order to discover what he intends for us to hear.

In reading the Bible, we cannot ignore the enormous distance that separates us from the thought world of ancient times. Not only the language, but the customs, concepts, and even theology differ vastly from our own. In order to determine what the Bible *means,* therefore, it is first necessary to find out just what it *meant.* For this purpose, several hermeneutical principles are indispensable.

**Literary
context**

The first of these is to observe the literary context, or more accurately, contexts. Suppose you read a statement in the Bible and you want to figure out what it means. The first thing to observe is the material surrounding the statement. Look at the passage in which it appears. Do the verses immediately before and after help to explain its meaning?

Keep expanding the literary contexts you take into account. Consider the chapter containing the statement. Then notice the general purpose of the book as a whole. You may need to refer to other works by the same author, if the Bible contains any of them.

As you consider the literary context of a biblical statement, you will also need to determine the kind of literature it represents. For example, is it a statement of historical fact or a prophetic prediction? Is it the report of a sermon or the account of a vision? Is it part of a letter, or a poem? Such questions are important in the attempt to figure out the intention of the passage. A look at the original language of the statement may be helpful, too. A good commentary will often explain the meaning of the original words.

**Historical
context**

As you look at the literary contexts, it is important to consider the historical contexts, too. What specific situation or circumstances does the passage reflect? Who and where was the author at the time of writing? Was he in prison or in exile, perhaps? And who was the original audience? One person, a group of people, or an entire nation? Why was he writing? Was the nation about to be destroyed (cf. Jeremiah)? Was the church threatened with heresy (cf. Galatians)? Were the readers facing persecution (cf. Revelation)? Were people concerned about Christ's return (cf. 2 Peter)? Such questions pertain to the immediate historical context—the specific situation in which the statement was originally made.

The remote historical context is equally important. It refers to the entire world of which the document, with its author and audience, is a part. It involves the cultural context of the times, including contemporary politics and economics, religious beliefs and practices, social customs, and ethical standards. A knowledge of the culture surrounding the ancient Israelites clarifies some of the bewildering passages of the Old Testament, just as familiarity with Roman laws and customs brings to life much of the New Testament.

**Comparing
Scripture**

After consulting the literary and historical contexts, the third step in biblical interpretation is to compare Scripture with Scripture. In a sense, this is an expansion of the literary context we consult in interpreting a passage. It involves taking into account the entire testimony of Scripture on a particular topic. The objective is to base doctrines on the broad themes of Scripture, not on isolated statements.

Try to do three things as you consider the broad range of biblical material dealing with an issue. First, remember that revelation is progressive. A spectrum of biblical statements may reflect a developing understanding of truth. On a single occasion, God does not necessarily say everything he intends us to know about a topic. We need to consider the accumulated evidence of the entire stream of revelation in order to grasp the full dimensions of truth.

Second, seek to harmonize the biblical writings. This does not mean manufacturing an artificial synthesis by overlooking obvious differences. Nor does it mean reading the same themes into every book of the Bible. But many apparent contradictions in Scripture can be resolved by looking for the underlying convictions which different authors share.

Third, let the Bible be its own interpreter. This is one of the best-known principles of biblical interpretation. It is also one of the most commonly misunderstood. It does not include the belief that we can totally eliminate our own perspective as we interpret the Bible. That would clearly be impossible. It does involve the practice of allowing one passage of Scripture to illuminate another. More specifically, however, it has to do with biblical authority. The idea that the Bible is its own interpreter means that we can never give something else authority over it. No church council or official interpreter can assign a meaning to the Bible. We must allow the Bible to speak for itself. This doesn't mean that we avoid consulting other writings in our attempt to understand the Bible. It simply means that we seek to base every interpretation of Scripture on the direct testimony of Scripture itself, not on the statements of some other source.

Another hermeneutical principle is to look for underlying principles within the details of time and place. We have already noticed this in connection with doctrine, but it is especially important when it comes to religious life. The Bible describes many religious practices, such as animal sacrifice, which Christians today no longer perform. There are others, including baptism, which we do. This principle helps us to make the distinction carefully. It also helps us in making ethical decisions. There are biblical precedents for polygamy and slavery. But these alone do not justify such practices for Christians today. We need to look at the basic principles of human relationships expressed in the Bible, not just the social customs it records.

A final suggestion for biblical interpretation comes from the overarching dynamic of revelation which has guided this discussion.

Principles versus details

Divine revelation, we noticed, fulfills its purpose only when God's people receive and respond to his messages. Hearing the Word of God is something we do as a group, not merely as individuals. Nothing can replace personal Bible study, and we should never allow others to decide for us what the Bible teaches. But we need to listen to the Word of God together. Biblical interpretation is the task of the church as a whole. Having other people respond to our interpretations may prevent us from entertaining erroneous ideas, and hearing what they have learned can enrich our own understanding of the Bible.

This corporate principle of biblical interpretation justifies listening to sermons, participating in Bible study groups, and taking religion courses. It also justifies reading Bible commentaries, theological works, and devotional literature. All these activities play a role in helping us to respond to divine revelation.

REVELATION AND THE REIGN OF GOD

The guiding principle of this project is the reign of God. This idea relates to the understanding of revelation outlined above in several different ways.

For one thing, we have seen that God takes the initiative in revelation. He is ultimately responsible for our knowledge of him. Moreover, God's purpose in revelation is not merely to inform us; it is to engage us. In revelation, God communicates himself, as well as information about himself.

Accordingly, receiving revelation involves more than acquiring information. It means entering into a personal relationship with God. It involves a total response to God's claim to our allegiance. The biblical admonition, "Hear!," as in, "Hear, O Israel" (Dt 6:4), and, "This is my beloved son. Hear ye him" (Mt 17:5), means more than simply, "Listen." It means "Obey." Responding to divine revelation is no mere intellectual exercise. It involves accepting God's sovereignty over our lives and committing ourselves to his purposes for us.

We can describe the purpose of God's reign in general, and of revelation in particular, as "salvific." This means that they are directed to human salvation. God does not crudely impose his reign upon human beings; rather, he seeks to awaken loyalty on our part. Similarly, revelation does not overwhelm us. It invites us to learn, and it invites us to respond to our Teacher in a personal way.

Another feature of God's reign which emerges in revelation is its subtle and cooperative character. We have seen that God employs human instruments as the means of communicating with us. The Bible represents the Word of God expressed in and through the words of men. God actually takes the personalities of his spokesmen into the process of revelation. Their contribution is inextricably involved in the final product. Similarly, God characteristically works in and through his creatures. God does not merely act upon creation. He cooperates with it.

The reality, the nature, and the purpose of the reign of God, therefore, are all apparent within the doctrine of revelation. They are even more apparent, of course, in the doctrine of God itself, which a good deal of this discussion presupposes. This is the next major doctrine we shall consider.

STUDY HELPS

1. Why is revelation necessary for a knowledge of God?

2. In what ways has God revealed himself to human beings?

3. What are the essential features of prophetic inspiration?

4. What are the major arguments for and against biblical inerrancy?

5. What factors led to the formation of the New Testament canon?

6. What steps must be taken to interpret a biblical passage correctly?

Questions for review

1. Compare the concepts of revelation expressed in the following statements:

a. "The category *revelation* . . . refers to the divine self-disclosure, the purpose of which is, by intervention in history and communication in language, the calling of men into fellowship with God" (Clark H. Pinnock, *Biblical Revelation—The Foundation of Christian Theology* [Chicago: Moody Press, 1971], p. 29).

b. "Revelation . . . is a process, an event, and indeed an event which happens to us and in us. Neither the prophetic Word of the Old Testament, nor Jesus Christ, nor the witness of the Apostles, nor of the preachers of the Church who proclaim Him, 'is' the revelation; the reality of the revelation culminates in the 'subject' who receives it" (Emil Brunner, *The Christian Doctrine of God* [Dogmatics, vol. 1], trans. Olive Wyon [Philadelphia: The Westminster Press, 1949], p. 19).

Questions for further study

2. What are the major similarities and differences between the documents of the Old Testament and those of the New Testament?

3. If one of Paul's "lost letters" were apparently discovered today (cf. 1 Cor 5:9; Col 4:16), what process would lead to its inclusion in the New Testament?

4. Along with other Protestants, Seventh-day Adventists accept the Bible as the final authority in matters of faith and practice. What are the effects of this attitude toward the Bible on the level of personal religious experience?

Suggestions for Bible study

1. Analyze the similarities among the following passages. What conclusions do they require concerning the nature of the Bible's inspiration?
   a. Isaiah 2:2–4; Joel 3:9–10; Micah 4:1–4
   b. Matthew 20:29–34; Mark 10:46–52; Luke 18:35–43
   c. Matthew 12:38–45; Luke 11:29–32, 24–26

2. According to the following passages, what do the Hebrew Scriptures represent from a Christian perspective?

   Romans 3:2; John 5:39; Luke 24:27, 44–47

3. How does a concept like "progressive revelation" help to explain the contrasts between biblical statements like these?

   Leviticus 7:37; Micah 6:6–8; and Hebrews 10:4, 11–14

4. What is the meaning for Christians today of biblical passages such as Ephesians 6:5–6 and 1 Timothy 2:11–15, which apparently condone slavery and encourage the subordination of women?

SUGGESTIONS FOR FURTHER READING

From Adventist writers

Ellen G. White presents a clear account of the nature of biblical inspiration in two important passages: *The Great Controversy*, pp. v–xii, and *Selected Messages*, bk. 1, pp. 15–23.

Arthur L. White includes an essay by Henry Alford, "The Inspiration of the Evangelists and Other New Testament Writers," as an appendix to *The Ellen G. White Writings* (Washington, D.C.: Review and Herald Publishing Association, 1973), explaining that members of Ellen G. White's staff found the piece helpful as they worked with her writings.

For the most part, Seventh-day Adventist writers have concerned themselves with the scientific and historical reliability of the Bible and with questions of biblical interpretation, rather than with the doctrine of revelation in general. The following works illustrate these interests: Siegfried Horn, *The Spade Confirms the Book* (rev. ed.; Washington, D.C.: Review and Herald Publishing Association, 1980); Gordon M. Hyde (ed.), *A Symposium on Biblical Hermeneutics* (Washington, D.C.: Biblical Research Committee, General Conference of Seventh-day Adventists, 1974), which deals with a number of historical and literary questions related to biblical interpretation; and Gerhard Hasel, *Understanding the Living Word of God* (Mountain View, Calif.: Pacific Press Publishing Association, 1980).

Sakae Kubo and Walter Specht discuss the important question of Bible translation in *So Many Versions? Twentieth Century English Versions of the Bible* (rev. ed.; Grand Rapids, Mich.: Zondervan Publishing House, 1983).

A. Graham Maxwell gives a readable account of the contents, transmission, translation, and interpretation of the Bible in *You Can Trust the Bible* (Mountain View, Calif.: Pacific Press Publishing Association, 1967).

A recent issue of *Spectrum* contains a special section entitled "Ways to Read the Bible." It includes the following articles: John C. Brunt, "A Parable of Jesus as a Clue to Biblical Interpretation"; Lawrence T. Geraty, "Beyond Fundamentalism: A Short History of Adventist Old Testament Scholarship"; Larry G. Herr, "Genesis One in Historical-Critical Perspective"; and Ottilie Stafford, "The Bible as Visionary Power" (*Spectrum,* vol. 13, no. 2, pp. 30–62).

The recently revised *Seventh-day Adventist Bible Commentary,* ed. Francis D. Nichol (7 vols.; Washington, D.C.: Review and Herald Publishing Company, 1953–1957), and Siegfried H. Horn, *Seventh-day Adventist Bible Dictionary* (rev. ed.; Review and Herald Publishing Association, 1979), remain the most extensive SDA contributions to Bible study. For the most part, their contents are accessible to the general reader.

From other writers

From a conservative, or evangelical, perspective, the definitive statement of the doctrine of revelation is Carl F. H. Henry's massive and rather ponderous work, *God, Revelation and Authority* (6 vols.; Waco, Tx.: Word Books, Publisher, 1976–1983). There are, of course, numerous books dealing with the issues that Henry discusses. A highly readable account of the origin and contents of the New Testament is F. F. Bruce, *The New Testament Documents: Are They Reliable?* (5th ed.; Grand Rapids, Mich.: William B. Eerdmans Publishing Co., 1960). Bernard Ramm analyzes the concept of special revelation in *Special Revelation and the Word of God* (Grand Rapids, Mich.: William B. Eerdmans Publishing Co., 1961). Clark Pinnock discusses the nature of divine revelation and its relation to the Bible and to Christian theology in *Biblical Revelation—The Foundation of Christian Theology* (Chicago: Moody Press, 1971). Stephen T. Davis analyzes the arguments for biblical inerrancy and finds them wanting in *The Debate About the Bible: Inerrancy Versus Infallibility* (Philadelphia: The Westminster Press, 1977).

Dutch theologian G. C. Berkouwer deals with various aspects of this doctrine in two volumes of his Studies in Dogmatics: *General Revelation* (Grand Rapids, Mich.: William B. Eerdmans Publishing Co., 1955), and *Holy Scripture,* trans. and ed. Jack B. Rogers (Grand Rapids, Mich.: William B. Eerdmans Publishing Co., 1975).

A penetrating and informative analysis of the phenomenon of prophetism, or prophetic inspiration, appears in Abraham Joshua Heschel, *The Prophets* (New York: Harper & Row, Publishers, 1962), pp. 324–473.

The doctrine of revelation receives extensive discussion in the writings of neo-orthodox theologians such as Karl Barth and Emil Brunner. H. Richard Niebuhr presents a clear statement of this general concept of revelation in *The Meaning of Revelation* (New York: The Macmillan Company, 1941). John Hick succinctly contrasts the conservative and neo-orthodox concepts of revelation, which he terms ''propositional'' and ''non-propositional,'' respectively, in ''Revelation'' (*The Encyclopedia of Philosophy,* ed. Paul Edwards [4 vols.; New York: Macmillan Publishing Co., 1967], 4: 189–191).

In recent years, scholars have devoted increasing attention to the function of the Bible as a whole in theology and in the life of the Christian community. Two examples are David Kelsey, *The Uses of Scripture in Recent Theology* (Philadelphia: Fortress Press, 1980), and Charles M. Wood, *The Formation of Christian Understanding: An Essay in Theological Hermeneutics* (Philadelphia: The Westminster Press, 1981). George W. Stroup summarizes the development of ''narrative theology,'' which emphasizes the narrative structure of Scripture and of Christian identity, in *The Promise of Narrative Theology: Recovering the Gospel in the Church* (Atlanta: John Knox Press, 1981).

3

THE DOCTRINE OF GOD: BASIC CONSIDERATIONS

"You shall have no other gods before me" (Exodus 20:3).

"He is not far from each one of us, for 'in him we live and move and have our being'" (Acts 17:27–28).

"He who does not love does not know God, for God is love" (1 John 4:8).

Genesis 1:1
Exodus 3:14–15
Exodus 20:3–7
Exodus 34:6–7
Leviticus 11:45
Deuteronomy 32:4
Psalm 53:1
Isaiah 6:3

Isaiah 45:15
Isaiah 55:8–9
Acts 14:16–17
Acts 17:22–31
Romans 1:20
Romans 2:14–15
Hebrews 11:6

Who and what is God? No question is more fundamental to religion, or to all of human life. Properly understood, it is not just one among many doctrinal questions. It is the only question there is.[1] Behind every theological issue stands the question of God.

1. The writings of contemporary theologians on the topic of God include assertions like the following: "Rightly understood, the problem of God is not one problem among several others; it is the only problem there is. Hence all our thinking, on whatever theme

We not only reach the heart of religion when we talk about God, we touch the most fundamental concerns of every human life. Everything depends on the question of God. What you think about God will affect your attitude toward everything else. Most important, it will determine your understanding of yourself. Is your life worthwhile? Do your choices really matter? Is there any hope for the future? What you think about God makes all the difference in your answer to these questions.

OUR KNOWLEDGE OF GOD

Some people will object to the attempt to construct a doctrine of God. If God is so great, they will ask, how can even the highest human thoughts do him justice? Wouldn't it be more realistic, and more reverent, to abandon the attempt to describe him?

There is a lot to say for this suggestion. In fact, an important strand in Christian history is called the *via negativa,* the "negative way." We cannot form any positive idea of God, its supporters reasoned; we can only know what he isn't. So their language about God consisted primarily of denials.

It is true that God lies forever beyond our powers of comprehension. His greatness surpasses all human descriptions. But to conclude that we should give up any attempt to understand him is a mistake. It overlooks several important things.

The first of these is the fact of revelation. If it is utterly impossible for us to know anything about God, there is no reason for him to try to communicate with us. Yet the Bible is the extensive record of God's attempt to help us obtain a knowledge of him. We undermine its value if we insist that this objective is unreachable.

It is also important to remember that understanding is the basis of personal trust.[2] If we can't understand God at all, it is useless to

---

and whether properly theological or not, is of some, at least indirect, relevance to clarifying and solving it" (Schubert M. Ogden, *The Reality of God and Other Essays* [New York: Harper & Row, Publishers, 1966], p. 1). The statement, "I believe in one God," "contains in an implicit way the whole of the Christian faith. . . . As far as their content is concerned, the other statements of the faith speak of many other things besides God. . . . But these many and varied statements are statements of the faith only to the extent that they are related to God. . . . God is therefore the sole and unifying theme of theology" (Walter Kasper, *The God of Jesus Christ,* trans. Matthew J. O'Connell [New York: Crossroad, 1984], p. 3).

2. As Wolfhart Pannenberg puts it, "Faith lives from the truth of its foundations" (*The Apostles' Creed in the Light of Today's Questions,* trans. Margaret Kohl [Philadelphia: The Westminster Press, 1972], p. 12).

think we can trust him. So if God wants us to have confidence in him, he must want us to have an understanding of him, too.

Consequently, we need to qualify the limits of our ability to understand God, impressive as they are. We can do this by making some distinctions as we think about God. One is the distinction between inadequate and inaccurate ideas of God. Our concepts of God are obviously inadequate; they will never do justice to the fullness of the divine reality. What we don't know about God will always be more than what we do know about him.

But this doesn't mean that our concepts of God completely misrepresent him. Our ideas of God can, and should, be accurate as far as they go. Human meaning and logic have their basis in divine creativity, the doctrine of creation assures us. God made the world and he made the human mind with the capacity to know the world and its maker. So even though we can't know everything about God, or even very much about him, we can know something. And we can rely on it.

Logic and God

It is also helpful to distinguish incomprehensibility from inconsistency. We can't avoid saying certain things about God that are incomprehensible to some extent. We say, "God made the world," but we don't know what his creative activity involved; it is beyond our understanding. We can know *that* he created, but we will never know *how*.

While we can't avoid incomprehensibility, we must eliminate inconsistency and incoherence from our language about God. It is one thing for a statement to go beyond our understanding; it is quite another for it to go against our understanding. Mozart, to illustrate, was able to compose music without putting pen to paper. On occasion he had an entire composition in his mind before he ever wrote it out. Now I find this incomprehensible; I don't understand how he could have the entire overture to Don Giovanni clearly in his mind, without having written a note of it. At the same time, this is not incoherent or inconsistent. There is nothing logically impossible about the feat. I just cannot understand how someone is able to do it.

In contrast, consider a statement like, "Mozart drew square circles." This is not merely incomprehensible, it is incoherent. The problem is not merely that I do not know how to draw square circles. I have no idea of what it is that is being done. The statement does not assert something that goes beyond my understanding; it asserts something that goes against it.

We must be careful to distinguish these two qualities in thinking about God. We can never eliminate incomprehensibility. God will always transcend the reach of our imagination. But we must eliminate inconsistencies, or we are not saying anything meaningful about God. We do not honor him by careless thinking.

Above all, we should never excuse an incoherent statement about God by appealing to God's incomprehensibility. It will not do to defend a statement like "God makes square circles" by arguing that God is incomprehensible. If our language about God can violate the fundamental rules of logic, then we can say anything about God—as long as we cover it with the shroud of "incomprehensibility." And if we can say just anything at all about God, we might as well say nothing, because nothing we say will be reliable.

THE REALITY OF GOD

For centuries—in fact, for most of human history—few people questioned the existence of God. Not everyone made a personal commitment to him, of course, and from time to time certain thinkers raised questions about his reality. But in general people believed that God presided over the universe. In biblical times, the presence of divine power in the world was evident to everybody. The great question of the Old Testament was not whether there is a God, but which is the true God? Where does he make himself known? How should we respond to him?

Things are very different today. People now find it much more difficult to believe in God. There are several reasons for this attitude.

The challenge of science
Historians agree that the rise of modern science has done more to change human life than anything else in history. In fact, some people maintain that science is the only part of human life that shows any real progress. We are certainly indebted to science and its application to the practical concerns of life for many of the comfortable features of our environment. But science not only affects the way we live, it also affects the way we look at the world.

Science operates on the assumption that the world is orderly. If we know enough about the present, we can make reliable predictions about the future. A procedure performed in Los Angeles, California, will yield identical results in Iceland or New Guinea, if the original conditions are duplicated.

Science also directs its attention to the physical world, the world of matter and energy. Scientific experiments employ our senses, such as sight and hearing, or the extension of our senses by sophisticated instruments like microscopes and telescopes.

So obvious are the gains of science and so influential are its results that people naturally hold the conclusions of science in very high esteem. In our society, a person in a white coat is practically an unquestioned source of truth. Statements beginning with the words, "According to the latest scientific evidence," or, "Scientists now believe," have the ring of final authority.

The enormous prestige of modern science tends to have a negative effect on belief in God. Although science itself doesn't require this conclusion, there are people who believe that the areas of life with which science deals are the only ones that count. They define reality as what is accessible to scientific investigation, and they equate truth with the results of scientific experiments. If science can't develop an explanation for something, then we are wasting our time worrying about it.

From such a perspective, the idea of God is hardly worth considering, because God isn't an object for scientific investigation. We can't see him, or hear him, or touch him. Astronauts do not attempt to locate him in outer space. No one expects electron microscopes to detect his presence in the atom.

Not only is God something that science cannot examine, but he is also no longer needed to explain how things work. For a while it was common to assign God responsibility for things that science couldn't explain. He accounted for the "gaps" in our understanding of the world. But scientific advances have done such a good job of filling in these gaps that there is less and less for God to do. This way of looking at God has very few supporters today.

If we are tempted to think that science affects people who are less religious than we are, we need to remind ourselves of how dependent we all are on the scientific perspective. If we develop a toothache or break an arm, we instinctively seek dental or medical help. We may pray on the way to the emergency room, but we will look for a medical solution to our problems rather than a miracle. By the same token, if we see some remarkable phenomenon, like a man apparently walking on thin air, we naturally expect a scientific explanation for it. We will be suspicious of appeals to angelic assistance. The scientific perspective is virtually unavoidable in our society, and it has an inevitable effect on our view of God.

The challenge of evil

Another obstacle to belief in God is much older than modern science, and is probably a greater threat to faith. This is the problem of evil. As we shall see, Christians believe that God is both supremely powerful and perfectly loving. So the presence of suffering in the world he has created poses a tremendous problem. If he is all-powerful, he could prevent or eliminate evil; if he is all-loving, he would certainly want to do so. Yet evil exists. So, the traditional objection goes, God must be less than perfect in either power or love. In other words, the God of Christian faith cannot be real.

If the problem of evil fails to move us on an intellectual level, eventually it touches everyone on the personal level. A serious injury, the death of a loved one, an academic or professional crisis—experiences like these inevitably lead us to wonder why God doesn't intervene to protect or rescue us from such calamities.

There are other factors which make it difficult for people to believe there is a God today, but we have probably said enough to indicate that a contemporary doctrine of God must address the question of God's existence. It is not enough to itemize his attributes according to some traditional list. We will therefore begin our doctrine of God by considering the evidence for his existence. Then we will review some important elements in the biblical portrayal of God. In the next chapter we will explore the understanding of God to which the Bible leads us.

The Bible deals with the reality of God, as it does with all great issues. And philosophy, too, can contribute to our confidence that he exists.

To begin with, the Bible knows that believing in God can be difficult. True, the writers of the Bible all assumed that God existed, but they did not assume that trusting God would always be easy for people. Some of God's closest followers found it hard to trust him at times. Not long after his great victory on Mount Carmel, Elijah was so discouraged that he wanted God to end his life. John the Baptist had doubts that Jesus was the Messiah. Jesus himself wondered why God had forsaken him. Faith in God has never been easy. So the problem of God's existence does not take us outside the concerns of the Bible.

**The evidence
of nature**

The Bible appeals to several kinds of evidence that supports the reality of God. For the most part, this evidence consists in the general or natural revelation we have already mentioned. It includes two major sources: the wonders of nature, and human experience. "The heavens are telling the glory of God," David wrote," and the firmament proclaims his handiwork" (Ps 19:1). Centuries later the apostle Paul expressed essentially the same idea: "Ever since the creation of the world, his invisible nature, namely, his eternal power and deity, has been clearly perceived in the things he has made" (Rom 1:20).

The Bible also cites human behavior as an indication of God's reality. In his sermon at Athens, Paul referred to the religious practices of his audience. ''Men of Athens, I perceive that in every way you are very religious, for as I passed along and observed the objects of your worship, I found also an altar with this inscription, 'To an unknown God.' What, therefore, you worship as unknown, this I proclaim to you'' (Ac 17:22–23).

The evidence of human experience

According to Paul, the religious experience of his listeners indicated an awareness of God, although he was not clearly understood. This awareness provided a contact point for the proclamation of God's revelation in Jesus.

Paul also found evidence that everyone experiences God in another aspect of human behavior. This is the area of conscience, or morality. Human beings everywhere have a sense of right and wrong. ''When Gentiles who have not the law do by nature what the law requires . . . they show that what the law requires is written on their hearts . . .'' (Rom 2:14–15).

PHILOSOPHICAL EVIDENCE

In passages like these the Bible appears to support the idea that there is evidence for the reality of God, and that this evidence is available to thinking people everywhere. Over the years, philosophers have also found evidence for the existence of a supreme personal being. It, too, comes from two major sources: the nature of reality and the characteristics of human experience.

The teleological argument

The most popular argument for God's existence is called the teleological argument, or the argument from design. Its starting point is the complexity and intricacy we find in nature. When we look at the beauty of a starry sky or consider the incredible mechanism of our own bodies, we find it difficult to believe that such things just happened, that they owe their existence to mere chance. They give every indication of being designed by an enormous intelligence.

If we found a watch on a deserted beach, we would naturally conclude that some intelligent being had made it, even if we had never seen one before and didn't know exactly what it was for. In the realm of nature we find things far more intricate than watches. So, if something like a watch leads us to affirm the existence of an intelligent maker, then the wonders of nature point to the existence of a supremely intelligent designer. and this is one of the activities that Christians have always attributed to God.

The cosmological argument

Besides the constitution, or construction, of the world, philosophers have also found evidence for God in the mere existence of a world. This is sometimes referred to as the cosmological argument. It begins with the observation that nothing in the realm of ordinary experience explains its own existence. Everything gets its existence from something else. In other words, its existence is dependent, or "contingent," to use a technical term.

If we think of the world, or the universe, as the entire collection of dependent things like this, we have to wonder about the origin of *its* existence. What accounts for the world as a whole? In other words, why is there something, rather than nothing?

One response is to find the ultimate cause of the universe in something whose existence is dependent, like everything else. But this won't work. Such an object can't be the reason for everything, because it needs an explanation itself. It would be just another part of the collection of dependent things.

Another response is to disallow the question. We can ask about the cause of things within the world, some say, but we can't ask about the origin of the world as a whole. But this answer is unsatisfactory, too. It is natural to look for the explanation of things. Asking such questions is what human intelligence consists of. There is no good reason to stop just because we arrive at the world as a whole. So this response arbitrarily limits the range of human inquiry.

A third answer arises from the elimination of the previous two. If there is something that accounts for the existence of the world as a whole, and if it can't be something that depends on anything else for existence, then it must be something that accounts for its own existence. It must be a self-existent being—one whose existence does not depend on anything else. This, too, is a quality Christians have always applied to God. If the world has an explanation, such a being must exist.

The ontological argument

The most famous and controversial argument for the existence of God is the so-called ontological argument. Unlike any of the other arguments, it begins with the mere idea of God, or the idea of a perfect being. It has taken many different forms, and philosophers have debated its merits for centuries. In its most effective form, the ontological argument concludes from the idea that God is the greatest being conceivable, that we cannot think of him as not existing. If we can think intelligently of God at all, if the very idea of God makes sense, then God must be real.

The reasons for this conclusion are fairly clear. If God did not exist, nothing could create him unless it were at least as great as he is. If he did exist, nothing could exterminate him without being at least as powerful as he is. In either case, God loses his status as the single greatest being. So we have to think of God, if we can think of him at all, as existing without the possibility of not existing.

The other major source of evidence for the reality of God is human experience. Philosophers have noticed the same two features mentioned in Paul's writings: religion and morality. They seem to be universal factors in human experience.

The argument from religion

Religion takes two forms. There are explicit religious experiences, such as acts of devotion, rituals, religious instruction, and the like. Throughout history, human beings have engaged in religious activities of one kind or another.

In addition to specific religious activities, there is a dimension in everyone's experience that can only be described as "religious." Human beings have a natural inclination to worship something, to invest something with ultimate importance. It may not be a traditional object of religious devotion. It may be one's career, one's country, or even something as relatively unimportant as the fortunes of a favorite baseball team or the antics of a celebrity. But everybody worships something. Worship is something distinctively and essentially human.

The best explanation for this aspect of human experience is the reality of its object. Most of our basic desires find their fulfillment in something that actually exists. Since the tendency to worship is so basic to human experience, it is logical to conclude that it, too, corresponds to something in reality. The existence of God provides the best explanation for this dimension of human experience. Augustine put it this way centuries ago: "Thou hast made us for thyself, and our hearts are restless until they find their rest in thee."[3]

Many thinkers believe that moral experience also points to the reality of God. Moral sensitivity is one of the essential characteristics of human beings. We are all aware that there is a difference between right and wrong. We sense that we ought to do certain things and avoid others, whether we follow this sense or not.

The moral argument

3. This famous statement is translated in many different ways. One is this: "Thou madest us for Thyself, and our heart is restless, until it repose in Thee." In *The Confessions of St. Augustine,* trans. Edward B. Pusey (New York: Washington Square Press, Inc., 1962), p. 1.

There are exceptions to this rule, of course, but they only prove it to be true. We do not regard individuals who lack this capacity as persons in the full sense of the word. We deny them the privileges of full-fledged members of society; we usually lock them up.

Besides this basic sensitivity, certain obligations are also well-nigh universal. They are difficult to specify, to be sure, and they are definitely few in number, but such moral standards do exist. The wanton taking of human life is forbidden in every culture. There is also a nearly universal obligation to tell the truth, unless there are good reasons not to.

The presence of moral sensitivity does not mean that everyone behaves in a moral way. It just means that people sense that they should do certain things, whether they actually do them or not. We often violate our sense of right and wrong. When this happens, however, we typically attempt to justify our actions. This tendency to excuse our behavior only shows how strong our moral sensitivity is.

There are many explanations for this part of human experience. It is especially popular to regard it as the product of social conditioning. According to this view, you believe something is wrong because your parents taught you it was wrong, because their parents taught them it was wrong, and so on. There is nothing objective about our moral standards.

But for others, moral experience points to the reality of God. To be moral is to feel responsible, and to feel responsible is to feel responsible to—well, to *what?* The only adequate answer is, to someone, to a person. As persons, we feel accountable to persons. If ultimate reality is impersonal, if the universe is nothing more than the arrangement of finite particles of matter, then there is no good reason for our sense of right and wrong. It has its only adequate explanation in the reality of a supreme person who is the ultimate source of our moral standards and who holds us accountable for our behavior. Such activity, of course, is precisely what Christians have always attributed to God.

There seems, then, to be reasonable evidence for the reality of God, from the world as a whole and from human experience in particular.

**The limits
of argument**
People often say that no one can *prove* the existence of God, because no amount of evidence can convince someone against his will. But this is true of many things, not just God's existence. And it is a mistake to think that this is what the arguments for God are trying to do. Instead of attempts to convince people that God exists, it is better to think of these arguments as indications that it is reasonable to

believe in God. Their effect is to show that religious faith is a genuine option for thinking people, not to persuade those who are convinced otherwise.

Besides, if the evidence of God's existence is less than compelling, this should not surprise us, considering the kind of person God is. God invites us to believe in him, but he will never force us. He always gives us room to make our own decisions about him. This is why all the evidence in the world will never make an airtight case for God's existence. He wouldn't want it to. Faith would be of little value if people had no conceivable alternative. The evidence is there—not enough to provide absolute proof but enough to make a reasonable conclusion— and it supports the conclusion that God is real.

Having considered the question of God's reality, we now need to examine some of the biblical descriptions of God.

THE BIBLICAL VIEW OF GOD

We can get an overview of the biblical concept of God by looking briefly at three related topics—the names of God, the activities of God, and the qualities attributed to him by the biblical writers.

The Names of God

The question of God's name was particularly important to the Hebrew people. When God called Moses to lead his people out of bondage, the reluctant prophet wondered what he should say when people asked him to name the God who had sent him (Ex 3:13). The disclosure of his name was one of the most important aspects of God's revelation to the Jewish people.

For ancient people, a name was more than a means to indicate something. It was the bearer of identity; it expressed the inner essence of its object. This is why naming a child was so important, and why naming the animals was an essential part of their creation. Nothing fully existed until it had a name.

Elohim

The two most important names of God in the Old Testament are *Elohim* and *Yahweh. El* was the word used by the peoples surrounding the ancient Israelites to refer to a divine being. *Elohim* is its plural form in Hebrew. *El* and *Elohim* are a little like the word *god* in English, which is used both to refer to a divine being (''god'') and as a proper name (''God'').

Elohim appears 2,570 times in the Old Testament, beginning with Genesis 1:1.[4] It is almost always treated as a singular noun. As a name for God, it indicates that all divine power is concentrated in him. He performs many of the functions attributed to the gods of other peoples, and he is the creator and sustainer of nature.

Yahweh

Yahweh is the most important of God's names in the Old Testament, where it occurs more than 6,800 times. Unlike *Elohim,* it never refers to other gods, but only to the God of Israel. God identifies himself as *Yahweh* especially in connection with the most important events in Hebrew history. As *Yahweh,* he delivered them from bondage, adopted them as a chosen nation, and guided them into the promised land.[5]

The most famous passage containing *Yahweh* is Exodus 3:14: "God said to Moses, 'I am who I am.'" The meaning of these words is widely discussed among biblical scholars and theologians. Some see them as an affirmation of divine self-existence, or eternity. Others observe that the Hebrew uses a future tense here—"I will be what I will be." They conclude that the words express God's freedom, his self-determining character. For still others, this statement speaks primarily of the presence of God, rather than his nature or reality. If the words are translated, "I shall be there as who I am," they portray God as a living presence, ready to act redemptively for his people.

The two primary names for God in the Old Testament point, respectively, to his sovereign power and redemptive presence. In general, *Elohim* designates the creator and *Yahweh,* the redeemer. Together, they identify the comprehensive work of God in the world.

"Jehovah"

The translation of the Hebrew word *Yahweh* has an interesting history. As originally written, it contained only the four consonants YHWH. We don't know just how it was pronounced. "Yahweh" is probably correct. By the time of Christ, Jews held this name of God in such awe that they refused to say it out loud. They spoke another word, *Adonai,* whenever YHWH appeared in a biblical passage they were reading. Later, when vowel marks were added in copying Hebrew manuscripts, scribes put the vowels for *Adonai* around the consonants YHWH to remind the reader of this practice.

A combination of the letters YHWH and the vowels in *Adonai* produces the word *Jehovah,* which occurs as one of God's names in the

4. Carl F. H. Henry, *God, Revelation and Authority* (6 vols.; Waco, Tx.: Word Books, Publisher, 1976–83), 2: 187.

5. Henry, *God, Revelation and Authority,* 2: 210.

King James Version of the Bible (cf. Ex 6:3; Ps 83:18). But there is really no such word in Hebrew. The name *Jehovah* does not appear in recent versions of the Bible. Some, like the Jerusalem Bible, use *Yahweh.* Others, like the Revised Standard Version, translate YHWH with "Lord" or "God" in all capital letters (cf. Ex 3:15, 16), as the King James Version often does.

Father

In the New Testament we find two interesting developments in the divine name. First, the use of one Greek word, *theos,* replaces the variety of proper names that appear in the Old Testament. *Theos* is the equivalent of "God" in English.

Second, the identification of God as "father" represents a significant advance on the Old Testament view of God. In many ways it summarizes the unsurpassable revelation of God in the person of Jesus. God is the Father of Jesus (Rom 15:6); Jesus is the unique Son of God (Jn 3:16). But more than this, in Jesus, God manifests and extends his fatherhood to all human beings. By responding to this gracious overture, we are brought into an intensely close and personal relationship with God. We, too, become the children of God. And we can speak of him and to him as our Father (Mt 6:9; 1 Jn 3:1–2). Jesus, in fact, used the Aramaic word *Abba* to show how intimate our relation to God can be. It is roughly equivalent to familiar English words like "Daddy" and "Papa."

We can learn several things from this biblical emphasis on the names of God. The most basic is the fact that God is a person. To name something is to elevate it from the realm of things to the realm of persons. We give names to people. We sometimes name animals and machines to indicate that they are more to us than mere objects in the physical world. The fact that God has names indicates that he is personal in nature. He is a "thou," not an "it."

Moreover, in revealing his names to us, God calls us into a personal relationship with him. When we exchange names with someone, or introduce ourselves, we have the beginning of a personal relationship. To identify yourself by name is to offer your friendship.

Third, in giving us his names, God gives us himself. Remember the importance of names in Hebrew thought. A name summarizes the essence of its bearer. God's nams, therefore, tell us what God is really all about. In sharing his names with us, God shares himself.

The Activities of God

Besides the names of God, the Bible also describes a number of God's actions, or activities. It is customary to develop a doctrine of God by defining a series of divine qualities. In the Bible, however, God's actions receive more attention than his attributes. Its writers identify God by describing what he does rather than what he is. We see this in the opening verse of Genesis: God created. It is evident in the confession Hebrew worshipers made when they offered their sacrifices: "The Lord brought us out of Egypt" (cf. Dt 26:5–11).

The New Testament continues this interest in divine actions. God was acting in the ministry of Jesus for human salvation (2 Cor 5:19). His resurrection, in particular, was a manifestation of divine power: "God raised him up" (Ac 2:24).

Creation and salvation are the two most important divine activities. But associated with them are a number of other things God does. He upholds the universe (Neh 9:6; Heb 1:3). He forgives sins (Ex 34:7). He communicates with human beings (Am 3:7; Heb 1:1–2). He makes and keeps promises (Dt 15:6; 2 Pet 3:9). He predicts the future (Isa 46:10). God also makes plans (Isa 46:11), and he occasionally changes his mind (Gen 6:6; Jer 18:7–9).

The personhood of God emerges in his actions as well as in his names. Only a person can make plans and work to fulfill them, and only a person can communicate with other persons.

The Attributes of God

Even though it is primarily interested in God's activity, the Bible does attribute a number of qualities to God. We can only call attention to some of the most important ones here.

God, of course, is supremely powerful (Jer 32:17). He is everlasting (Ps 90:2), or immortal (1 Tim 6:16). He is everywhere (Ps 139:7–8; Ac 17:27–28). And he knows everything (1 Jn 3:20). Because of his unrivaled greatness, God is utterly unique, unlike anything or anyone else (cf. Isa 45:5; 46:9). Other supposed gods are vastly inferior, and in the final analysis they amount to nothing at all. He alone is God (Dt 6:4).

The fact that God is different from anything else lies behind the quality of divine holiness (Lev 11:44; Isa 6:3). We tend to think of "holy" as meaning "pure," "undefiled," or "morally upright," and it does include these ideas. But more basically, it refers to the quality of being utterly different from ordinary things. Something holy gives a sense of the uncanny. It is mysterious. We find it fascinating and terrifying at the same time.

God's love   The Bible attributes many personal qualities to God. None of them, however, is more important than love. The English word "love" covers an enormous range of meaning. We use it to describe our attitudes toward everything from our favorite food to the people who mean the most to us. In Greek, the original language of the New Testament, there are several different words for love. Two of them are particularly important for understanding the nature of divine love. They are *eros* and *agapē*.[6]

Eros is the Greek root for such English words as "erotic" and "eroticism." While these derivations have distinctly sexual overtones, the original meaning of *eros* is not necessarily sexual at all. It refers to the attraction a person feels for something he finds desirable and wants to possess. *Eros* may refer to the desire one has for another person, but it can also refer to one's attraction for anything, such as knowledge, money, or power.

Agapē, in contrast, is love which flows entirely from the nature of the lover. It does not depend on desirable qualities in its object. Instead of seeking to possess its object, *agapē* leads to self-giving, self-sacrificing actions. It is untainted by self-interest; it is unconditional. To use Shakespeare's words, it does not "bend with the remover to remove."[7] It continues whether or not it is ever returned.

The New Testament uses the second of these words to describe God's attitude toward human beings, as many familiar texts indicate (cf. Jn 3:16). "We love, because he first loved us" (1 Jn 4:19); "In this is love, not that we loved God but that he loved us . . ." (1 Jn 4:10). We see God's love in the lavish gifts he bestows upon us: "For God so loved the world that he gave his only Son" (Jn 3:16). We also see it in the fact that God loves the totally undeserving: "But God shows his love for us in that while we were yet sinners Christ died for us" (Rom 5:8). God's love, then, is his unconditional commitment to the well-being of his creatures. It is aggressive, generous, and uncalculating.

From its unconditional character, we may be tempted to think of God's love for us as a benign indulgence. We may suppose that God doesn't really care what we do, because he will go on loving us no matter what. But nothing is farther from the truth. The Bible speaks of God in several ways that prevent us from drawing this conclusion.

---

6. The word *eros* does not appear in the Greek New Testament, but it was part of the vocabulary available to the apostolic writers. It is illuminating that they avoided it in favor of *agapē* in describing both divine and human relationships.

7. "Love is not love which alters when it alteration finds or bends with the remover to remove" (William Shakespeare, Sonnet CXVI, in *The Portable Shakespeare* [New York: The Viking Press, 1944], p. 754).

God's wrath   God is relentlessly opposed to sin and determined to eliminate it from the universe. He is a "jealous God" (Ex 20:5), "who will by no means clear the guilty" (Ex 34:7). He will bring "every deed into judgment" (Ecc 12:14), and finally destroy the wicked in a lake of fire (Rev 20:14–15).

Some people see a contradiction between God's love and his relentless opposition to sin. They wonder how the same being can be at once a merciful and compassionate parent and a stern judge of evildoers. Some, in fact, have gone so far as to maintain that the God of the Old Testament and the God of the New are entirely different beings. They could not identify the loving Father of Jesus Christ with the seemingly vengeful God of the Hebrews.[8]

However, there is no contradiction between these aspects of God's character if we recognize the true nature of his love. It is unconditional, to be sure, but it is also deadly serious. We cannot say that God loves us so much that nothing we do really matters to him. We have to say that God loves us so much that everything we do matters to him. As far as he is concerned, there is nothing insignificant about us. Our thoughts, our behavior, our desires, our attitudes—everything about us is important to him.

Because he loves us, he is satisfied with nothing less than the best for us. He is distressed when we are willing to settle for less. This explains why God is utterly ruthless in the face of sin throughout the Bible. It never goes unnoticed and unresponded to. This isn't because God is determined to even the score, to take revenge for every slight he has suffered. It is because he cannot stand idle while the people he loves destroy themselves.

God's desire for the best can make life uncomfortable for people if they don't share this objective. His numerous commands and prohibitions seem to some like so much meddling in the incidentals of life. But against the background of God's enormous concern for human beings, we can see these requirements as expressions of his desire that we enjoy the best life possible. Nothing related to our happiness escapes his attention.

In this chapter we have examined some concerns that are basic to the Christian view of God. We have explored the possibility of knowing God and considered the question of his existence. We have reviewed some of the important features in the biblical portrayal of God.

8. This was the view of the second-century heretic Marcion, for example (Bengt Haegglund, *History of Theology*, trans. Gene J. Lund [St. Louis: Concordia Publishing House, 1968], p. 41).

With this discussion in mind, we can now attempt a more formal statement of the doctrine of God.

STUDY HELPS

Questions for review

1. How and why is our knowledge of God limited?

2. What should we require of our language about God?

3. Why is it difficult for people to believe in God?

4. What evidence supports God's existence?

5. What are the biblical names for God and what do they signify?

6. What actions and qualities does the Bible attribute to God?

7. What is the nature of God's love and how does it react to sin?

Questions for further study

1. How is the language about God in a book like this different from the language about God we use in prayer, or in singing hymns?

2. In sharing their faith in God, should Christians appeal primarily to personal experience or to rational evidence?

3. The French thinker, Blaise Pascal (1623–1662) proposed the following wager in response to the question of God's existence. Do you think it provides a good basis for believing in God?

   "Let us weigh the gain and the loss in wagering that God is. Let us estimate these two chances. If you gain, you gain all; if you lose, you lose nothing. Wager, then, without hesitation that He is." (*Pensées: Thoughts on Religion and Other Subjects,* trans. William Finlayson Trotter, ed. H. S. Thayer [New York: Washington Square Press, Inc., 1965], p. 72).

4. How does our concept, or understanding, of God affect our relationship to God? What experience of God does each of these terms suggest: "father," "judge," "shepherd," "uncaused cause"?

5. The concept people have of God generally changes as they grow. How is the view of God you have now different from the one you had as a child or as an adolescent?

6. Many people see changing ideas of God in human history. How has the idea of God changed since biblical times? Do Seventh-day Adventists have a different view of God today from what they had a hundred years ago? What factors could contribute to such changes?

Suggestions for Bible study

1. Scholars sometimes distinguish three types of language about God: Literal language means exactly what it says. Symbolic language uses what is obviously a figure of speech. And analogical language applies to God terms that also apply to creaturely objects. Which of these categories would you use to describe each of the following biblical statements about God?

Genesis 1:1	1 John 3:20
1 Timothy 6:16	Matthew 19:26b
John 4:24	Genesis 6:6
1 John 4:8	Psalm 23:1
Malachi 3:6a	Psalm 18:2
Exodus 34:14	Isaiah 46:11b
Psalm 90:2b	Exodus 34:7

2. Read Genesis 1. Write a list of all the things you can learn about God from this one chapter of the Bible.

3. In several passages describing or written by Paul, the apostle appeals to the evidence for God in nature. Analyze the following examples in light of these questions: (1) To whom is Paul speaking/writing? (2) What things does he mention as evidence of God's existence? (3) How do people respond to this evidence?

Acts 14:14–18
Acts 17:22–32
Romans 1:18–25

4. Some people see a developing concept of God in the Bible. Do you think the following passages support this idea?

a. Exodus 18:11; Exodus 20:3; Psalm 86:8; Isaiah 37:19–20
b. Genesis 1:1; John 1:3; Hebrews 1:2
c. Exodus 20:5–6; Psalm 103:8–14
d. Genesis 3:8; Exodus 25:8; John 1:14; Revelation 21:3
e. 1 Samuel 16:14; Isaiah 45:7; Romans 8:28; 1 John 1:5

SUGGESTIONS FOR FURTHER READING

Ellen G. White discusses the nature of God in *Steps to Christ,* pp. 9–15 and 85–91, and in *Testimonies for the Church,* vol. 8, pp. 255–289.

From Adventist writers

A. Graham Maxwell emphasizes the trustworthiness of God in *Can God Be Trusted?* (Nashville, Tenn.: Southern Publishing Association, 1977).

Richard Rice analyzes some recent arguments for the reality of God in "Does God-Talk Make Sense Today? Facing the Secular Challenge," *Spectrum,* vol. 7, no. 4, pp. 40–45.

Fritz Guy examines evidence for the existence of God in "Affirming the Reality of God: Some Observations," in *The Stature of Christ: Essays in Honor of Edward Heppenstall* (privately printed, 1970), pp. 13–22.

The topic of God-language, or theistic discourse, has received a great deal of attention during the last thirty years. Two readable accounts of the discussion are Frederick Ferré, *Language, Logic, and God* (Chicago: University of Chicago Press, 1981), and Terrence W. Tilley, *Talking of God: An Introduction to Philosophical Analysis of Religious Language* (New York: The Paulist Press, 1978). An anthology containing some of the most important contributions to this discussion is *The Logic of God: Theology and Verification,* ed. Malcolm L. Diamond and Thomas V. Litzenburg, Jr. (Indianapolis: The Bobbs-Merrill Company, Inc., 1975).

From other writers

Over the years the question of evidence for God's existence has probably attracted more philosophical and theological discussion than any other single topic. Introductions to the various proofs for God's existence appear in John Hick, *Philosophy of Religion* (2d ed.; Englewood Cliffs, N.J.: Prentice-Hall, Inc., 1973), pp. 15–30; William L. Rowe, *Philosophy of Religion: An Introduction* (Belmont, Calif.: Wadsworth Publishing Company, Inc., 1978), pp. 16–59; and Charles Hartshorne, *A Natural Theology for Our Time* (La Salle, Ill.: The Open Court Publishing Company, 1967), pp. 29–89.

John Hick provides a more extensive analysis of the classical arguments in *Arguments for the Existence of God* (New York: The Seabury Press, 1971). Anthologies of these arguments include *The Ontological Argument from St. Anselm to Contemporary Philosophers,* ed. Alvin Plantinga (Garden City, N.Y.: Anchor Books, 1965); and *The Cosmological Arguments: A Spectrum of Opinion,* ed. Donald R. Burrill (Garden City, N.Y.: Anchor Books, 1967).

The most comprehensive discussion of this issue in recent years from a theological perspective is Hans Kung, *Does God Exist? An Answer for Today,* trans. Edward Quinn (New York: Vintage Books, 1981). Christian apologist C. S. Lewis presents a readable argument for the reality of God in *Mere Christianity* (New York: The Macmillan Company, 1960), pp. 3–25.

The biblical concept of God is the subject of many scholarly and popular books. One of the most important discussions in recent years is Samuel

Terrien, *The Elusive Presence: Toward a New Biblical Theology* (San Francisco: Harper & Row, Publishers, 1978). Another recent proposal is Dale Patrick, *The Rendering of God in the Old Testament* (Philadelphia: Fortress Press, 1981).

Rudolf Otto's famous analysis of the primary attribute of God is *The Idea of the Holy: An Inquiry into the Non-rational Factor in the Idea of the Divine and Its Relation to the Rational,* trans. John W. Harvey (New York: Oxford University Press, 1958). The single most influential discussion of divine love remains Anders Nygren, *Agape and Eros,* trans. Philip S. Watson (New York: Harper & Row, Publishers, 1969).

4

THE DOCTRINE OF GOD:
A CONSTRUCTIVE PROPOSAL

"Before the mountains were brought forth, or ever thou hadst formed
the earth and the world, from everlasting to everlasting, thou art God"
(Psalm 90:2).

"God is spirit, and those who worship him must worship in spirit and
truth" (John 4:24).

"Worthy art thou, our Lord and God, to receive glory and honor and
power, for thou didst create all things, and by thy will they existed and
were created" (Revelation 4:11).

Exodus 34:6–7
Nehemiah 9:6
Job 38–41
Psalm 33:6–9
Psalm 103:13–14
Psalm 139
Isaiah 6:1–6
Isaiah 46:8–11
Jeremiah 10:10
Jeremiah 18:1–11
Daniel 2:20–21

Matthew 28:19
Romans 4:17
Romans 8:28
Romans 11:33
1 Corinthians 1:9
2 Corinthians 13:14
1 Timothy 2:4
1 Timothy 6:15–16
James 1:17
Revelation 14:7

Our objective in this chapter is a coherent description of God which is
faithful to the Bible, sensitive to the experience of the church, relevant

to thinking people today, and helpful to religious experience. Whether we reach this objective or not, it is the standard by which our work should be judged. Moreover, we have taken for our guiding theme the reign of God. This is the appropriate place to develop this idea more fully.

God in relationship

If we think of God primarily in terms of his reign, or his sovereignty, we must think of him in relation to something else. To reign is to reign over something; no one reigns in isolation. Consequently, we can understand God only in relationship. We cannot conceive of him as an utterly independent, solitary object of thought.

Our doctrine of God will therefore develop as an account of his relation to the world. We may affirm God's essential independence of the world. He does not need it in order to exist. But everything we know about God derives from his relation to our world. This is clear from the first thing the Bible describes about God—his creative activity. There is no better place to begin in our attempt to formulate a Christian concept of God.

According to the Bible, God brought into existence the world of finite beings by a free creative act: "In the beginning God created the heavens and the earth" (Gen 1:1). From this comprehensive statement and the descriptions that follow, the basic elements in a doctrine of God emerge. They are: (1) God's basic identity, or what makes him God; (2) God's character, or his disposition toward the creaturely world; (3) God's activity in the world, or the way God affects his creatures; and (4) God's experience of the world, or the way God's creatures affect him. We will examine each of these topics. First, however, we should observe the fundamental relation between God and the world which the biblical concept of creation provides.

GOD AND THE WORLD

The word "world" is often a synonym for the planet earth. But it can also refer to the entire universe. We will use it here in the second sense. Genesis 1–2 describes the origin of life on this planet, but it also provides a basis for understanding God's relation to all of reality.

The idea of creation presents us with a fundamental distinction which lies behind every aspect of Christian faith—the distinction between creator and creation. This distinction is all-inclusive, and it is permanent. Everything that exists belongs to one or the other of these categories. It is either creator or creature. As creator, God is the source of all reality. He alone exists independently; everything else owes its existence to him. Morever, what is creaturely is always creaturely. A creature can never become a divine being.

This basic distinction between God and the world, between creator and creation, rules out two other world views that have had great influence in human history. One is known as monism. The other is dualism.

As the word suggests, monism is the belief that all reality is one. It also affirms that all reality is divine, so everything real is a part of God. According to monism, the distinctions that seem so important on the level of ordinary experience—between different persons, between pain and pleasure, life and death, good and evil—all these differences are illusory. They arise from our misinterpretation of things.

Monism

The way of salvation this world view implies is one of self-realization. It consists in discovering one's essential divinity, and usually includes a method for overcoming the distinctions suggested by ordinary experience. The great religions of the East typically present a monistic view of reality.

As a religious force, dualism is not nearly as influential as it once was, but at times it has represented a serious rival to the biblical view of God and the world. According to dualism, there are two ultimate principles, rather than one, which are engaged in permanent conflict with each other. One principle is good, usually symbolized by light. The other is evil, or darkness.[1]

Dualism

Dualism provides a convenient solution to the problem of evil, because it attributes all suffering to the evil principle in reality. In its pure form, it promises no end to suffering, since evil is just as powerful as good. Understandably, almost all dualistic religions, such as Zoroastrianism, affirm the ultimate victory of good over evil, even though this compromises the basic idea.

With its affirmation of the creaturely world, the doctrine of creation excludes monism. On the one hand, the world is real, even though it is not divine. Our experience of things in time and space is not an illusion. (How could we know if it were?) On the other hand, the world is

Doctrine of creation

---

1. The opposition between God and the devil, or Satan, described in the Bible differs significantly from dualism, because the conflict is not eternal. According to Christianity, the devil is not a primordial evil power, but a creature who fell into sin from an exalted position (cf. Isa 14:12–15; Ezek 28:12–19), and his rebellion against God will eventually come to an end (Rev 20:10).

not evil merely because it is not God. The distinction between God and the world does not coincide with the distinction between good and evil. The created world is good because it was created by a good and loving God.

The doctrine of creation also conflicts with dualism in two ways. First, it allows for only one supreme being: God. He is the single source of all that exists. His power is unrivaled, so there is no chance of a permanent conflict between God and anything else. Second, God is wholly good, and what he creates is essentially good, too. Evil doesn't belong in the scheme of things. It isn't something God created. In fact, it isn't a "something" at all; it is a distortion of what was meant to be.

The unity of God

As creator, God enjoys universal sovereignty over the world, as statements like the following affirm: "The earth is the Lord's and the fulness thereof, the world and those who dwell therein" (Ps 24:1). Everything belongs to God. Because God's reign is all-inclusive, he is the only being who deserves to be worshiped. This is the single most important theme in the Old Testament—there is only one God. We find it in the first of the ten commandments: "You shall have no other gods before me" (Ex 20:3). We see it in this great confession: "Hear, O Israel, the Lord our God, the Lord is one" (Dt 6:4; the Hebrew allows for several translations).

Because it emphasizes that God is one, the religion of the Old Testament is often identified as "monotheism," in contrast to "polytheism," the belief that there are many gods. Polytheism and monotheism involve divergent views of life and of reality as a whole.

Polytheism

In polytheism reality is divided up, or parceled out, among many divine beings. Each god has a different sphere of influence, or a limited range of power. One is in charge of the sea. Another is responsible for war. Still others preside over hunting, planting, building, and so on. In ancient times, for example, each nation had its favorite god, which looked after its interests. When one country defeated another in war, the people attributed this to the superiority of one god to the other.

Monotheism

According to monotheism, a single divine being rules over everything and everyone. Reality is not divided up among different centers of divine influence, competing with each other for human allegiance. Reality is "of a piece." It forms a coherent whole.

This means that our personal, individual lives can have coherence, too. The various facets of our existence find unity in a single object of devotion: the one true God. This is precisely why the so-called first great commandment directly follows the confession of faith in the oneness of God: "Hear, O Israel: The Lord our God is one Lord; and you shall love the Lord your God with all your heart, and with all your soul, and with all your might" (Dt 6:4–5). The universal sovereignty of God makes it possible to love him with every fiber of our beings, because nothing we can do takes us outside his domain.

Although the oneness of God is basic to biblical religion, it apparently took the Hebrew people a long time to grasp its meaning and importance. In early years, God was identified with the patriarchs of Israel, the nomadic herdsmen Abraham, Isaac, and Jacob. After the Exodus, he was identified as the one who had delivered the Israelites from Egyptian bondage. For many years polytheism posed a great threat to monotheism. The people of Israel were constantly tempted to participate in the religious practices of surrounding nations, and they were finally subjected to Babylonian captivity because of their failure to worship God alone (see Jer 1:14–16).

The Old Testament reveals a developing understanding of God's true status. At times, God is described as greater than other gods, a sort of first among many: "Now I know that the Lord is greater than all gods" (Ex 18:11); "There is none like thee among the gods, O Lord, nor are there any works like thine" (Ps 86:8). Eventually the recognition emerges that if God is infinitely greater than all others, he must be the only God there is: "They [idols] were no gods. . . . Thou alone art the Lord" (Isa 37:19–20).

The emphatic distinction between God and creation excludes idolatry. Idolatry is the practice of identifying God with some finite reality. In its most rudimentary form, it is an attempt to depict divinity by means of some physical reality. An idol may be an object existing naturally, such as a stone or a tree, or it may be a human artifact. Either way, it consists in crossing the boundary, or blurring the distinction, between creator and creature. It brings God down to the level of a creature, or it elevates some finite being to the status of divinity. Because God is the creator of all, no physical object adequately represents him. As Paul said in Athens, "We ought not to think that the Deity is like gold, or silver, or stone, a representation by the art and imagination of man" (Ac 17:29).

Idolatry

Idolatry also involves an attempt to limit and manipulate God. If God is restricted to some specific object or place, then we can control him to some extent. We may be able to appease his anger with sacrifices or curry his favor with expensive gifts. At least, we can limit his control over us by running away. But Jonah discovered that you can't run away from God; he rules the sea as well as the land. Neither is his love restricted; he loves the Ninevites along with the Israelites.

The real problem with idolatry is an inadequate conception of God, which leads to an inappropriate response to him. This is by no means restricted to primitive or ancient peoples. In contemporary Western society, few people actually worship idols, but many people have a distorted view of God. They regard him as someone or something to be called upon to meet their needs from time to time, or as a source of personal gratification. They try to manipulate him to get what they want. Other people give finite things their ultimate devotion. They place their trust in human potential, scientific knowledge, or military strength. So in its essence, idolatry is still with us. It is the perpetual rival of genuine religion.

We have seen that the doctrine of creation gives us a basic understanding of God's relation to the world. It excludes a variety of religious beliefs and practices. Now we turn to the first of the four major elements in our doctrine of God.

GOD'S IDENTITY

As we have seen, the biblical view of creation involves a certain understanding of God. Theologians traditionally express the idea of God by means of several divine attributes or qualities. In this section we are particularly interested in the things that establish God's basic identity—in other words, what it is that makes God God.

Self-existence, or "aseity," as it is sometimes called, is probably the most fundamental divine attribute. It refers to the quality of independent existence we have already mentioned. The relation between God and creation is assymetrical. The world needs God, but God doesn't need the world. Its existence is derivative, but his is original, underived, and originating.

Because God is self-existent, he is also eternal. He has always existed and he always will. Nothing could threaten him, because there is nothing that he has not made.

Omnipotence   The most famous divine attributes are omnipotence, omnipresence, and omniscience. They all contain the Latin root meaning "all." God's omnipotence, or power, is logically related to his self-existence. As the source of reality, God must be supremely powerful, of course. But omnipotence means not merely that God is more powerful than anything else. It means that he could not be more powerful than he is. In other words, his power is perfect.

Just what perfect power involves is a matter of considerable discussion. If we insist that perfect power is "power to do anything," we soon run into difficulties. Can God make a rock so big he couldn't lift it? Can God add two and two and get five? Can God make a square circle? Can God create uncreated creatures? If God can do anything, then we have to answer yes to all such questions, because there is nothing God can't do. So this definition of omnipotence leads to absurd statements about God.

For this reason, most theologians identify perfect power as "power to do the logically possible." In denying that God can do what is logically impossible, we do not limit his power. We simply insist that our language about him make sense. The reason God cannot make square circles, add two and two and get five, or create uncreated creatures is not because his power is inadequate. It is because such things aren't doable. They are arrangements of words with no meaningful content. We do not honor God by attributing nonsense to him or detract from his glory by denying it.

Omnipresence

Omnipresence describes God's involvement in the world spatially; it is the quality of being everywhere. Like omnipotence, it follows from the idea that God is the universal sovereign, and it means that there is no part of the universe from which God is excluded. On the practical religious level, this gives us the assurance of God's presence wherever we are. Nothing can separate us from him. It also reminds us that we can never hide from him; all we do is open to his gaze.

The characteristic of omnipresence raises the question of whether or not God has a body of some kind, a question on which Christians differ. Those who believe that God has a body often appeal to the biblical statement that man was created "in the image of God" (Gen 1:27), which seems to suggest a physical similarity between man and God. If human beings resemble God, they reason, and if human beings have bodies, then it is logical to assume that God, too, exists in bodily form.

In addition, many biblical passages attribute physical characteristics to God. Adam and Eve heard the sound of God walking in the garden of Eden (Gen 3:8). Moses saw God's back as he passed by on Mount Sinai (Ex 33:23). Isaiah and Daniel saw God sitting on a throne (Isa 6:1; Dan 7:9). There are numerous references to God's eyes, his hand, and his mouth, and he is often described as speaking, and sometimes as weeping.

On the other hand, many Christians attribute to God the quality of ''incorporeality,'' to use the technical term. They believe that important considerations prevent us from concluding that God exists in bodily form. One is the strong biblical condemnation of any attempt to depict God by physical means. The second of the ten commandments, for example, prohibits both the manufacture and worship of images (Ex 20:4–5). Another factor is God's status as creator of the universe. He inhabits all of reality, not just a part of it (cf. Isa 57:15). He is present to human beings everywhere; he is no more available in one place than in another. In answer to the question of where one should worship God, Jesus said, ''God is spirit, and those who worship him must worship in spirit and truth'' (Jn 4:24). Since God is accessible anywhere, worship is a matter of heart and mind rather than physical location.

Those who believe that God is incorporeal appeal to other considerations as well. It is hard to see how God could be everywhere if he had a body, they reason, for to exist as a body is to be somewhere in particular; it is to be here, rather than somewhere else.

In addition, a body as we know it depends on its environment. All our physical organs—eyes, nose, mouth, hands, feet, etc.—enable us to function within our specific environment. They wouldn't be necessary if we didn't need to move around and weren't dependent on such things as food, water, and air to survive. If we say that God has a body, we seem to imply that he is similarly dependent on an environment, when the Bible clearly indicates that God does not depend on anything outside himself in order to exist. Consequently, many believe that we cannot identify God with a bodily form.

Those who affirm God's incorporeality usually interpret biblical passages which attribute physical characteristics to God as ''anthropomorphisms.'' An anthropomorphism describes God as if he had human qualities. It is a literary device, which should not be taken literally.

Perhaps we can harmonize these different views of God if we distinguish between ''having a body'' and ''assuming a physical form.'' This enables us to say that God himself is not essentially physical, but he may assume a characteristic form from time to time when he manifests himself to physical creatures. This might explain the similarities among the various descriptions of God we find in prophetic visions.

Omniscience

Omniscience is the quality of perfect knowledge. There is nothing that God does not know. In fact, we can define reality as what is known by God. His knowledge is the standard of truth.

Omniscience, like omnipotence, is the subject of much discussion. Some people insist that it means God knows everything; others argue that it means that God knows everything that is logically knowable. In either case, God knows everything there is to know. The question is whether certain things are unknowable, and therefore unknown even by God. The heart of this issue is divine foreknowledge, or God's knowledge of the future.

If God knows literally everything, the traditional argument goes, then he knows past, present, and future. He knows everything that ever will happen, just as surely as he knows everything that ever has happened. So, to deny that God knows the future in all its detail is to deny his omniscience and compromise his perfection.

But if God knows the future in all its detail, the counter-argument runs, then everything that will ever happen is already definite. Everything will happen just as God foresees, and there is nothing left to be decided. And if nothing remains to be decided, there is no such thing as freedom, for freedom involves selecting between genuine alternatives. If all our choices are known by God in advance, then we do not really make them when we choose; we merely find out what they are.

We shall not attempt to settle this complicated issue here. But you should keep in mind that supporters of both sides of the question agree that God's knowledge is perfect. They differ as to whether the future—in particular, whether future free decisions—can be genuine objects of knowledge.

The idea of creation not only establishes the essential identity of God, it also suggests the kind of being God is. And it implies a certain attitude on God's part toward the world he has made.

GOD'S ATTITUDE TOWARD THE WORLD

As we said earlier, God brought the world into existence by a free, creative act. God created because he chose to do so, not because he was compelled to do so. We see his freedom clearly in the fact that he finished his creative activity when it reached its conclusion (Gen 2:2). It didn't go on and on indefinitely.

Person

Because God is free and self-determined, we can speak of him as a personal being. The concept of "person" is one of the most significant ideas we have. It plays an important role in our understanding of both God and man. But it is a difficult concept to define. We will try to identify some of the things it involves.

To be a person, something must first of all be a unity. It must be an individual being, not a mere collection of beings. A forest, for example, is not a person. To be a unity, something must have a center which organizes and determines its activities. The central nervous system, including the brain, determines the activities of the entire organism in higher forms of animal life and human beings. In addition to unity, or individuality, a person is also characterized by self-consciousness. It is not only a unity, but it is aware of itself as a unity.

Unity and self-consciousness enable a person to experience relationships with other persons, relationships in which there is reciprocity. When you and I encounter a person, we encounter something that can affect us and be affected by us in similar ways.

A personal being is also free or self-determined, to some extent. It is never entirely the product of factors outside its control. Each person is at least partly the result of his own choices. For this reason, we hold persons responsible for their behavior.

Because a person is free and self-determined, there is always an element of mystery in a person's behavior. His actions are never entirely predictable. He may decide to do something he has never done before or express himself in an original way. Think of people you know well and admire. One of the things that make them interesting is their capacity to surprise you. The more you know them, the more you appreciate their creativity.

Finally, a person has dignity and value. We place a higher value on persons than anything else. We can't express the importance of a person in monetary terms. We would never compare the value of a person with that of a building, or an automobile, for example. Personal worth is incalculable.

To summarize, a person is self-conscious and free, capable of relationships and characterized by responsibility, mystery, and dignity. When we speak of God as a person, we think of him as free and as capable of relationships with us similar to our relationships with each other.

The Bible clearly conceives of God as a person. It endows him with many personal qualities, and it employs personal relationships to describe his attitude toward his creatures. The most powerful of these is the symbol of ''father,'' which we mentioned earlier in connection with the names of God. This suggests that God's interest in creation goes far beyond a craftsman's or an artist's interest in some product of his ingenuity. God not only values and admires what he has made; he also commits himself to its welfare and seeks to establish a relationship with his creatures. This is the significance of God's creating human beings in his image. It reveals the depth of God's commitment to what he creates.

God's personal interest in creation separates the Christian view of God from two other concepts of God's relation to the world. They are deism and pantheism. Both of these affirm the reality of the world and the oneness of God, so they fall roughly under the category of "monotheism" we employed earlier. But each view, in its distinctive way, denies that God is personally related to the world.

Deism

Deism attributes the origin of the world to God, but it denies that he has any present interest in its activities. Like a master craftsman, God started the universe running. Since he designed it perfectly, he never needs to adjust its operation. The common metaphor for this view of God is the absentee landlord. It suggests that God is ultimately or originally responsible for the existence of the world, but he takes no part in its current operation. In a deistic world view, there is no place for supernatural revelation and miraculous divine intervention. Everything operates according to fixed natural law.

Pantheism

Whereas deism separates God from the world, pantheism goes to the opposite extreme and identifies the two as one. For all practical purposes, pantheism takes "God" and "world" as references to the same all-inclusive reality. The problem with pantheism is what it denies about God. It maintains correctly that God is the power which sustains all reality, but it denies that he is anything more than this. It reduces God to his function within the world.

It is clear that both views exclude a personal relationship between God and creation. If, as with deism, God is unaware of the world, he has no relationship with it at all. On the other hand, if, as with pantheism, God is essentially identical to the world, his relation to the world can never be truly personal. There is no possibility of reciprocity between God and any of his creatures.

Immanence and transcendence

The terms "immanence" and "transcendence" often play a role in discussions about God. We can use them to summarize the two views of God just described and to distinguish the Christian idea of God. Immanence refers to God's participation or involvement in the world. Transcendence refers to his difference or separation from it.

The God of deism is wholly transcendent, and the God of pantheism is wholly immanent. Each view emphasizes one attribute to the exclusion of the other. The Christian view of God is different because it attributes both qualities to God. God indeed transcends the world. He is unlike anything he has made and infinitely superior to anything finite. At the same time, he is immanent. He is actively involved in the world, momentarily sustaining its operation and guiding it toward the fulfillment of his purposes for it. The term "theism" is often used to refer to this view of God, especially in contrast to deism and pantheism.

The discussion of these different concepts of God leads us into the third essential part of our doctrine of God. God's personness requires a certain kind of relation to the world, and it implies the reality of divine activity in the world.

GOD'S ACTIVITY IN THE WORLD

We tend to identify creation with the divine activity which brought the world into existence, but it also refers to God's present relation to the world. In fact, this may be its most basic meaning. According to Martin Luther, to say, "I believe in God the Father, maker of heaven and earth," is really to say, "I believe that God has created *me.*"[2] We have not grasped the true significance of divine sovereignty if we think of God only as *the* Lord. We must each think of him as *my* Lord.

God in nature
The term "providence" is often used to refer to God's ongoing activity in the world. As described in the Bible, this activity takes several different forms. First, God sustains and guides the natural order of things on a moment-by-moment basis. There is no place in the biblical view for the absentee landlord of deism. God never takes a vacation. It is direct divine power that maintains the universe. "Thou hast made heaven, the heaven of heavens, with all their host, the earth and all that is on it, the seas and all that is in them; and thou preservest all of them" (Neh 9:6).

God's role in sustaining the universe provides us our most fundamental means of identifying him. This divine function lies behind the traditional arguments for God's existence, and it provides the minimal definition of God as the source of reality. In this vein, Paul Tillich defines God as the "ground of being," or the "power of being."[3]

The idea of nature that figures so prominently in Western thought is closely related to the Christian view of God's relation to the world. Modern science developed from the basic presupposition that our

2. Quoted by Helmut Thielicke, *Man in God's World,* trans. and ed. John W. Doberstein (New York: Harper & Row, Publishers, 1963), pp. 15, 86.
3. Paul Tillich, *Systematic Theology* (3 vols.; Chicago: University of Chicago Press, 1951–63), 1:235.

environment is orderly and predictable. This idea emerged from the belief that an orderly God is responsible for its operation. He constructed the world to behave in certain ways, and with careful study, we can figure out what they are.

Although it can refer to God's sustaining relation to the natural world, "providence" usually designates God's relation to human history. Divine providence is the activity by which God directs the course of history toward the fulfillment of his purposes. For the most part, he suggests, influences, and responds to human decisions and actions. On occasion, however, he assumes a more direct role and causes specific things to happen.

God in history

Often apparently negative, even disastrous developments wind up fulfilling his purposes. In a fit of jealousy, Joseph's older brothers sold him into slavery. Years later, as a powerful figure in Egypt, Joseph was able to save his family from starvation. God thus used an act of treachery to bring about something beneficial. At least, this was Joseph's conviction. "Do not be distressed, or angry with yourselves," he told his brothers. "God sent me before you to preserve for you a remnant on earth, and to keep alive for you many survivors. So it was not you who sent me here, but God" (Gen 45:5–8).

The crucifixion of Jesus is the most dramatic instance where God used something negative to fulfill a positive purpose. Here the consummate act of human injustice was the very means by which God saved the world. "Christ redeemed us from the curse of the law, having become a curse for us—for it is written, 'Cursed be every one who hangs on a tree' " (Gal 3:13). "For our sake he made him to be sin who knew no sin, so that in him we might become the righteousness of God" (2 Cor 5:21).

So great is God's ability to work for good that there is nothing, however bad in itself, that cannot ultimately serve his purposes. This seems to be Paul's conviction in the most famous biblical statement on divine providence: "We know that in everything God works for good with those who love him, who are called according to his purpose" (Rom 8:28).

For obvious reasons, these words, and the concept of providence they express, have been a tremendous source of strength to Christians over the years. They assure us that God can work for good in every situation, no matter how negative it seems to be.

We must be careful to distinguish this view of providence from divine determinism, which makes God directly responsible for everything that happens to us. Some people have the idea that God specifically plans every event in their lives. They believe that nothing takes place that he has not intended. They may even find support for this view in another translation of Romans 8:28: "And we know that all things work together for good to them that love God, to them who are the called according to his purpose" (KJV).

But this view of God can have disastrous consequences because it makes him responsible for all the suffering and evil in the world. This is something which Christian faith emphatically denies. It is faithful to the Bible to say that God works through certain events—even negative ones—for our good. But it is not accurate to say that God directly causes all the events he uses. God frequently works in spite of circumstances, as well as through them.

God's role in superintending the course of human history is most evident in the prophetic books of the Bible. Here we see God actively involved in national and international developments. The prosperity of a nation is shown to be the result of divine favor; conversely, its misfortunes are a form of divine judgment. The overall theme of Daniel, for example, is God's ultimate supremacy over every other power, including the mightiest nations on earth.

Prophecy

The phenomenon of prophecy is closely related to the concept of providence. Prophecy expresses God's perspective on the future, and, like many aspects of the doctrine of God, it is interpreted in different ways.

A familiar approach is to view prophecy as an expression of divine foreknowledge. Many people think of prophecy as "history in advance." They believe that God looks into the future, sees what is going to happen, and shares his knowledge with us.

An alternative approach is to view prophecy primarily as an expression of God's intentions. From this perspective, prophecy gives us an indication of God's plans for the future, rather than a description of what will inevitably take place.

There are biblical passages that lend support to each approach to prophecy. The remarkable fulfillment of certain predictions recorded in the Bible corroborates the view that prophecy is God's announcement of what lies ahead. Seventh-day Adventists see a close correspondence between the prophecies of Daniel 2 and 7 and the course of ancient history, with its succession of four great kingdoms. For many, this provides strong evidence that the Bible is divinely inspired.

In addition, certain features of Jesus' life recall specific statements in the Old Testament. These include his mother's virginity (Isa 7:14), his place of birth (Mic 5:2), and the circumstances surrounding his death (Ps 22:16–18; Isa 53:7, 9).

Perhaps most striking are various predictions of individual behavior. Isaiah, for example, foretold Cyrus' role in repatriating the Jewish people and restoring Jerusalem well over a hundred years before he lived, according to conservative biblical reckoning (44:28–45:4). On the eve of his crucifixion Jesus described the future activities of his disciples, including Judas' betrayal and Peter's threefold denial (Mt 26:21, 25, 31–34; Jn 13:21, 26).

In view of such predictions, we can see why many regard prophecy as the announcement of what is bound to transpire. However, there are also passages which base God's announcement of what is to come on his intention to take personal action and directly cause things to happen. One example is Isaiah 46:9–11: "I am God, and there is no other; I am God, and there is none like me, declaring the end from the beginning and from ancient times things not yet done" (vss. 9–10a). By themselves these verses may suggest that God is a passive observer of the future. But the next few words give us a different picture: " 'My counsel shall stand, and I will accomplish all my purposes. . . .' I have spoken, and I will bring it to pass; I have purposed, and I will do it" (vss. 10b–11). In this passage, what God foretells will not happen on its own; he is going to make it happen.

According to this view, the basic purpose of prophecy is to express God's intentions. In prophecy, God reveals his ultimate objectives for human existence and presents the course of action he plans to follow in order to reach them.

God's course of action often changes in response to human behavior, and for this reason we speak of many biblical prophecies as "conditional" in nature. This means that their fulfillment depends on certain human factors. The prophet Jeremiah gives us one of the clearest descriptions of conditional prophecy:

> "If at any time I declare concerning a nation or a kingdom that I will pluck up and break down and destroy it, and if that nation, concerning which I have spoken, turns from its evil, I will repent of the evil that I intended to do to it. And if at any time I declare concerning a nation or a kingdom that I will build and plant it, and if it does evil in my sight, not listening to my voice, then I will repent of the good which I had intended to do to it" (Jer 18:7–10).

These verses indicate that God's actions often depend on the behavior of human beings. Since God modifies his plans to accommodate human decisions, many prophetic predictions do not provide an ironclad forecast of coming events. Instead, they describe what God will do in the event that certain things happen. This view of prophecy supports the same concept of God's relation to history that we find in the doctrine of providence. It portrays God as an active participant in human affairs.

In spite of their differences, the two views of prophecy just described are not incompatible. We can harmonize them by observing that there are different kinds of prophecy. Some prophecies describe what God foresees as things that will inevitably come to pass. In contrast, other prophecies express God's intention to do certain things. He does not foresee their occurrence as inevitable; he intends to cause them to happen, but he may change his plans according to human actions.

The fact that God characteristically acts in, through, and in response to the actions of others gives us an important insight into the nature of the reign of God. God does not customarily exercise his sovereignty by directly imposing superior force. He may, of course, interrupt the normal course of events with dramatic displays of sheer power. His preferred mode of operation, however, is to allow his creatures to make decisions and then respond to these decisions in the way that best serves his purposes. To put it another way, God cooperates with his creatures. His actions do not nullify ours. Instead they incorporate them into a higher synthesis. This gives us the privilege of participating in God's activity. We can be among the means through which he reigns.

Miracles

Christians believe that God is involved in the entire course of human history, but they attribute certain events or occurrences to specific divine activity. We usually refer to such events as miracles. A miracle is a definite occurrence, frequently an interruption in the normal course of events, which happens as the direct result of God's power.

As C. S. Lewis observes in his book on miracles, the possibility of miracles presupposes two things. One is the presence of some power capable of intervening in nature. The other is the willingness of this power to do so.[4] Our attitude toward miracles therefore depends on our understanding of what and who God is.

Our concept of the reign of God certainly fulfills the first of these conditions. It affirms the superiority of God to what he has made and the interest he maintains in creation. As sovereign, God is not bound to relate to the natural sphere in only one way. He may, on occasion, interrupt his normal course of operation if it suits his purposes.

In this view of God's relation to the world, the laws of nature are not like logical rules which allow no exceptions. They simply describe

4. C. S. Lewis, *Miracles: A Preliminary Study* (New York: The Macmillan Company, 1947), cf. p. 65.

the customary way God operates. Miracles do not violate the laws of nature; rather they are departures from God's ordinary way of doing things.

But even in the view that there is a power superior to nature, the possibility of miracles remains in question. Why would God want to intervene? Wouldn't miracles somehow repudiate or invalidate the order he originally created? If he set things up the right way to begin with, why would he want to alter their operation?

It actually obscures the nature of miracles to define them merely as interruptions in the normal course of events, because this focuses on their exceptional character rather than their purpose. The basic purpose of miracles is to awaken and strengthen human faith in God. They focus attention on the real source of all that is good in the world; they remind us that God is indeed alive and well.

Miracles played a prominent role in the ministry of Jesus. In that context their purpose was to illustrate the nature of the kingdom of God. In feeding the hungry, healing the sick, casting out demons, and raising the dead, Jesus provided vivid examples of what takes place when the reign of God is realized in this world. His miracles were previews of what life will be like when the kingdom of God is fully established.

When properly viewed, then, miracles are not violations of nature, but revelations of it. They provide us a window on the true character of reality.

GOD'S EXPERIENCE OF THE WORLD

The fourth major aspect of this doctrine concerns God's experience of the world. In this area the Christian view of God differs sharply from other ideas. For example, many Greek philosophers, such as Aristotle, believed that God is totally indifferent to the world. In their view the creaturely world is unworthy of God's attention, so he exists in the splendid isolation of eternity, where he thinks of nothing but himself.[5]

In contrast, Christians believe that God is completely aware of the finite world and intimately involved in its events. This is certainly the biblical view. From Genesis to Revelation, we see God's intense interest in this world. He is the supreme actor on the stage of history,

5. Aristotle, *Metaphysics*, Book XII, chs. 6–9; in *Introduction to Aristotle*, edited and introduced by Richard McKeon (2d ed. rev.; Chicago and London: University of Chicago Press, 1973), pp. 315–326.

as we noticed in the previous section, and he is keenly interested in what happens to his creatures. Indeed, according to Jesus, he numbers the very hairs of our head and even takes note when a sparrow falls (Mt 10:29–30).

Contrasting views of God's experience

Although Christians universally believe that God knows and cares about his creatures, they do not agree as to the precise nature of his experience. Many hold the view that God's experience of the world is static. They believe that God experiences the course of history all at once—in a single, timeless perception. From the vantage point of eternity, therefore, he enjoys the value of all reality—past, present, and future.[6]

Others are convinced that God's experience of the world is dynamic. They believe that God is so closely related to his creatures that he experiences their lives in a temporal way. In other words, he experiences the events of this world successively, as they occur, rather than all at once. This means that things make a contribution to God's experience precisely when they happen. Interestingly, there is biblical evidence for both ideas.

Evidence for a static divine experience

Texts like the following play an important role in this discussion: "I the Lord do not change" (Mal 3:6); "Jesus Christ is the same yesterday and today and for ever" (Heb 13:8); and "Every good endowment and every perfect gift is from above, coming down from the Father of lights with whom there is no variation or shadow due to change" (Jas 1:17).

When the Bible speaks of God as changeless, it seems to support the idea that God's experience of the world is static. This is because a dynamic experience is one that grows or develops, and a changeless God remains the same in every way no matter what happens.

The Bible also states that God is "perfect" (Mt 5:48). Indeed, "perfection" is the essential attribute of God. It means that God is the greatest being imaginable; nothing about him could be better than it is. In the thinking of many people, God's perfection supports the idea that his experience is static because it excludes the possibility that he could change in any way. A God who changed in the slightest, even in

---

6. A number of important Christian thinkers have taken this position. One interpreter describes Augustine's view of God's relation to the world in these terms: "In one single, unchangeable glance God contemplates every being, every truth, every possible or real object. This knowledge is an eternal intuition before which the past and the future are as real as the present . . ." (Eugene Portalié, *A Guide to the Thought of St. Augustine,* trans. Ralph J. Bastian [Chicago: Henry Regnery Company, 1960], p. 128).

his experience of the world, cannot be perfect, they maintain; he cannot be the greatest possible being.

This is because something can change in one of two ways, they reason, either for better or for worse. If God could improve in any way, then he must be less than perfect now; if he got worse, obviously, he would become less than perfect. Consequently, a perfect being cannot change, and God's experience of the world must therefore be static—forever exactly the same.

Many biblical prophecies lend support to the view that God's relation to the world is static, because they seem to indicate that God experiences the future ahead of time. Certain important prophecies chart the general course of coming history (Dan 2, 7; Mt 24; Rev 13). Others accurately predict the behavior of certain individuals, such as Pharaoh, who rejected God's demand to release the Israelites (Ex 4:21), and Cyrus, the Persian king who supported the rebuilding of Jerusalem (Isa 44:28–45:4). Jesus' predictions of Judas' betrayal and Peter's denial belong to this category (Jn 13:21–30; Mk 14:29–30). Perhaps most remarkable are the numerous "messianic" prophecies in the Old Testament that were fulfilled in the life of Jesus (e.g., Ps 22; Isa 7:14; 53; Mic 5:2). We could extend the list considerably, but the pattern of prediction and fulfillment convinces many that God experiences the future, along with the past and the present, all at once.

Personal religion seems to require a changeless God, so this, too, contributes to the idea that God's experience is static. If God changes, how can we trust him? How can we be confident that he will not alter his attitude toward us? In order to commit ourselves to God completely, many believe, we need the assurance that nothing about him could ever be different, including his experience of the world. To use traditional language, he must be "immutable."

Evidence for a dynamic divine experience

Evidence that God's experience of the world is static is impressive, but there is significant evidence on the other side of the discussion, too. Numerous biblical passages seem to indicate that God's experience of the world is dynamic. These texts describe God as reacting to events as they occur. They also show that God is highly sensitive to his creatures. What they do and what happens to them has a powerful effect on him.

At creation, for example, God was delighted with what he had made; he saw that it was "very good" (Gen 1:31). Before the flood, however, he was sorry that he had created human beings; indeed, "it grieved him to his heart" (Gen 6:6). Later on God was distressed by Israel's apostasies (Jer 3:20), and he was anguished with the thought of having to give his people up (Hos 11:8). Such passages attribute different emotions to God at different times. They support the idea that his experience changes in response to what happens in the creaturely world.

The many "conditional" prophecies of the Bible present God as responding and reacting to events in human history (cf. Jer 18:7–10). The most famous conditional prophecy is probably Jonah's prediction of Nineveh's destruction (Jon 3:4). According to the Bible, the city's inhabitants repented when they heard this message, and "when God saw what they did, how they turned from their evil way, God repented of the evil which he had said he would do to them; and he did not do it" (3:10). This statement gives the strong impression that God decided to spare the Ninevites in direct response to their repentance. In other words, he experienced their repentance when it happened, not before.

During his ministry, Jesus heightened this portrait of God's sensitivity to the experiences of his creatures. In a passage we referred to above, Jesus claims that our heavenly Father notices the falling of a sparrow (Mt 10:29). In the most dramatic and moving stories he told, Jesus described how God reacts when sinners return to him (Luke 15). According to Jesus, God feels what the shepherd, the woman, and the father in the respective parables felt when they recovered what was lost. In his words, there is "joy in heaven over one sinner who repents" (Lk 15:7).

Further support for the view that God's experience is dynamic comes from the important biblical statement, "God is love" (1 Jn 4:8). Christians believe that God's love is fundamental to the entire plan of salvation (Jn 3:16). If God's basic attitude toward his creatures is one of love, then he must be responsive to their experiences, for love is nothing if not sensitive to its objects.

Human relations demonstrate this principle. The greater our affection for someone, the more responsive we are to that person's experiences. If we are deeply in love, we care about the slightest fluctuations in another's moods and feelings. There is nothing about the person that does not concern us. If, as we believe, God loves us more than any human being does, then our experiences have a greater effect on him than on anyone else. He is infinitely sensitive to everything that happens to us.

For many Christians, biblical passages like the ones just mentioned support a dynamic concept of God's experience of the world. They indicate that various feelings or emotions apply to God's response to events as the events actually happen. God sorrows *when* the sparrow falls; he rejoices *when* the sinner repents. He shares our joy and suffers our sorrow precisely with us. He has the experience when the event takes place, and not before. To do justice to such descriptions, they believe, we must view God's experience of the world as temporal, or dynamic, rather than timeless.

The question of God's relation to the world is closely related to the question of divine foreknowledge. Christians who believe that God's knowledge of the future is not exhaustive are obviously committed to the view that his experience of the world is dynamic. To be consistent, those who believe that God's experience of the world is static must also maintain that God knows the future in all its detail.[7] Many, perhaps most, Christians today take yet another position. They believe that God knows the future in advance but is still affected by events as they occur. In other words, God's knowledge of the world is static, but his experience of the world is dynamic. Knowing that something is going to happen, they observe, is not the same as actually experiencing it.[8]

These are complicated issues, to say the least, but they deserve careful attention because they can have a profound effect on our attitude toward God and on our relationship to him. We shall not attempt to settle the question of how God experiences the world here, but perhaps our discussion provides a starting point from which to think the issues through and find satisfactory answers.

In conclusion, our fourfold division of this doctrine enables us to make some important distinctions in our understanding of God. After reviewing the basic relation between God and the world, we discussed the essential being of God, or what it is that makes him God. Then we analyzed God's basic attitude, or disposition, toward the world. After

Foreknowledge and God's experience

A fourfold view of God

---

7. John Calvin, for example, attributed to God both absolute foreknowledge and a static relation to the creaturely world. In his words, "When we attribute foreknowledge to God, we mean that all things always were, and perpetually remain, under his eyes, so that to his knowledge there is nothing future or past, but all things are present. And they are present in such a way that he not only conceives them through ideas, as we have before us those things which our minds remember, but he truly looks upon them and discerns them as things placed before him" (*Institutes of the Christian Religion,* III.xxi.5, trans. Ford Lewis Battles [Philadelphia: The Westminster Press, 1960], 2:926).

8. In this vein, contemporary theologian Donald Bloesch claims that "although God knows the future before it happens, he does not literally know the concrete event until it happens" (*Essentials of Evangelical Theology* [2 vols.; New York: Harper & Row, Publishers, 1978], 1:29). For the implications of this position, see my discussion in *The Openness of God: The Relationship of Divine Foreknowledge and Human Free Will* (Washington, D.C.: Review and Herald Publishing Association, 1980), pp. 15–20.

that we turned our attention to God's activity in the world; and we have just considered God's experience of the world.

We can see the importance of these distinctions in light of our discussion of God's experience of the world. They make it possible to assert that God is static, or absolute, in some ways and dynamic, or relative, in others. Certainly, the fundamental being and character of God are absolute. They are incapable of change. It is inconceivable that God should not exist, or that the quality of his knowledge, goodness, and power should be less than perfect. Nor can Christians think of God as ever changing in his attitude toward his creatures; constant love is an essential quality of his character.

At the same time, we subtract nothing from the majesty of God if we regard his activity in the world as dynamic. Indeed, it is impossible to think of God's activity as static. To act is to effect a change; that is part of what the word means. To act without anything changing would be a contradiction in terms. Similarly, it need not detract from God's glory to think of his experience as dynamic, responsive to the experiences of his creatures.

To summarize, we *must* think of God's essential being and fundamental character—the things that make him God—as absolute, or static. At the same time we *may* think of his activity in the world and his experience of his creatures as dynamic. The important thing to remember is that we can speak of God as both static and dynamic, as both absolute and relative, if we apply these qualities to different aspects of God.

Our fourfold conception of God achieves logical consistency, but more important, it enables us to develop a view of God that is faithful to the full range of descriptions we find in the Bible. Furthermore, in presenting us with a God who is completely reliable and at the same time loving and lovable, it helps to meet the deepest needs of personal religious experience.

THE TRINITY

So far we have said nothing about the trinity, even though it represents the distinctively Christian understanding of God. This should not create the impression that we can formulate a doctrine of God without the idea of the trinity, because in fact the opposite is true. A truly Christian doctrine of God is unavoidably trinitarian. The threefoldness which the idea of the trinity involves underlies everything we have already said about God.

The role of the trinity in a doctrine of God always raises questions. One reason is that the word itself does not appear in the Bible, nor is there any clear statement of the idea. But the Bible does set the stage for its formulation, and the concept represents a development of biblical claims and concepts. So even though the doctrine of the trinity is not part of what the Bible itself says about God, it is part of what the church must say to safeguard the biblical view of God.

People also wonder whether the idea of the trinity makes sense. It seems to present us with a mathematical absurdity. How can something be three and one at the same time? Furthermore, some people feel that the idea of the trinity is a relapse into polytheism, the belief in a plurality of gods. How can we reconcile the claim that God is somehow three with the strong Old Testament emphasis on divine oneness?

Questions about the trinity

The doctrine of the trinity is not a numbers game. It is not an attempt to restore by sleight of hand what monotheism excludes from the idea of God. It is, instead, an attempt to do justice to the complexity of divine revelation. Indeed, this is really what the concept of the trinity is all about. With all the unfamiliar terminology and the intricate argumentation we find in its historical development, the concept of the trinity expresses one fundamental conviction, namely, that God reveals himself as he really is. God's revelation in the history of salvation is a genuine *self*-revelation. As Emil Brunner says, "The unity of the *nature* and the *revelation* of God is what is meant by the doctrine of the Trinity."[9]

With this in mind, we can summarize the essential meaning of the doctrine rather easily. The threefold manifestation of God in the history of salvation discloses and corresponds to distinctions within the inner being of God himself. To explain this we need to anticipate the doctrine of salvation, because the doctrine of the trinity arises from the claims that Christians make about Jesus.

The meaning of the trinity

The earliest Christians, the ones who had personal contact with Jesus, found God unbelievably close to them in his life—so close, in fact, that they had to speak of God as being personally present in him. Jesus was not simply a messenger from God. He was God. There was no other way to say it and do justice to their experience.

At the same time, all the early Christians were confirmed monotheists. They never spoke of Jesus as another god, besides, or in

God in Christ

9. Emil Brunner, *The Christian Doctrine of God,* Dogmatics, vol. 1, trans. Olive Wyon (Philadelphia: The Westminster Press, 1949), p. 220, italics original.

addition to, the ruler of the universe. They experienced God *in* Jesus, not God *and* Jesus. But even as they identified Jesus with God, they made a distinction between the Father and the Son, as Jesus himself had done. Jesus was aware of the Father as another. He prayed to the Father, for example, and he urged his followers to do so in his name.

Christ in the Spirit

The experience of God as personally present in the life of Jesus was the first moment in the development of the doctrine of the trinity. The second was the experience of Jesus' personal presence through the power of the Holy Spirit. This is the meaning of Pentecost, when the Holy Spirit came upon the early Christians and enabled them to fulfill the gospel commission (Ac 2:1–4; cf. 1:8). The experience assured them that Jesus was with them at that very time, guiding and leading in their activities. Though physically absent, Jesus remains with his people through the Spirit to the end of the age (Mt 28:20). Once again, there is distinction as well as identity. In the fourth Gospel, Jesus speaks of the Spirit as the Comforter, one who will come (Jn 14:16, 17, 26; 15:26; 16:7–14).

To summarize, the doctrine of the trinity expresses the belief that the one God is present in Jesus through the Holy Spirit. Further, to repeat our earlier point, it is the belief that God is Father, Son, and Spirit in himself, as well as in our experience of him.

Biblical evidence for the Trinity

We can find hints of this doctrine in the Old Testament and preliminary expressions of it in the New. The Old Testament speaks of the "spirit of God" and the "word of the Lord" in connection with the creation of the world (Gen 1:2; Ps 33:6). There is also a famous passage in the book of Proverbs where "wisdom" seems to enjoy near-divine status (8:22ff.). These expressions suggest a complexity within the being of God. God is something more than sheer undifferentiated unity.

The complexity or differentiation in God is much more apparent in the New Testament. There are two texts which mention the three together: the baptismal formula of Matthew 28:19, "baptizing them in the name of the Father and of the Son and of the Holy Spirit,"; and the benediction that concludes 2 Corinthians, "The grace of the Lord Jesus Christ and the love of God and the fellowship of the Holy Spirit be with you all" (13:14). In addition, there are several New Testament references to Jesus and to the Holy Spirit as divine (e.g., Ac 5:3–4).

As these passages indicate, the idea of the trinity has precedents in the Bible, even though a full-fledged doctrine of the trinity is not to be found there.

Christian thinkers formulated the doctrine of the trinity largely during the fourth and fifth centuries after Christ. They sought to express more fully the threefold manifestation of God we find in the New Testament and to safeguard the experience of God essential to Christian faith. They faced two heretical tendencies. Some Christians emphasized God's unity so much that all divine plurality was lost. They regarded Father, Son, and Spirit merely as modes through which the one God manifested himself, not as real distinctions within God.

In contrast, there were those who emphasized divine plurality at the expense of divine unity. They typically subordinated the Son to the Father in such a way that he was less than fully God, and thus there seemed to be more than one divine being.

Heretical views of God

As you can imagine, it is no simple task to describe God in a way that avoids both of these extremes. The basic challenge facing the early church was to account for both the unity and the plurality of God at the same time. There were two approaches to this problem.

The major thinkers of the Eastern church began by assuming God's plurality and set about to account for his unity. How can the three be one? was their way of posing the problem. As a solution, they formulated the "principle of coinherence." We typically associate each member of the Godhead with a different activity. We think of the Father in connection with creation; the Son, with redemption; and the Spirit, with the work of sanctification. According to the principle of coinherence, the whole trinity, all there is of God, is operative in each activity. Whenever God works, all of God works. Father, Son, and Holy Spirit are not parts of God, somehow added together to make the total divine reality. Each is wholly God.

The prominent theologians of the Western church took the opposite tack. They assumed the unity of God's being and attempted to account for the divine plurality. The question they addressed was, How can the one be three? Their answer was to specify certain relations within the being of God. Among the important terms they used were "generation" and "procession." They asserted that the Father generates the Son, and the Holy Spirit proceeds from both the Father and the Son. It is not easy to determine just what these expressions mean, but the basic intention is fairly clear. They were attempts to show that each member of the Godhead relates to the other two in a distinctive way. The relation between the Father and the Son is different from their relation to the Holy Spirit. The terms "Father," "Son," and "Spirit" point to something real in God.

Two approaches to the Trinity

**The orthodox
formula**

Out of this complicated discussion came a number of terms which we still use to express the idea of the trinity. Two of them appear in the comprehensive formula, "one substance, three persons." The term "substance" refers to what makes something what it is. Father, Son, and Holy Spirit are one in their essential divinity. But as persons, the three are distinct.

The Latin word *persona,* the origin of the English word "person," first referred to the mask an actor wore to identify his part in a play. In the trinitarian formulas, it referred to the distinct manner of subsisting characteristic of each of the three. It did not indicate an independent center of will and consciousness, as the word "person" does today.

Because "person" means something different now, some of the familiar analogies for God break down rather quickly. We cannot, for example, think of God as a family of three, or as a committee that always votes unanimously. This separates the persons and compromises God's unity.

On the other hand, we obscure the distinctions within God if we think of the three persons merely as three different functions. A single individual, for example, may be a teacher, a parent, and an amateur radio operator, all at once. Similarly, some people think, the one divine person variously functions as Father, Son, and Spirit. But this view fails to recognize how essential these distinctions are to God.

The doctrine of the trinity is one of those areas where faith affirms what reason cannot totally comprehend. Some people are tempted to dismiss the idea as a theological word game unworthy of serious thought. But its formulators weren't playing games. They were trying to safeguard the essential Christian experience of God.

Consequently, when we reflect on the meaning of the trinity, it is best to return to the basic conviction it expresses. The history of salvation reveals God as he really is. The threefold manifestation of God as Father, Son, and Spirit is not a mere expedient, or an affectation, on God's part. It is a disclosure of God's inner reality. God gives himself to us in the work of salvation.

STUDY HELPS

**Questions for
review**

1. According to Christian thought, what is God's relation to the world? How does this concept differ from monism, dualism, polytheism, pantheism, and deism?

2. What do the following divine attributes mean and what question(s) does each raise: omnipotence, omnipresence, and omniscience?

3. What do these divine activities involve: providence, prophecy, and miracle?

4. What is the evidence for and against the idea that God somehow changes?

5. What is the essential meaning of the doctrine of the trinity and how did this doctrine develop?

Questions for further study

1. According to Theodore Parker, man worships either God or an idol.[10] What idols in our society compete with God for our worship?

2. Voltaire once stated, "If God did not exist, it would be necessary to invent him."[11] What is the relation between our ideas of God and the needs and desires of human beings?

3. Philosophers typically develop an understanding of God from a careful analysis of the world. What are the possibilities and problems of this approach to God?

4. Conservative Christians believe that God not only upholds the world as a whole, but occasionally performs certain actions within the world, too. Why does God perform such actions? How can we identify an event as "an act of God"?

5. Conservative Christians also believe that "God has a plan for our lives." What do God's plans for us involve? How can we find out what they are?

6. We often speak of "the power of prayer." What effect does prayer have on God? What is its effect on us?

Suggestions for Bible study

1. According to the following passages, what is the primary means of God's manifestation in the world? What can we learn from this about the nature of God?

---

10. "Yet if he would, man cannot live all to the world. If not religious, he will be superstitious. If he worships not the true God, he will have his idols" (*Critical and Miscellaneous Writings,* Essay 1: "A Lesson for the Day").

11. "Épître à l'auteur du Livre des Trois Imposteurs" (Nov. 10, 1770).

Jeremiah 2:1; Hosea 1:1; Joel 1:1; Jonah 1:1; Micah 1:1
Isaiah 40:8; Ps 33:6; John 1:1–3; Hebrews 1:3; Hebrews 4:12

2. Some scholars maintain that the Hebrew view of God is distinctive in the ancient world in attributing supreme power and supreme goodness to the same divine being. What do we learn from the following passages about God's goodness and righteousness?

Exodus 34:6–7; Psalm 100:5; 106:1; 107:1; Isaiah 40:10–11; 45:21; Hosea 2:19

3. Two important Old Testament passages express our fundamental responsibilities to God. Deuteronomy 6:5 is often identified as "the first great commandment" (cf. Matthew 22:37). Similarly, Exodus 20:3–11 is widely referred to as "the first table of the decalogue." What understanding of God do these verses present? What are the implications of this view of God for human existence?

4. This chapter interprets the doctrine of the trinity as the expression of the distinctive Christian experience of God. According to the following passages, what are the essential features of this experience?

2 Corinthians 13:14; Matthew 28:19–20; cf. Galatians 5:25 and 2 Corinthians 5:17; 1 Corinthians 3:16–17; Galatians 4:4–6; Romans 8:15–17

SUGGESTIONS FOR FURTHER READING

From Adventist writers

There are not many books by Adventist authors devoted specifically to the doctrine of God, but two recent proposals are Edward W. H. Vick, *Speaking Well of God: A Statement of the Christian Doctrine* (Nashville, Tenn.: Southern Publishing Association, 1979), which deals with a range of topics, including the trinity and arguments for God's existence; and Richard Rice, *The Openness of God: The Relationship of Divine Foreknowledge and Human Free Will* (Washington, D.C.: Review and Herald Publishing Association, 1980), which concentrates on the question of God's relation to the creaturely world.

From other writers

Discussions of the doctrine of God can be found in every systematic theology. A stimulating treatment of the doctrine, which emphasizes the biblical names of God and reviews the major divine attributes, is Emil Brunner, *The Christian Doctrine of God,* Dogmatics: vol. 1, trans. Olive Wyon (Philadelphia: The Westminster Press, 1949). Heinrich Ott concentrates on the personness of God in *God,* trans. Iain and Ute Nicol (Richmond, Va.: John Knox Press, 1971). An illuminating discussion of the changing forms the question of God has taken in human history is John Courtney Murray, S.J., *The Problem of God Yesterday and Today* (New Haven and London: Yale University Press, 1964). J. B. Phillips examines inadequate conceptions of God and proposes a corrective in his highly readable *Your God is Too Small* (New York: The Macmillan Company, 1961).

In *The Concept of God* (New York: St. Martin's Press, 1974), Keith Ward explores the intimate relation between our experience of God and our understanding of him.

Contemporary Christian theologians have also undertaken revisionary interpretations of this fundamental doctrine. Two examples are Schubert M. Ogden, *The Reality of God and Other Essays* (New York: Harper & Row, Publishers, 1966), especially the title essay; and Gordon D. Kaufman, *Constructing the Concept of God* (Philadelphia: The Westminster Press, 1981).

The following works both contain a philosophical analysis of the concept of God which examines each of the important divine attributes: Stephen T. Davis, *Logic and the Nature of God* (Grand Rapids, Mich.: William B. Eerdmans Publishing Co., 1983); and Ronald H. Nash, *The Concept of God* (Grand Rapids, Mich.: Zondervan Publishing House, 1983).

Hardly any discussion of the trinity will be easy reading. Two probing treatments of this subject are Eberhard Jungel, *The Doctrine of the Trinity: God's Being Is in Becoming* (Grand Rapids, Mich.: William B. Eerdmans Publishing Co., 1976); and Karl Rahner, *The Trinity,* trans. Joseph Donceel (New York: Herder and Herder, 1970).

A remarkably clear and informative study of the Holy Spirit, which examines the biblical, historical, and contemporary expressions of the topic, is Alasdair I. C. Heron, *The Holy Spirit* (Philadelphia: The Westminster Press, 1983).

The nature of God's relation to the creaturely world is a topic that concerns a great many thinkers. G. C. Berkouwer offers a Calvinist interpretation of the subject in *The Providence of God,* trans. Lewis B. Smedes (Grand Rapids, Mich.: William B. Eerdmans Publishing Co., 1952). C. S. Lewis also examines the topic in his most highly regarded book, *Miracles: A Preliminary Study* (New York: The Macmillan Company, 1947). One of the most important books in this area in recent years is Langdon Gilkey, *Reaping the Whirlwind: A Christian Interpretation of History* (New York: The Seabury Press, 1976).

5

THE DOCTRINE OF MAN:
ESSENTIAL HUMANITY

**Biblical
basis**

"Then God said, 'Let us make man in our image, after our likeness'"
(Genesis 1:26).

"What is man that thou art mindful of him, and the son of man that
thou dost care for him? Yet thou hast made him little less than God,
and dost crown him with glory and honor" (Psalm 8:4–5).

Genesis 1:26–30
Genesis 2:4–25
Psalm 8
Psalm 90
Psalm 103:13–16
Psalm 104:23
Proverbs 4:23

Proverbs 22:6
Isaiah 45:12
Matthew 10:28
Matthew 19:3–9
Acts 17:26
Romans 1:26–27
1 Corinthians 7

THE PROBLEM OF BEING HUMAN

"Man has always been his own most vexing problem." With these
words Reinhold Niebuhr begins his famous work, *The Nature and Destiny of Man.*[1] His insight is valid. No matter what we learn about the
vastness of the universe or the intricacy of the atom, we ourselves are

---

1. Reinhold Niebuhr, *The Nature and Destiny of Man: A Christian Interpretation* (2
vols.; New York: Charles Scribner's Sons, 1941, 1943), 1:1.

the greatest mystery of all. And the more we learn about ourselves, the more mysterious we seem to become.

When we look at ourselves, we confront paradoxes on every hand. We can say little about human beings that is simple and straightforward. Every description seems to require qualification, and in some sense its denial is probably true as well.

Paradoxes of human existence

It is obvious, for example, that human beings are finite, that we have enormous limitations. At the same time, we are aware of these limitations, and in this very act we go beyond them to some extent. Because we know what it is to be limited, we have an idea of what it is to be unlimited, too.

Again, we exist. No one can deny that. Yet we might not exist. We might never have been born, and we can easily think of circumstances that would end our lives. So our hold on existence is tenuous. Our situation in the scheme of things is precarious, to say the least.

Another remarkable feature is the way we live both as individuals and as groups. Most of us are acutely aware of the things that make us different from other people. We feel that we have a personal significance that nothing can take away from us. But we also live in groups, or communities, and their reality is just as basic as our own—maybe more so, in fact. After all, we owe our existence to others, and without a community our lives would have little meaning.

We also feel free and determined at the same time. I know that there is a great deal about me that I haven't chosen—my race, my sex, my nationality, the color of my eyes and hair, my basic I.Q., and so on. Yet there is a lot about me that could be different if I wanted it to be. I could have chosen another occupation. I could have married somebody else. I could have decided to live in another part of the country. To a significant degree I am self-determined; I am responsible for many of the things about myself.

I feel responsible for my behavior most of the time. I believe there are things I should do and things I should avoid. I am pleased when my behavior conforms to this sense of obligation, and I am upset when it doesn't. I may then blame myself and feel guilty, or I may try to justify my actions to escape the blame of others.

These universal human feelings indicate that we are both good and evil at the same time, never entirely one or the other. We can't be merely good, because our behavior so obviously refutes that idea. But we're not wholly evil either. If we were, we wouldn't condemn evil when we see it in others or try to excuse it when we find it in ourselves.

**The biblical
view of man**

These paradoxes of human existence underscore the complexity of our task. Nothing is more difficult than to formulate an adequate understanding of human being. But when we look to Christian faith, that is precisely what we find—a description of human existence that takes everything into account. The contrasting qualities of good and evil, dependence and independence, freedom and destiny—they all get the attention they deserve. The Bible provides us with an explanation of human life that covers the full sweep of human experience. It tells the story of each one of us.

In fact, so fundamental to Christian faith is its view of humanity that we could view all of Christian theology as a doctrine of man. We said the same thing about the doctrine of God, you may remember, but both statements are true. The two doctrines are intimately connected. We really can't think of God or man without thinking about the other, too. As John Calvin said, "Nearly all the wisdom we possess . . . consists of two parts: the knowledge of God and of ourselves. . . . [W]hich one precedes and brings forth the other is not easy to discern."[2]

The interrelation of the doctrines of God and man illustrates the complexity of Christian faith in its entirety. It is impossible to explore any part of it without reaching into all of it. Each point of faith brings us into contact with others.

"Creature" and "image of God" are the most basic descriptions of human being. They appear with the very first mention of human beings in the Bible: "Then God said, 'Let us make man in our image, after our likeness'" (Gen 1:26). These expressions point, respectively, to what we have in common with other forms of life and to what distinguishes us within the natural world. Let's begin our study of man by exploring what it means to be a creature.

MAN AS CREATURE

**Purposeful
existence**

To say that we are creatures implies that our existence has a purpose. The biblical account of human origins assures us that we belong in the scheme of things; we were meant to be here. It also implies that we are not alone. To speak of a creature is to speak of its creator at the same time. There is another in the universe to whom we owe our existence.

2. John Calvin, *Institutes of the Christian Religion*, I.i.1, trans. Ford Lewis Battles (2 vols.; Philadelphia: The Westminster Press, 1960), 1:35.

The concept of human creatureliness excludes purely naturalistic accounts of human origins. It rules out a view like that of Jacques Monod, a Nobel-Prize-winning biologist: "Man knows at last that he is alone in the universe's unfeeling immensity, out of which he emerged only by chance. His destiny is nowhere spelled out, nor is his duty."[3]

As these words suggest, there is a great deal at stake in the issue of human origins. It is not merely a question of how our species arrived on this planet. It involves the larger issues of purpose and destiny, as well as the principles that should guide our lives. Do we decide what we are meant to be? Or is the goal of our existence given to us by someone else? The doctrine of creation asserts that there is a transcendent meaning to our lives. It is not blind chance or good luck that accounts for our existence, but the power and purpose of a personal God. We cannot ignore his wishes for us as we attempt to understand the meaning and purpose of our lives.

The concept of creatureliness involves the idea that God brought human beings into existence. The question of how he did it is another matter, and Christians give a variety of answers to this question.

There are those who believe that God created human beings by guiding the process of evolution. They agree with the widely held view that our species developed from pre-human life forms over a vast period of time, but they maintain that it is God who directed this process to its climax in the emergence of human beings.

Others accept the general picture of evolutionary development, but they believe that human creation involves more than divine guidance in the overall process. In their view, God created human beings by acting in a special way on pre-human forms of life. True, the process of evolution produced man-like, or hominoid, animals. But man as such did not exist until God acted upon these life-forms in a distinctive way. One theologian expresses the concept in these words: "Though man came *through* the brute, he did not come *from* the brute. . . ."[4] Many generally conservative Christians have held this view of human origins.

Seventh-day Adventists typically reject such accounts of human creation. They believe that the biblical narrative provides a literal description of how human beings came into existence, namely, by a definite act of God which did not involve pre-human forms of life. Only

3. Jacques Monod, *Chance and Necessity: An Essay on the Natural Philosophy of Modern Biology,* trans. Austryn Wainhouse (New York: Vintage Books, 1972), p. 180.

4. Augustus Hopkins Strong, *Systematic Theology: A Compendium Designed for the Use of Theological Students* (Valley Forge, Pa.: The Judson Press, 1907), p. 469.

this view, they believe, does justice to the biblical account of human origins and safeguards the Christian view of man. Attempts to accommodate the biblical account to evolutionary theories detract from human dignity and divine power.

A place in the world

The idea of human creatureliness not only imparts a sense of purpose to our lives; it also reminds us that we are part of a larger creation. We belong to the natural world, and we participate in the various conditions and limitations of creaturely life in general. We can say, therefore, that the doctrine of creation does two things for us. It locates human beings in the scheme of things; it gives us a home. But in so doing, it circumscribes or defines our lives, setting boundaries on our activities and aspirations. It implicitly warns us against violating any of the basic conditions of our existence.

We can summarize the idea that we participate in the larger sphere of creation by describing human beings as finite. Finiteness, or finitude, has a number of different dimensions.

Human finitude

As finite, human beings are dependent, or contingent. That is, we owe our existence to something else. Something greater than we are brought us here and continues to keep us going. We are reminded of our finitude, or dependence, when we think about the importance of our environment. Our survival depends on the right set of circumstances. To maintain physical health, we need certain nutrients. An absence of water would end our lives in a matter of days. Take away oxygen, and we would die immediately. Our existence is radically dependent on things outside ourselves.

Human frailty is a prominent theme in the Bible, particularly in the Old Testament. The psalms, especially, recall the tenuous character of our lives, which they set in striking contrast to the power and eternity of God. "[Men] are like a dream, like grass which is renewed in the morning: in the morning it flourishes and is renewed; in the evening it fades and withers" (90:5–6).

As finite, human beings are limited in time and space. We are physically restricted: we can't be in more than one place at the same time. We are temporally restricted, too: we cannot avoid the passage of time. We grow older whether we want to or not. We are also limited to this particular time. We can't decide to live in the nineteenth century, or in the twenty-second. Our historical situation is not something we control.

HUMAN CORPOREALITY

We can summarize many of these features of our existence by stating that human being is essentially corporeal. We exist in bodily form. It is not merely that we *have* bodies. More accurately, we *are* bodies. We find this fundamental character of human existence in one of the most important biblical statements about man: "Then the Lord God formed man of dust from the ground, and breathed into his nostrils the breath of life, and man became a living being" (Gen 2:7).

The body, then, the physical organism, is a constitutive aspect of human existence. We cannot conceive of human life apart from some kind of body. Indeed, a human being without a body would be a contradiction in terms.

We see the importance of the body to human existence in the biblical accounts of the resurrection of the dead. "So is it with the resurrection of the dead. What is sown is perishable, what is raised is imperishable. . . . It is sown a physical body, it is raised a spiritual body" (1 Cor 15:42, 44). For Paul, the transition from this life to the future life involves a dramatic transformation, but it does not involve leaving bodily existence behind.

The goodness of life

Because human existence is essentially corporeal, the body is something good. It deserves to be taken care of. In themselves, the things that make our lives physically enjoyable are good. There is certainly nothing wrong with eating and drinking as far as the Bible is concerned. God himself provided food for Adam and Eve (Gen 2:9, 16). Jesus promised to eat and drink with his disciples in the kingdom of God (Lk 22:16–18), and John says the redeemed will never hunger or thirst (Rev 7:16).

So there is no place in the Christian view of man for the idea that natural physical needs and desires should be denied. In the pursuit of holiness, people sometimes go without enough to eat and drink, in certain cases for years at a time. The Bible endorses fasting, but only as a temporary measure for spiritual benefit. It never encourages us to submit to unnecessary physical hardship in the hope of improving our spiritual condition. To the contrary, the Bible urges us to attend to our health.

The unity of life

A second implication of our corporeality is the unity of human life. It is true that human beings are multidimensional. We are more than mere physical organisms, as we shall see. But whatever our other characteristics, we can never separate them from the physical; they can never exist by themselves.

This contradicts the influential idea that there is a part of human beings that has independent reality and can survive the body. There are those who believe that the "spirit" or the "soul" can exist without the body. But according to the Bible, the body and everything else associated with human life exist together as an indivisible unit.

These contrasting views of man are sometimes referred to as "wholism" and "dualism." Wholism is the idea that man is a complex unity of many facets. They are interrelated, and none can exist in isolation. Dualism is the view that man is a composite being, a union of things that are essentially different, such as body and soul. According to dualism, one of these parts is the real bearer of personal identity, and it does not need the other to exist. As we shall see, these views lead to strikingly different concepts of death.

"Soul" and "spirit"

An examination of the biblical terms applied to man supports the wholistic concept. The Bible employs a number of words to describe human beings, including "soul" and "spirit." Both appear in Genesis 2:7, quoted above. The Hebrew word for "breath" in this text is often translated "spirit." It refers to the animating power within a physical organism which comes from God. It isn't something that can exist apart from the body; in fact, it isn't even distinctively human. According to one passage, human beings and animals have the same breath (Ecc 3:19).

The Hebrew here for "living being" is rendered "living soul" in the King James Version. It is the same expression that appears in Genesis 1:21 and 24, where it refers to various forms of animal life. Human beings, then, are not the only souls around. Animals are souls, too, in the biblical sense of the word.

Moreover, the word translated "soul" in this verse refers to the organism as a whole, not to some part of it. The soul is not something that can be separated from the person. It is the person in its entirety. A human being doesn't *have* a soul, in other words; it *is* a soul.

HUMAN SOCIALITY

Human beings are essentially social as well as corporeal. We exist as groups, not merely as individuals, and our being together is just as important as what we are by ourselves.

The social dimension of our humanity is easy to overlook, especially if you grow up in one of the Western nations of the world, like the United States. In our society, we value nothing more highly than individual accomplishments, particularly when they set a person apart from others. The most popular figure in American folklore is the cowboy, who rides into town unannounced and single-handedly cleans up the place with his fists and his six-shooter. We know nothing of his family or his background; we may not even know his real name. But we have little interest in these things. We admire his independence and unconventionality. Our approach to sports also reflects this preoccupation with individuals. We sometimes speak of "team efforts," but we are more often interested in the achievements of individual players.

Emphasis on individual accomplishments begins early in life. In a typical grade-school classroom we notice who is best at reading and arithmetic, who is best at sports, and who is best in music. We grow up thinking that the most important things about us are the ways in which we are different from other people.

It is difficult, then, for some of us to sense the importance of sociality. However, several things about us clearly point to this dimension of our lives. One is the obvious fact that we owe our existence to other people—not just our physical origin, although that is indispensable, but our intellectual and cultural origins, too. We learn to speak, for example, because we are spoken to. According to child psychologists, we derive our basic self-concept from the way other people, especially our parents, treat us during the early months of life.

When you think about it, people with exceptional accomplishments are also enormously dependent on others. Without teachers they would never acquire the skills they display. Without a society where the work of others provides life's basic necessities, they would never have the time to perfect their abilities. So when someone sings, "I Did It My Way," to praise his individuality, remember how much he owes to those around him.

We are fully human, then, only in relation to others. The Bible affirms our fundamental sociality in its account of human creation. When God made man, he created two different individuals. The primary unit of human existence is the group, not the individual.

The people of biblical times attached much more importance to the group than we do in the Western world today. For them, the significance of the group was fundamental, and that of the individual was secondary and derivative.

"Corporate personality"

The concept of "corporate personality" plays a prominent role in biblical thought. This is the idea that an important human group, such as a nation or a tribe, has an identity of its own, more important than that of any individual. Individual members participate in the life of the group and partake of its significance. On occasion, certain individuals bear the identity of the group as its representatives. This is particularly true of important figures like the priest and the king.

The concept of corporate personality lies behind many of the incidents in the Bible which initially perplex us. It helps us to understand why entire families sometimes suffered for the misdeeds of one member. In one instance a man was guilty of looting when Jericho fell, against God's direct instructions. His family was punished along with him (Josh 7). In another case, Saul defied God's command to wipe out the Amalekites when he spared their king (1 Sam 15:1–10). The nation survived as long as the king was alive. On the positive side, all the soldiers of Israel participated in David's victory over Goliath, the champion of the Philistines (1 Sam 17).

The concept of corporate personality can be extremely helpful in understanding such important New Testament themes as the meaning of Jesus' death and the relation between Christ and the church. It reminds us of the intimate relation between individual and group that existed in the minds of the biblical writers.

The corporate, or social, character of human existence relates to our guiding theme of the reign of God. It calls to mind the fact that God's reign extends to all human beings and unites us all into one. It also points to the fact that God's original intentions included the population of this planet with human beings.

Human solidarity

Our basic sociality goes beyond relationship with others to solidarity. Our lives are intertwined with those of other human beings. In the familiar words of John Donne, "No man is an island."[5] We inevitably influence other people, and their behavior has an inevitable effect on us. For this reason, we participate to some extent in the actions of others. As much as we deplore such things as materialism and violence in our society, they reflect something about us, too.

We find the corporate dimension of human experience in the biblical concept of resurrection, which we mentioned in our discussion of human corporeality. The biblical descriptions of the resurrection of the dead indicate not only that the future life involves some form of bodily

---

5. John Donne, Devotion Number XVII (quoted in *Some Poems and a Devotion of John Donne: The Poet of the Month* [Norfolk, Ct.: New Directions, 1941]).

existence; they show that it also includes social existence. The dead rise together to receive immortality. Their eternal inheritance is something shared; it isn't given to them one by one. This leads us to believe that social life, just as bodily life, will be dramatically transformed by the power of God. Our closest relationships here may represent dim reflections of the intimacy available in the life to come.

HUMAN SEXUALITY

The biblical account of creation indicates that human beings are essentially sexual, as well as physical and social. It states that God created man "male and female" (Gen 1:26). In a sense, this dimension of human existence incorporates the other two and promotes them to another level. On one level, sexuality is something physical. The bodies of males and females have different features, and they are capable of different functions. On another level, sex is social, too. Sexual activity is the means by which human beings create other human beings. It is also the means for expressing the most intimate human emotions.

Besides emphasizing that we are physical and social beings, sexuality points to the essential differentiation within human existence. The things that make us different should not create distances between us. Human beings are meant to complement each other. The fact that sexuality is fulfilled in the union of male and female reminds us that no one individual can be everything human beings are meant to be. It takes a social unit to display humanity at its fullest.

The Bible is realistic and affirmative in its approach to human sexuality. It never obscures the fact that sexuality is an essential part of human existence. In fact, people are sometimes startled by the frankness with which the Bible refers to sexual activity. The Bible also affirms the value of sexuality. It honors its procreative function and generally reflects the attitude that sex is something natural and therefore good (Gen 1:28). The Bible does not urge us to deny our sexuality.

Mistaken sexual attitudes

These features separate the Christian view of sex from two familiar attitudes. We can call one the "puritanical" view of sex, although it is doubtful whether it applies to the Puritans themselves. According to this view, sex is something evil and ought to be avoided. The less we hear of it, the better. Needless to say, enforced ignorance does not eliminate an interest in sex; it only leads to misunderstanding.

At the opposite end of the spectrum we find the "playboy" attitude toward sex. According to this view, sex is more than something to celebrate. It is a reason for living. For the playboy mentality, sexual liberation contains the key to meaning in life. Give your sexual drives free rein, it insists, and you will find happiness and peace of mind.

Oddly, this attitude contains two conflicting views of sex. On the one hand, it exaggerates its significance; it glorifies this dimension of experience and leads people to expect more from sex than it can possibly provide. At the same time, however, the playboy mentality trivializes sex. Instead of pondering its profound significance for human life, it treats sex as a form of entertainment. The writers of the Bible thought a lot more of sex than that.

The Christian view of sex stands apart from both of these attitudes. In contrast to the puritanical view, Christianity regards sex as an essential part of human life, as something good and purposeful. In contrast to the playboy attitude, it maintains that the sexual part of life is exactly that—just a part of life, not all of it. We can realize its value only as we keep it in perspective and relate it to the other aspects of life.

Sexual behavior

In recent years the question of appropriate sexual behavior has received a lot of attention. It is a much larger subject than we can do justice to here, but our treatment of sex as a dimension of human creatureliness would not be complete without at least mentioning some of the issues.

Marriage

According to traditional Christianity, the only acceptable framework for sexual relations is heterosexual monogamy—marriage involving two individuals, one male and one female. In different places, the Bible seems to tolerate certain departures from this norm. Many of the central figures of the Old Testament practiced polygamy, including Abraham, Jacob, David, and Solomon. According to the first Gospel, one of Jesus' statements on marriage permits divorce in the case of adultery (Mt 19:9).

The Bible denounces other practices much more straightforwardly. The seventh of the ten commandments prohibits adultery, sexual intercourse between a married person and someone other than his/her spouse (Ex 20:14). In his letters, Paul admonishes Christians to avoid fornication, sexual intercourse between unmarried people (cf. 1 Cor 6:18; Eph 5:3; 1 Thess 4:3). Several biblical statements condemn homosexual activities (Lev 18:22; 20:13; Rom 1:26–27; 1 Cor 6:9; 1 Tim 1:10).

People today often raise questions about divorce, premarital sex, and homosexuality. Up until 1950 prevailing Seventh-day Adventist church policy permitted a member to remarry following divorce only if the other party had been guilty of adultery. The guilty party might be reinstated following a period of contrition, but could never remarry. In 1950 the policy was modified to allow a "guilty" party who had remarried to reenter church fellowship through rebaptism after a period of time, if there was evidence of genuine repentance.[6] The policy may undergo further modification. One large Adventist congregation has formulated a new policy on divorce and remarriage. The policy provides for a period of time following divorce when the parties involved have the status of "affiliate membership." After two years or so, the policy implies, they may remarry without jeopardizing their relation to the church.[7]

Divorce

From current motion pictures and television programs one could easily conclude that sexual activity among unmarried people is the norm rather than the exception today. Whatever the statistics are, there is certainly widespread acceptance of the idea that people may experiment with several sexual partners. Many believe that such activity is not only normal and healthy, but helpful in preparing for marriage.

Premarital sex

A simple biblical statement on the matter is unlikely to satisfy many people today.[8] But there are good reasons for waiting until marriage and staying faithful afterwards. There is the risk of pregnancy or venereal disease, which is still with us in spite of modern medicine. Even more important, it is impossible to duplicate or perfectly anticipate a marriage relationship. Marriage involves a total commitment between two people, a commitment that is permanent and exclusive. It is impossible to make a permanent commitment on a trial basis, or an exclusive commitment to more than one person.

6. Gerald Winslow carefully reviews the complicated discussions of this issue in Seventh-day Adventist history, including the relevant statements in various editions of the *Church Manual*, in "Divorce, Remarriage and Adultery," *Spectrum*, vol. 7, no. 2, pp. 3–7.

7. One version of the policy, which has undergone numerous revisions, is entitled, "A Proposed Policy for Marriage, Divorce, and Remarriage," by the University Church of Seventh-day Adventists, Loma Linda, California. For a summary of the contents of this policy and a description of its reception by the General Conference of Seventh-day Adventists, see "LLU Church Proposes New Divorce Guidelines," by Bonnie Dwyer and Gene Daffern, *Forum*, Winter 1982, pp. 5–6.

8. Two such statements are the seventh commandment, "Thou shalt not commit adultery" (Ex 20:14, KJV), and Paul's straightforward admonition, "Flee fornication" (1 Cor 6:18, KJV), also translated, "Shun immorality" (RSV).

Most important of all, sex has the capacity both to express and to generate the deepest feelings of which human beings are capable. Any sexual activity which ignores or seeks to avoid this capacity is destructive. We may think of it as recreational sex, or just fooling around, but it inevitably lowers our respect for ourselves and the other person involved. And it empties the experience of real meaning.

Homosexuality

The unprecedented willingness of homosexuals in our society to identify themselves, both inside and outside the church, requires Christians today to confront the question of Christianity and homosexuality. Traditionally condemned for their behavior, homosexuals are pressing for the recognition that homosexuality is a valid alternative to heterosexuality within the Christian community. Their arguments frequently turn on a distinction between homosexual practices and a homosexual orientation. They reason that our basic sexual orientation is not something we choose for ourselves. It is something we each acquire early in life, largely as the result of factors we cannot control. Once set, it is virtually impossible to change.

If we allow for a basic homosexual orientation in this sense, the argument goes, we must look at homosexual practices in two different ways. If a person's basic orientation is heterosexual, it is a perversion of his/her sexuality to engage in homosexual practices. But if the basic orientation is homosexual, then such practices can be a valid expression of affection.

Because no one in ancient times understood the nature of sexual orientation, the argument continues, biblical writers viewed all homosexual practices as perversions. That is why the biblical statements about homosexual practices are all negative. But we have to remember, homosexuals assert, that they speak only of homosexual practices, not of the homosexual orientation. This is therefore an issue that biblical interpretation alone cannot settle. We need the help of contemporary insights into human sexuality.[9]

---

9. An influential statement of the argument summarized here appears in John H. McNeill, S.J., *The Church and the Homosexual* (New York: Pocket Books, 1978). "We must distinguish," McNeill writes, "between the invert and the pervert. The pervert is not a genuine homosexual; rather he is a heterosexual who engages in homosexual practices. This distinction between the condition of inversion and the behavior of perversion is indispensable for a correct interpretation of biblical and traditional sources. . . . [T]here is ample evidence that in most instances where Scripture deals with homosexuality the author probably had in mind what today we would call perversion, namely, the indulgence in homosexual activity on the part of those who were by nature heterosexually inclined" (p. 51).

It is clear that Christians must respond to homosexuality today with something other than blind condemnation. Whatever a person's sexual background, he or she deserves to be treated with sympathy and respect. Unfortunately, homosexuals have often found nothing but prejudice, insensitivity, and rejection on the part of supposed Christians.

It is not so clear that the Bible has nothing to say to the issue of sexual orientation or that a person's sexual orientation cannot be changed. The biblical accounts of creation affirm the fundamental distinction between male and female, and its fulfillment in procreation. The rest of the Bible presupposes this distinction. So the general sweep of biblical testimony, in addition to several specific statements, stands against homosexuality.[10]

In addition, even if homosexuality is an orientation, not merely a practice, this does not remove it from biblical condemnation. The Bible condemns certain conditions as well as various actions. The fact that sin corrupts our natures does not relieve us of divine condemnation, for example.

At the same time, the gospel promises deliverance from all the consequences of sin, conditions as well as actions. So there may be reason to believe that a homosexual orientation is not unchangeable. There are those, in fact, who claim to be delivered from it, although we should add that some seriously question such testimony.[11]

HUMAN DEVELOPMENT

There is a final aspect of human creatureliness that deserves our attention. This is the fact that human beings are developmental by nature. We are creatures of growth or nurture. This is obvious during the early years when physical and mental development are so conspicuous, but it is also characteristic of human beings generally. We are always on the way; we are never through growing and changing.

10. For an informed, sensitive, and biblically based discussion of homosexuality by a Seventh-day Adventist theologian, see Raoul Dederen, "Homosexuality: A Biblical Perspective," *Ministry,* September 1981, pp. 14–16.

11. Colin Cook, director of Quest Counseling Center in Reading, Pennsylvania, asserts, "There *is* deliverance from homosexuality," in "Homosexual Healing," an interview with J. R. Spangler published in *Ministry,* September 1981 (p. 7; italics his). Others are highly skeptical of Cook's claim. Their views are often expressed in the periodical *SDA Kinship Connection:* Newsletter of Seventh-day Adventist Gay Men and Women and Their Friends.

This dimension of creatureliness has many facets. We noticed earlier that our basic sociality is reflected in our dependence on others for guidance and help. But there are other aspects, too. One is the fact that ideal humanity is something we must constantly aim for. Some thinkers argue that human nature is not something given to us, something we possess. Rather, it is a possibility which we must strive for, something we must consciously seek to attain.

MAN AS THE IMAGE OF GOD

In general, human creatureliness refers to things which human beings have in common with other forms of life on this planet. All its dimensions have their counterpart in other created beings. Animals, too, are finite. They are all corporeal. Many of them also exhibit social, sexual, and developmental qualities.

Although human beings share many characteristics with other forms of life, it is just as obvious that we are remarkably different, too. There is something qualitatively unique about human existence. We are undeniably a part of nature, but we are more than nature, too. Certain characteristics exclude the idea that we are nothing more than a highly developed form of animal life. In the Christian doctrine of man, these distinctive qualities are embodied in the symbol of ''the image of God.'' We can develop the Christian view of human uniqueness by exploring the meaning of this idea.

The expression first appears in Genesis 1:26–27: ''Then God said, 'Let us make man in our image, after our likeness; and let them have dominion over the fish of the sea, and over the birds of the air, and over the cattle, and over all the earth, and over every creeping thing that creeps upon the earth.' So God created man in his own image, in the image of God he created him; male and female he created them.''

Two related questions about this idea have occupied Christian thinkers for centuries. First, just what is the image of God in man?, and second, what happened to the image of God as a result of the fall?

Image and likeness

The prevalent view in the church before the Protestant Reformation of the sixteenth century made a distinction between the ''image'' and the ''likeness'' of God in man. The image included certain natural powers, but the divine likeness was an additional, supernatural gift. It included powers that enabled human beings to know God and retain immortal life. At the fall, the likeness was lost, but the image of God remained intact.

The Protestant Reformers rejected this distinction between image and likeness. From their knowledge of the Hebrew language they concluded that the two terms refer to the same thing. They also maintained that the image of God was not a set of qualities, but a positive orientation of the will toward God. They believed that the image of God was devastated by the fall. In John Calvin's words, it was "so corrupted that whatever remains is frightful deformity."[12]

Contemporary theologians seem to disagree as to whether the image of God is better understood as a certain quality human beings possess, or a particular relationship in which they stand. We can try to answer this question for ourselves by taking a close look at the context in which the expression first appears.

Dominion over creation

Directly after the words "Then God said, 'Let us make man in our image, after our likeness,' " we find the words " 'And let them have dominion. . . .' " This suggests that the image of God involves a specific relationship between human beings and the rest of creation. The expression refers primarily to a function, rather than a quality. Human beings enjoy the status of dominion, or sovereignty, over other forms of reality. One theologian describes the image of God as man's "creative mastery of existence."[13]

This function, or office, is fulfilled as human beings modify their environment in accordance with their will. We see it in the pursuits of art, science, and technology. Art suggests imaginative ways of looking at the world; science seeks explanations for the various phenomena we encounter; and technology employs the discoveries of science to alter certain features of our world. By these means we can shape and fashion our environment to suit our purposes. We utilize the chemical and biological resources of the earth to provide ourselves with food, shelter, and clothing, along with the means of transportation and communication.

Human beings not only inhabit a material environment, they also inhabit a *world,* a structure of meaning. The image of God also manifests itself in the diverse cultural forms we find on the earth. The structures of our social life, our relations with other people, are largely

12. *Institutes of the Christian Religion,* I.xv.4, trans. Ford Lewis Battles (Philadelphia: Westminster Press, 1960), p. 189.

13. Wolfhart Pannenberg, *What Is Man? Contemporary Anthropology in Theological Perspective,* trans. Duane A. Priebe (Philadelphia: Fortress Press, 1970), p. 15.

subject to our dominion. They are the products of human creativity and imagination.

Stewardship

The expression "image of God" not only suggests a certain relationship between humanity and the rest of creation; it also suggests a particular relationship between human beings and God. For one thing, it reminds us that humans are God's representatives in the world. They are not his replacement. In creating man in his image, God did not abandon the world to human whims. The earth is still the Lord's, and human beings, too, are subject to his sovereignty.

For this reason, we must think of our relation to the world's resources in terms of stewardship. God entrusts the world to our care, but he holds us accountable for the use we make of it. We are responsible to him for what he has given us.

Furthermore, as God's representatives in the world, human beings should exercise their dominion in a way that resembles the sovereignty of God. God enjoyed and valued the products of his creative power. Human beings should treat the objects of their sovereignty in a similar way. For these reasons, the concept of man as the image of God provides a basis for concern about the environment. God intends us to use the resources of the earth, but not to abuse them.

This excludes two unacceptable attitudes toward natural resources. One attitude sees everything in light of its potential for human use; the earth is solely an object for exploitation. This view ignores the fact that other things have a basic right to exist, too. It is clearly opposed to the biblical affirmation of the goodness of all creatures, and it conflicts with the concept that we are accountable for the use we make of things in this world.

The other extreme bemoans any indication of human presence on this planet. It idealizes wilderness and severely restricts the extent to which human beings can shape the environment to suit their purposes. But the biblical view gives us permission to utilize nature, although it challenges us to find a way of using natural resources responsibly. As creatures, humans, too, have a legitimate place on this planet. We must, however, find a way of meeting our needs without destroying the rest of creation in the process.

Limits to human dominion

There are other limits to human sovereignty. God never intended human beings to exercise dominion over other human beings. The idea of the image of God confers a dignity on every individual. Since all bear the image of God, one human being should never be the property of another. Neither race, nor sex, nor age elevates one person or group to a position of sovereignty. The concept of the image of God rules out all forms of slavery—economic, political, and sexual.

We can illustrate the way the Bible situates human beings in the order of things with the diagram below. As a creature, man is subject to divine sovereignty along with the rest of creation. As the image of God, he enjoys a relation to other creatures that resembles God's sovereignty. And because all human beings bear the image of God, we are not to exercise dominion over each other. We might say that our dominion does not extend to the realm of the personal.[14]

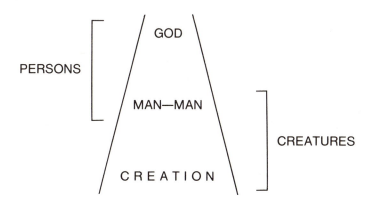

HUMAN UNIQUENESS

We have identified the image of God as a function rather than an attribute. According to this view, it refers to a position human beings occupy, rather than a quality which they possess. At the same time, we can't avoid thinking of certain characteristics in connection with the image of God, since human beings can fulfill their function only if they have the necessary abilities to do so. People have tried to indicate just what characteristics distinguish human beings from other creatures in many different ways. It will be helpful to look at a few of the most important suggestions.

14. As one might expect, there are many other interpretations of the image of God. One of the more interesting is the view that human sexuality is intrinsic to the image of God—a position that Karl Barth advanced. For a readable discussion of this view, see Ray S. Anderson, *On Being Human: Essays in Theological Anthropology* (Grand Rapids, Mich: William B. Eerdmans Publishing Co., 1982), pp. 104–129.

Reason

It is popular to describe "reason" as the distinctive human quality. We often speak of humans, in contrast to animals, as "rational" beings. Our reasoning ability is our capacity for general concepts and abstract thought. Because we can reason, we can use the word "chair," for example, whether there are any chairs in sight or not. We have a mental image which does not have to refer to any one chair in particular.

Symbolism

While reason is obviously important, there are thinkers who believe that it doesn't fully account for human uniqueness. An alternative suggestion is the human capacity for symbols. For human beings, immediate physical surroundings, no matter how pleasant, are never enough to satisfy our needs. Our lives must have meaning, not merely duration. Symbols are the means by which we structure our lives. They provide us with categories for understanding ourselves; they locate us in the scheme of things.

Others identify the uniquely human with our capacity for self-transcendence. No matter how much we know, we can always ask more questions, and every answer becomes a basis for still further questions. So there is no standpoint beyond which we are incapable of moving. Human thought never reaches a dead end.

Self-determination

"Self-determination" is another way of designating human uniqueness. Most creatures have no choice about what they are. Their basic "nature" is something given to them, and they simply live in harmony with the established laws of their being. They do by instinct everything they are capable of doing. In contrast, our humanity isn't something given to us once and for all. It is something we choose; we "appropriate" it voluntarily. Being human is not something we just do naturally. We have to be taught to be human, as any parent knows. Sometimes our behavior is conspicuously subhuman. In addition, human beings have few instincts. Our reaction to different situations isn't predetermined; it is something we can change with a little imagination.

As self-determined or self-creative beings, we are essentially free. Human freedom is a vast area for investigation, and we can scarcely venture into a thorough discussion of it here. But there are a few aspects of the subject that we should not bypass in our attempt to describe human uniqueness.

HUMAN FREEDOM

The basic meaning of freedom is that our decisions "make a difference." What we choose is not caused, or determined, by factors we cannot control. Our actual choices contribute something to the scheme of things that would otherwise be missing. In an important sense, therefore, we create our choices. They have no explanation beyond the fact that we make them.

At the same time, our freedom is by no means unstructured or unlimited. A choice is not a random occurrence. We usually have reasons and motives in choosing as we do, and they provide a basis for our choices. Strictly speaking, however, our motives do not cause or produce our choices.[15] As a parent, for example, I am motivated by the desire to do what is best for my children, but this motive does not automatically produce behavior that is beneficial to them. The motive informs and guides my choices, but I still have to make them.

Our freedom is limited by several different things. One is the fact that we are creatures and therefore finite. Because of the kind of creature I am, living without oxygen or water is not one of the options available to me. Nor can I choose to inhabit Los Angeles and New York City at the same moment.

Heredity and environment place further restrictions on our freedom. A lack of size prevents me from pursuing a career in professional sports. If you live in the midwestern United States, you won't be able to choose surfing as a regular pastime.

Previous choices also affect the range of options available to us. If you major in business at college, you can't apply for a job as a hospital nurse. On the other hand, if you are musically talented and decide to practice diligently, you may someday have the option of becoming a professional musician.

In various ways, then, our freedom is qualified or conditioned. For the most part, our choices lie within a limited range of options we can do little to control.

Limits to freedom

15. The following statements offer a helpful account of the relation between motives and choice: "Motivating factors may impel, urge, incline, dispose, stimulate to certain acts of the will. They cannot compel. Motives do not make free acts impossible but meaningful, since they provide reasons for them. They do not determine, in the sense of excluding freedom, but motivate, by giving the 'I' a reason for its self-determination—a reason for *willing* something" (Peter Rohner, "Will," in *Encyclopedia of Theology: The Concise Sacramentum Mundi,* ed. Karl Rahner [New York: The Seabury Press, 1975], p. 1816; italics original).

Different kinds of freedom

Among the options available to us, we make choices of two different kinds. The biblical account of creation suggests two kinds of freedom. The more obvious is moral freedom: freedom to do right or wrong. God told Adam and Eve not to eat of the tree of knowledge of good and evil (Gen 2:17). They were capable of doing so, and therefore in a sense free to do it, but it was clearly God's desire that they obey him and refrain. Freedom to obey or disobey God is typically called "moral freedom." In moral choices, the options are right and wrong.

Other choices do not involve options that are right and wrong. When God told Adam and Even to avoid the tree of knowledge of good and evil, it was clear what he wanted them to do. But when God invited Adam to name the animals, he would have been equally pleased with any selection. No moral issue was at stake in the names chosen. There are areas in which the choices available to us are neither right nor wrong in a moral sense.

Responsibility

This analysis of freedom has some important practical implications. Because freedom is essential to being human, its exercise in concrete personal decisions is never something we should avoid. Oddly, some people try to do this by seeking God's will. Confronted with alternatives, they want God to decide for them, rather than making the decision themselves. To know God's will, of course, is the first priority of every Christian, and there are many times when God has something specific in mind for us. But there are also instances where God does not have a preference. He may be equally pleased, for example, if a person chooses one of several careers. If praying over a decision leaves us with no clear impression as to what God wants us to do, we should consider the possibility that he is leaving the matter up to us and will be happy with any responsible choice.

Personal qualities

Freedom is the most important characteristic which human beings share with God. It allows us to apply the category of the personal to both human and divine beings. As we saw in our doctrine of God, a person exhibits several essential qualities. A person is first of all a unity, a being distinct from other beings. Second, a person enjoys self-consciousness; a person is aware of being a person. And third, a person is capable of relationships with other persons; in fact, a person exists as such only in relation to others.

In his famous book *I and Thou,* Martin Buber describes the two fundamental relationships which characterize our experience.[16] One is

16. Martin Buber, *I and Thou,* trans. Ronald Gregor Smith (2d ed.; New York: Charles Scribner's Sons, 1958), cf. p. 3.

our relation to objects, which he calls an "I-It" relationship. We treat objects as things to be examined, analyzed, and used. In contrast, we experience persons in an "I-Thou" relationship. The essential characteristic here is reciprocity. In an I-Thou relationship, you experience the other as a counterpart to yourself, not as something to be merely analyzed or used.

Buber's insights into the unique qualities of the personal point to three other aspects of personal being. One is dignity. We value persons more highly than anything else. We also rightly refuse to compare the value of different persons. The life of an inner-city infant has just as much absolute value as that of a United States senator. Second, persons have responsibility; we hold persons accountable for their behavior. Our legal system rests on the fundamental conviction that people choose to behave as they do. A third aspect of personal being is mystery. Because they are free, the actions of a person are never entirely predictable. A person can always choose to do certain things differently.

In creating persons among the inhabitants of this planet, God took an enormous risk, for he brought into existence beings whose actions could not be entirely predicted. They could do things that would disappoint him severely. But He created personal beings anyway, because only persons could respond to him as a person. Only persons are capable of love.

Summary: The human situation

In summary, Christianity attributes great complexity to human being. It locates man at the boundary, so to speak, of nature and spirit. As creatures, we share many characteristics with other forms of life on this planet. We, too, are finite and corporeal. But we are "more than nature" in certain important respects. Our intelligence is superior to that of other forms of life. More important, we have the quality of freedom, which gives us the capacity for self-determination, elevates us to the realm of the personal, and enables us to master our environment. We are creatures, then, but we are unique creatures. As persons we bear the image of God.

Humanity and the reign of God

To express these ideas in terms of our guiding theme, we can understand ourselves only in relation to the reign of God. His creative sovereignty assigns us our place in the scheme of things. We are his creatures, subject to his lordship; we are dependent on him for making us the way we are. Yet he has assigned us a special work to do. We are his representatives in the world. In certain important respects we resemble him. And we are a major means by which God continues to exercise his sovereignty in the world. Our creative mastery of existence is an extension of the creative activity of God himself. God thus reigns over, in, and through human beings.

STUDY HELPS

Questions for review

1. What are the most important biblical characterizations of human beings?

2. What are the essential qualities of human creatureliness?

3. How does the Bible understand the relation between the individual and the group?

4. What is the biblical view of the human body?

5. What is the biblical attitude toward human sexuality? What framework for sexual activity does the Bible support?

6. In what sense are human beings "in the image of God"?

7. What are the nature and limits of human freedom?

Questions for further study

1. How can creationists account for the structural similarities between human beings and various animals? How much can we learn about human beings from the study of animals?

2. In *Moral Man and Immoral Society* (New York: Charles Scribner's Sons, 1932), Reinhold Niebuhr contends that individual human beings have moral resources that human groups do not have. Love, he maintains, is possible for an individual, but not for a group. Do you agree or disagree with this view? Why?

3. If bodily existence is part of our essential humanity, what attitude should we have toward our personal appearance?

4. In what ways does sexuality affect human life, besides its obvious reproductive function?

5. How do the following enterprises manifest the image of God in man: natural science, social science, fine art, applied art, business and industry, athletic activity?

6. What form(s) of government is/are most compatible with the concept that freedom is an essential dimension of human life?

1. The first chapter of the Bible not only tells us a great deal about God, it also says a lot about human beings. Make a list of the things we can learn about human existence from Genesis 1.

2. When the serpent tempted Eve in the garden of Eden, she had no evil tendencies. So, what essential human qualities did the serpent's utterances to her presuppose (Genesis 3:1–5)?

3. Does God deal with human beings primarily as individuals, or as members of the group to which they belong? What do the following passages indicate?

   a. Exodus 20:5; Joshua 7:22–25; 1 Samuel 15:3; Job 1:6–19; Jonah 1:4–15
   b. Deuteronomy 24:16; Ezekiel 18:1–4, 20; Matthew 10:30; Luke 15:7; Matthew 10:34–37
   c. Genesis 18:22–33; Matthew 5:13
   d. Ephesians 1:4; 2 Peter 2:9–10

4. People disagree as to whether the ideal human environment is the city or the country. What light on this question do the following passages shed?

   a. Genesis 2:8, 10, 15; 4:17; 11:1–8
   b. Numbers 14:7–8; Psalm 48:1–2; 137:5–6
   c. Numbers 14:32–33; Jeremiah 4:23–26; Matthew 3:1; 4:1; Luke 1:80; 2:39–40
   d. Genesis 13:12–13; Revelation 18:21–24
   e. Isaiah 11:6–9; 35:1–2; Revelation 21:2–3; 21:9–22:5

5. Most people believe that our lives should contain periods of both work and leisure. What attitudes toward these activities do the following passages suggest?

   a. Genesis 2:15; 3:17
   b. Proverbs 10:4; Ecclesiastes 9:10; Colossians 3:23
   c. Deuteronomy 24:14–15; Ephesians 6:9
   d. Isaiah 65:21–22
   e. John 5:17; 9:4
   f. Matthew 6:25–31
   g. Exodus 20:9–10; Mark 6:30–31

6. One of the most perplexing issues facing people today is the proper relation between the sexes. Are women subordinate, equal, or perhaps superior to men? What do the following passages indicate?

   a. Genesis 1:27; 2:21–24; 3:16
   b. Proverbs 31:10–31

    c. Ephesians 5:21–33
    d. 1 Corinthians 14:33–35; 1 Timothy 2:11–15
    e. Galatians 3:28; Mark 12:25

7. We generally think of sexual activity as a privilege, or right, provided it takes place in the proper context. When, according to the Bible, is sex a responsibility? Read Genesis 1:28; Deuteronomy 25:5–10; 1 Corinthians 7:3–5. When is abstinence from sexual activity desirable? Read 1 Corinthians 7; Matthew 19:10–12.

SUGGESTIONS FOR FURTHER READING

From Adventist writers

Ellen G. White comments on various aspects of human nature throughout her writings. She describes the different dimensions of our essential humanity in *Patriarchs and Prophets,* pp. 44–51.

The unity of man, or the non-immortality of the soul, has always been one of the distinctive doctrinal concerns of Seventh-day Adventists. LeRoy Edwin Froom accumulates a massive amount of historical material on the subject in *The Conditionalist Faith of Our Fathers: The Conflict of the Ages Over the Nature and Destiny of Man* (2 vols.; Washington, D.C.: The Review and Herald Publishing Association, 1966, 1965). Two philosophical discussions of the topic are Carsten Johnsen, *Man the Indivisible: Totality Versus Disruption in the History of Western Thought* (Oslo: Universitetsforlaget, 1971), and J. R. Zurcher, *The Nature and Destiny of Man: Essay on the Problem of the Union of the Soul and the Body in Relation to the Christian Views of Man,* trans. Mabel R. Bartlett (New York: Philosophical Library, 1969).

Seventh-day Adventists have also been highly interested in the question of origins over the years—a topic closely related to the concept of human creatureliness. Three books dealing with this subject are Harold Coffin, *Creation—Accident or Design?* (Washington, D.C.: Review and Herald Publishing Association, 1969); Richard M. Ritland, *Meaning in Nature* (Washington, D.C.: The Department of Education, General Conference of Seventh-day Adventists, 1966); and Gerald W. Wheeler, *The Two-Taled Dinosaur: Why Science and Religion Conflict Over the Origin of Life* (Nashville, Tenn.: Southern Publishing Association, 1975). Articles discussing the biological and geological questions concerning the creation-evolution discussion have appeared in various Adventist periodicals, such as *Adventist Review* and *Spectrum. Ministry* recently devoted an issue to the topic, "Creation/Evolution: The Issues and the Evidence" (May 1984).

There is a growing number of books and articles by Adventist authors dealing with human sexuality. The most popular is probably Charles Wittschiebe, *God Invented Sex* (Nashville, Tenn.: Southern Publishing Association,

1974). Others include Alberta Mazat, *That Friday in Eden: Sharing and Enhancing Sexuality in Marriage* (Mountain View, Calif.: Pacific Press Publishing Association, 1981), and Nancy Van Pelt, *The Compleat Courtship* (Nashville, Tenn.: Southern Publishing Association, 1982), and Nancy Van Pelt, *The Compleat Marriage* (Nashville, Tenn.: Southern Publishing Association, 1979). Sakae Kubo seeks a more comprehensive perspective on the topic in *The Theology and Ethics of Sex* (Washington, D.C.: Review and Herald Publishing Association, 1980). A recent issue of *Spectrum* contains a section devoted to sexuality (vol. 15, no. 1, pp. 2–23).

Adventists are also facing the question of homosexuality more openly. *Ministry* has devoted an issue to the topic (September 1981). There is also a series of articles on homosexuality in *Spectrum,* vol. 12, no. 3 (pp. 32–48).

The quarterly journal *Origins,* of the Geoscience Research Institute of the General Conference of Seventh-day Adventists, discusses various aspects of the creation-evolution issue on a regular basis.

From other writers

Some of the most important theological writing of this century has been concerned with the doctrine of man. Two outstanding works are Emil Brunner, *Man in Revolt: A Christian Anthropology,* trans. Olive Wyon (Philadelphia: The Westminster Press, 1939), and Reinhold Niebuhr, *The Nature and Destiny of Man* (2 vols.; New York: Charles Scribner's Sons, 1941, 1943).

Besides these "classics," there are many less ambitious efforts. Ray S. Anderson's *On Being Human: Essays in Theological Anthropology* (Grand Rapids, Mich.: William B. Eerdmans Publishing Co., 1982) develops a doctrine of man that is heavily indebted to Karl Barth's thought. Marianne H. Micks presents a readable series of reflections on various topics in *Our Search for Identity: Humanity in the Image of God* (Philadelphia: Fortress Press, 1982). More rigorous and stimulating is Wolfhart Pannenberg's *What Is Man? Contemporary Anthropology in Theological Perspective,* trans. Duane Priebe (Philadelphia: Fortress Press, 1970). Helmut Thielicke explores the related themes of man's place in creation and God's relation to the world in *Man in God's World,* trans. and ed. John W. Doberstein (New York: Harper & Row, Publishers, 1963).

The subject of human sexuality—not merely sexual relations but relations between the sexes in general—has attracted increasing attention lately. Two books dealing with this topic are Erhard S. Gerstenberger and Wolfgang Schrage, *Woman and Man,* trans. Douglas W. Stott (Nashville, Tenn.: Abingdon, 1981), and Paul K. Jewett, *Man as Male and Female* (Grand Rapids, Mich: William B. Eerdmans Publishing Co., 1975).

Students of Christian theology can also learn a great deal from biblical scholarship in this area. Rudolf Bultmann's discussion of Paul's doctrine of man is especially valuable (*The Theology of the New Testament,* trans. Kendrick Grobel [New York: Charles Scribner's Sons, 1951–1955], 1:190–269).

John A. T. Robinson's work, *The Body: A Study in Pauline Theology* (Philadelphia: The Westminster Press, 1952), is also informative.

6

THE DOCTRINE OF MAN: THE HUMAN CONDITION

"All we like sheep have gone astray; we have turned every one to his own way" (Isaiah 53:6).

"Therefore as sin came into the world through one man and death through sin, and so death spread to all men because all sinned" (Romans 5:12).

"Then death and Hades were thrown into the lake of fire" (Revelation 20:14).

Genesis 2:15–17	John 5:25–29
Genesis 3	John 11:21–26
Genesis 4:6–7	Romans 1:18–3:20, 23
Psalm 51:4–5	Romans 5:12–21
Psalm 115:17	Romans 6:16–18, 20, 23
Psalm 146:2–4	Romans 7:8–20
Ecclesiastes 9:5, 12:7	1 Corinthians 15:12–57
Isaiah 14:12–14	1 Thessalonians 4:14
Ezekiel 28:1–23	1 John 3:4–10
Micah 2–3	Revelation 20:4–5

In the preceding chapter we looked at the essential qualities of human being. We examined the Christian view of what men and women were originally meant to be as creatures in the image of God. But it is obvious that more discussion is needed to describe human beings as they actually exist, because there is an enormous contrast between the world God first created and the world we live in now. The Bible attributes this tragic discrepancy to sin. Sin is one of the most profound biblical concepts, and there is clearer evidence for it in our experience than for any other Christian idea.

THE MEANING OF SIN

The human predicament

The Bible attributes the origin of all that is evil in the earth to an act of human disobedience, a willful departure from God's express intentions for human life. This indicates that the fundamental human problem originates in what man has done, not in what he is. We might say that our predicament is moral rather than metaphysical. This is important, because certain religions find something wrong with what man basically is. Specifically, they believe that our basic problem is the fact that we are distinct, or separate, from God. But the Bible finds nothing wrong with the fact that we are not divine. We were never meant to be. The basic problem is our lack of harmony with God, our unwillingness to accept his sovereignty over us. The human predicament is something we are responsible for.

The fall

We often speak of the origin of sin as "the fall." This points to another important aspect of sin: the fact that it is accidental. Sin is an interruption in God's design, a departure from his plans for the world. It isn't something that was meant to be or that has a positive place in the scheme of things. Some views of reality treat evil as an illusion; they deny it exists. Others assign positive significance to everything, including suffering and disappointment. Christianity differs from both of these approaches. It acknowledges the existence of evil, but it denies that evil belongs in the world. For Christians, life has a tragic quality. There is a drastic discrepancy between the way things are and the way they were meant to be.

Sin and sins

Paul's frequent use of the word *sin,* singular, as opposed to *sins,* plural, indicates another aspect of this doctrine: the conviction that sin is fundamentally a condition of our existence. It is true that the Bible speaks of sins and identifies various actions as sinful, but specific sins are symptoms of a deeper human problem: our basic lack of harmony with God. The solution to the problem of sin involves much more than attempts to modify our behavior. Nothing less than a transformation of human nature itself will suffice.

With these general considerations in mind, we can examine the inner content or essence of sin. We are looking for what it is that makes sin sinful.

From the serpent's conversation with Eve in the Garden of Eden, we see that unbelief, or distrust, is an essential aspect of sin. "Did God say . . . ?'' the tempter began, planting seeds of doubt as to God's interest in human beings. Sin therefore involves doubting God's trustworthiness, or reliability. We also see that sin involves assuming divine prerogatives for ourselves. "You will be like God," the serpent lied, encouraging Eve to deny her essential dependence on God. Pride, or self-centeredness, also lies at the heart of sin.

Unbelief

Pride

Another, perhaps more familiar, aspect of sin is disobedience, or transgression of the law (1 Jn 3:4). The first human sin presupposed God's command not to eat from the tree of knowledge of good and evil (Gen 2:17). Sin involves disregarding God's will for human beings. Some people reject the expression of God's will in the law, while others reject the revelation of his will in creation. One way or another, however, sin always involves disobedience.

Disobedience

Sin is also a matter of rebellion against the sovereignty of God. The biblical doctrine of sin presupposes the doctrine of creation. As our creator, God has a right to our allegiance. Sin is the rejection of God's rightful claims on us.

Rebellion

A further aspect of sin is ingratitude. Sin is the violation of a personal relationship. This is a familiar theme in recent discussions of sin and salvation. It provides a helpful balance to the tendency to "quantify" or "objectify" sin, which treats sin as something separate from the sinner. There is a certain objectivity to sin. Every action, including sinful ones, sets in motion a chain of consequences which the agent can never entirely control. But this should not obscure the fact that sin is fundamentally the breakdown of our relationship with God. This is why David cried, "Against thee, thee only, have I sinned" (Ps 51:4). His crimes of adultery and murder hurt a great many people, but the recognition that he had let God down caused him the greatest distress.

Ingratitude

The five aspects of sin we have just discussed pertain to its spiritual or vertical dimension. They refer to alterations in our relationship to God. But sin has a horizontal or social dimension as well. It

Injustice

involves our relationship with other human beings. Rejecting the sovereignty of God inevitably leads us to ignore the rights of other people. This is because the two great commandments—love to God and love to the neighbor—are inseparably linked together. We cannot observe one without observing the other, and failing to keep one inevitably leads us to violate the other.

In summary, the fundamental meaning of sin is "failure," as both the Greek and Hebrew words for "sin" imply. It is a rupture in our relationships with God and other human beings, involving unbelief, pride, disobedience, rebellion, and ingratitude.

THE RESULTS OF SIN

Condemnation
Sin has disastrous consequences. It distorts every aspect of the human situation. One effect is "condemnation" (cf. Rom 5:8). As sinners we stand under the judgment, or wrath, of God; a "guilty" verdict hangs over our heads. This result of sin plays an important role in Paul's understanding of man, as his letter to the Romans indicates. For Paul, sin places every human being under the judgment of God.

Corruption
Our condition in sin is also one of corruption, or disintegration. Sin is like a disease which destroys the harmony and balance of things. Because it distorts our fundamental relationship to God, it distorts everything else about us, too. It leads to physical decay, to illness, and ultimately to death (Rom 5:12). It also leads to spiritual decay and to idolatry, the substitution of false objects of worship for the true God (Rom 1:23–25; 7:23, 25). As already noted, it leads to social disruption, or injustice (Rom 1:29–31), and to lust, or sexual corruption (Rom 1:26–27).

Alienation
We can express this idea with more contemporary terms like "estrangement," or "alienation." The reaction of Adam and Eve to their original transgression suggests a breakdown in the several relationships which are basic to human existence (Gen 3:10–13). Their effort to hide themselves implies a rupture in their relationship with God. Their willingness to blame each other shows that their human relationships were fractured. Their exile from the garden and the curse of the ground indicate their alienation from creation in general (Gen 3:24, 17). The shame which Adam and Eve felt also suggests self-rejection or alienation (Gen 3:10). So sin corrupts every essential human relationship.

The human situation is truly desperate, because the consequences of sin are comprehensive, irreversible, and inevitable.

The theological concept of "total depravity" emphasizes the comprehensive effects of sin. As used by the great Reformers, the expression "total depravity" does not indicate that human beings are as bad as they could possibly get, or that there isn't a trace of goodness left. It means that sin affects everything about us. There is nothing that it doesn't touch. In John Calvin's words, "The whole man is overwhelmed—as by a deluge—from head to foot, so that no part is immune from sin and all that proceeds from him is to be imputed to sin" (*Institutes of the Christian Religion,* II.i.9).

"Total depravity"

The irreversibility of sin appears in Paul's description of our condition in sin as one of slavery, or bondage (Rom 6–7). As he sees it, sin holds us captive; we are powerless under its spell. It is possible to interpret the famous conflict Paul describes in Romans 7:7–25 as an account of the sinner's desperate plight. Sin so dominates the sinner's faculties that he is powerless to do good. In fact, he cannot even will to do good. All his striving proceeds from the sinful desire to attain righteousness on his own. His motives, as well as his actions, therefore, are all wrong.

Slavery

The controversial concept of "original sin" points to the inevitability of sin in human experience. This does not mean that sin could not have been avoided to start with; but once it was introduced, there is no escaping its influence. Along with the idea of total depravity, this concept locates sin on the level of human nature. The fact is, we all sin. No Christian belief has more practical evidence to support it than this one.

Original sin

In spite of this, people question the inevitability of sin from time to time. Like Pelagius in the fourth century, there are those today who believe that we all have the natural ability to choose between good and evil. Morally speaking, they maintain, we start where Adam and Eve did when they were first placed in the Garden of Eden. In contrast, a long stream of thinkers, ranging from Augustine to Ellen White (cf. *Patriarchs and Prophets,* p. 61), claims otherwise. The fall of our first parents does more than give us a bad example. It has an effect on our very nature.

We cannot accept Augustine's notion that sin is biologically transmitted through sexual procreation.[1] But the essential concept of

---

1. Because Adam and Eve covered their genitals with fig leaves after eating the forbidden fruit, Augustine reasoned, sexual activity is the means by which sin is

original sin is permanently valid. Sin affects human nature, not merely behavior. It is a basic condition of our existence and has an influence on everything about us.

THE GREAT CONTROVERSY

No Adventist doctrine of sin would be complete without a discussion of "the great controversy," for this idea provides the comprehensive framework with which Seventh-day Adventists often think of the entire course of human history, including the plan of salvation. The title of Ellen G. White's most influential series of books, "The Conflict of the Ages," along with that of its most important volume, *The Great Controversy,* reflects the significance of this concept in her own mind.

The origin of the conflict

According to the great controversy theme, human sin is part of a cosmic conflict between superhuman powers of good and evil, with the destiny of the entire universe at stake. The controversy began with the rebellion of Lucifer, the highest of created beings, who, as a covering cherub, ministered in the very presence of God (Ezek 28:14). Lucifer envied God's power, resented his authority, and sowed dissension among his angelic colleagues. His animosity ripened into open revolt (Rev 12:7), and he ultimately persuaded one-third of the angels to join him in rebellion (Isa 14:13–14; Ezek 28:17; Rev 12:3–4). As a result, they were expelled from heaven (Isa 14:12; Rev 12:9).

Now called the devil, or Satan, this fallen angel tempted Adam and Eve and led human beings into sin (Rev 12:9). He continues to tempt and harass human beings (cf. Mt 4:1), and he bears ultimate responsibility for all the evil in the world. His eventual defeat was insured by the death of Jesus, but he is now working desperately to take as many people as possible to destruction with him before his time runs out (1 Pet 5:8; Rev 12:12).

The issue in the conflict

The sovereignty of God is the central issue of the great controversy. This may seem strange, since God is supremely powerful. All

transmitted to succeeding generations (Peter Brown, *Augustine of Hippo* [Berkeley and Los Angeles: University of California Press, 1969], pp. 388–389; W. H. C. Frend, "Augustinianism," in *The Westminster Dictionary of Christian Theology,* ed. Alan Richardson and John Bowden [Philadelphia: The Westminster Press, 1983], p. 58).

his creatures depend on him for their very existence, and he could annihilate them as easily as he created them. But the reign of God does not rest on superior power. Its basis is love. As we saw in our examination of the image of God in man, God created beings with a capacity to appreciate his character and reciprocate his love for them. He desires the allegiance that arises from an intelligent appreciation of his character, not merely respect for his power. God gave these creatures freedom because he didn't want their loyalty to be mechanical.

What is at stake in the great controversy, therefore, is not God's supremacy; it is his character. More precisely, it is his reputation. Because Lucifer resented his authority, he accused God of being a tyrant who lords over his creatures, depriving them of dignity. Lucifer thus threatened God's government by raising doubts about God's real attitude toward his creatures.

Lucifer evidently reached the point where he was willing to sacrifice himself to achieve his purposes. This is the only way to account for his open revolt against God. Intelligent as he was, he must have realized that God could end his life in a moment, but he knew that this would appear to substantiate his charges against God. It would make God look just like the tyrant he accused him of being and make him, Lucifer, look like a hero. After all, the courageous response to tyranny is resistance, even if it costs you your life.

Having created a world with free creatures in it, God committed himself to its preservation, even at the cost of rebellion. He knew that he could not meet Lucifer's charges with a display of superior power; he could refute them only by demonstrating the depth of his love. What the great controversy required, therefore, was a revelation of God's character so vivid, so compelling, that it would convince even his enemies and forever silence questions about his love. **God's response to the challenge**

In the context of the great controversy, this is precisely what the plan of salvation represents—an unmistakable manifestation of God's love for sinners. The cross of Christ shows how deeply God cares for us. It reveals his willingness to risk everything, even the life of his only Son, in order to overcome the alienation of sin. It reveals the true nature of his sovereignty, one that has only our best interests at heart. It allows no conclusion but that God deserves to be God.

The great controversy is a powerful theological idea. It dramatizes the human situation, and it properly focuses theological attention on the doctrine of God. It also provides a way of integrating many important themes in Christian faith, including the fall of man, the meaning of the cross, and the end of history.

Questions about the great controversy

As helpful as it is, the idea of the great controversy also raises some important questions. One of these is the very possibility of questioning the character of God. According to the great controversy, Lucifer raised doubts about God's reliability, and these doubts are settled by the plan of salvation. Overwhelming evidence accumulates to show God's love for his creatures.

There is a problem, however, with the status of this evidence, because it is related to the character of God. To decide any issue, we need to trust the data and the ability of our minds to interpret it accurately. In other words, we have to trust the nature of things, or the structure of reality. To settle the issue of the great controversy, therefore, we have to assume that the evidence before us is reliable and that our minds will not deceive us. But God is the creator. Since he is ultimately responsible for the structure of reality, including our minds, we cannot trust any part of reality unless we trust in God. We must be convinced that he is not manufacturing the evidence or manipulating our thoughts.

Here we find ourselves in a predicament. We have to trust God, it seems, in order to find out if God is trustworthy. But this is begging the question; it assumes the very point to be proved. As every student of logic knows, this is fallacious reasoning. Because God is creator, his trustworthiness can never be a matter of genuine doubt. It is impossible not to trust him, if we are to believe anything. Indeed, every claim to know something expresses a fundamental trust in God.

The concept of the great controversy, therefore, deserves further theological attention. We may need to modify our understanding of it in light of God's status as creator of the world.

THE NATURE OF DEATH

Our ignorance of death

Death is something most of us think about very little. We don't have to, thanks largely to the advances of medical science, and we don't want to because it isn't a pleasant topic. But we pay a price for our ignorance. We tend to be unprepared when we are finally forced to face it. We may be unsure about what happens when someone dies, and we may not understand our own feelings about death.

Unfamiliarity with death is a modern phenomenon. A hundred years ago the death rate was much higher, and there was hardly anyone who hadn't lost a parent, or a brother or sister. When couples promised to love each other "till death do us part," someone has calculated, they could look forward to an average of twelve years together before one of them died.

Some people have remarked that death and sex have switched places in the shift from Victorian consciousness to our contemporary outlook. In the last century, everyone knew about death, but they found sex utterly mysterious. Today we hear a great deal about sex, but we hardly ever speak about death.[2]

Death was certainly familiar to the people of biblical times. The writers of the Bible have a good deal to say about it. We shall conclude our doctrine of human being with a consideration of this important topic. As we attempt to place death in the perspective of Christian faith, there are two fundamental questions that face us: What is death? and, What does it mean? To put them another way, What happens at death? and, What should our attitude toward death be?

A wholistic view of life and death

The biblical view of death is closely related to the biblical view of man. As we noticed earlier, the Bible presents a "wholistic" view of human being. Although multidimensional, a human being is essentially a unity; none of his components can exist in isolation from the others. Consequently, when someone dies, the whole person dies. Part of him does not keep going in some other mode of being. Death, in other words, is the complete cessation of life. When a person dies, experience comes to an end, mental as well as physical.

Numerous texts illustrate this view, including Psalm 146:4, "When his breath departs he returns to his earth; on the very day his thoughts perish"; Ecclesiastes 9:5, "The living know that they will die, but the dead know nothing"; and Ecclesiastes 12:7, "The dust returns to the earth as it was, and the spirit returns to God who gave it." This last verse suggests that death reverses the process of human creation, where God formed man of dust from the ground, and breathed into him the breath of life (Gen 2:7).

Because death is a cessation of life, the future beyond death involves the recovery, or resumption, of life, not merely an extension, or continuation, of it. For this reason, the resurrection of the dead is comparable to the creation of human beings. It occurs only by virtue of a specific divine activity (cf. Rom 4:17).

We can illustrate the biblical view of death with the following diagram. It shows that death is a void, an emptiness, the absence of all experience. The future beyond death is the restoration of life.

2. "In the permissive society of today sex is a topic of unrestricted conversation but death has for some time been almost unmentionable in polite society" (John Hick, *Death and Eternal Life* [New York: Harper & Row, Publishers, 1976], p. 81).

THIS LIFE | DEATH | THE FUTURE LIFE

The biblical view of death contrasts sharply with the popular conviction that life somehow continues after death. This belief draws support from some recent reports of so-called "near death" experiences. In certain cases, people who are "clinically dead" recover and display a remarkable awareness of what happened to them. Occasionally they describe feelings of utter tranquility. Sometimes they feel the presence of people who have previously died. There are biochemical explanations for such experiences, but to many, these reports confirm mankind's oldest fantasy—that we don't really die.

A dualistic view of life and death

The dualistic view of man, which entered Christian thought from Greek sources, also supports the idea that life continues after death. According to dualism, human beings are composite creatures—a union of two quite different things. Besides the physical body, which is mortal and doomed to perish, there is the immaterial soul, or spirit, which is immortal. It is the true bearer of personal identity. At death the soul escapes the body, which ceases to function, and goes on to exist in another realm.

As the following diagram illustrates, dualism views death, not as the cessation of life, or even an interruption of it. It is merely the transition between one phase of life and the next. Personal experience never stops, and the future life is a continuation of the present one.

THIS LIFE   DEATH   THE FUTURE LIFE

Belief in natural immortality, the idea that we don't really die, exerts a powerful influence on conventional views of death. It resonates to our instinctive rejection of death, and it often comforts and reassures people when their loved ones die.

The concept of natural immortality conflicts with the biblical view of death, of course, but it also contradicts some of our basic feelings about death. It denies the finality of death. It also denies its fundamentally tragic character, for if the dead are really happier now, why do we feel wretched when they die? Clearly, we need to examine the meaning of death, as well as its nature.

THE MEANING OF DEATH

The Bible not only describes what happens at death, it also interprets the meaning of death. Its perspective rings true to personal experience and provides a basis for hope as well.

For biblical faith, death is an enemy, an intruder. It was never meant to be. It is true that human beings are essentially mortal; we are capable of ceasing to exist. But it was never God's plan that we should. He intended for us to live forever, as the presence of the tree of life in Eden indicates.

Death as an enemy

Instead, death is a consequence of sin. People began to die as a result of violating the will of God. As Paul states, "Sin came into the world through one man and death through sin" (Rom 5:12). This recalls the prohibition in Eden from eating of the tree of knowledge of good and evil. "In the day that you eat of it," God said, "you shall die" (Gen 2:17). This expression does not mean that death would occur within a few hours. It means that with the act of disobedience, death became inevitable.

We should not think of death as an arbitrary penalty for sin, as if God is out to get even with people for offending him. The true nature of death appears in light of our basic relation to God. God is the source of life, and our existence depends on his sustaining power. Consequently, rejecting his sovereignty means cutting ourselves off from life. Rebellion against God is a kind of suicide (Prov 8:36).

The unnatural, or intrusive, character of death justifies our instinctive rejection of it. We are right to think of death as something that is horrible and frightening. It doesn't belong in the world God made. We are also right to feel that something real is lost at death, for death is the great antithesis of life. When a person dies, he is gone, and we are entitled to our feelings of bereavement.

This realistic assessment of death contradicts various attempts to give death a happy face. One popular view is that death has nothing for us to fear. As one poet put it, "There is nothing to trouble any heart, nothing to hurt at all. Death is only an old door in a garden wall."[3] Another encourages us to approach death "like one who wraps the drapery of his couch about him, and lies down to pleasant dreams."[4]

Popular views of death

3. Nancy Byrd Turner, "Death Is Only an Old Door," in *Light From Many Lamps*, edited and with commentary by Lillian Eichler Watson (New York: Simon and Schuster, 1951), p. 119.
4. William Cullen Bryant, "Thanatopsis," in *Light From Many Lamps*, p. 112.

In her recent and widely read studies of dying, psychiatrist Elisabeth Kübler-Ross observes that people approaching death move through a series of predictable stages, beginning with denial and ending with acceptance.[5] The healthy approach to death, she implies, is one which accepts it as a natural part of life. We have nothing to be afraid of when it comes.

Other people take a sharply different view of death. They confront it with clenched fists. As his father's death drew near, for example, Dylan Thomas urged, "Do not go gentle into that good night. Rage, rage against the dying of the light."[6] Death may be inevitable, but we do not have to submit to it meekly. The courageous thing is to defy it to the bitter end.

There is something attractive about a person standing up bravely to a superior foe. We admire a fighter, even if defeat is a foregone conclusion. In many ways this approach to death is more praiseworthy than the benign acceptance we just noticed. At least it doesn't try to cover the horror of death with a smile. At the same time, it does nothing to reassure us. It leaves us open to the enormous threat that death represents: the threat that life is ultimately meaningless.

If death can bring our lives to a final end, then it can also destroy everything we do. None of our accomplishments can have permanent value. The people we love and serve will someday die. Sooner or later the human race itself will cease to exist. Our having done good or evil, our having existed at all, makes no final difference in such a scheme of things. Death confronts us with the specter of utter meaninglessness.

The Christian view of death

A Christian view of death avoids both of these extremes. It acknowledges the inherent negativity of death, but it denies death the last word about human beings. It affirms the reality of a future beyond death.

The Bible portrays death as an enemy (1 Cor 15:26). We have a right to feel frightened by it and a duty to resist it. The touching scene of Jesus weeping at the tomb of Lazarus reinforces this negative view of death (Jn 11:35). The horror he felt as his own death approached does the same (Mt 26:37–44).

At the same time, the Bible describes death as a conquered enemy. Its power over us is broken by the victory of Christ and will

5. Elisabeth Kübler-Ross, M.D., *On Death and Dying* (New York: The Macmillan Company, 1969), pp. 34–121.
6. In *The Collected Poems of Dylan Thomas* (New York: New Directions Publishing Corporation, 1957), p. 128.

ultimately come to an end (1 Cor 15:26, 54–55; Rev 20:14). For this reason we can be hopeful, even confident, in the face of death, in spite of its ominous character. This is not because death itself is any less horrible than it first appears. Rather, it is because something more powerful has conquered it.

THE FUTURE BEYOND DEATH

The biblical expression "resurrection" points to the recovery of life after death which Christian hope anticipates. Because death is the complete absence of life, its recovery must be viewed as a resumption, rather than a continuation, of our present existence. Personal experience begins again with nothing less than an act of divine creative power.

The meaning of the resurrection

There are other aspects of the resurrection that deserve our attention, too. For one, the resurrection is eschatological—it occurs at the end of the age, when Christ returns to this earth (Jn 5:28–29; 1 Thess 4:16). It is thus part of a cluster of events with which the plan of salvation will reach its conclusion.

Another feature of the future life is its transformative character. Resurrection involves glorification, as Jesus' resurrected form indicates. Paul describes the bodies of the resurrected as "imperishable" and "immortal" (1 Cor 15:42, 53). Evidently the resurrection will restore human existence to the quality it had before the entrance of sin. Our bodies will be impervious to disease and death and all our physical powers will be fully developed.

The future life also involves the fulfillment of this life. It transforms and glorifies it, but it does not negate it. It brings the positive aspects of this life to completion. There is, for example, personal continuity between this life and the next. While it transforms our appearance, the resurrection also preserves personal identity. Those who are resurrected are the same individuals who existed before.

It is contrary to the Bible to think of human beings entering their eternal destiny at the moment of death. As the Bible describes the resurrection, it happens to everyone at once; all the redeemed receive their eternal inheritance together. Paul asserts that the living will not precede those who have died. Instead, living and dead enter the presence of Christ together (1 Thess 4:16–17).

The idea of recovering personal identity after death raises some deep philosophical questions, for how can we attribute to the same

The possibility of life after death

person a life lived, say, between 1900 and 1975 and an existence that begins at a later date and continues through eternity? What makes these time spans one life, rather than two? How can we say that it is a previously existing person who comes to life, rather than a new human being?

The resurrection is clearly a miracle, of course. Nothing less than divine power could bring it about, so we can hardly expect to comprehend it. But a little reflection may help us to see its credibility.

Our sense of personal identity basically depends on two things: bodily continuity and memory. I am convinced that I am the same person I was yesterday because I have the same physical form and because I remember my past. I recall certain events as happening to me.

In the case of other individuals, bodily continuity provides a basis for affirming identity, too. I recognize someone I know by his physical appearance. But personality traits are also important. I may not have seen a former classmate for twenty years, but if someone I see today bears a physical resemblance to that person, displays some of the same characteristics, and shares some of my recollection of our experiences together, I will feel justified in concluding that this is my classmate.

The question the resurrection raises is whether personal identity can be maintained over an interruption in which there is no physical or mental experience. There is no compelling reason why not. We experience physical transformations of a sort in this life, and they do not prevent us from affirming personal identity. A woman in her twenties looks hardly anything like her baby pictures, but this doesn't prevent us from saying she is the same person who was photographed years before. Physiologists tell us that the cells of our body are replaced about every seven years. We are therefore not the same, materially or physically, as we were ten years ago, but we are still the same persons. Personal identity does not require absolute physical continuity.

Nor does personal identity require uninterrupted mental continuity, either. Whenever we sleep, our mental activity is suspended to a certain degree. (We won't get into the phenomenon of dreams here.) Yet after a good night's sleep we think of ourselves as the same persons who dozed off the evening before.

The resurrection of the dead is not simply a matter of replacing the cells in our body or waking up from sleep, of course. But it is not entirely unlike these things, and they help us to see that a considerable lapse of time between death and resurrection is not an insurmountable obstacle to believing that the dead will indeed rise again.

A SUMMARY OF THE CHRISTIAN VIEW OF MAN

The biblical doctrine of human being has led us to consider a number of challenging topics. In the last chapter we explored essential human being by examining the biblical descriptions of man as creature and as image of God. A concern for actual human existence led us in this chapter to reflect on the meaning of sin and death. These topics set the stage for the central concern of Christian theology, the doctrine of salvation. In a sense, salvation, like sin, is a complicating factor in human existence. We never find essential human being, because sin affects every part of our experience. But we never find sinful human being, pure and simple, either, because salvation permeates our present situation, too. As soon as sin entered the world, God was at work to mitigate its consequences and restore humanity to fellowship with him.

The reign of God relates to the doctrine of man in several important ways. It accounts for the ultimate origin and basic purpose of human life. It situates human beings in the world, subject to the sovereignty of God, the creator, yet uniquely representative of God. Man's unique situation and abilities show that God is willing to share his sovereignty and that he reigns in and through creaturely activity.

Humanity and the reign of God

Sin is the willful rejection of God's reign, and it leads to disastrous consequences. But the fact that human beings did not experience all the results of sin immediately indicates that God's reign continues in the world after the fall, though in a qualified, fragmentary way. Salvation is the restoration of God's reign in human affairs. In the next chapter we begin our study of this central aspect of Christian faith.[7]

7. *A Word About Organization.* After the doctrines of revelation, God, and man, systematic theology traditionally takes up the doctrines of salvation, the church, and last things—in that order. This arrangement is somewhat arbitrary, however, because each of these topics can be described in a way that includes the other two.

The doctrine of salvation typically contains two major parts: (1) the doctrine of Christ, including discussions of both his person and his work; and (2) an examination of the experience of salvation, which usually contains a consideration of such topics as justification and sanctification. But the doctrine of salvation could also include a discussion of the church, as the corporate, or social, dimension of salvation; and of last things, as its historical, or future, dimension.

One could also incorporate the doctrines of salvation and last things within a comprehensive doctrine of the church. The doctrine of Christ provides an account of the origin of the church; the doctrine of last things, an account of its destiny. The topics

STUDY HELPS

Questions for review

1. What view of the human predicament does the concept of "sin" involve?

2. What are the essential dimensions of sin and what are its consequences?

3. What view of sin does the concept of the great controversy involve?

4. According to the Bible, what happens when a person dies? What view of man does this concept presuppose?

5. What attitude toward death does the Bible support?

6. What view of the future beyond death does the Bible present?

7. What factors provide a basis for continuity between this life and the future one?

Questions for further study

1. Many theologians maintain that "sins of the spirit" are ultimately more serious than "sins of the flesh." What do you think?

2. Langdon Gilkey explains the relation between the religious and moral dimensions of sin this way: "Injustice to other men . . . is the

---

generally considered in connection with the experience of salvation describe the identity and activity of the church's members.

Finally, the doctrine of last things, too, could serve as a comprehensive organizational theme. This would lead to an emphasis on the new age inaugurated by Jesus' life, death, and resurrection. It would describe the church as the eschatological community and would portray the experience of salvation as eschatological existence—as "life in the Spirit," conceived as an eschatological gift.

Because of their close relationship, it is better to think of the doctrines of salvation, the church, and last things as overlapping, or even as concentric circles, rather than as lying side by side, more or less independent of each other.

Our discussion here follows the traditional sequence, with one notable exception. It begins by considering the person and work of Christ, the subjects of Chapters 7 and 8, respectively. But it then turns to the doctrine of the church, which here includes the topics associated with the experience of salvation. The doctrine of last things follows that of the church, as usual.

social consequence of an inward idolatry, the worship of one's own self or group'' (*Shantung Compound: The Story of Men and Women Under Pressure* [New York: Harper & Row, Publishers, 1966], p. 232). Do you think he's right?

3. Our society tends to explain a person's behavior as the result of psychological and social factors. Does this practice erode our sense of sin, or is it compatible with it?

4. According to Albert Camus, ''There is but one truly serious philosophical problem, and that is suicide'' (*The Myth of Sisyphus and Other Essays,* trans. Justin O'Brien [New York: Vintage Books, 1955], p. 3). What views of reality make suicide reasonable? What views make it unacceptable?

5. Many scholars maintain that the concept of life after death, though occasionally mentioned, does not play a major role in the religion of the Old Testament. What gave the figures in the Old Testament a sense of meaning in life? In what circumstances is the concept of a future beyond death essential for a sense of meaning in life?

Suggestions for Bible study

1. In harmony with the Bible we generally think of life as a blessing and death as a curse, or an enemy. Is the opposite ever true? Is death ever a blessing? or life a curse? See 1 Kings 19:4; Job 3:1–5, 11–12; Matthew 26:24.

2. How do you reconcile the biblical emphasis on individual responsibility (cf. Deuteronomy 24:16) with assertions that the consequences of sin extend to several generations (cf. Exodus 20:5; 34:7b)?

3. Does a concept like ''corporate guilt'' help to explain the destruction of entire groups of people, along with their children and possessions? Genesis 6:5–7; 7:21–23; Deuteronomy 7:1–2; 1 Samuel 15:1–3. What contemporary application(s), if any, does such a concept have?

4. According to the Bible, an appropriate response to sin includes several elements. What are they? See Leviticus 4–6; Psalm 32:1–5; James 5:16; 1 John 1:9.

5. In David's experience, genuine repentance did not forestall the conseqences of his sin (see 2 Samuel 11:2–12:23; Psalm 51). Is this always the case? Why, or why not?

6. A number of passages seem to contradict the fundamental biblical belief that the dead are unconscious. How can these texts be explained: 1 Samuel 28:8–25; Luke 16:19–31; Luke 23:39–46; 2 Corinthians 5:1–10; Philippians 1:19–26; Revelation 6:9–11?

7. Although unconscious, the dead are not nonexistent, according to the Bible. What do the following verses suggest as to their status: Luke 20:37–38?

8. What view(s) of life does the prospect of death generate in passages such as the following? Psalm 90:9–17; Psalm 103:15–16; Ecclesiastes 3:19–20; 9:2–10; 1 Corinthians 15:19, 32.

SUGGESTIONS FOR FURTHER READING

From Adventist writers

Ellen G. White discusses the origin, nature, and consequences of sin in many passages. Some of the better known are: *Patriarchs and Prophets,* pp. 33–43, 52–62; *The Great Controversy,* pp. 492–504. Her most influential books, of course, form the "Conflict of the Ages" series, whose pervasive theme is the cosmic struggle between God and Satan for the allegiance of the universe. Joseph Battistone analyzes the role of this theme in her writings in *The Great Controversy Theme in E. G. White Writings* (Berrien Springs, Mich.: Andrews University Press, 1978).

Ellen G. White also has a good deal to say about death and about erroneous concepts of death. An important statement of her views in this area appears in *The Great Controversy,* pp. 531–562.

Articles and booklets in great numbers have appeared presenting the Seventh-day Adventist understanding of "the state of the dead." A recent discussion which takes into account the reports of so-called "near death" experiences is Jack W. Provonsha, M.D., Ph.D., *Is Death for Real?* (Mountain View, Calif.: Pacific Press Publishing Association, 1981).

Two recent treatments of the problem and evil and suffering are Jerry Gladson, *Who Said Life Is Fair?* (Hagerstown, Md.: Review and Herald Publishing Association, 1985), and Richard Rice, *When Bad Things Happen to God's People* (Boise, Idaho: Pacific Press Publishing Association, 1985).

From other writers

Many of the books on the doctrine of man mentioned at the end of the previous chapter deal with the topics of sin, death, and resurrection. But each of these items is the subject of an extensive literature of its own.

G. C. Berkouwer presents a massive study of the topic in his book *Sin* (Grand Rapids, Mich.: William B. Eerdmans Publishing Co., 1971). Langdon

Gilkey corroborates the Christian doctrine of sin in the personal account of his internment during World War II, *Shantung Compound: The Story of Men and Women Under Pressure* (New York: Harper & Row, Publishers, 1966).

The problem of evil has generated a long history of philosophical and theological reflection, extending as far back as the biblical book of Job. Recent discussions of this perplexing issue include John Hick, *Evil and the God of Love* (rev. ed.; San Francisco: Harper & Row, Publishers, 1978); Stephen T. Davis (ed.), *Encountering Evil: Live Options in Theodicy* (Atlanta: John Knox Press, 1981); and Alvin Plantinga, *God, Freedom, and Evil* (New York: Harper & Row, Publishers, 1974). More readable are a couple of books dealing with the problem on a personal level, namely, C. S. Lewis, *The Problem of Pain* (New York: The Macmillan Company, 1962), and Harold S. Kushner, *When Bad Things Happen to Good People* (New York: Schocken Books, 1981).

Like the problem of evil, the subjects of death and immortality have attracted widespread philosophical as well as theological attention. Christian theologians frequently deal with them in connection with a general discussion of last things, or eschatology. But they are often the objects of independent studies, too. A famous discussion of alternative concepts of death and immortality is Oscar Cullmann, *Immortality of the Soul or Resurrection of the Dead? The Witness of the New Testament* (London: The Epworth Press, 1958). This essay, along with three others, appears in Krister Stendahl (ed.), *Immortality and Resurrection* (New York: Herder and Herder, 1970). By far the most informative and influential discussion of the issues in recent years, with a highly controversial proposal of its own, is John Hick, *Death and Eternal Life* (New York: Harper & Row, Publishers, 1976).

7

THE DOCTRINE OF CHRIST:
WHO JESUS WAS

**Biblical
basis**

"And the Word became flesh and dwelt among us, full of grace and truth; we have beheld his glory, glory as of the only Son from the Father" (John 1:14).

"He who has seen me has seen the Father" (John 14:9).

Deuteronomy 18:18

Micah 5:2

Matthew 16:15–16

Luke 2:52

John 1:1–18

John 3:16

John 6:35

John 8:12; 11:25–26; 14:6–9

Acts 2:22–24

Romans 1:4

1 Corinthians 15:3–5; 13–17

Philippians 2:5–8

Hebrews 1:1–3

Hebrews 2:17–18; 4:15

2 Peter 1:16

1 John 1:1–3

CHRISTIANITY AND JESUS

**Christianity and
other religions**

Every religion contains two essential elements. One is an analysis of our fundamental problem as human beings. The other is a description of its solution. All religions agree that there is something deeply wrong with us, that our lives are not what they were meant to be. We are alienated from the source of meaning and value. Every religion also describes a way of overcoming this separation and achieving our destiny.[1]

1. Cf. William James's twofold analysis of religion: "Were one asked to characterize the life of religion in the broadest and most general terms possible, one might say

For the great religions of the East, such as Hinduism and Buddhism, the basic human problem is finitude, or finiteness. As finite individuals, we are distinct from ultimate reality. Salvation therefore consists in transcending the conditions of creatureliness and achieving undifferentiated unity with the divine. Our destiny is to merge our lives with the all-inclusive One. Religions of this kind typically prescribe courses of self-discipline to assist us in losing self-consciousness in our consciousness of the Eternal.

For the great religions of Semitic origin—Judaism, Christianity, and Islam—the basic human problem is moral, not metaphysical. It is what human beings have done, not what they are. Salvation therefore consists in overcoming the consequences of sin, not in transcending the conditions of creatureliness. But at this point Christianity differs from Judaism and Islam, as well as from other religions. For Christianity, salvation is not the result of prodigious self-discipline, as with religions of the East, nor is it our reward for living a good moral life, as with Judaism and Islam. In Christianity, salvation is entirely the gift of God. It is something God does for us, not something we achieve or deserve.[2]

Another distinguishing feature of Christianity is the role which the founder plays in its doctrines. Almost every great religion traces its

Jesus more than a founder

---

that it consists of the belief that there is an unseen order, and that our supreme good lies in harmoniously adjusting ourselves thereto. This belief and this adjustment are the religious attitude in the soul" (*The Varieties of Religious Experience: A Study in Human Nature* [New York: The New American Library, 1958; A Mentor Book], p. 58.

2. The study of comparative religions has developed dramatically within the past three decades. It is now a full-fledged discipline in its own right, with a large and growing bibliography. Huston Smith gives a helpful review of the major beliefs of some of the world's great religions in *The Religions of Man* (New York: Harper & Row, Publishers, 1958). J. N. D. Anderson examines the divergent concepts of salvation among the world's prominent religions in *Christianity and World Religions* (Downers Grove, Ill.: Inter-Varsity Press, 1984), pp. 82–111.

Along with this growing interest in the specific beliefs and practices of the world's various religions, scholars have devoted increasing attention to the phenomenon of religion *per se,* as a distinctive human activity or experience. The foremost student of religion in this century is probably Mircea Eliade. Two of his more accessible works are *The Myth of the Eternal Return, or Cosmos and History,* trans. Willard R. Trask (Princeton, N.J.: Princeton University Press, 1971; New York: Harper Torchbooks, 1959), and *The Sacred and the Profane: The Nature of Religion,* trans. Willard R. Trask (New York: Harper Torchbooks, 1961). Introductory texts on the study of religion include Robert S. Ellwood, Jr., *Introducing Religion: From Inside and Outside* (Englewood Cliffs, N.J.: Prentice-Hall, Inc., 1978), and Ninian Smart, *The Phenomenon of Religion* (New York: The Seabury Press, 1973).

origin to the experience of some outstanding personality. For Buddhism, it is Gotama; for Judaism, Moses; and for Islam, Mohammed. But in each case, the identity of the founder is incidental to the content of his teachings. The teachings deserve to be believed because they are true, it is held, not because this particular person happened to discover or proclaim them for the first time. The founder is important because of his teachings. Their significance is primary, his is secondary.

With Christianity, however, Jesus is not simply the one who first discovered or proclaimed its beliefs. He is himself the basic object of its beliefs, the essential content of its doctrines. The heart of Christian faith consists in certain claims about the significance of Jesus.[3] For Christianity, then, it is the identity of the founder that makes his teachings important. This reverses the customary relation between a religion's founder and its doctrines. What Jesus said is important, Christians believe, because of who and what he was. At the center of Christianity lies a particular understanding of Jesus, and in the final analysis, the Christian doctrine of salvation is nothing other than the interpretation of Jesus' significance for human existence. Soteriology is christology.

The person and the work of Christ

Christian theology traditionally divides the doctrine of Christ into two parts. The first concerns the nature, or person, of Christ, and the other discusses his work, or what he accomplished. Recent Christian thought places a priority on the work of Christ.[4] Many scholars believe

---

3. Rudolf Bultmann puts it this way: "Jesus was more than [a teacher and prophet] to the Church: He was also the Messiah; hence [the earliest] Church also proclaimed him, himself—and that is the essential thing to see. He who formerly had been the *bearer* of the message was drawn into it and became its essential *content. The proclaimer became the proclaimed . . .*" (*Theology of the New Testament;* trans. Kendrick Grobel [2 vols.; New York: Charles Scribner's Sons, 1951, 1955], 1:33; italics original). J. N. D. Anderson makes a similar observation concerning the unique proclamation characteristic of Christianity in *Christianity and Comparative Religion,* pp. 31–51.

4. Schubert M. Ogden, for example, a contemporary Protestant theologian, describes Jesus as "re-presenting" to human beings the possibility for authentic existence that God's grace always makes available (*The Point of Christology* [San Francisco: Harper & Row, Publishers, 1982]). In his view, Jesus' significance is entirely a matter of his function in human experience and has nothing to do with his nature or person. In contrast, another contemporary Protestant theologian, Wolfhart Pannenberg, reasserts the traditional priority of the person to the work of Christ. In his words, "Christology, the question about Jesus himself, about his person, as he lived on earth in the time of Emperor Tiberius, must remain prior to all questions about his significance, to all soteriology [the doctrine of salvation]. Soteriology must follow from Christology, not vice versa. Otherwise, faith in salvation itself loses any real foundation" (*Jesus—God and Man,* trans. Lewis L. Wilkins and Duane A. Priebe [2d ed.; Philadelphia: The Westminster Press, 1977], p. 48).

that this is closer to the spirit of the earliest Christians, whose primary interest was in what Jesus did, rather than who he was. A preoccupation with the person of Christ developed later, they argue, in response to various Christian heresies.

In some ways this is a healthy emphasis. It prevents us from slighting the work of Christ because of an interest in his person. In reality, however, it is impossible to separate the two. It would be unfaithful to the New Testament to ignore the question of his identity; its writers were certainly concerned with the question of who Jesus was. It is also possible to view the "christological formulas" that came several centuries later as expressions of the basic New Testament belief about Jesus, rather than departures from or distortions of it.

JESUS AND GOD

The basic Christian belief about Jesus concerns his unique relation to God. It arose from the powerful manifestation of God's presence in Jesus' life, combined with his own testimony and that of the Old Testament scriptures about his identity, and it claims that God comes closer to us in the life and ministry of Jesus than he does anywhere else in human history.[5]

Some of the most familiar and most important statements in the New Testament express the unique relation between Jesus and God. "In the beginning was the Word, and the Word was with God and the Word was God. . . . And the Word became flesh and dwelt among us . . ." (Jn 1:1, 14). "In Christ God was reconciling the world to himself . . ." (2 Cor 5:19). " 'I am the way, and the truth, and the life; no one comes to the Father, but by me' " (Jn 14:6). As these and similar verses indicate, the earliest Christians found that God came incredibly close to them in Jesus—so close, in fact, that the only way they could adequately express their experience was to speak of Jesus as the personal presence of God himself.

---

5. A recent statement of Christian faith expresses the point this way: ". . . [T]he New Testament's answer to the question 'Who is Jesus?' is that he is the man in whom God himself and his love have come unbelievably close to men" (*The Common Catechism: A Book of Christian Faith* [New York: The Seabury Press, 1975], p. 221). "The conclusion which the New Testament writers drew from the Easter event runs as follows: The nearness of God, which believers experience in Jesus Christ, transcends all previous experience men have had of God" (ibid., p. 232).

**The titles
of Jesus**

The New Testament does not develop this idea at length in any one place, even though certain passages have the elements of a christological treatise. For the most part, its view of Jesus emerges from the numerous titles which it applies to him. In their distinctive way, the expressions "prophet," "suffering servant," "high priest," "Messiah," "Son of man," "Lord," "Savior," "Word," and "Son of God" all point to Jesus as the one who brings human beings and God together. The most comprehensive of these expressions is probably "Messiah." Its Greek equivalent, "Christ," became another name for Jesus early in Christian history.

The basic meaning of the words "Messiah" and "Christ" is "anointed." From ancient times, Hebrew kings and priests were anointed as an indication that they were set aside for a special work. In the last couple of centuries before Jesus lived, the expectation developed among the Jewish people that a special leader would arise, an anointed one, or messiah, who would restore the fortunes of Israel. With his leadership, Israel would gain her independence and the prophetic promises of national greatness would be fulfilled. In short, the Messiah would inaugurate the kingdom of God.

Jesus began his ministry surrounded with these messianic expectations. They provided a receptive atmosphere for his ministry, but they also generated widespread preconceptions as to what his mission involved. The content of Jesus' teaching and the events of his life both fulfilled and disappointed the messianic hopes of his contemporaries. The four Gospels were written to demonstrate that he was indeed the Messiah (cf. Jn 20:30–31).

**Jesus and the
kingdom of God**

According to the first three Gospels, the kingdom of God was the theme of Jesus' ministry. It was the central topic of his preaching (Mk 1:14–15), as the Sermon on the Mount indicates (Mt 5–7), and it was the subject of many of his famous parables. His miracles served as signs that the kingdom of God was near. They also illustrated the nature of life in the kingdom. When the kingdom fully arrives, the miracles reveal, there will be no hunger or disease. We will have nothing to fear from the natural elements. Most important, there will be no death. In short, all the consequences of sin will be removed, and human life will reach its full potential.

Much of what Jesus said and did encouraged the belief that he was the hoped-for Messiah, but other factors led to widespread disillusionment. One was his emphasis on the priority of the spiritual dimension of the kingdom of God to its material and political dimensions. As the Sermon on the Mount illustrates, the kingdom of God is fundamentally a matter of values and attitudes, rather than power and position. Until certain spiritual conditions were fulfilled, the kingdom of God would not be visibly manifested.

Another source of disillusionment was the close connection which Jesus claimed between himself and the kingdom of God. The so-called "crisis in Galilee" came shortly after Jesus fed the five thousand, one of the few miracles recorded in all four Gospels. Enthusiasm for his mission abounded, and large numbers of people were ready to proclaim him king. Jesus frustrated their plans by insisting that their relation to the kingdom depended entirely on their personal response to him. Only if people accepted him as the source of spiritual life could they enter the kingdom of God (Jn 6:26–59). Faced with such remarkable personal claims, many people lost hope that Jesus was the Messiah.

By far the greatest obstacle to believing that Jesus was the Messiah was the manner of his death. His crucifixion shattered the hopes of his closest followers and was the major difficulty which early Christians faced in convincing Jews to believe in him. None of their expectations prepared them for a suffering Messiah. In fact, the very idea seemed a contradiction in terms. After all, the law of Moses places the curse of God on those who are hanged (Dt 21:23). The crucifixion was indeed a stumblingblock to the Jews (1 Cor 1:23).

JESUS' RESURRECTION

The importance of Jesus' resurrection

The strongest evidence of Jesus' special relation to God was his resurrection from the dead (e.g., Rom 1:4). The claim that Jesus had risen lay at the very heart of apostolic faith. In one of his letters, Paul summarizes early Christian preaching by listing four items: Jesus' death, burial, resurrection, and subsequent appearances (1 Cor 15:3–5). The apostles described themselves as witnesses to the resurrection (Ac 2:23).

It is impossible to overemphasize the importance of the resurrection. The event transformed the apostles' perspective on Jesus. It corrected their earlier misunderstanding of his mission and gave them courage to fulfill the gospel commission. The resurrection overturned the verdict which human authorities had rendered against Jesus, vindicating him and showing instead that his executioners were lawless men (Ac 2:23).

Besides confirming his identity, Jesus' resurrection is significant for every human being. It proves that death is not the last word about human existence; there is a future beyond death (1 Cor 15:12–20). His resurrection gives substance to our hope for resurrection.

Jesus' resurrection also illuminates the nature of the future life, as we mentioned in the previous chapter. It shows that its relation to our present life is one of both continuity and change. After his resurrection, Jesus continued to exist in a physical, or corporeal, form. He still had a body. People could see him, hear him, and touch him. He still bore the marks of his crucifixion. But at the same time, his body was transformed in certain ways. He mysteriously appeared and disappeared from the presence of his disciples, for example (Jn 20:19; Lk 24:31).

The evidence for Jesus' resurrection

Over the years there have been many questions about history's greatest miracle. The recovery of life after death is so out of harmony with ordinary experience that many people doubt that it really happened. After all, the only reports we have of the event come from Jesus' ardent followers, and their stories of the resurrection could be accounted for in other ways.

There are two major sources of evidence that Jesus rose from the dead. One is the empty tomb; the other is the fact that he was seen. We can see how they form a strong case for the resurrection by examining some of the other explanations of each phenomenon.

The empty tomb

To account for the empty tomb, people have suggested three different theories. One is that the women went to the wrong tomb. Grief-stricken, they lost their way in the early morning, found an empty tomb, and jumped to the conclusion that Jesus was not dead, but alive.

Another explanation is that Jesus never really died. Sometimes called the "swoon theory," it proposes that Jesus entered a coma on the cross and was taken down as dead. In the cool of the night, he revived and made his escape from the tomb.

The oldest explanation of the empty tomb is that someone removed the body. The embarrassed guards blamed his disciples. Other possibilities include the Roman or Jewish authorities, who understandably wanted to prevent a theft by Jesus' followers.

None of these theories stands up under scrutiny. It is unlikely that the women found the wrong tomb, for several reasons. First, some of them were present when Jesus' body was first interred. Second, sorrowful as they must have been on that Sunday morning, they were not disoriented by grief. They were in a practical frame of mind, as their concern about having the stone removed indicates. Third, their testimony alone would not have been taken seriously in a male-dominated society. As soon as they heard of the empty tomb, Jesus' disciples rushed to examine it for themselves.

The idea that Jesus left the cross alive is even more implausible. Pilate was startled to hear that he had died within a few hours of his crucifixion, and he confirmed these reports before releasing the body to Jesus' friends (Mk 15:44–45). Moreover, the Roman soldiers surely knew their business well and would not have let him escape alive.

The idea that Jesus' body was removed is equally unconvincing. The disciples were certainly in no condition to attempt such a feat. Jesus' death dashed their hopes and left them fearful for their own safety. There is no reason to believe that the Roman or Jewish authorities had the body in their possession. If so, they could have squelched the rumors of his resurrection by putting it on public display. The gospel could never have been preached in Jerusalem if Jesus' body had been in the hands of those who had put him to death.

Consequently we are left with the simplest, most convincing explanation of the empty tomb. It is the one first given to Jesus' followers: "He is not here; for he has risen" (Mt 28:6).

The empty tomb is important evidence for Jesus' resurrection, but by itself it would never have convinced his skeptical and disillusioned disciples. They believed he was alive not merely because his tomb was empty, but because they saw him with their own eyes.

There are other ways to account for the reports of Jesus' resurrection appearances. One is the possibility that Jesus' followers were simply lying. Embarrassed by the failure of their expectations, and/or unwilling to return to a life of toil, they decided to tell people that Jesus was really alive after all.

The resurrection appearances

Practically no one finds this explanation plausible. Jesus' followers fully believed that they saw him after his death. Their accounts of the story certainly appear to be straightforward and uncontrived. More important, many of them suffered persecution, imprisonment, and death for maintaining that Jesus had come to life from the dead. It is highly unlikely that a sizable group of people would face death for a claim they knew to be false. The suggestion that the disciples were deliberately lying is absurd.

A more popular suggestion is that the disciples were hallucinating when they thought they saw Jesus. They experienced something, but they mistakenly interpreted their experiences as encounters with the risen Christ. They were psychologically disoriented.

This explanation, too, is seriously flawed. The reports of Jesus' appearances fail to conform to hallucinatory experiences. For one thing, the mental outlook of the disciples was not conducive to hallucinations. They were devastated by Jesus' crucifixion and never expected to see him again. They were skeptical of accounts that he was alive. Thomas' attitude was typical: "Unless I see in his hands the print of the nails, and place my finger in the mark of the nails, and place my hand in his side, I will not believe" (Jn 20:25). This mentality would not lead to hallucinations.

Another important factor is the frequency and duration of the appearances. There were several appearances, with days or weeks between them. Then, after about six weeks, they abruptly stopped, with the exception of Paul's vision on the road to Damascus (1 Cor 15:8; Ac 9:4–5). If the appearances arose from overactive imaginations, we would expect a different pattern: either one dramatic experience by itself, or a rapid succession of appearances—a kind of "chain reaction"—propelled by the rumor that Jesus was alive, or a continuation of appearances well into the future. But none of these occurred.

Here again, the clearest, most satisfactory explanation is the one offered by the New Testament. After his crucifixion Jesus came back to life and during the next forty days appeared to his followers from time to time in different locations. Then he ascended to heaven from the Mount of Olives (Ac 1:9), and his disciples turned to the work he had given them to do.

Did Jesus really rise from the dead? No amount of argument will convince someone who rejects such a thing as utterly impossible, but the evidence of the empty tomb and the appearances obliges us to consider the question carefully. Together, these phenomena support the conviction that Jesus is alive. They show that believing in Jesus' resurrection is an intelligent, responsible position.

The resurrection has an important bearing on the identity of Jesus, as we mentioned above. It provided the strongest evidence of his unique relation to God. It supported the conviction of those who knew him that God was personally present in his life and ministry. This basic Christian claim emerges from the New Testament, but it was not fully elaborated until many years later in the doctrine that Jesus had two natures, human and divine. This doctrine deserves our attention, because it influences the way most of us think about Jesus, and it provides the framework for most conservative christologies.

THE DEVELOPMENT OF CHRISTOLOGY

Christological heresies

Christian theology often develops in reaction to heresy, just as you and I often discover what we believe by responding to views we disagree with. This was certainly true with the doctrine of Christ. The orthodox formula, "two natures in one person," emerged as early Christians reacted to views that would have weakened the fabric of Christian faith.[6]

Several heretical tendencies threatened the faith of the early church in Jesus. One of the first was the tendency to slight the humanity of Jesus in favor of his divinity. A version of this heresy is called "docetism," from the Greek word meaning "to seem," or "to appear." Docetists held that Jesus was really a divine being who merely seemed or appeared to be human. Some evidently held such views during the days of the apostles themselves, for we find them rejected in the writings of the New Testament: "Every spirit which confesses that Jesus Christ has come in the flesh is of God, and every spirit which does not confess Jesus is not of God" (1 Jn 4:2–3).

Slighting humanity

People with a background in Greek thought might have found docetism attractive. Greek philosophy typically drew a sharp distinction between spirit and matter, regarding the former as vastly superior. With such a view, the incarnation—the idea of God taking on human nature, with its physical, material qualities—is repulsive. Hence, the conclusion that Jesus only seemed to be human; he was really nothing but divine the whole time.

There were also tendencies to slight the divinity of Jesus. One, called "adoptionism," held that Jesus was merely human to begin with, but at some point he was elevated, or adopted, to the status of God's Son.

Slighting divinity

Another extremely influential view was called "Arianism," after its leading proponent, Arius, a fourth-century church leader in Egypt. This was probably the most widespread christological heresy in the history of the church, and there are those today who hold similar views.[7] Arians believe that Jesus was the incarnation of the Logos, a

---

6. See "The Definition of Chalcedon," in *Creeds of the Churches: A Reader in Christian Doctrine from the Bible to the Present*, ed. John H. Leith (Garden City, N.Y.: Anchor Books, Doubleday & Company, Inc., 1963), pp. 35–36. An understanding of the nature of Christ was the church's most important theological achievement during the first few centuries following apostolic times. And this development has received enormous scholarly attention. A reliable and readable account of the major issues appears in J. N. D. Kelly, *Early Christian Doctrines* (rev. ed.; San Francisco: Harper & Row, Publishers, 1960), pp. 138–62; 280–343.

7. There is evidence of Arianism among early Seventh-day Adventist writers. In the following description of Christ's origin, E. J. Waggoner implies the Arian view that there

pre-existent, divine being, but they deny that this being existed forever with the Father. In other words, they deny his eternity. They believe that he began to exist sometime in the distant past, long before the creation of the world.

The Council of Nicea rejected Arianism in A.D. 325. Its participants insisted that the Son was of "one substance" with God the Father and that there was never a time when he did not exist.[8]

Confusing the natures

Instead of slighting one nature in favor of the other, some heresies combined, or confused, the two natures so that one or the other was effectively distorted. It was typically the human nature that suffered more. According to one such view, the divine nature replaced the human will in Jesus and made his decisions. Such a theory not only denies that Jesus was fully human and fully divine; it leaves us with a Christ who is really neither. Like the myth of the centaur, who, as half man and half horse, was neither one nor the other, this view portrays Jesus as an amalgamation of humanity and divinity.

Dividing the person

Another kind of christological heresy seemed to divide the divine and the human into separate individuals. The result was a kind of schizophrenia, in which the consciousness of Jesus was controlled by his divinity at certain times, and by his humanity at others. In reaction, the view that prevailed insisted on the unity of Christ's person. It held that Jesus was a single center of consciousness, or a well-integrated ego, to use contemporary language.

The church's consensus

It is tempting to dismiss the ancient christological controversies as so much theological hair-splitting, but this overlooks the enormity of the issue. The question of the person of Christ is not just a topic for rarefied technical debate. It touches the very heart of Christian experience. Nothing less than the survival of Christian faith was at stake in these discussions. By turning away from one misconception after another, the church sought a way to describe Jesus that would

---

was a time when Christ was not: "There was a time when Christ proceeded forth and came from God, from the bosom of the Father (John 8:42; 1:18), but that time was so far back in the days of eternity that to finite comprehension it is practically without beginning" (*Christ and His Righteousness* [Oakland, Calif.: Pacific Press Publishing Company, 1890; reprinted, Nashville, Tenn: Southern Publishing Association, 1972], pp. 21–22).

8. "The Creed of Nicea," in Leith, *Creeds of the Churches,* pp. 30–31.

faithfully express its experience of him as the personal presence of God. It concluded that he is at once fully divine and fully human, and that he is a single person.

THE BIBLICAL DOCTRINE OF CHRIST

It is certainly appropriate to ask if this doctrine is biblical. The terminology and sometimes the pattern of thought seem different from what we find in the New Testament. We need to see if we can locate any precedents for these ideas in the biblical descriptions of Jesus.

For the most part, the humanity of Jesus was not an issue for the writers of the New Testament. The Gospels all portray Jesus with typically human characteristics. He had a physical form, with familiar human needs. On occasion, he grew weary (Jn 4:6), hungry (Mt 21:18), and thirsty (Jn 19:28). He ate and drank (Mk 14:22–23; cf. Mt 11:19), and slept (Mk 4:38). He also exhibited human emotions. On one memorable occasion, he wept out of sympathy for his friends (Jn 11:35). He appreciated human companionship and was hurt when people rejected him (cf. Jn 6:66–67). In short, although he was an extraordinary personality, there is nothing about the picture of Jesus which emerges from the Gospels that would lead us to describe him as "abnormal," or "unhuman."

Jesus was human

We also see the humanity of Jesus in the Gospel accounts of his childhood and youth, brief though they are. According to two of the Gospels, his mother did not become pregnant in the normal manner (Mt 1:18; Lk 1:30–35), and unusual circumstances accompanied his birth (Mt 2:1–12; Lk 2:8–13). But we know who his family was (Mt 1:1–16; Lk 3:23–38) and where he grew up (Mt 2:32), and we are told that his growth followed the pattern of normal human development.

Perhaps the best summary of his youth is this statement: "And Jesus increased in wisdom and in stature, and in favor with God and man" (Lk 2:52). It indicates that Jesus matured symmetrically in all the essential dimensions of human existence: mental, physical, spiritual, and social. Equally important, it implies that he did not possess superhuman powers, physically or mentally. As a first-century Jew, he shared the world view of his time. He acquired a sense of his unique mission in life gradually, over a period of years; it wasn't something he was born with.

No doubt the most significant aspect of Jesus' humanity was his moral experience. He was susceptible to temptation and underwent severe spiritual struggles. The Gospels describe these experiences in graphic terms (Mt 4:1–12; 26:36–44; Mk 14:32–39; Lk 4:1–13; 22:39–42), and the book of Hebrews refers to the reality of his temptations as a source of encouragement to us (2:18; 4:15). As our high priest, Jesus can help us in facing temptation, because he himself knows what it is like to be tested.

The book of Hebrews develops the theological significance of Jesus' humanity at considerable length. It is his humanity which qualifies him to serve as our high priest. To represent us before God, he must be one of us, and he is. He submitted to all the essential conditions of human existence. Consequently, his priestly ministry opens up "the new and living way" that gives us access to the presence of God (Heb 10:20).

Jesus was more than human

Jesus was unquestionably a human being, as far as the New Testament is concerned. But he was also an exceptional human being; there were things that distinguished him from everyone else. The New Testament records of things he said and did, along with its various descriptions of him, put him in a class all by himself. He was every bit a man, but he was more than man as well.

For one thing, Jesus did things that no ordinary human could do. He not only healed the sick, raised the dead, and subdued the forces of nature, but more significantly, he forgave sin, a prerogative of God alone (Mk 2:7, 10).

The things he said also distinguished Jesus from other human beings. The title "prophet" fit him naturally (cf. Jn 4:19), yet his manner was unlike that of the prophets before him. He spoke on God's behalf with unprecedented power and immediacy. Jesus never said things like, "The Word of the Lord came to me." What he said *was* the word of the Lord.

His unique relation to God also appears in some of the titles the New Testament applies to him: "Lord" (Ac 2:36); "God" (Jn 20:28); "I am" (Jn 8:58; cf. Ex 3:14).

Finally, and most prominently, there are references to his preexistence as a divine being. The most familiar appears in the opening verses of the fourth Gospel. This passage applies several significant qualities to the Word (*logos* in Greek): eternity ("in the beginning"); closeness to God ("with God"); divinity ("was God"); creative power ("all things were made through him"); and life, or self-existence ("in him was life").

Other passages also mention preexistence, such as John 8:58: "Before Abraham was, I am" (cf. Ex 3:14). Some of them describe Christ as the agent of creation. According to Colossians 1:16, "All things were created through him and for him." Similarly, the author of Hebrews states that God created the world through the Son (Heb 1:2).

The idea of the incarnation presupposes Christ's preexistence. It affirms that God the Son, coexistent and coeternal with the Father, assumed human nature, or became a human being, at a specific point in time. Furthermore, he remains divine during his earthly life. He also continues to exist as a human being after his resurrection and ascension, so the incarnation is forever. When God gave his Son to the world, it was a permanent gift.

JESUS' DIVINITY

The idea that Jesus was (and is) both human and divine raises two obvious questions: What was the condition/status/function of his divinity? And what was the condition/status/function of his humanity? Put another way, what did the Son give up when he assumed humanity? And what did he take on?

A famous passage in Philippians indicates what the incarnation involved for Christ's divinity (2:5–8). According to these verses, which some scholars describe as a hymn,[9] Christ Jesus was originally in the form of God and enjoyed equality with God. But he emptied himself in taking human form, humbled himself, and became obedient to the point of accepting death by crucifixion.

The Son's condescension

He did not cease to be divine when he became human, as we have seen, but something happened to his divinity, all the same. Even though God was in Christ, we might say, not all of God was in him.[10]

9. Ernest F. Scott mentions the arguments for and against this view in his exegesis of the Epistle to the Philippians in *The Interpreter's Bible* (12 vols.; Nashville, Tenn.: Abingdon Press, 1951–1957), 11:46–47.

10. Russell F. Aldwinckle gives this answer to the question, "Is all of God in Jesus?": "Some self-limitation of God in His act of incarnation in Jesus Christ seems to be required both by Scripture and reason. The difficulties of ascribing omnipotence, omniscience, and omnipresence to Jesus of Nazareth are so enormous that no satisfactory doctrine of the Incarnation can be built on this basis" (*More Than Man: A Study in Christology* [Grand Rapids, Mich.: William B. Eerdmans Publishing Co., 1976], p. 88). "Jesus of Nazareth does not exercise all the functions of deity, nor was He in His historical actuality in the full possession and exercise of what we have called the metaphysical attributes" (ibid., p. 192).

Some things clearly had to change. Among them were certain qualities that are incompatible with genuine human experience. Because human existence is essentially bodily, or corporeal, Jesus could not retain the divine attribute of omnipresence. Similarly, human knowledge is essentially finite, or limited, so Jesus could not have been omniscient, or all-knowing, and genuinely human at the same time.

The emphasis in Philippians is on the enormous condescension involved in the incarnation. It calls attention to the dramatic change in status which Christ underwent in becoming human, rather than to divine qualities he left behind. He descended from a position of supreme sovereignty to one of complete submission; he went from Lord of all to servant of all. Instead of giving orders, he received them. He submitted his will to the direction of his Father, to the point of accepting death in the most humiliating manner.

So complete was this change in position that Paul says he *emptied* himself in the process. He became completely subservient to his Father's will. Throughout his life, Jesus acted only with a divine mandate, consistently refusing to take matters into his own hands. As he said on one occasion, "I can do nothing on my own authority" (Jn 5:30). Jesus exercised tremendous authority, of course—in fact it was the mark of his teaching (Mt 7:29)—but he evidently did so only with his Father's direction.

Divine power   Jesus also possessed divine power. Otherwise, he could never have said such things as "I am the resurrection and the life" (Jn 11:25), and "I have the power to lay [my life] down and I have power to take it up again" (Jn 10:18).

If Jesus had divine power, many people believe, then he enjoyed an advantage over other human beings. He could escape from any difficulty and easily resist temptation. This would be true if Jesus used his power for personal benefit or relied on it to transcend his human limitations. In fact, however, he did neither. He never performed a miracle to benefit himself or merely to satisfy curiosity (cf. Lk 23:8, 9). To do so would have removed him from servant status and defeated one of the purposes of the incarnation.

Instead of giving him an advantage, Jesus' possession of divine power was really a liability: it provided an avenue for temptation. In fact it was precisely at this point that Jesus was first tested in the wilderness. "If you are the Son of God," the tempter said, "command these stones to become loaves of bread" (Mt 4:3). The suggestion was pointless unless Jesus had the power to do what he said. Its objective was to entice Jesus to take matters into his own hands and abandon the position of a servant.

We can thus draw the following conclusions in answer to the question, What did the Son give up in becoming human? He gave up the status and prerogatives of divinity, along with certain qualities that are incompatible with genuine human experience. Divine power was available to him, but he never used it on his own.

The manifestation of divinity in Jesus' ministry tells us a great deal about the reign of God. It indicates that God wants to serve us, rather than rule us, and he wants love from us, not mere submission. He wants us to respond to him from an appreciation of his character. For this reason God's glory was "veiled" in the person of Jesus, as Ellen G. White often said. Instead of overpowering our senses with a display of his glory, Jesus manifested the true character of God by a life of service and sacrifice. "The Son of man also came not to be served but to serve," he said, "and to give his life as a ransom for many" (Mk 10:45).

The incarnation and the reign of God

JESUS' HUMANITY

The status, or condition, of Jesus' humanity is also an object of widespread discussion. Among Seventh-day Adventists, for example, there is a strong difference of views as to whether he assumed a sinless or a sinful human nature. The issue turns on the question of how much like us Jesus must be in order to be our savior. Here we face an apparent dilemma. On the one hand, it seems, he must be one of us in order to save us; but on the other, he must be different, or he himself will need salvation.[11] Those who emphasize the importance of similarity attribute a sinful humanity to Jesus; those impressed with the necessity for difference maintain that his humanity was sinless.

Several factors favor the view that Jesus' humanity was sinless, rather than sinful. One is Jesus' account of his own disposition. According to the fourth Gospel Jesus said, "My food is to do the will of him who sent me, and to accomplish his work" (Jn 4:34); and,

Reasons for the sinless view

---

11. John Knox states "the dilemma of early Christian thought about the humanity of Jesus, and indeed our dilemma still," in this way: "How could Christ have saved us if he was not a human being like ourselves? How could a human being like ourselves have saved us?" (*The Humanity and Divinity of Christ: A Study of Pattern in Christology* [London: Cambridge University Press, 1967], p. 52).

"The ruler of this world . . . has no power over me" (Jn 14:30). Such statements suggest that Jesus' fundamental orientation to God was one of obedience. He was naturally inclined to do God's will. This doesn't mean he couldn't sin, of course, but it means that he would have departed from his natural bent of mind in doing so.

Another reason to attribute sinlessness to Jesus is his relation to the human race. Paul compares Jesus with Adam in an important passage in Romans (5:12–21). The effects of their actions are sharply different, of course. Adam brought us condemnation and death, while Christ brings us acquittal and life. But their relation to humanity is the same: what they accomplished affects the entire race. It is therefore reasonable to conclude that they began with the same moral posture. They were naturally loyal to God, and this loyalty was tested for both. Adam failed the test, and Christ passed it.

The strongest indication of Jesus' sinlessness is the content of his temptations. A spiritual nature dulled by the effects of sin often blunders into disobedience without realizing it. But Jesus had the spiritual sensitivity of unfallen humanity. Only a superior moral character could discern the issues involved in his great temptations.

The force of his temptations also indicates an unfallen nature. On two occasions his spiritual struggles were so severe that they actually threatened his life. He would have died after his temptation in the wilderness without the ministry of angels (Mt 4:11), and his experience in Gethsemane left him similarly weakened (Mk 14:33–34).

Jesus' capacity to exhaust the tempter's power reveals superior moral strength and also makes him the only human being to feel the full force of temptation. Only an athlete who completes a marathon knows what it takes to run the distance, not one who quits after five, ten, or even twenty miles. Only Jesus, who never yielded, knows what it really takes to withstand temptation. There are several reasons, then, to believe that Jesus' humanity was sinless.

Problems with the sinful view

It is also significant that attributing a sinful human nature to Jesus fails to achieve its purpose. Many who advocate this position feel that the major purpose of Jesus' mission was to provide us an example in overcoming sin. Only if he had a sinful nature like ours, they believe, could he be our example. His moral struggle must begin where ours does if his achievement is to be within our reach.

One problem with this position is that we can never put Jesus on our level. To start where we do, Jesus would have to be not only sinful but sinning, and this is something even the most ardent supporter of his sinful humanity would not accept.

Another problem is the idea that Jesus' achievement is within our reach, for if others could duplicate what he did, then we could conceivably have several examples to follow, rather than one. In fact, their examples would be even better, because they have more in common with us than he does.

In short, the notion of a sinful savior creates more problems than it solves. If we make Jesus entirely one of us, then he needs salvation as much as we do. If we place his achievements within our reach, then others could save as well as he.

We need to recognize that there is much more to Christ's work than giving us an example. A drowning man needs more than swimming lessons; he needs a lifesaver. Lost as we are in sin, only a dramatic rescue can help us, and only someone vastly superior to us can effect it.

Although Jesus shared the moral posture of our original parents, in other respects he did experience the consequences of sin. Physically and mentally, his condition was similar to that of other people of his time. Socially, of course, he could not avoid the effects of sin. He was surrounded by negative influences.

We have mentioned two ways in which Jesus' temptations were different from ours. Some of them focused on his unique access to divine power, and they were much more intense than anything we shall ever have to face. But his temptations were also similar to ours in several important ways. In fact, according to the book of Hebrews, he is able to help us as we face temptation, because "in every respect [he] has been tempted as we are, yet without sin" (4:15).

**Jesus'
temptations**

These words require careful interpretation. Clearly they cannot mean that Jesus faced literally every temptation that ever afflicted other human beings. Living when he did, he was never tempted to watch the wrong things on television or drive a car recklessly. These words must refer, not to the occasion of Jesus' temptations, but to the underlying issues involved.

The occasion, or avenue, of temptation varies from person to person. It depends on opportunity and personality. But when it comes to the underlying issues, all temptations are the same—from the ones facing Adam and Eve in the garden, through the ones Jesus met in the wilderness, to the ones we encounter every day. The fundamental issues are trust and obedience. Will we trust God? Will we believe what he says? Will we obey him? Will we accept his sovereignty over our lives? Every temptation presents us with one or both of these issues, and the fundamental issues of Jesus' temptations were the same, even though the avenues of temptation were different.

Perhaps the most important similarity between Jesus' moral experience and ours is the potential source of victory over temptation. As we have seen, neither his inherent divinity nor his sinless humanity assisted him in meeting temptation. If anything, they intensified the experience. What enabled him to overcome was implicit trust in the power of God. Jesus gained the victory by faith, something available to all of us.

A summary of the doctrine of Christ

We need to summarize our reflections on the nature of Christ. It is important for us to find the fundamental theme, or guiding thread, that runs through the many questions this topic raises. The characteristic Christian tendency to identify Jesus with God originated with the experience of the earliest believers. It arose from their own encounter with Jesus. They found in the life and ministry of Jesus a revelation of God so complete and so clear that nothing could conceivably equal or surpass it. As Jesus himself once claimed, "He who has seen me has seen the Father" (Jn 14:9). As a result, they found that the only way they could adequately, faithfully describe what they saw in Jesus was to speak of God himself. Jesus was not merely God's representative; he was God himself in human form.

With this firmly in mind, we can put the long history of discussions about the nature of Christ into perspective. All christology is an endeavor to safeguard the essential Christian experience of Jesus. It seeks to express his identity in ways that are faithful to this basic experience. In doing so, it reacts to, and rejects, descriptions that threaten to undermine this experience, either explicitly or implicitly. It is true that the classic christological formulas employed terms and concepts drawn from the context of Greek thought, but their fundamental claims are faithful to the biblical perspective. They have served the church well ever since their formulation in its perpetual attempt to describe who Jesus is.

Important as it is, the question of Jesus' identity is not the only element in the doctrine of Christ. As it is generally formulated, this doctrine considers what he did, as well as who he was. As we have noted, in the thinking of many people the question of his work is even more important than that of his person.

STUDY HELPS

Questions for review

1. What is unique about Jesus' relation to the religion he founded?

2. What evidence supports the reality of Jesus' resurrection?

3. What is the orthodox Christian view of the person of Christ? What factors led to its formulation?

4. How does the New Testament attest to both Jesus' humanity and his divinity?

5. How did the incarnation affect the divinity of the Son of God?

6. What was the condition of Jesus' humanity?

7. How were Jesus' temptations similar to those of other human beings, and how were they different?

1. What is the significance of the fact that the four Gospels stand at the beginning of the New Testament? Why do you suppose Matthew comes first? **Questions for further study**

2. The Gospels, it is often said, are not true biographies, but testimonies of faith (cf. John 20:31). Why are the Gospels silent about so much of Jesus' life?

3. What are the benefits and the liabilities of emphasizing Jesus' role as our example?

4. In the fourth and fifth centuries A.D., the Christian church expressed its understanding of the nature of Christ by using terms and concepts drawn from Greek thought. Was this development necessary? Were its consequences for the church positive or negative?

5. In recent years a number of films and musicals have appeared portraying the life of Jesus. Is your reaction to such productions positive or negative? Why?

6. Officially, Seventh-day Adventists do not attach religious significance to the traditional Christian holidays of Christmas and Easter. Why is this so? In your view, is this attitude toward these holidays good or bad?

1. Examine the two genealogies of Jesus which appear in the Gospels (Matthew 1:2–17 and Luke 3:23–38). Notice the similarities and differences between them. What do they tell us about Jesus' identity? What background to his ministry do the other Gospels provide? **Suggestions for Bible study**

2. The virgin birth is specifically mentioned only twice in the New Testament (Matthew 1:18–21; Luke 1:26–35). What does the concept of the virgin birth contribute to our understanding of Jesus? Is the virgin birth essential to the Christian doctrine of the incarnation?

3. According to some scholars, the Gospel according to John is an extended response to the question, Who is Jesus? The author answers this question by presenting a series of "signs" and recording a number of Jesus' claims about himself. What do we learn about Jesus' identity from each of the following passages?

   a. John 2:1–12; 4:46–54; 5:1–16; 6:5–13; 9:1–41; 11:1–44; 12:32
   b. John 6:35; 8:12; 10:7; 10:11; 11:25; 14:6; 15:1

4. The writers of the New Testament also establish Jesus' identity by applying various titles and offices to him, many of them drawn from the Old Testament. What does each of the following expressions tell us about Jesus?

   a. Deuteronomy 18:15, 18; Matthew 16:14; 21:11, 46; Luke 7:16; John 6:14
   b. Genesis 49:10–12; 2 Samuel 7:8–17; Psalm 2:7–9 (Hebrews 1:5); Psalm 110:1 (Hebrews 1:13); Micah 5:2–4; Matthew 22:42; Matthew 16:13–20
   c. Matthew 1:21; Luke 2:11; John 4:42; 1 John 4:14; Titus 2:13
   d. Mark 2:10; 2:28; 13:26; 8:31; 9:31; John 3:13; 5:27; 8:28
   e. Luke 1:35; Matthew 4:3, 4; 8:29; 14:33; 26:63–64; John 5:25; 9:35; 11:4
   f. Romans 5:12; 1 Corinthians 15:21–22, 45–49

5. Jesus is identified as the creator in the "high christology" presented in such passages as Colossians 1:15–20, Hebrews 1:1–3, and John 1:1–5. Study these verses carefully. What are the reasons for assigning this divine work to Jesus? How do statements like this relate to such Old Testament texts as Genesis 1:1 and Psalm 33:6, 9?

SUGGESTIONS FOR FURTHER READING

From Adventist writers

For Seventh-day Adventists, the most influential book on Jesus Christ is undoubtedly Ellen G. White, *The Desire of Ages* (Mountain View, Calif.: Pacific Press Publishing Association, 1898), probably the most cherished of her writings.

A number of other Adventists have also written on the nature of Christ. Some of the more recent offerings include Thomas A. Davis, *Was Jesus Really Like Us?* (Washington, D.C.: Review and Herald Publishing Association, 1979); Edward Heppenstall, *The Man Who Is God: A Study of the Person and Nature of Jesus, Son of God and Son of Man* (Washington, D.C.: Review and Herald Publishing Association, 1977); and Edward W. H. Vick, *Jesus the Man* (Nashville, Tenn.: Southern Publishing Association, 1979). These works reflect some of the divergent opinions among Seventh-day Adventists concerning the nature of Christ. According to Davis, for example, Jesus possessed a fallen human nature, with certain qualifications, and is therefore qualified to serve as our example. To the contrary, Heppenstall insists that Jesus' humanity could not have been sinful. Vick maintains that Jesus participates in the sinful structures of human existence, but he opposes an exemplarist approach to christology.

From other writers

Not surprisingly, the person of Christ has been the object of extensive theological reflection, as much if not more in recent years than in the past history of the church. A brief but sweeping overview of developments from the New Testament to the early part of the twentieth century is Sydney Cave, *The Doctrine of the Person of Christ* (London: Gerald Duckworth & Co., Ltd., 1925). Oscar Cullmann, *The Christology of the New Testament,* trans. Shirley C. Guthrie and Charles A. M. Hall (rev. ed.; Philadelphia: The Westminster Press, 1959), analyzes the various christological titles that appear in the New Testament. John Knox, *The Humanity and Divinity of Christ: A Study of Pattern in Christology* (Cambridge: Cambridge University Press, 1967), identifies and interprets the main types of christology that emerged during the early experience of the Christian church. Aloys Grillmeier, *Christ in Christian Tradition From the Apostolic Age to Chalcedon,* trans. John Bowden (2d ed., rev.; Atlanta: John Knox Press, 1975), is the definitive study of christological developments up to the mid-fifth century. A more accessible account of the same period appears in various chapters of J. N. D. Kelly, *Early Christian Doctrines* (rev. ed.; San Francisco: Harper & Row, Publishers, 1960).

Contemporary christological proposals include D. M. Baillie, *God Was in Christ: An Essay on Incarnation and Atonement* (New York: Charles Scribner's Sons, 1948), which is still influential after forty years; Emil Brunner, *The Mediator: A Study of the Central Doctrine of the Christian Faith,* trans. Olive Wyon (Philadelphia: The Westminster Press, 1947), considered one of the theologian's most important works; and Wolfhart Pannenberg, *Jesus—God and Man,* trans. Lewis L. Wilkins and Duane A. Priebe (2d ed.; Philadelphia: The Westminster Press, 1977), a major work which reaffirms the priority of the person to the work of Christ and argues for the historicity of Jesus' resurrection.

More conservative interpretations of the doctrine of Christ are G. C. Berkouwer, *The Person of Christ,* trans. John Vriend (Grand Rapids, Mich.: William B. Eerdmans Publishing Co., 1954), and Russell F. Aldwinckle, *More Than Man: A Study in Christology* (Grand Rapids, Mich.: William B. Eerdmans

Publishing Co., 1976). The latter is a sophisticated reaffirmation of traditional christology which is sensitive to contemporary biblical and theological scholarship.

At the liberal end of the theological spectrum one finds the following works: Rudolf Bultmann, *Jesus Christ and Mythology* (New York: Charles Scribner's Sons, 1958), which explains the author's famous concept of "demythologizing"; Schubert M. Ogden, *The Point of Christology* (San Francisco: Harper & Row, Publishers, 1982), which insists that Christian faith in Jesus has everything to do with his work and really nothing to do with his person; and John Hick, ed., *The Myth of God Incarnate* (Philadelphia: The Westminster Press, 1977), whose contributors maintain that the incarnation is appropriately understood as "myth," but not as literal truth.

The topic of Jesus' resurrection deserves special mention. There are many discussions of the evidence that Jesus came to life from the dead. Christian apologists who have considered the subject include: Norman Anderson, *A Lawyer Among the Theologians* (Grand Rapids, Mich.: William B. Eerdmans Publishing Co., 1973), pp. 66–149; Wilbur M. Smith, *Therefore, Stand: Christian Apologetics* (Grand Rapids, Mich.: Baker Book House, 1974), pp. 359–457; and John R. W. Stott, *Basic Christianity* (rev. ed.; Grand Rapids, Mich.: William B. Eerdmans Publishing Co., 1971), pp. 46–60. Contemporary theologian Wolfhart Pannenberg examines the question in *Jesus—God and Man,* trans. Lewis L. Wilkins and Duane A. Priebe (2d ed.; Philadelphia: The Westminster Press, 1977), pp. 88–114. New Testament scholar George Eldon Ladd studies the historicity of the resurrection, giving special attention to the relevant biblical materials, in *I Believe in the Resurrection of Jesus* (Grand Rapids, Mich.: William B. Eerdmans Publishing Co., 1975).

8

THE DOCTRINE OF CHRIST:
WHAT JESUS DID

"For God so loved the world that he gave his only Son, that whoever believes in him should not perish but have eternal life" (John 3:16).

Biblical basis

"In Christ God was reconciling the world to himself" (2 Corinthians 5:19).

"He himself bore our sins in his body on the tree" (1 Peter 2:24).

Genesis 3:15	Luke 22:39–23:56
Exodus 25–30	John 1:29
Leviticus 1–7; 16	John 3:14–17; 12:32
Psalm 22	John 18–19
Isaiah 53	Acts 4:12
Matthew 1:21	2 Corinthians 5:19–21
Matthew 16:21–24	Galatians 6:14
Matthew 26:36–27:61	Ephesians 1:7–8
Mark 10:45	Hebrews 5:7–10
Mark 14:32–15:47	1 Peter 2:21–25
Luke 15	1 John 2:2; 4:10
Luke 19:10	Revelation 5:6

The Christian doctrine of atonement, as the work of Christ is often called, expresses the fundamental conviction that Jesus is the means of human salvation. In his life and particularly in his death, God was acting to deliver all humanity from the consequences of sin. As Paul put it in one important passage, "In Christ God was reconciling the world to himself" (1 Cor 5:19).

JESUS' LIFE AND WORK

Jesus' identity

There are three things about Jesus that bear upon his saving work. We have already touched on two of them—the incarnation and his sinless life. According to the first, salvation involved the condescension of God himself to assume human form. This is why we devoted so much attention to the person of Christ. He could not have accomplished what he did had he not been who he was. Consequently, Christ is not merely the only one who saves us; he is the only one who could save us. As Peter exclaimed, "There is salvation in no one else, for there is no other name under heaven given among men by which we must be saved" (Ac 4:12). The belief that Jesus is the eternally preexistent Son of God is integral to the Christian doctrine of salvation.

Jesus' ministry

Jesus became our Savior not only because of who he was, but also through what he did. His earthly life and ministry, too, contribute to his saving work. By his words and works, Jesus proclaimed the kingdom of God. He presented God's offer of salvation to all people—particularly those who are unimportant by conventional standards. His ministry transcended every human barrier: race, sex, age, education, culture, money, class, health, occupation, reputation. He excluded no one. Every human being, in his view, was a potential citizen in the kingdom of God.

His numerous teachings explained the principles of God's kingdom. In particular, they emphasized that everyone is a guest in the kingdom of God. No one enters because he deserves to. Salvation is a gift.

Jesus' works illustrated the nature of the kingdom of God. The Greek word for "salvation" also means "healing," and Jesus' miracles of healing were signs of salvation. They showed that the kingdom of God was near and what life in the kingdom is like. Where God reigns, all is joy and peace. There is no suffering, disease, or death.

Jesus' sinlessness

Jesus' moral experience also contributed to his role as Savior. He faced temptation in common with all human beings. His struggles were severe, but he never yielded. His trust in and obedience to God were never interrupted. The New Testament uniformly asserts his sinlessness (2 Cor 5:21; Heb 4:15; 1 Pet 2:22; 1 Jn 3:5).

Jesus' sinlessness has several implications. For one thing, it gives us a valuable example as we face temptation. It assures us that moral victory is possible. It further shows us how victory can be achieved. From his life we learn that complete openness to God's leading is the key to spiritual success.

Jesus' life in general provides a pattern for human behavior. Everything about him deserves our imitation—his sense of values, his compassion for human beings, his self-forgetful service, his courage in the face of personal danger. These and other qualities make Jesus the ideal for every human life.

The meaning of Jesus' sinlessness emerges against the background of Hebrew worship. Offering sacrifices was an important element in that system; it was part of the process by which sins were forgiven. Furthermore, for many sacrifices the animals offered had to be faultless, not diseased or deformed in any way. The New Testament often refers to Jesus as the Lamb of God (Jn 1:29, 36; 1 Cor 5:7; 1 Pet 1:19; Rev 5:6, 12; 13:8). It frequently speaks of his death as a sacrifice (Eph 5:2; Heb 7:27; 9:26–28; 10:12), and it also describes his blood as the means of salvation (1 Jn 1:7).

As the ultimate sacrifice for sin, Jesus had to be spotless. The slightest blemish would have disqualified him as our Savior. Had Jesus sinned in any way, he himself would have needed salvation.

We have said that Jesus is our Savior because of who he was and what he did. But he is also our Savior because of what happened to him. As we just noticed, his death was central to his saving work.

JESUS' DEATH

For Christian faith, the cross is the single most important event in all of human history. Jesus' mission would not have been complete without the cross. The cross guarantees the eventual fulfillment of the plan of salvation—the eradication of sin from the universe. Thus everything before the cross is preparation, and everything after it is consequence. This does not mean that the cross could stand alone. It had to be prepared for, and its consequences must be developed. But the cross is the center of God's entire work of salvation. It was here that God secured our salvation—finally, fully, and for all time.

There are several different ways to look at the cross. First of all, we can look at it from the outside, as a means of execution. Although it

The cross

is not pleasant to recall the details, it is sometimes worth remembering what Jesus suffered. Second, we can try to envision the experience from within. We can ask what Jesus must have gone through during his crucifixion. Third, we can take a theological perspective and ask what the experience meant for human salvation. What, in fact, did the cross accomplish? In an effort to understand the cross, we will examine it from each of these vantage points.

Death by crucifixion

Crucifixion was common in the first century.[1] The four Gospels tell us little about its details because when they were written everyone knew what it involved. The Carthaginians first used crucifixion as a means of execution, and the Romans adopted and refined the practice. Crucifixion could not be inflicted on Roman citizens. It was reserved for slaves and provincials—the lowest elements of society. Everything about it was designed to inflict as much pain and humiliation as possible.

Once condemned, the victim of crucifixion was first scourged with a whip made of leather straps to which bits of bone and metal were attached. Repeated lashes reduced his back to ribbons of bleeding flesh. Then he had to carry part of the cross with him to the place of execution, which was usually outside of town. There, soldiers stripped him and fastened his hands and feet to the wooden beams with nails or ropes.

With limbs extended and immobile, the victim was unable to care for his bodily needs and vulnerable to the elements and the taunts of spectators. Since no vital organ was injured, death was often long in coming. Victims of crucifixion almost never died sooner than a day and a half; most lasted three or four days. A few lived as long as a week. They finally succumbed from exposure or from tetanus resulting from their wounds.

If soldiers had to end the process for some reason before the victim died as a result of crucifixion, they usually smashed his arms and legs with something heavy, like a hammer. This was to intensify

---

1. Any Bible dictionary will contain a description of crucifixion. The brief account offered here is drawn largely from the following sources: C. Milo Connick, *Jesus: The Man, the Mission, and the Message* (2d ed.; Englewood Cliffs, N.J.: Prentice-Hall, Inc., 1974), pp. 386–393; Sherman E. Johnson, Exegesis of Matthew in *The Interpreter's Bible* (12 vols.; Nashville, Tenn.: Abingdon Press, 1951–57), 7:599–611; Pierson Parker, "Crucifixion," in *The Interpreter's Dictionary of the Bible* (4 vols.; Nashville, Tenn.: Abingdon Press, 1962), 1:746–47; D. H. Wheaton, "Crucifixion," in *The New Bible Dictionary* (Grand Rapids, Mich.: William B. Eerdmans Publishing Co., 1962), pp. 281–282.

suffering as a compensation for shortening its duration. Then they delivered the *coup de grace* with a spear thrust to the side.

Such practices understandably offend our sensibilities, in spite of the prevalence of cruelty in our world. But it is also significant to recall the stigma attached to crucifixion, along with the suffering it involved. No form of death was more revolting, and, as we have noticed, the Jews of Christ's time felt that a curse rested on those who were its victims.

Jesus did not die from the effects of crucifixion. He cried, "It is finished," only six hours after reaching Calvary. It was mental and emotional rather than physical suffering that ended his life. He died, it is sometimes said, of a broken heart.[2] The peculiar nature of Jesus' anguish appeared at several different times during his final hours. His struggle in Gethsemane was one. Here we see Jesus shrinking from the prospect of death, begging God to release him from this destiny—"If it be possible, let this cup pass from me" (Mt 26:39)—and finally submitting to the Father's will (Mt 26:39). His suffering seemed to reach its deepest point when he cried from the cross, "My God, my God, why have you forsaken me?" (Mt 27:46). What evidently ended Jesus' life, then, was separation from God—a separation so severe that it left him, literally, hopeless and lifeless.[3]

What Jesus suffered

2. In *The Desire of Ages,* Ellen G. White provides the moving account of Jesus' suffering and death on which this analysis is based. In her words, "It was the sense of sin, bringing the Father's wrath upon Him as man's substitute, that made the cup He drank so bitter, and broke the heart of the Son of God" (Mountain View, Calif.: Pacific Press Publishing Association, 1898), p. 753.

3. Ellen G. White employs the expressions "agony" and "struggle" to describe the different elements in Jesus' suffering identified here. As she uses the word, "agony" refers to the sense of divine condemnation which Jesus experienced and which eventually ended his life. She further describes this aspect of his experience with various metaphors of pressure and isolation: "The sins of men weighed heavily upon Christ, and the sense of God's wrath against sin was crushing out His life" (*Desire of Ages,* p. 687); "He felt that by sin He was being separated from His Father. The gulf was so broad, so black, so deep, that His spirit shuddered before it" (ibid., p. 686); "The withdrawal of the divine countenance from the Saviour in this hour of supreme anguish pierced His heart with a sorrow that can never be fully understood by man. . . . He feared that sin was so offensive to God that Their separation was to be eternal" (ibid., p. 753).

Besides this "agony," or "anguish," Jesus also suffered from a terrible "conflict," or "struggle," with the temptation to abandon his mission: "Terrible was the temptation to let the human race bear the consequences of its own guilt, while He stood innocent before God" (ibid., p. 688). According to Ellen White's account, this aspect of Jesus' suffering reached its climax in Gethsemane with his decision to "save man at any cost to Himself" (ibid., p. 693). At that time, "Christ's agony did not cease, but His depression

The temptation to avoid this horrible experience compounded Jesus' torment, as his Gethsemane experience also indicates. It was a temptation he had faced before—in the wilderness and during his ministry (cf. Mt 16:21–23). But on the eve of his crucifixion he felt its force more keenly than ever.

These factors lead us to conclude that Jesus experienced God's judgment against sin. He bore the full force of divine condemnation (1 Pet 2:24; 2 Cor 5:21), and he felt utterly and irreversibly excluded from the presence of God. Only in this way can we account for the mysterious suffering his words and behavior expressed.

Several biblical statements point to this conclusion, such as 2 Corinthians 5:21: "He made him to be sin who knew no sin." A number of them apply to him portions of the famous "suffering servant" passages of Isaiah (especially 53:5–6). According to 1 Peter 2:24, for example, "He himself bore our sins in his body on the tree."

WHAT JESUS ACCOMPLISHED

We now face what is probably the most important question of all: What did Jesus' death accomplish? How does it solve the problem of sin? The New Testament gives no single answer to this question. There is no one theory of atonement in the apostolic writings; in fact, there are no *theories* at all. What we find instead are several striking metaphors, or symbols, describing what Jesus did. There are too many to survey here, so we will concentrate on only a few of the most important.[4]

Salvation   The most general and comprehensive term for the work of Christ is "salvation," an expression we have already used a number of times. Romans 1:16 identifies the gospel as "the power of God unto

---

and discouragement left Him" (ibid., p. 694). His agony intensified until it eventually ended his life on the cross.

4. Leon Morris provides an extensive analysis of the various New Testament descriptions of salvation in *The Apostolic Preaching of the Cross* (Grand Rapids, Mich.: William B. Eerdmans Publishing Co., 1955). In addition to "reconciliation" and "redemption," he also discusses the meaning of "covenant," "the blood," "propitiation," and "justification." Morris's view of the atonement is noteworthy for its emphasis on divine wrath and for preferring the use of the English word "propitiation," rather than "expiation," to interpret some important biblical passages (cf. p. 154).

salvation,'' and ''savior'' is one of the important titles early Christians applied to Jesus (cf. Phil 3:20). The very name ''Jesus,'' in fact, points to his work of salvation (cf. Mt 1:21).

This expression recalls the long history of God's activity on behalf of the Hebrew people. According to the Old Testament, God is the deliverer, or savior, of his people, especially from Egyptian bondage and at the Red Sea (Ex 15:2).

The Greek word for ''save'' can also mean ''heal,'' or ''make whole,'' as we have noted. This suggests that salvation involves both rescue and restoration. Christ not only delivers us from the power of sin, but also restores us to complete spiritual health.

Reconciliation

''Reconciliation'' is another important description of Christ's work in the New Testament. ''In Christ God was reconciling the world to himself'' (2 Cor 5:19; cf. Rom 5:10–11; Eph 2:16; Col 1:20). In Christ God overcomes the alienation which sin causes and restores a condition of peace. Because Christ brings us the peace of God, we are able to live at peace with all men (Rom 12:18).

The biblical idea of reconciliation has many facets. For one thing, it is cosmic in scope; it includes everything on earth and in heaven. It is also significant that the New Testament always speaks of God as the subject of reconciliation, never as the object. God reconciles us to him; we do not reconcile him to us. Moreover, God seeks us while we are still hostile to him. He makes the first move to establish fellowship with us. Reconciliation, then, emphasizes God's initative in the work of salvation.

Redemption

The New Testament also speaks of Christ's work as ''redemption'' (Eph 1:7; Rom 3:24). This word had powerful connotations for people in ancient times. It referred to the act of delivering captives, or liberating slaves from bondage, and meant to pay a price for freedom. Like ''salvation,'' this word has a vivid Old Testament background. It, too, described God's deliverance of Israel from Egypt. Mark 10:45 is the most important New Testament text to use this expression: ''The Son of man came . . . to give his life as a ransom for many.''

Scholars are divided as to whether the New Testament concept of redemption includes the idea of paying a price, or whether it is simply another word for deliverance. Either way, this description of Christ's work makes several important points. For example, it indicates that the work of Christ delivers us from hostile powers, specifically, from sin and its effects. This reminds us of the freedom that Christians enjoy (Gal 5:1); we are no longer dominated by the forces of darkness or in bondage to sin. At the same time, ''redemption'' emphasizes the cost of this deliverance. God's solution to the problem of sin is enormously expensive. For this reason, Paul tells his readers that they were bought with a price; they belong to God (1 Cor 6:20).

WHY JESUS DIED

We have reviewed several ways in which the New Testament describes the work of Christ, and before that we examined the atoning experience, or the means by which he achieved these things. We now come to what many regard as the most perplexing question in the doctrine of salvation: *How* does the death of Jesus solve the problem of sin? Granted that God was active in Christ for human salvation, and granted that his effort succeeded, the question remains, just how did Christ's work achieve its results? What, precisely, made it effective?

Theories of Atonement

Christians have never reached a consensus in answer to this question. There is an orthodox doctrine of the person of Christ, but there is no corresponding doctrine of his work. Looking at the history of Christian thought, we find instead several prominent theories of atonement. Each has influenced the thinking of the church from time to time, but none has ever enjoyed unanimous support. It will be helpful to review the three most important types.[5]

The ransom theory   One of the oldest interpretations of Christ's work is the ransom theory. Leaning heavily on biblical passages that speak of ransom, early Christian thinkers graphically portrayed Christ battling with the devil and defeating him once and for all. Sometimes they even described Christ as the worm on the hook which finally caught Satan. The atonement, for this theory, is God's dramatic victory over the hostile forces of sin and death.

---

5. The most influential discussion of the three major theories of atonement is Gustaf Aulen, *Christus Victor: An Historical Study of the Three Main Types of the Idea of Atonement,* trans. A. G. Hebert (New York: The Macmillan Company, 1969).

The satisfaction theory has probably been more influential than any other. It received its classic formulation in the writings of Anselm, a churchman of the eleventh century, and it reflects the thought world of medieval times, with feudal lords and vassals.

The satisfaction theory

According to this theory, sin is an outrage to the honor of God, which demands satisfaction. This puts man in a serious predicament, for, to use Anselm's words, "Sinful man owes God a debt for sin which he cannot repay, and at the same time . . . he cannot be saved without repaying it."[6] Man cannot be saved unless God's honor is satisfied, but this is something man is in no position to do. He is finite, his debt is infinite.

Christ solves the problem by virtue of his twofold nature. As a human being Christ pays the debt which humans owe; his divinity gives the payment an infinite value. Thus the incarnation is essential to the atonement. This answers the question of Anselm's famous essay, "Why the God-Man?" According to the satisfaction theory, then, Jesus Christ, as man, bore the penalty for human sin and made satisfaction on behalf of all of us.

The moral influence theory arose in reaction to the satisfaction theory. It emphasizes the effects of Christ's death on man, rather than God. According to this view, the atonement is a revelation of the love of God, intended to call forth an answering love in man. Christ's death saves us by giving us a vivid portrayal of God's love for us and moving us to love God in return.

The moral influence theory

We can specify the central differences in these three important positions by noting where each of them locates the obstacle to divine-human fellowship. Each theory has a distinctive view of what it is that makes atonement necessary. According to the moral influence theory, the obstacle to reconciliation lies within man; our misperception of God's character needs to be corrected. Christ removes this obstacle by clarifying God's attitude toward us.

The theories compared

The satisfaction theory places the primary object of atonement within God himself. According to views of this type, Christ's death satisfies the demands of God's own nature. Some of these views describe a tension within God between two contrasting qualities. His love, or mercy, makes him eager to forgive, but his justice, or wrath, or holiness, makes it impossible for him to forgive freely. Christ's death

6. Anselm, *Why God Became Man*, Bk. 1, ch. 25; trans. Eugene R. Fairweather, in *A Scholastic Miscellany: Anselm to Ockham* (Philadelphia: The Westminster Press, 1956), pp. 145–146.

resolves this tension. With it, God's love provides the atonement which his holiness demands. God is merciful and just at the same time.

The ransom theory seems to place the object of atonement outside both God and man. It lies, instead, in the desperate human situation. We are captive to the alien powers of sin and death, and Christ's death breaks their hold over us.

The theories evaluated

Each of these views has its strengths and its weaknesses, and each view can distort certain features of Christ's work. The strength of the ransom theory is its emphasis on God's saving activity. Salvation is God's work from first to last. He is the source, not the object, of atonement. Furthermore, with its emphasis on the dramatic victory Christ achieved over man's enemies, this view has tremendous psychological value. It reminds us that everything has been done to secure our salvation.

The weakness of this theory is its literalistic imagery. It tends to portray the atonement as a transaction between God and the devil. Some versions even suggest that God pays off the devil in order to set us free.

There are objections to the satisfaction theory, too. Many people find it too calculating, too much like a bookkeeping system, as if Christ accumulated credit by dying to pay off our debts to God. Sin, they insist, is a matter of personal relationship. It can't be disposed of by manipulating various accounts.

The idea of Christ as our substitute also raises questions. People have wondered about the ethics of this arrangement, because personal guilt isn't something that can be transferred from one person to another. No judge in our legal system would allow an innocent citizen to go to prison in place of a convicted criminal. How would that serve the interests of justice?

The most important objection to this theory is that it makes God the object of reconciliation. In the satisfaction theory, man makes atonement (in the person of Christ), and God receives it. This is contrary to the consistent biblical theme that it is God who reconciles. For the writers of the New Testament, atonement is not something man does for God; it is something God does for man.

On the other hand, the satisfaction theory underscores the seriousness of sin, as far as God is concerned. It suggests that a part of the process of forgiveness is a manifestation of his judgment against it. Surely no understanding of Christ's work is adequate which fails to appreciate how repulsive sin is to God.

The moral influence theory has the merit of emphasizing God's initiative in salvation, which is certainly faithful to the Bible. However, some people feel that it slights the costliness of forgiveness. It fails to account for the enormity of sin in the sight of God. It also has a tendency, its critics believe, to detract from the uniqueness of Christ's accomplishments. It treats the cross as one of many ways God seeks to communicate his love to the world, not as something that made an unprecedented impact on God himself.

Toward an Adequate Theory of Atonement

As these observations indicate, there is no simple answer to the question, How does Christ's work solve the problem of sin? No single proposal seems adequate to the task. It is tempting to try to pull all the theories together to form one comprehensive explanation, but we could do this only by ignoring their basic differences. A better approach may be to look for several themes which every responsible interpretation of the work of Christ must consider.

The love of God

The most fundamental theme in any Christian doctrine of salvation must be the love of God. His vast and intense concern for every human being is the basis of his saving activity. This explains why God takes the initiative in meeting the problem of sin. As soon as sin entered the world, God acted to mitigate its consequences. In other words, salvation went into effect the moment it was needed. Some texts even suggest that God formulated a response to sin before it was actually needed. The book of Revelation, for example, describes Jesus as the Lamb slain from the foundation of the world (Rev 13:8; cf. 1 Pet 1:20).

The cost of forgiveness

God's willingness to forgive must not obscure the spontaneity, or freedom, of his love. His response to sin is not a mechanical process, nor is it a matter-of-fact reaction. People sometimes assume that it is easy for God to forgive. One such was a notorious sinner who, at the point of death, showed no concern for the hereafter. "God will forgive me," he said. "That is his business."[7] There is no place in the Christian doctrine of salvation for such a casual attitude. We must not overlook the "difficulty" of God's forgiveness. Our salvation is costly to him. Only the agony of the cross reveals the scope of God's suffering as a result of sin.

7. Quoted in D. M. Baillie, *God Was in Christ: An Essay on Incarnation and Atonement* (New York: Charles Scribner's Sons, 1948), p. 172.

It may seem odd to insist that forgiveness is both natural and difficult for God at the same time. However, it is not always easy to do what comes naturally. A loving parent will "naturally" risk his own life to save his child, but this doesn't make the action "easy" for him. So it was with God: even though he responded instantly to meet the problem of sin and willingly gave his only Son for our salvation, he did so at an inestimable cost. We must not lose sight of "love's hard work."

The wrath of God

A careful analysis of divine love also helps us to understand the nature of divine wrath, or justice. As we saw, some views of the atonement assume that God's love and holiness are contrary forces, pulling in different directions. His love makes him willing to forgive, but his holiness makes him reluctant to do so. The atonement, then, provides a way of meeting the demands of both motives. The problem is that this idea equates wrath with vengeance and love with indulgence. There is a better way to interpret their relationship, and that is to see wrath as the expression, not the antithesis, of love.[8]

Genuine love takes its object with utmost seriousness. Because God loves us, everything about us matters to him. He therefore cannot ignore our sins. As one theologian writes, "God must be inexorable towards our sins; not because he is just, but because he is loving; not in spite of his love, but because of his love; not because his love is limited, but because it is unlimited. . . ."[9] God's wrath, then, is his loving response to sin. He finds it repulsive, disgusting. It distresses him to see the ones he loves destroying themselves.

The influence of God's love

Knowing how much God loves us awakens our love in response. Moreover, knowing how seriously he takes our sins can also help us to accept forgiveness. Suppose you deliberately said something to hurt a friend's feelings. Later you were sorry about it and asked forgiveness. Would you feel forgiven if he passed off the incident as if nothing had happened? Probably not. A flippant, casual attitude toward sin does not communicate forgiveness. To experience forgiveness, we need to know that our sins are taken seriously. A manifestation of God's

8. Many theologians have made this point, among them Anders Nygren. Nygren rejects the idea that the atonement resolves a tension within God between holiness and love, in favor of the view that "atonement is necessary, not because God's love is holy, but because it is love" (*Essence of Christianity: Two Essays,* trans. Philip S. Watson [Grand Rapids, Mich.: William B. Eerdmans Publishing Co., 1960], pp. 117–118).

9. D. M. Baillie, *God Was in Christ: An Essay on Incarnation and Atonement* (New York: Charles Scribner's Sons, 1948), p. 173.

attitude toward sin therefore plays an important role in communicating his love to us. It shows us how important we are to him.

This leads us to the conclusion that atonement is not something an angry God demands, but something a loving God provides. As the supreme manifestation of his judgment against sin, it is the supreme demonstration of his love for sinners. His wrath is part and parcel of his love; it affirms the immense value God places on us.

A synthetic view of the atonement

This view of the atonement emphasizes the impact of Christ's work on our perception of God. In some respects, then, it resembles the moral influence theory. But it also stresses the importance of divine judgment in the process of forgiveness, and it insists that reconciliation is entirely the work of God. Thus it shares some of the characteristics of the satisfaction and ransom theories, too.

Perhaps we need a variety of views of Christ's work. A great natural wonder, like the Grand Canyon, invites us to look at it from many vantage points. It never ceases to impress us, and no one perspective allows us to capture its beauty. To a far greater degree, Christ's accomplishments defy our powers of description. The more we reflect on the meaning of the cross, the more amazing it becomes. God's condescension in assuming humanity and his mysterious willingness to bear the consequences of sin will challenge our minds and stir our emotions forever. Eternity will not be time enough to plumb the depths of love revealed at Calvary.

STUDY HELPS

1. What qualifies Jesus to be our Savior?

Questions for review

2. What is the significance of the manner of Jesus' death?

3. How does the New Testament describe the work of Christ?

4. What are the principal theories of atonement and how does each explain why Jesus died?

5. What criteria must an acceptable doctrine of atonement satisfy?

6. How are divine love and wrath related?

1. The crucifixion of Jesus figures prominently in the New Testament, especially in Paul's writings, and in the history of the church. Could

Questions for further study

Jesus have fulfilled his mission had he died in any other way?

2. Christians often refer to Jesus as our "substitute," since he died "for us," or "in our place." Are there problems with this view? For example, would a respectable judge today set a condemned criminal free and execute an innocent person in his place? Does it help to think of Jesus as our "representative," rather than our "substitute"? Is there any difference between these two ideas?

3. People speak of Jesus' death in contrasting ways—both as a voluntary sacrifice on his part and as the obedient fulfillment of his Father's will. Could Jesus have abandoned his mission and avoided death without violating God's will? If so, why was this the major issue in his temptations? If not, was his sacrifice truly voluntary?

4. According to Reinhold Niebuhr, "It is because the cross of Christ symbolizes something in the very heart of reality, something in universal experience, that it has its central place in history" (*Leaves From the Notebook of a Tamed Cynic* [Cleveland and New York: The World Publishing Company, Meridian Books, 1957], p. 106). Do you think the cross symbolizes something within every person's experience? If so, what?

5. In *The Problem of Christianity,* American philosopher Josiah Royce describes an act of atonement as "some new deed which makes the human world better than it would have been had [the precise sin it responds to] not been done" (2 vols.; Chicago: Henry Regnery Company, 1968), 1:308. Did Jesus' death achieve something that would not have existed unless sin entered the universe? Is the universe ultimately better off for having experienced sin than it would have been otherwise?

Suggestions for Bible study

1. Study the following verses in several English translations of the Bible: Romans 3:25; Hebrews 2:17; 1 John 2:2; 4:10. Why do some versions use the word "expiation" and others, "propitiation"? Which term do you prefer? (You may find dictionaries and Bible commentaries helpful for this.)

2. Carefully read the story of the prodigal son (Luke 15:11–24). Imagine that you are the father in this story. Can you think of anything that might have made it "difficult" for him to forgive his son?

3. Paul called Christ crucified a "stumbling block to Jews and folly to Gentiles" (1 Corinthians 1:23). Chapter 7 briefly suggests some

reasons for the Jewish reaction. How can we explain the Gentile reaction? Why was the cross "folly" to the Greek mind? How do people think of the cross today?

4. The "suffering servant" of Isaiah strongly influenced the way early Christians looked at Jesus. What did they learn about Jesus from this prophetic figure?

   Isaiah 52:13–53:12 (1 Peter 2:21–25); Isaiah 61:1 (Luke 4:21); Luke 18:31–33; 24:25–27.

5. How are the nature and the work of Christ related to each other in these passages? Hebrews 2:14–18; 4:14–16; 5:8–9; 10:19–22.

SUGGESTIONS FOR FURTHER READING

From Adventist writers

Ellen G. White, *The Desire of Ages* (Mountain View, Calif.: Pacific Press Publishing Association, 1898), includes important chapters on the suffering and death of Jesus and its significance for human salvation. See especially, "Gethesemane" (pp. 685–697); "Calvary" (pp. 741–757); and "It Is Finished" (pp. 758–764).

Edward Heppenstall concentrates on the present work of Christ in *Our High Priest: Jesus Christ in the Heavenly Sanctuary* (Washington, D.C.: Review and Herald Publishing Association, 1972).

Jack Provonsha offers a stimulating interpretation of the atonement which emphasizes the impact of the cross on our perception of God in *You Can Go Home Again* (Washington, D.C.: Review and Herald Publishing Association, 1982).

Edward W. H. Vick discusses the doctrine of atonement in portions of two of his works: *Let Me Assure You: Of Grace, of Faith, of Forgiveness, of Freedom, of Fellowship, of Hope* (Mountain View, Calif.: Pacific Press Publishing Association, 1968); and *Is Salvation Really Free?* (Hagerstown, Md.: Review and Herald Publishing Association, 1983).

The most extensive discussion of this doctrine to date by Adventist scholars is the symposium volume, *The Sanctuary and the Atonement: Biblical, Historical, and Theological Studies,* ed. Arnold V. Wallenkampf and W. Richard Lesher (Washington, D.C.: Review and Herald Publishing Association, 1981). In general, the essays included are descriptive rather than constructive.

From other writers

Many works on the doctrine of salvation discuss both the person and work of Christ. This is true of the books by Baillie, Brunner, and Pannenberg referred to at the end of chapter 7. Other works, including some mentioned below, discuss the way we receive, or experience, salvation, along with what God has done to make it possible.

Leon Morris, *The Apostolic Preaching of the Cross* (Grand Rapids, Mich.: William B. Eerdmans Publishing Co., 1955) contains an extensive analysis of the various concepts the New Testament employs to describe the work of Christ.

John Murray gives a staunchly Calvinist interpretation of Christ's work in the atonement in *Redemption: Accomplished and Applied* (Grand Rapids, Mich.: William B. Eerdmans Publishing Co., 1955). Though less emphatic on certain points, G. C. Berkouwer, *The Work of Christ* (Eerdmans, 1965), also stands in the Reformed tradition.

In his classic work, *Christus Victor: An Historical Study of the Three Main Types of the Idea of Atonement,* trans. A. G. Hebert (New York: The Macmillan Company, 1969), Gustav Aulen emphasizes the merits of the ransom theory, or, as he variously calls it, the classic, patristic, or dramatic idea of atonement, over its two great rivals in the history of Christian thought.

Two other discussions written in the first part of the twentieth century are noteworthy for brevity and clarity, as well as their enduring value: P. T. Forsyth, *The Cruciality of the Cross* (Grand Rapids, Mich.: William B. Eerdmans Publishing Co., 1909); and Anders Nygren, "The Atonement as a Work of God," in *Essence of Christianity: Two Essays,* trans. Philip S. Watson (Grand Rapids, Mich.: William B. Eerdmans Publishing Co., 1960).

F. W. Dillistone explores the relations between the doctrine of atonement and various facets of general human experience in *The Christian Understanding of Atonement* (Philadelphia: The Westminster Press, 1968).

No contemporary theologian gives the cross a more prominent place in his theology than Jurgen Moltmann, author of *The Crucified God: The Cross of Christ as the Foundation and Criticism of Christian Theology,* trans. R. A. Wilson and John Bowden (New York: Harper & Row, Publishers, 1974).

9

THE NATURE AND PURPOSE
OF THE CHRISTIAN CHURCH

Biblical basis

"Now you are the body of Christ and individually members of it" (1 Corinthians 12:27).

"On this rock I will build my church, and the powers of death shall not prevail against it" (Matthew 16:18).

"Christ loved the church and gave himself up for her" (Ephesians 5:25).

Genesis 12:1–4
Deuteronomy 7:6–11; 9:4–5
Deuteronomy 26:1–11
Isaiah 5:1–7
Isaiah 49
Hosea 11:1–9
Joel 2:28
Matthew 16:13–19

Matthew 21:33–43
Acts 1–15
1 Corinthians 1:26–31
1 Corinthians 12, 14
Galatians 3:28–29
Ephesians 1–3
Ephesians 4:11–16
Revelation 12:17; 19:10

SALVATION AND THE CHURCH

The doctrine of Christ is only one part of the doctrine of salvation. It describes God's activity in making salvation available to fallen humanity. The other part of the doctrine describes the reception, or the experience, of salvation. For human beings to be saved, obviously, they must respond to God's gracious gift in Jesus Christ.

There are many ways to approach the experience of salvation. One is to concentrate on the effects of salvation in individual lives. We generally think of biblical expressions like "new birth," "justification," and "sanctification" as descriptions of what happens to the individual Christian. We are accustomed to hearing about the necessity of making a personal response to the gospel. Having Christian parents or grandparents won't do, we are told; we have to make a definite decision for Christ ourselves in order to be saved.

Spiritual individualism

Nothing should detract from the importance of personal religious experience, but a preoccupation with it can have unfortunate consequences. For one, it can encourage too much self-analysis, or introspection. It can lead us to become overly concerned with our attitudes or feelings at the moment, which often results in insecurity. People who worry unduly about their physical health often feel less well than they are. The same is sometimes true of people too concerned about their spiritual health.

Another result of overemphasizing personal religious experience is the tendency to lose interest in other people. The driving force of Jesus' life was ministry, or service. He did not neglect his own relation to God, certainly, but the good of others was uppermost in his mind. Those whose first priority is their own welfare may attempt to serve others, but their objective is often to gain personal benefit or discharge some personal responsibility. It isn't really to enhance the well-being of other people.

The most serious theological consequence of spiritual individualism is the failure to appreciate the larger dimensions of salvation. Such an attitude obscures the fact that God's work in the world is larger than personal salvation. His purpose is to establish his sovereignty over all creation. This certainly includes personal salvation, but it is not exhausted by it.

Spiritual individualism makes the social, or corporate, aspects of salvation seem secondary, even artificial. If we think of salvation as essentially an individual matter, then the church—the togetherness of God's people—will always be less important. We may urge people to attend church to receive a personal blessing or to fulfill their personal obligations, but we will never appreciate the full significance of the corporate life in Christ that the New Testament describes.

What do you say to someone who feels closer to God by himself than with others? or to the family that goes camping every weekend instead of to worship services? Are they really missing anything? Perhaps they are not, if salvation is essentially for individuals. But if it isn't, if it involves unique relationships with other people as well as with God, then they are missing a great deal. What they need is a better understanding of salvation and all that it means.

An adequate doctrine of salvation, therefore, requires a doctrine of the church. Accordingly, to do justice to the work of Christ in all its dimensions and to correct some prevalent misconceptions, we will treat the experience of salvation as part of the doctrine of the church.

FACETS OF THE DOCTRINE OF THE CHURCH

In many ways the doctrine of the church is the most complicated aspect of Christian faith, perhaps because the church is the most vivid spiritual reality we encounter, and the concrete is often more difficult to describe than the abstract. In discussing the church, we must consider a number of themes. One is its spiritual identity. We need to explore the relation of the church to Christ, and to examine his role as head of the church and as high priest of his people. In addition, we need to look at the gifts of the Spirit to the church.

Another important topic is the membership of the church. What is the essential identity of church members? What distinguishes Christians as a group from other human beings? What are the implications for their behavior? What does "life in the Spirit" consist of?

We also need to reflect on the role of the church in the world. The church's mission takes it into the world, bringing it into contact with other religions and with different social and political structures. Just what is the church's mission? What sort of organization does it call for? How can Christians fulfill their spiritual, social, and political responsibilities at the same time? These questions call for a wholistic view of the church, not unlike the wholistic doctrine of man proposed above. The church is both a spiritual reality and a visible, social-historical institution. We can't reduce it to one or the other.

The subject of Christian worship also deserves consideration. What is the essential purpose of worship? What forms should it take? What is the meaning of activities like baptism and the Lord's Supper?

Finally, we cannot ignore the question of the true church. The church has taken many turns during its long history, and there are many groups today that call themselves "Christian." Are they all entitled to that name? Are any of them entitled to it? Seventh-day Adventists often describe themselves as the "remnant church." What does this mean, and what does it say about the relation of Adventism to other Christian groups, past and present?

THE GOSPEL AND THE CHURCH

The church is part of the gospel. The heart of the good news is that God acted in Jesus for human salvation, and he offers it to everyone as a gift, free of charge. But the good news doesn't stop there. Christ not only died for our sins and rose to life from the dead, he also created a community to whom and through whom his presence in the world continues. In the church he fulfills his promise, ''Lo, I am with you always, to the close of the age'' (Mt 28:20).

The church is the sphere of salvation. God is active in the church to accomplish reconciliation, and he adds to the church those who are being saved (Ac 2:47). The church is also the means of salvation. Its mission is to extend the offer of salvation to the entire world (Mt 28:19–20), and the plan of salvation will not be complete until this is accomplished (Mt 24:14). Thus it is evident that the church plays an essential role in God's work of salvation.

Christ in the church

The book of Acts shows how the work of Christ continues in the church. Originally part of a longer work, Luke-Acts, it joins the Gospels to provide a comprehensive account of Christian beginnings. The description of Pentecost is crucial to the purpose of the book (Ac 2). This miraculous display of the Holy Spirit's power accomplished several important things: it fulfilled the promise of Jesus (Ac 1:8); it assured the early Christians not only of Christ's continuing care for them, but of his actual presence among them; and it empowered them to fulfill the mission he had given them. Peter's greatest sermon directly followed this manifestation. In it he proclaimed Jesus as the Messiah who was presently alive, sitting at the right hand of God. The further words and works of the apostles also testify to the abiding power of the Spirit in their midst. The story of Pentecost underlines the fact that the church is not a human creation, but owes its existence to the power of God.

God's power in the church

The church, then, is a kind of community which human beings cannot produce. What happens among members of the church, the spirit of fellowship which they enjoy, is something only the unique presence of God can explain. In the wake of Pentecost, for example, early Christians held their possessions in common (Ac 2:44–45). What united them was so compelling that the normally important distinctions between ''mine'' and ''yours'' seemed insignificant.

Because it owes its existence to the power of God, the church is unlike any other group. Most organizations arise because people have similar interests or needs. People who enjoy photography may form a camera club, for example. Students who need academic help may form study groups. Groups like this exist to meet the needs or stimulate the interest of the individual members.

Other groups arise from deeper human needs. Families and nations, for example, reveal a fundamental human need for fellowship. In such groups the interests of the community are more important than those of the individual. With a club it is individuals that make the group important, but in a community the individual derives significance from the group. In addition, the community as a whole generally has a personality of its own, distinct from those of the individuals who make it up.

Obviously the church is more like the second kind of group than the first. It is more important than the individual members who comprise it, and it has a personality of its own, derived from Christ, its head. But it is much more than the natural fulfillment of a human need. Only God could create the kind of fellowship available in the community of the Spirit, and only the power of God can account for its remarkable history. The Christian church is the primary means by which God reestablishes his reign among human beings.

THE CHURCH AS THE PEOPLE OF GOD

As it appears in the New Testament, the word "church" has several different meanings. It can refer to a group of people called together for a particular purpose, a community of Christian believers in a specific area, or to all of God's people, whenever and wherever they lived. It is never used in the Bible to refer to a building, and it never refers to one branch of Christianity as opposed to another. Early Christian congregations typically met in private homes, and different denominations did not yet exist.

Symbols for the church

Besides using the term itself in a variety of ways, the New Testament also employs a host of different symbols, or metaphors, for the church. For example, members of the church are sometimes called "saints," "believers," and "slaves." The church itself is variously referred to as a "kingdom," "temple," "household," "vineyard," and "flock." But among the many biblical descriptions of the church, two are particularly important. One is the "people of God"; the other is the "body of Christ." The first calls attention to the church's place in history, while the second emphasizes its intimate relation to Christ.

The covenant

The expression "people of God" reminds us that God has been working for human salvation ever since the fall. He characteristically operates within the framework of a certain relationship with human beings, one the Bible calls a "covenant." A covenant is like a formal agreement, or a contract. It sets down the terms of a relationship between different parties and lists the privileges and responsibilities involved on both sides. In the Bible, God always makes the covenant. In doing so, he promises certain things to people, and he indicates what he expects of them in return.

The word itself first appears in the story of Noah, where God tells the patriarch to take his family into the ark: "I will establish my covenant with you; and you shall come into the ark" (Gen 6:18). Later, God made a covenant with Abraham and with his descendants (Gen 17:7), promising to bless all the families of the earth through them (Gen 28:14). He reaffirmed this covenant with the people of Israel at Sinai, after he delivered them from Egypt. He promised that Israel would be his special people among the nations of the earth (Ex 19:5). He promised to give them the land of Palestine (Dt 4:37–38), and he stipulated obedience to his commandments as a condition of this relationship (Ex 19:5–8; Dt 7:9, 12).

The election of Israel

God's call to Israel has two important features. In the first place, it was not something Israel deserved. God didn't select the Jews to be his special people because they were larger or stronger than other nations (Dt 7:7), nor because they were spiritually superior (Dt 9:6). As a nation they were most unimpressive: they had been in bondage for generations, and they were stubborn (Dt 9:6). In short, there was nothing about the Hebrew people that qualified them for special consideration. Their call had its basis entirely in God's love and faithfulness. He intended to keep the promises he had made to their ancestors (Dt 7:8). Israel's election, then, was a matter of divine grace; it was totally undeserved.

A second feature of Israel's call was its distinct purpose. God was not playing favorites when he chose Israel; he did not intend to set them apart from other people as the exclusive objects of his love. Instead, he wanted them to be the means of extending salvation to others. In other words, God didn't love Israel *instead* of other people; he wanted to love all people *through* Israel. Israel was called to service, not elevated to a privileged status.

The prophets expressed God's hopes for Israel in glowing terms. God saw them as "a covenant to the people, a light to the nations, to open the eyes that are blind, to bring out the prisoners from the dungeon" (Isa 42:6–7). In Israel God wanted to put the effects of his saving power on public display so that, through Israel, salvation would reach the entire world. "I will give you as a light to the nations, that my salvation may reach to the end of the earth" (Isa 49:6; cf. 52:10).

The election
of the church

The New Testament refers to the Christian church as the "people of God": "But you are a chosen race, a royal priesthood, a holy nation, God's own people" (1 Pet 2:9). The features of the church's call are identical to those of Israel's. There was nothing about the members of the early church that qualified them for special consideration: "For consider your call, brethren; not many of you were wise according to worldly standards, not many were powerful, not many were of noble birth" (1 Cor 1:26). They owed their position entirely to the grace of God. "He is the source of your life in Christ Jesus" (vs. 30).

Moreover, the church is not an exclusive group. Its purpose is to extend salvation to the entire world. It does this by proclamation and demonstration. The church is to preach the the gospel, the good news that God has acted in Jesus Christ for the salvation of all human beings. It is also intended to display the effects of salvation for all to see, to "declare the wonderful deeds of him who called you out of darkness into his marvelous light" (1 Pet 2:9).

Differences
between
the church
and Israel

There are things about the church, however, that distinguish it from Israel. One of these is its international composition. The New Testament divorces the church from all national, ethnic, or social groups. Ideally, it is the most inclusive society on earth. "There is neither Jew nor Greek, there is neither slave nor free, there is neither male nor female; for you are all one in Christ Jesus" (Gal 3:28).

The most important characteristic of the church that distinguishes it from Israel is its attitude toward Jesus. It regards him as the Messiah, or Christ, and it looks back on his life, death, and resurrection as the climax of God's saving activity in human history. As a group, of course, Jews do not accept these claims for Jesus. He was rejected and put to death by the Jews of his day, and the messianic branches of contemporary Judaism still await the coming of the Messiah.

The question
of Israel today

The Jews' rejection of Jesus raises the perplexing question of their subsequent status. As a people, do they still have a distinctive role to play in the plan of salvation, or has the Christian church entirely superseded them as God's chosen people? There are strong differences of opinion among Christians over this question, and the testimony of the New Testament itself is not free from ambiguity.

In a famous section of his letter to the Romans, Paul insists that God has not rejected his people. Stimulated by the response of Gentiles to the gospel, he believes, the Jews, too, will accept Jesus (11:14). At the same time, Paul states that "not all who are descended from Israel belong to Israel, and not all are children of Abraham because they are his descendants" (9:6–7). He also speaks of those who have accepted Christ as true Israel: "If you are Christ's, then you are Abraham's offspring, heirs according to the promise" (Gal 3:29). In addition, Jesus' famous parable of the wicked tenants concludes with these dramatic words to the Jewish leaders of the time: "Therefore I tell you, the kingdom of God will be taken away from you and given to a nation producing the fruits of it" (Mt 21:43).

Coupled with the application to the church of expressions like "chosen race," "holy nation," and "God's own people" (2 Pet 1:9–10), such biblical statements convince many Christians that the church is now the principal means through which God is at work in the world. Jews may join the church, of course, but as a separate ethnic or national group, they have no distinctive spiritual significance.[1]

In contrast, some Christians believe that the Old Testament promises to Israel will be literally fulfilled someday, and many Jews will accept Jesus as the Messiah.[2] Others view the whole idea of the church replacing, or "superseding," Israel as anti-Semitic.[3] They regard Judaism as a parallel route to salvation.

The cumulative witness of the New Testament seems to favor the first of these three positions. As the people of God, the Christian

---

1. *The Seventh-day Adventist Bible Commentary* makes this emphatic statement: "Whatever the Jews, as a nation, may do, now or in time to come, is in no way related to the former promises made to them. With the crucifixion of Christ they forever forfeited their special position as God's chosen people. Any idea that the return of the Jews to their ancestral home, that is, to the new state of Israel, may in any way be related to Bible prophecy is the product of wishful thinking on the part of misguided, even if sincere, religious enthusiasts, and is without valid scriptural foundation" (in "The Role of Israel in Old Tstament Prophecy," in *The Seventh-day Adventist Bible Commentary,* ed. Francis D. Nichol [7 vols.; Washington, D.C.: Review and Herald Publishing Association, 1953–57], 4:33).

2. This is the position of those who accept "Dispensationalism" (see Charles Caldwell Ryrie, *Dispensationalism Today* [Chicago: Moody Press, 1965], pp. 158–59; and Hal Lindsey, *The Late Great Planet Earth* [Grand Rapids, Mich.: Zondervan Publishing House, 1970], pp. 42–58).

3. Paul Van Buren encourages his readers to see a positive relationship between Christianity and Judaism in *Discerning the Way: A Theology of the Jewish-Christian Reality* (New York: Seabury Press, 1980).

church is the recipient of the promises and the responsibilities earlier given to Israel.

Because God acted decisively in Jesus, salvation is now a certainty. This gives members of the church unprecedented assurance of God's love, and confidence in his acceptance of them. The new situation which this creates is nothing less than a "new covenant," according to the book of Hebrews (8:13; 9:15). It is superior to the old covenant, and the system of worship it involved, in several ways. Its revelation of God is more vivid (1:1–2). As God's Son, Jesus revealed God more effectively than the prophets could. In contrast to animal sacrifices, Jesus' death was a sacrifice that really solved the problem of sin (Heb 7:27; 9:26; 10:4). Unlike the priests who entered the apartments of the Hebrew sanctuary periodically, Jesus ministers constantly in the very presence of God (9:6–10, 24; 10:12). He thus provides a "new and living way" that gives us direct access to God (10:19). In view of all this, we can approach God with confidence and receive all the help we need (4:16; 10:22).

The new covenant

As our high priest, Christ serves as our representative, or advocate (1 Jn 2:1). Because he is human and knows what it is like to be tempted, he understands the difficulties we face. He is able to sympathize with us (Heb 2:18; 4:15), and he can help us (4:16). Jesus' position, therefore, is that of a mediator or intercessor. He is our go-between with God (1 Jn 2:1).

Our high priest

This description of Jesus' work should not lead us to feel that God is hostile to us. After all, he is the one who provides the mediator. Instead, it gives us further assurance of God's love for us. He has done everything necessary, everything possible, in fact, to establish fellowship with us. The high priestly ministry of Jesus reminds us that God is on our side.

As high priest, Jesus is not only close to God; he is also extremely close to us. Through the work of the Holy Spirit, in fact, he is personally closer to us than he could be if he were physically present somewhere on earth. The New Testament expresses this intimate connection between Christ and the church in several different ways. One is with the important symbol, the "body of Christ" (1 Cor 12:27).

THE CHURCH AS THE BODY OF CHRIST

The symbol of the body illuminates several important aspects of the relation between Christ and the church. As Christ's body, the church

Christ as Head of the church

depends on him for its existence. He is the source of the church, not only as its founder, but as the power that sustains it moment by moment. The church continually depends on Christ.

As Christ's body, the church also derives its essential identity from him. Individual church members participate in the life of the church, but they do not determine what its life shall be. It is Christ who makes the church important, not the other way around. As his body, the church derives its significance from him. The church is what it is because of who Jesus is, not because of who its members are.

The symbol of the body also suggests subordination. As Christ's body, the church is subject to his authority. He is "the head over all things for the church" (Eph 1:22). Recognizing that Christ's authority in the church is supreme prevents us from exaggerating the importance of any church official or organizational structure. The church needs organization, of course, but no organizational structure should obscure Christ's authority.

Apostolic authority

Many believe that Jesus' statement "You are Peter, and on this rock I will build my church" (Mt 16:18) gives Peter and his presumed successors, the bishops of Rome, supreme authority over the church on earth. But several things prevent us from drawing this conclusion. One is the fact that the New Testament elsewhere speaks of Christ, not Peter, as the rock, or the cornerstone, on which the church is built (Eph 2:20; 1 Pet 2:7). Another is the role Peter himself played in early Christianity. He was certainly a major figure, and the Gospels consistently portray him as the leader of the disciples, but he was by no means the single most important authority in the church. On one memorable occasion, the church met in council to settle some important issues (Acts 15). Peter's voice was one among several that were heard, but it was James who expressed the consensus of the group. On another occasion, Paul publicly criticized Peter for refusing to eat with Gentiles (Gal 2:11–14).

This interpretation of Jesus' statement also misunderstands the nature of apostolic authority. What made the apostles—and their writings—important was their firsthand testimony to Jesus. They spoke out of personal experience. They were also organizational leaders, but it was their function as witnesses that mattered most, not the office they occupied. Because this function depended on a certain personal experience, it could not be passed on. Others could assume their organizational responsibilities, but their witness to Christ was irreplaceable. In view of what really made them apostles, then, the conventional notion of "apostolic succession" is a mistake. Doctrinal agreement with the apostles is much more important than organizational continuity.

Members of the body

The image of the body not only illuminates the relation between Christ and the church; it also has powerful implications for the relation of church members to each other. A body is a complex unity, a single thing made of many different parts. Its oneness and its differentiation are both important—in fact, they require each other. A body is nothing without its members, but it is togetherness that makes the members important. None of them could exist, or would have any purpose, apart from the others.

Paul uses these ideas to encourage unity among the Christians at Corinth in one of the most picturesque passages in his letters (1 Cor 12:12–27). The tendency of certain individuals to emphasize their unique abilities threatened to disrupt that early congregation. Paul compared the church to a human body to remind these people of their dependence on others and to encourage those with different, perhaps less conspicuous abilities to think of themselves as essential parts of the church, too.

He begins by affirming the essential unity of the body: "For just as the body is one and has many members, and all the members of the body, though many, are one body, so it is with Christ" (12:12). Next, he asserts that each member is a part of the body, regardless of how it feels (12:15–16). He then shows how important differences among members of the body are. A body would be seriously handicapped without organs that have different functions (12:17–20). If we were nothing but an eye, for example, how would we hear? The point is that the different members of the body need each other; none of them can survive by itself. Finally, what they experience, they experience together, as one. "If one member suffers, all suffer together; if one member is honored, all rejoice together" (12:26). "Now you are the body of Christ," he concludes, "and individually members of it."

This striking illustration emphasizes the uniqueness and the importance of each church member. At the same time, it upholds the priority of unity, for it is only togetherness that gives individual abilities their purpose.

SPIRITUAL GIFTS

Paul's basic concern in 1 Corinthians 12–14 is church unity, but he speaks specifically to the issue of spiritual gifts (cf. 12:1), the presence of different abilities among members of the church. From Paul's rather extensive discussion we learn several things about this important and often perplexing topic.

**The source
of spiritual gifts**

To begin with, the gifts all have the same source; they all come from God. Since we aren't responsible for our gifts, we can't take credit for them or congratulate ourselves for having them. We should also recognize that the abilities of other people likewise come from God, so there is no basis for personal rivalry in the differences that exist among church members.

In the second place, it is God who decides which abilities we receive. He gives different abilities to different people, so it should not surprise or discourage us to find that others have abilities we don't.

**The purpose
of spiritual gifts**

Third, the purpose of the gifts is to contribute to the good of the entire church. In a sense, the gifts are given to the church as a whole, not to the individuals within it. This has great practical significance. It should lead us to view people in the church who can do important things as gifts to the rest of us. If someone has a remarkable ability to explain the Word of God, for example, our reaction shouldn't be to wonder why he can do something we can't. Instead, we should regard his ability as God's gift to the entire congregation. The gifts are to benefit the church, not to glorify the individual member.

**The importance
of spiritual gifts**

Fourth, all of the gifts are important as far as God is concerned. There is no such thing as an insignificant spiritual gift, just as there is no such thing as an unimportant talent. The fact that some gifts are less conspicuous than others is no indication that they are less important. Some of the least impressive gifts, in fact, may be downright vital to the life of the church, as Paul's analogy of the organs of the body indicates. The church needs all its gifts, just as the body needs all its members.

At the same time, some gifts are more important than others—not because they are the only ones that count, of course, but because they are more fundamental to the mission of the church, or because their influence is more extensive than that of other gifts. Paul's list suggests a certain hierarchy among spiritual gifts: ''And God has appointed in the church first apostles, second prophets, third teachers, then workers of miracles, then healers, helpers, administrators, speakers in various kinds of tongues'' (1 Cor 12:28). Apostles head the list because their witness to Christ is the very basis of the church. The gift of tongues comes last, some believe, because those with this gift had created problems at Corinth by exaggerating their importance and making others feel inferior. So Paul puts them in their place. He assures them that they are part of the church, but they have no reason for personal pride.

Paul's discussion of spiritual gifts contains two additional elements that deserve our attention here. One is the magnificent hymn to love, one of the most famous of all biblical passages (1 Cor 13). Its purpose in this context is to show that a spirit of self-forgetful service is the most important thing anyone can have. It will outlast every other gift (13:8), and without it, tongues, prophetic powers, understanding, and even faith are worthless (13:1–3). This relativizes the whole question of spiritual gifts by showing that the most important question is not, What have I received?, but, What am I giving? What motivates my activity?

Love: the greatest gift of all

Paul also makes a series of suggestions about the appropriate exercise of the gift of tongues. He does not discourage the manifestation of this gift, but he doesn't want it to disrupt worship services, and he indicates that other gifts, such as prophecy, are more beneficial to the congregation. The important thing to keep in mind, he says, is that "all things should be done decently and in order" (1 Cor 14:40).

The gift of tongues

The gift of tongues is a widely discussed religious issue today. The charismatic movement, as it is often called, has many followers, not only within various Pentecostal groups, but among Catholic and mainline Protestant churches, too. Charismatics typically identify speaking in tongues with the baptism of the Holy Spirit. They believe that this phenomenon is an important indication of personal salvation.

It is not entirely clear from the New Testament just what the gift of tongues means. At several points in the book of Acts, a remarkable manifestation of the Holy Spirit indicated that certain people had experienced God's saving power. This was true of the group meeting in the upper room at Pentecost (2:1–4). It occurred in Samaria following the baptism of several converts to Christianity (8:17), and it happened to Cornelius and members of his household during Peter's visit (10:44–46). Such passages suggest that every genuine Christian should have the experience.

On the other hand, as we have just seen, Paul describes tongues as one of several gifts of the Spirit to the church. Since different members have different gifts, it isn't something everyone should expect to receive. We shouldn't view this particular gift as an essential part of everyone's experience of salvation.

There is a further difference of opinion as to what "speaking in tongues" involved. In Acts 2 it evidently enabled listeners from different countries to hear what the apostles had to say in their own languages (2:6), so it facilitated the communication of the gospel. In 1 Corinthians 12–14, however, it seems to be an ecstatic phenomenon rather than intelligible speech, and it doesn't particularly benefit other people (14:2-5, 9, 11, 19). To further complicate the situation, some scholars believe that Pentecost was an example of ecstatic utterance, while others maintain that the gift of tongues at Corinth consisted of speaking different human languages.[4]

We may never know exactly what speaking in tongues originally involved. It may be significant that the Gospels never mention the phenomenon and that Jesus never instructed his disciples on the matter. This, coupled with Paul's discussion of spiritual gifts, prevents us from concluding that everyone should seek the experience. In addition, linguistic studies of contemporary glossolalia have failed to find the characteristics of a genuine language.[5] We are therefore justified in being cautious about the phenomenon. At the same time, we should not be eager to discredit the experience out of hand. We must be open to different manifestations of the Spirit's power. God may have some surprises for us, just as he did for his people in apostolic times.

ELLEN G. WHITE AND THE GIFT OF PROPHECY

The gift of prophecy is particularly important to Seventh-day Adventists. They believe that the presence of this gift is one of the identifying marks of God's people in the last days (Rev 12:17; 19:10), and they regard the ministry of Ellen G. White as a manifestation of this gift in their history.

4. For a clear discussion of the various New Testament passages which refer to speaking in tongues see Frank W. Beare, "Speaking With Tongues: A Critical Survey of the New Testament Evidence," *Journal of Biblical Literature,* 83 (1964):229–246.
5. John P. Kildahl remarks, "Speaking in tongues does not sound like gibberish. It has the rhythm and qualities of a language" (*The Psychology of Speaking in Tongues* [New York: Harper & Row, Publishers, 1972], p. 2). But, he also observes, "Linguistic scholars work with precise definitions of what constitutes a natural human language. Glossolalia fails to meet the criteria of these definitions" (ibid., p. 47).

The general features of Ellen White's life are well known.[6] She was born in 1827, one of eight children of Robert and Eunice Harmon. At the age of twelve, she accepted William Miller's message, along with her family, and looked forward to the soon return of Jesus. She was among the "little flock" of believers who survived the devastating disappointment of October 22, 1844, still believing that the Lord had led them.

Two years later she married James White, a young Adventist preacher some six years her senior. They had four children, all boys, and only two of them survived to adulthood. She and James labored tirelessly during the formative years of the Seventh-day Adventist church. After he died in 1881, her work not only continued, but expanded. She spent two years in Europe in the mid 1880s and lived in Australia from 1890 to the turn of the century. Returning to the United States, she made her home in California, where she died in 1915 at the age of eighty-seven.

Ellen White regarded public speaking as her particular talent,[7] but she is best known today as a prolific writer. During her lifetime, she contributed well over four thousand articles to various denominational publications. She authored several dozen books on a wide range of topics, and she conducted a vigorous correspondence with people all over the world.

The most remarkable aspect of her life consisted in the unusual experiences to which she attributed her messages. She typically referred to them as "visions." The first occurred in December 1844, a few weeks after the Great Disappointment, when she was barely seventeen years old. There were hundreds in the years that followed. During these experiences she received spiritual instruction or messages of practical religious value in the form of vivid sensory impressions. She

Ellen White's life

Ellen White's visions

---

6. Arthur L. White is currently preparing a definitive, multi-volume biography of Ellen G. White. Volumes 5 and 6 of the projected six-volume work have now been published: *Ellen G. White: The Early Elmshaven Years, 1900–1905* and *Ellen G. White: The Later Elmshaven years, 1905–1915* (Washington, D.C.: Review and Herald Publishing Association, 1981, 1982). Ellen G. White recounts her own experience in much of *Life Sketches of Ellen G. White* (Mountain View, Calif.: Pacific Press Publishing Association, 1915). Selected biographical material also appears in Arthur L. White, *Ellen G. White: Messenger to the Remnant* (Washington, D.C.: Ellen G. White Publications, 1956), and T. Housel Jemison, *A Prophet Among You* (Mountain View, Calif.: Pacific Press Publishing Association, 1955).

7. In 1905 Ellen G. White said, "For many years I was known as a speaker on temperance" (*Temperance* [Mountain View, Calif.: Pacific Press Publishing Association, 1949], p. 259).

was instructed to communicate their contents to certain individuals, in some cases, and to the church at large, in others.

Ellen White never assumed the title "prophet" for herself,[8] but she did not object when others applied it to her. She did claim that divine authority lay behind her instruction. Seventh-day Adventists believe that her ministry is a manifestation of the gift of prophecy described in the New Testament. In fact, Adventists often assert that they believe in Ellen White's prophetic status precisely because they believe in the Bible. The doctrine of spiritual gifts, including the gift of prophecy, is one of the teachings of Scripture.[9]

The Biblical Tests of a Prophet

The New Testament encourages believers to examine purported prophetic claims in at least two different passages. Paul urges his readers to avoid skepticism (1 Thess 5:19–23); John urges his to avoid being gullible (1 Jn 4:1). They both recommend testing a person's messages to see if they are from God.

Faithfulness to the Bible   Assuming that the Bible is divinely authoritative, Seventh-day Adventists have traditionally applied several different biblical tests

---

8. This famous disclaimer appeared in *The Review and Herald,* July 26, 1906, and is reprinted in *Selected Messages,* vol. 1, pp. 31–35. The words, "I do not claim to be a prophetess," need to be carefully interpreted in light of Ellen White's own explanation of them. She says that she does not object if others describe her as a prophetess, and she gives the following reasons for not making the claim herself: "Because in these days many who boldly claim that they are prophets are a reproach to the cause of Christ; and because my work includes much more than the word 'prophet' signifies" (*Selected Messages,* vol. 1, p. 32). So she clearly attributed divine authority to her work, even though she did not apply the word "prophet" to herself.

9. A fascinating and informative selection of articles by early Seventh-day Adventists dealing with the gift of prophecy in Ellen G. White's experience and setting forth reasons for accepting the gift as valid appears in *Witness of the Pioneers Concerning the Spirit of Prophecy: A Facsimile Reprint of Periodical and Pamphlet Articles Written by the Contemporaries of Ellen G. White* (Washington, D.C.: The Ellen G. White Estate, 1961). These various articles make the following points: (1) The Bible affirms the perpetuity of the prophetic gift to the Christian church; (2) Ellen G. White's visions are genuine manifestations of the prophetic gift; (3) the visions provide proof that the Seventh-day Adventist Church is the remnant church foretold in the Bible; (4) the visions are subordinate to the Bible and are not employed as a test of fellowship by the Seventh-day Adventist Church; and (5) the visions are highly regarded by Seventh-day Adventists for their great spiritual value.

to the work of Ellen White.[10] Perhaps the most important is agreement with Scripture (cf. Isa 8:20). If the Holy Spirit lies behind a person's work, his or her teachings will harmonize with the teachings of the Bible, because God will not contradict himself. He will not say one thing in the Bible and another through a later prophet.

A biblical view of Christ

The second test is really an extension of the first. It consists of agreement with the biblical doctrine of the incarnation. "Every spirit which confesses that Jesus Christ has come in the flesh is of God" (1 Jn 4:2). A true prophet will affirm the genuine humanity of Jesus.

A beneficial ministry

The third test involves the effects of a person's ministry. Jesus warned against false prophets, saying, "You will know them by their fruits" (Mt 7:16, 20). A divinely authorized ministry will yield positive results; an imposter's ministry will not. To early Adventists, one of the most convincing features of Ellen White's ministry was the fact that the work of the church prospered when they followed her advice and suffered when they ignored it.[11]

When you consider most of the things that Seventh-day Adventists are known for, her influence is clearly visible. She urged her husband to start a publishing work; she strongly supported denominational schools; she encouraged the development of work in other countries of the world; and she led out in health reform and in establishing medical training facilities.[12]

10. T. Housel Jemison presents four "tests of a prophet" in *A Prophet Among You* (Mountain View, Calif.: Pacific Press Publishing Association, 1955), pp. 100–111.

11. In the words of George I. Butler, at the time president of the General Conference of Seventh-day Adventists, "We have tested them [the visions] for nearly a quarter of a century, and we find we prosper spiritually when we heed them and suffer a great loss when we neglect them" (*The Advent Review and Herald of the Sabbath,* June 9, 1874; reprinted in *Witness of the Pioneers Concerning the Spirit of Prophecy,* p. 47).

12. Francis D. Nichol credits Ellen G. White's ministry with the remarkable growth of the Seventh-day Adventist Church and its impressive accomplishments in publishing, medical, educational, and mission work: "But we had in our midst a most singular woman. She marked out what we ought to do in the different branches of our work. She was specific, emphatic, insistent. We accepted her counsel and direction, for we believed she had visions from God. That is the reason we have this marvelous organization and why we've grown" (*Why I Believe in Mrs. E. G. White: Some Reasons Why Seventh-day Adventists Believe That Ellen G. White Possessed the Gift of "the Spirit of Prophecy"* [Washington, D.C.: Review and Herald Publishing Association, 1964], p. 127).

**Fulfilled
prophecies**

Last, and probably least in importance, is the test of fulfilled predictions. According to certain biblical passages, the predictions of a true prophet will come to pass (cf. Jer 28:9), while those of a false prophet will not. There are important qualifications for this test, however. On the one hand, fulfilled predictions do not always guarantee the reliability of a prophet's ministry. The Israelites were instructed to ignore any suggestion to follow other gods, even if its author predicted something remarkable that came to pass (Dt 13:1–3).

On the other hand, unfulfilled predictions do not necessarily discredit a prophet. A message borne from God may not always come to pass. Jonah, for example, had God's command to forecast Nineveh's destruction, but the city was not destroyed. This doesn't mean that Jonah was not a true prophet. God decided to preserve Nineveh because its inhabitants repented.

The principle involved here is that of "conditional prophecy," which we mentioned in the doctrine of God. There are predictions, both promises and threats, whose fulfillment depends on the response of human beings. If, as in Jonah's case, people turn from their sins, threats of destruction will not be fulfilled. Similarly, turning away from God will thwart his desire to bless (cf. Jer 18:1–11).

Seventh-day Adventists have applied these different tests to Ellen White's life and work for nearly a century and a half. The process has strengthened their belief that God was directly involved in her ministry, and that she deserves to be regarded as a prophet. At the same time, however, her status in the church has always been widely discussed and carefully qualified. From the beginning, for example, Seventh-day Adventists have refused to make belief in her a formal "test of fellowship," although the statement of fundamental beliefs voted in 1980 may represent a departure from this practice.[13] For Seventh-day Adventists today, two of the questions surrounding Ellen White's prophetic status are particularly pressing. One is the relation of her writings to the Bible, and the other concerns the nature of her inspiration.

13. As voted by the General Conference of Seventh-day Adventists in the quinquennial session of 1980, "Fundamental Beliefs of Seventh-day Adventists" contains the following as number 17, entitled "The Gift of Prophecy": "One of the gifts of the Holy Spirit is prophecy. This gift is an identifying mark of the remnant church and was manifested in the ministry of Ellen G. White. As the Lord's messenger, her writings are a continuing and authoritative source of truth which provide for the church comfort, guidance, instruction, and correction. They also make clear that the Bible is the standard by which all teaching and experience must be tested. (Joel 2:28, 29; Acts 2:14–21; Heb. 1:1–3; Rev. 12:17; 19:10.)" (*Seventh-day Adventist Church Manual* [General Conference of Seventh-day Adventists, 1981], pp. 39–40).

ELLEN G. WHITE AND BIBLICAL AUTHORITY

Seventh-day Adventists have always identified themselves as Protestants. They affirm the Reformation principle of *sola Scriptura,* as it is sometimes called. This is the conviction that the Bible alone is the authoritative guide for Christian faith and practice. The first item in the church's latest statement of fundamental beliefs, for example, asserts, "The Holy Scriptures are the infallible revelation of His [God's] will. They are the standard of character, the test of experience, the authoritative revealer of doctrines, and the trustworthy record of God's acts in history."[14]

At the same time, Seventh-day Adventists regard Ellen G. White as a prophet. They believe that the Spirit who inspired the writings of the Bible is also responsible for her messages. This creates an apparent dilemma. If we place Ellen White on the same level as the Bible, then we seem to compromise the Protestant principle of the Bible only. On the other hand, if we subordinate her writings to Scripture, we seem to undermine her prophetic status.[15] Is it possible to accept the Bible alone as supremely authoritative and also to regard Ellen White as a prophet? What, precisely, is her relation to Scripture?

Ellen White's own comments are helpful on this point. She has a great deal to say about the Bible, and about its relation to her own

Ellen White's view of the Bible

Compare this formulation with number 19 in "Fundamental Beliefs of Seventh-day Adventists" which appeared in the 1963 edition of the *Church Manual:* "That God has placed in His church the gifts of the Holy Spirit, as enumerated in 1 Corinthians 12 and Ephesians 4. That these gifts operate in harmony with the divine principles of the Bible, and are given 'for the perfecting of the saints, for the work of the ministry, for the edifying of the body of Christ.' Eph. 4:12. That the gift of the Spirit of prophecy is one of the identifying marks of the remnant church. (1 Cor. 1:5–7; 1 Cor. 12:1–28; Rev. 12:17; Rev. 19:10; Amos 3:7; Hosea 12:10, 13.) They recognize that this gift was manifested in the life and ministry of Ellen G. White" (*Church Manual* [General Conference of Seventh-day Adventists, 1963], p. 34).

The 1980 version of Fundamental Beliefs devotes an entire section specifically to "The Gift of Prophecy," rather than including this gift in the section dealing with spiritual gifts in general (number 16 is entitled "Spiritual Gifts and Ministries"). Moreover, the later version straightforwardly asserts that this gift "was manifested in the ministry of Ellen G. White," in contrast to the seemingly parenthetical statement mentioning Ellen G. White in the earlier version.

14. *Seventh-day Adventist Church Manual* (General Conference of Seventh-day Adventists, 1981), p. 31.

15. Herold D. Weiss brilliantly analyzes this problem and formulates the general solution presented here in his article, "Are Adventists Protestants?" *Spectrum,* vol. 4, no. 2 (Spring 1972), pp. 69–78.

writings. To begin with, she strongly supports the importance of the Bible and asserts that the Bible is indispensable as a source of knowledge about God. It contains everything we need to know for salvation (*Counsels to Teachers*, p. 448; *Testimonies for the Church*, vol. 8, p. 286). It is the supreme religious authority; nothing will ever replace or supersede it. It is the test of all other manifestations of the Spirit (*The Great Controversy*, p. vii).

Ellen White also spoke about the appropriate interpretation of the Bible. She urged Christians to engage in personal Bible study (*Testimonies for the Church*, vol. 5, p. 686); in fact, she described this as the highest duty of every rational being (*The Great Controversy*, p. 598). According to her, the meaning of the Bible is available to every honest student (*Testimonies for the Church*, vol. 5, p. 663). We must lay aside our preconceptions and allow the Bible to be its own interpreter (*Testimonies to Ministers*, p. 100; *The Great Controversy*, p. 354).

Ellen White's view of herself

When it comes to her own writings, Ellen White maintained that she received her messages from God and that they deserve to be carefully studied. But she clearly subordinated them to the Bible. Their essential purpose, she said, is to emphasize what we find in the Bible. "The written testimonies are not to give new light," in her words, "but to impress vividly upon the heart the truths of inspiration already revealed" (*Testimonies for the Church*, vol. 5, p. 663). In fact, they would not even be needed if people had paid enough attention to the Bible itself to start with (*Testimonies for the Church*, vol. 5, p. 667).

We can summarize Ellen White's own position, then, by saying that the Bible is the supreme and comprehensive source of religious knowledge. The purpose of her writings is to enhance our appreciation of the Bible by emphasizing, explaining, and applying its contents.

The supremacy of biblical authority

If we are faithful to Ellen White's own position, we will avoid placing her on a level with Scripture. In practice, as well as in theory, we will give the Bible the first and last word in religious matters. It is not enough to assert that we judge Ellen White by the Bible, and not the Bible by Ellen White. If the authority of the Bible is truly supreme for us, it will do more than establish Ellen White's prophetic status. It will continue to serve as our primary object of study, and we will support our doctrinal positions by direct appeals to Scripture.

This will keep us faithful to the classical Protestant position. The Reformation emphasis on the primacy of Scripture did not elevate the Bible to a position of supreme authority for the first time, nor, for that matter, does it imply that the Bible is the only thing of religious interest that Christians should ever read. What it really did was remove everything standing between the Bible and the church in the way of an authoritative guide or interpreter. The prevalent position of the day acknowledged the supreme authority of the Bible, but it insisted that the Bible must be interpreted by the church. In so doing, it interposed tradition, or church doctrine, between believers and the Bible. The principle of *sola Scriptura* removes this intermediary. It insists on direct contact with the Bible.

If Seventh-day Adventists adhere to this important principle, they will not treat Ellen White as an infallible interpreter of the Bible. They will not allow her writings to distract them from the study of the Scriptures, or regard them as a shortcut to their meaning. They will support every biblical interpretation, including those of Ellen White, by appealing directly to the Bible itself.

ELLEN G. WHITE AND PROPHETIC INSPIRATION

Recent developments have focused widespread attention on the question of Ellen White's inspiration. During the past dozen years, and especially during the past two or three, students of her writings have discovered that her literary indebtedness is a more complicated phenomenon than most people ever realized.

Ellen White's literary indebtedness

For years it has been general knowledge that she employed various historical works in writing *The Great Controversy*. The 1911 edition, in fact, gave credit to her sources. We now know that she used written sources extensively in composing many of her other books, too. Her writings on health, for example, closely resemble views held by others in her time.[16] Some have suggested that a few of her best-loved devotional books, such as *Desire of Ages,* are more like compilations of material than original compositions.[17] There is even

16. Ronald L. Numbers offers an extensive analysis of Ellen G. White's involvement in the health reform movement in *Prophetess of Health: A Study of Ellen G. White* (New York: Harper and Row, Publishers, 1976). The staff of the Ellen G. White Estate has prepared a detailed response to Numbers' book entitled, *A Critique of the Book Prophetess of Health* (Washington, D.C.: The Ellen G. White Estate, 1976).

17. Ellen G. White's use of sources in *Desire of Ages* has been the subject of a multi-year research project under the direction of Fred Veltman, while on leave from the Religion Department of Pacific Union College. Entitled "The E. G. White Life of Christ

evidence that she sometimes employed words she had previously read somewhere in transcribing what she received in vision.[18]

In addition, the role of her literary assistants, such as Marian Davis, now appears larger than before. They did not merely proofread her manuscripts for grammatical errors and transpose paragraphs. They collected material for her books, and sometimes they deleted large portions of what she herself had written (though not without her approval).[19]

These discoveries make it impossible for many Seventh-day Adventists to accept the familiar view that she received the content of her writings in vision and turned to other sources for occasional assistance in expressing herself.[20] There are those who believe that we have largely misunderstood the nature of Ellen White's work, and a few have lost confidence in her prophetic ministry.[21] Many believe, however, that we can modify our understanding of inspiration to accommodate the available data. There are several possible approaches.

Proposed solutions: The guidance of the Holy Spirit

A familiar suggestion is that she used sources under the guidance of the Holy Spirit. The Spirit not only imparted a message to her, but directed her to select material that would aid her in expressing it effectively. This is possible. It is also possible that the content of

---

Research Project'' and funded by the General Conference of Seventh-day Adventists, the study has involved the careful examination by a number of scholars of the written sources Ellen G. White used in selected chapters of *Desire of Ages*. (See Bonnie Dwyer, ''EGW Project Extended,'' *Spectrum,* vol. 12, no. 4 [June 1972], p. 64.)

18. Warren H. Johns, ''Ellen White: Prophet or Plagiarist?'' *Ministry,* June 1982, p. 10. Johns's fifteen-page article is a candid and constructive treatment of the question of Ellen White's literary indebtedness. It contains a number of figures comparing selected passages from Ellen White's writings to those from books in her library. It also contains a table listing various references to her borrowing over the years, and it concludes with a bibliography of seventeen items for further study. Johns's discussion is a good place to begin examining this difficult question.

19. See Eric Anderson's discussion of Donald R. McAdams's research in ''Ellen White and Reformation Historians,'' *Spectrum,* vol. 9, no. 3, pp. 23–26.

20. Donald R. McAdams reviews some of the recent developments in research into Ellen White's literary indebtedness and their impact on the concept of her prophetic inspiration in ''Shifting Views of Inspiration: Ellen G. White Studies in the 1970s,'' *Spectrum,* vol. 10, no. 4, pp. 26–41. Probably the single most influential factor in the SDA Church's reassessment of Ellen White's prophetic gift was the publication of the minutes of the 1919 Bible Conference (*Spectrum,* vol. 10, no. 1, pp. 27–57). The records of that conference clearly show that in the early twentieth century a number of prominent Seventh-day Adventists were aware of her literary indebtedness and the questions it poses for the concept of her prophetic inspiration.

21. See, for example, Walter T. Rea's caustic critique, *The White Lie* (Turlock, Calif.: M&R Publications, 1982).

some of her visions coincided with material already familiar to her. There is nothing about the simple idea of inspiration that requires total originality. But this approach requires us to abandon a familiar argument for her inspiration. We can no longer regard her as an uneducated woman who couldn't possibly have developed her materal by any natural means.

There is also a problem with the view that the Spirit guided in her selection of sources. Historians generally regard some of *The Great Controversy*'s sources as rather poor history. In the opinion of many scholars, for example, Wylie and d'Aubigne are not reliable historians, and they were not the best historians available in Ellen White's time.[22]

Others' words, her ideas

A similar suggestion is that Ellen White incorporated the words of others to express ideas she received in vision. Much of the material was derived, but the overarching framework of thought was her own. One problem with this is the difficulty of separating Ellen White's concepts from the ideas in some of the works she employed. In many cases, she seems to include the ideas as well as the verbal formulations of her sources.

On the other hand, there is an important precedent for such a distinction in the Bible itself. The consensus among biblical scholars is that Matthew and Luke copied extensively from Mark.[23] They follow Mark's overall outline of Jesus' ministry, and they reproduce many of its passages virtually word for word. Yet in spite of their similarities, each of the so-called Synoptic Gospels has its distinctive perspective on the life of Jesus. Literary dependence does not exclude considerable originality. Perhaps further literary analysis will reveal an originality in Ellen White's works that the current preoccupation with her use of sources obcures.

Unconscious indebtedness

One striking proposal is that Ellen White did not realize the extent of her dependence on other writers. We often meet some of our "original" ideas in books we have read and forgotten about. Ellen White

22. This is William S. Peterson's contention in "A Textual and Historical Study of Ellen G. White's Account of the French Revolution," *Spectrum,* vol. 2, no. 4, pp. 57–69.

23. For a discussion of the so-called "Synoptic Problem," see D. T. Rowlingson, "Synoptic Problem," in *The Interpreter's Dictionary of the Bible* (4 vols.; Nashville, Tenn.: Abingdon Press, 1962), 4:491–495. Discussions of the literary relationships among the first three Gospels can easily be found in other Bible dictionaries and in New Testament introductions.

may have had similar experiences. Perhaps she expressed as her own, ideas which she first encountered in other writings, because she had made them her own. Besides, Ellen White was primarily concerned with the content of ideas, rather than their source. She believed that God was the ultimate author of all truth. Accordingly, when she read something that impressed her, she naturally attributed it to God.[24]

The note of divine authority

There is another response to the similarity between much of Ellen White's writings and other material. This is to emphasize the tone, rather than the content, of her messages. According to this suggestion, we see inspiration primarily in the note of divine authority with which she wrote. Others may have said similar things, but when she spoke, the church listened and obeyed.[25]

This response shifts the focus of attention from the production of Ellen White's messages to her role in the community. In the final analysis, this may be where the question of her inspiration must be decided. Each person evaluates the impact of her ministry on his own life, and the community as a whole reaches a consensus as to her prophetic status.

One merit of this approach is its concern with the larger question of revelation. Instead of concentrating narrowly on the production of her writings, its perspective takes into account her role in the larger cycle of God's communication with his people.

The nature of Ellen White's ministry is one of those areas where the church's thinking is currently developing. What we have learned requires us to reexamine our concept of prophetic inspiration. But

---

24. These are suggestions Jack W. Provonsha presents in his unpublished essay entitled, "Was Ellen G. White a Fraud?" (2d printing, June 1980). In answer to this question Provonsha writes, "No. I think the more likely possibility is that this godly woman was so sensitive to the many voices of God and responded to them so intensely that she tended to overlook customary amenities like saying thanks to the ordinary writers who provided the occasion" (p. 22). Provonsha addresses "the more pressing ethical question," as he describes it, in another, more recent, essay, "Did Ellen White Attempt to Conceal the Fact That She 'Borrowed' From the Writings of Others?" (unpublished manuscript, p. 1). Here Provonsha asks us to shift our concern from the origin to the content of Ellen White's messages. "In this matter," he states, "we have been focusing our attention largely on the wrong issue. Ellen White and her moral perfection are not on trial! It is the *truth* with which she is associated that concerns us. Ellen White is only incidental to that truth" (p. 11; italics his).

25. Ron Graybill explores the distinctiveness of prophetic authority as it applies to Ellen G. White, in contrast to scriptural and exegetical authority, in "Ellen White's Role in Doctrine Formation" (*Ministry*, October 1981, pp. 7–11).

those for whom her writings have been of great spiritual benefit are hardly inclined to discard them. Clearly, this is an area where more theological work needs to be done, and where the community needs to be sensitive to the views of all its members.

STUDY HELPS

Questions for
review

1. What is the relation between personal salvation and church membership?

2. What makes the church unique among human groups and organizations?

3. What are the primary symbols the New Testament applies to the church?

4. How is the church like the nation of Israel? How is it different?

5. What is the nature and source of authority in the church?

6. What are the characteristics of spiritual gifts?

7. What do the gift of tongues and the gift of prophecy, respectively, involve?

8. What biblical tests do Seventh-day Adventists apply to Ellen G. White's ministry?

9. What are some of the recent questions concerning Ellen White's writings?

Questions for
discussion

1. Certain people insist that they don't need the church. They say they can get more out of worshiping God by themselves than being with other Christians. How do you respond to this attitude?

2. Sometimes a group of people with modest abilities can accomplish more than an equal number of more talented individuals. (You can probably think of examples in areas like sports and music.) Why is this so? What does this imply about the Christian church?

3. In apostolic times, the Christian church thrived in the face of intense opposition. In contrast, there is little interest in religion in much of the so-called "Christian" world today. When is adversity spiritually beneficial? Why?

4. Of all ancient peoples, only the Jews survive today, and modern Israel has a remarkable history. Is there a religious explanation for these phenomena? Are there other explanations?

5. How can a person find out what his or her spiritual gifts are?

6. How would you go about explaining the ministry of Ellen G. White to someone for the first time?

Suggestions for Bible study

1. What do we learn about the church from the following biblical symbols?
   a. Romans 1:7; 1 Corinthians 1:2; Ephesians 1:1; Philippians 1:1; Colossians 1:2
   b. 2 Corinthians 4:5; Galatians 5:13
   c. 1 Peter 2:4–5; Colossians 1:13; Matthew 5:3; 2 Corinthians 6:16
   d. 1 Timothy 3:15; Ephesians 2:19; Matthew 23:8; 1 Corinthians 6:5; 1 Peter 2:17; Romans 9:26; Ephesians 5:25–27
   e. 1 Corinthians 3:5–9; Acts 20:28; 1 Peter 5:2; John 10:16
   f. 2 Corinthians 5:17; Ephesians 2:15

2. People sometimes think of the apostolic church as relatively free from internal difficulties. But what do the following passages indicate about some of the problems early Christians faced? How do their difficulties compare with those of Christians today?
   a. Acts 6:1; Acts 15:36–40; 1 Corinthians 1:10–12
   b. Acts 11:1–3; Galatians 2:11–16; Philippians 3:2–3
   c. 2 Corinthians 11:2–5; Galatians 1:6–9; 1 John 4:1
   d. 1 Corinthians 5:1–2; 1 Timothy 1:19–20

3. Read through the first twelve chapters of Acts. List the ways in which the Holy Spirit operated in the life of the earliest Christian community.

4. Some people make a sharp distinction between the gift of the Holy Spirit mentioned in Acts (e.g., 2:38; 8:17; 10:44–47) and the spiritual gifts referred to in Paul's letters (e.g., 1 Corinthians 12:4–11, 28; Ephesians 4:11). In your view, how are these related?

5. How do you reconcile the equality among church members presented in texts such as Galatians 3:28 with the apparent affirmation of social and sexual differences within the church in texts such as Ephesians 5:22–23; 6:5–9; 1 Timothy 2:11–15?

6. Romans 9–11 is one of the most important New Testament passages dealing with the spiritual destiny of the people of Israel. From your study of these chapters, what is the relation between Israel and the church?

SUGGESTIONS FOR FURTHER READING

From Adventist writers

The doctrine of the church has been one of the least-developed aspects of Seventh-day Adventist theology. But although Adventist writers have devoted relatively little attention to the doctrine as such, certain aspects of it have received a good deal of study.

Ellen G. White discusses the nature of the church in several important passages, especially in some of her later works. She describes the purpose of God's call to Israel and the relation between Israel and the church in *Prophets and Kings*, pp. 15–22, 703–721. She considers the origin and destiny of the church in *Acts of the Apostles*, pp. 9–16, 593–602.

I know of no book-length discussion of the doctrine of the church by an Adventist writer, but there are several articles that deserve mention. One is Raoul Dederen, "Nature of the Church," in a supplement to *Ministry*, vol. 52, no. 2 (February 1978), pp. 24B–24F. Another is Charles Teel, Jr., "What Is Church?" in *Scope*, November–December 1978, pp. 12–17. Richard Rice argues for the importance of church fellowship in "Is Going to Church All That Important?" *Insight*, January 11, 1972.

Edward Heppenstall has done as much to shape Adventists' understanding of the covenants as any other thinker. For a statement of his views, see "The Covenants and the Law," in *Our Firm Foundation: A Report of the Seventh-day Adventist Bible Conference Held September 1–13, 1952* (2 vols.; Washington, D.C.: Review & Herald Publishing Association, 1953), 1:435–492.

Understandably, the topic of spiritual gifts, in particular the gift of prophecy, has stimulated extensive discussion among Adventist writers. There are numerous works supporting Ellen G. White's prophetic status. The standard textbook on the subject is T. Housel Jemison, *A Prophet Among You* (Mountain View, Calif.: Pacific Press Publishing Association, 1955). Similar works include Francis D. Nichol, *Why I Believe in Mrs. E. G.. White* (Washington, D.C.: Review and Herald Publishing Association, 1964), Denton E. Rebok, *Believe His Prophets* (Washington, D.C.: Review and Herald Publishing Association, 1956), and F. M. Wilcox, *The Testimony of Jesus: A Review of the Work and Teachings of Mrs. Ellen Gould White* (Washington, D.C.: Review and Herald Publishing Association, 1934). These and many other studies deal with the critical questions that Ellen G. White's ministry raises. Some of the more recent books and articles are mentioned in the footnotes to this chapter. The most extensive defense of Ellen G. White's prophetic status remains Francis D. Nichol, *Ellen G. White and Her Critics: An Answer to the Major*

Charges That Critics Have Brought Against Mrs. Ellen G. White (Washington, D.C.: Review and Herald Publishing Association, 1951). However, it appeared before some of the pressing questions of the current discussion were raised.

Three volumes have now appeared of Arthur L. White's projected six-volume biography of Ellen G. White, published by the Review and Herald Publishing Association: Volume 6, *The Later Elmshaven Years: 1905–1915* (1982); Volume 5, *The Early Elmshaven Years: 1900–1905* (1981); and Volume 4, *The Australian Years: 1891–1900* (1983).

From other writers

The literature on the subject of the church is vast, and much of it inaccessible to the average reader. Nevertheless, some very helpful works have appeared in recent years intended for a general audience. One is David Watson, *I Believe in the Church* (Grand Rapids, Mich.: William B. Eerdmans Publishing Co., 1978), which admirably covers the broad range of topics this doctrine involves.

C. Norman Kraus, a Mennonite theologian, explores the essential nature and purpose of Christian community in two readable works: *The Community of the Spirit* (Grand Rapids, Mich.: William B. Eerdmans Publishing Co., 1974) and *The Authentic Witness: Credibility and Authority* (Grand Rapids, Mich.: William B. Eerdmans Publishing Co., 1979).

Catholic theologian Hans Kung examines the question of church authority in his well-known work *Infallible? An Inquiry,* trans. Edward Quinn (New York: Image Books, 1972).

Rudolf Schnackenburg studies the early history and theology of the Christian church in *The Church in the New Testament,* trans. W. J. O'Hara (New York: Seabury Press, 1965). Eric G. Jay reviews developments in the concept of the church from the first to the twentieth centuries in *The Church: Its Changing Image Through Twenty Centuries* (Atlanta: John Knox Press, 1980).

Langdon Gilkey discusses the relation of the church to the world, specifically in America, in *How the Church Can Minister to the World Without Losing Itself* (New York: Harper & Row, Publishers, 1964).

10

THE MISSION
OF THE CHRISTIAN CHURCH

**Biblical
basis**

"I will give you as a light to the nations, that my salvation may reach to the end of the earth" (Isaiah 49:6).

"You shall be my witnesses in Jerusalem and in all Judea and Samaria and to the end of the earth" (Acts 1:8).

"Then I saw another angel flying in midheaven, with an eternal gospel to proclaim to those who dwell on earth, to every nation and tribe and tongue and people" (Revelation 14:6).

Matthew 10	Ephesians 4:5–6
Matthew 28:19–20	1 Timothy 2:4
John 17:20–21	1 Timothy 3:1–13; 4:6–5:22
Acts 2	2 Timothy 2:1–13; 3:14–4:5
Acts 6:1–6	Titus
1 Corinthians 14:40	2 Peter 3:9
Galatians 3:28	Revelation 12:17

We have looked at the basic portrait of the church in the New Testament and have explored what it means to call the church "the people of God" and "the body of Christ." This sets the stage for the most important part of the doctrine of the church: a consideration of the church's mission in the world.

The church is not merely a group of people united by common experiences, as significant as they may be. Nor does it exist primarily to celebrate its own existence, as worth celebrating as this is. The church exists to do something. Its life is its work. Everything about the church must find its ultimate justification in relation to this fundamental task.

THE SCOPE AND CONTENT OF CHRISTIAN MISSION

The essential work of the church is to continue the work of Christ himself. The ministry of Jesus did not end with his earthly life; it really just began. It continues in the community which he established. We noted earlier that the church is part of the gospel. It owes its origin to the special activity of Christ, and through it Christ continues the work of salvation in the world. In terms of our guiding theme, the purpose of the church is to display and extend the sovereignty of God in the world. To understand more fully what this means, we need to discuss both the purpose and scope of the church's mission, as well as its form and content.

The church bears witness to the reign of God in two important ways: by proclamation and by demonstration. It communicates a certain message about God, identifying who he is, describing what he is like, and explaining what he has done for human beings. In addition, it illustrates the truth of its message by the corporate life it establishes in the world.

The church's message

The basic message of the Christian church is that God acted in Jesus Christ for the salvation of all men. This assures human beings of God's love and care for them, and it expresses his intense desire for intimate, personal fellowship with them. There is also an exclusive element in this message, for Christians claim that salvation is available only in Jesus Christ. He provides our one and only avenue to God. According to the fourth Gospel, Jesus said, "No one comes to the Father, but by me" (Jn 14:6; cf. Ac 4:12). The mission of the church, then, presupposes the unique activity of God in Christ.

Christian mission also presupposes the importance of hearing about what God has done. It is not enough for God to have acted. In order for this activity to achieve its purpose, people must hear about it and respond to it. Only then can there be genuine fellowship between God and man. This is why the command to preach receives such emphasis in the New Testament. The gospel commission, as it is often called, is the climax of the Gospel according to Matthew (28:19–20), and according to Paul it is the preaching of Christ that generates faith

(Rom 10:17). Thus it is the proclamation of the gospel that makes the experience of salvation available.

The task of proclaiming the good news of what God has done in Jesus is the first duty of the church. Both the commands of Jesus and the record of the apostles' activities in Acts emphasize this. But it is also the church's greatest privilege. The apostles rejoiced in fulfilling their task by telling others what they had seen and heard (cf. 1 Cor 9:16). When something wonderful happens, it is natural to want to share it with other people (cf. Mk 5:19). Thus the experience of salvation naturally leads to the proclamation of the gospel (Ac 4:20).

The proclamation of the gospel includes several different things. One is the work of education. Jesus told his followers to "make disciples of all nations, . . . teaching them to observe all that I have commanded you" (Mt 28:19–20). Besides relating the good news, the apostles instructed those who accepted it about what it meant for their lives and organized them into congregations. Teaching was a major function of Paul's letters, for example. With one exception he sent them to churches or individuals with whom he had previously worked. The last part of each letter typically contains material about how Christians should live, now that they have received salvation. Education played an important part in Paul's ministry, and it is important to the mission of the church as a whole.

The scope of Christian mission is universal; the entire world is to hear the gospel. From Matthew to Revelation, the New Testament emphasizes the full extent of the church's task: "This gospel of the kingdom will be preached throughout the whole world" (Mt 24:14); "You shall be my witnesses . . . to the end of the earth" (Ac 1:8); "Then I saw another angel flying in midheaven, with an eternal gospel to proclaim to those who dwell on earth, to every nation and tribe and tongue and people" (Rev 14:6).

The scope of the church's mission

The scope of Christian mission is as large as the scope of Christ's work. It includes all mankind. The early Christian church took this responsibility with utmost seriousness. There are indications that Paul intended to cary the gospel himself to all the countries surrounding the Mediterranean Sea (cf. Rom 15:19, 24). In one place, the New Testament seems to indicate that the first generation of Christians reached the whole world with the gospel (Col 1:23).

It is important for us to remember that the mission of the church is intensive, as well as extensive. Its scope includes our present locations, as well as the distant parts of the earth. In the 1800s most "foreign missionaries" went from England and North America to other countries, and we tend to think of these other parts of the world as the "mission field." But the church faces its mission wherever there is unbelief. This certainly includes the secular, sophisticated, and largely decadent culture of the Western world. It includes the great cities of Europe and America. It may even include our own families.

The scope of its mission presents the Christian church today with a tremendous challenge. In fact, the number of people alive right now who have never heard the gospel is many times higher than the population of the entire world when Jesus lived. Not only that, but the proportion of the world's population that is Christian is steadily declining. The task facing the church becomes more formidable with every passing year.[1]

There is no way the church can meet this challenge with its present rate of activity. We may look hopefully to the speed of modern communication, with devices like television and satellites. We may encourage church leaders to formulate new evangelistic programs. We may calculate how quickly the work could be finished if each church member engaged in active witnessing. But the fact is that the church will never complete its mission with human means or human plans alone. Only a surge of spiritual power, like the one that launched the church at its beginning, will enable it to do the enormous work before it now.

THE SALVATION OF NON-CHRISTIANS

We noticed that the church's mission presupposes that Jesus is the only means of human salvation. We also described the tremendous challenge the church faces in communicating the gospel. These factors raise an important question: What is the fate of those who never hear the gospel? Can non-Christians be saved, or will they all be lost?

Christians seem to face a dilemma in answering this question. If non-Christians can be saved, then preaching the gospel doesn't seem to be as important as it first appeared. On the other hand, if non-Christians cannot be saved, then literally billions of people have no chance of salvation, and this is hard to reconcile with the love of God.

1. The most important Seventh-day Adventist publication to date on the topic of Christian mission is Gottfried Oosterwal, *Mission Possible: The Challenge of Mission Today* (Nashville, Tenn.: Southern Publishing Association, 1972). Oosterwal's concepts lie behind much of what I have said about mission.

When we ask about the salvation of non-Christians, it is important to formulate the question very clearly. The question is not whether God has some other means for saving sinners besides Jesus Christ. He doesn't. The New Testament is emphatic that Christ is the only means of salvation, so this is not the issue. The issue is whether a person must actually hear the gospel preached in order to be saved. In other words, can a human being receive the salvation God makes available in Jesus without an explicit knowledge of what he has done in Christ? There is evidence to support both positive and negative answers to this question.

Posing the question

Those who maintain that no one can be saved without actually hearing and responding to the gospel give several reasons for their position.[2] One is the biblical portrayal of Jesus as the exclusive source of salvation; another is the biblical emphasis on the importance of preaching, or evangelism (Rom 10:14–17). If people can be saved without hearing the gospel, they argue, there is little point in proclaiming it. In fact, there may even be reason not to. Hearing the gospel only increases a person's responsibility, so it may actually diminish rather than improve the hearer's chances of being saved. On the other hand, if people are doomed to be lost unless they hear the message of Christianity with their own ears, we have a powerful incentive for aggressive mission work, because our presentation of the gospel provides their only possible hope of salvation.

Evidence against the salvation of non-Christians

Those who believe that non-Christians may be saved without personally hearing the gospel also appeal to biblical evidence. The most important is the magnificent biblical theme sometimes referred to as "the universal salvific will of God." This is the very motive that accounts for the plan of salvation in the first place: God's ardent desire to save every human being. According to the Bible, God does not wish that any should perish (2 Pet 3:9). He "desires all men to be saved and to come to the knowledge of the truth" (1 Tim 2:4). This portrayal of God makes it difficult to imagine him rejecting billions who, through no fault of their own, never hear the gospel.

Evidence for the salvation of non-Christians

Other biblical themes also support the notion that non-Christians can be saved. One is the universality of divine revelation. According to the Bible, God has never left himself without witness (Ac 14:17). The

2. SDA theologian Edward Heppenstall presents a vigorous defense of this position in his lecture, "Has the Natural Man Access to God Apart From Jesus Christ or Special Revelation?" (The Edward Heppenstall Endowment Lecture [Loma Linda, California: Division of Religion, Loma Linda University, 1974]).

natural world bears the stamp of its maker, as it has ever since creation (Rom 1:20). True, the typical effect of this revelation has been to render men and women inexcusable in their sins (Rom 1:20), but God's hope was that human beings would seek him, "feel after him and find him" (Ac 17:27).

Another important theme is the universality of divine activity in human lives. The fourth Gospel describes Jesus as the "true light that enlightens every man" (Jn 1:9). This suggests that God is involved in every human life, imparting spiritual insight and influencing the person for good. Certainly the possibility exists that some will respond favorably to his activity.

Those who believe in the possible salvation of non-Christians also appeal to certain biblical passages describing the experience of similar individuals. The Syro-phoenician woman, with only a faint grasp of religious truth, exercised faith in Jesus (Mt 15:21–28). According to Acts 10, God accepted Cornelius, the centurion, before he had an opportunity to hear and respond to the preaching of the apostles. In addition, Christian missionaries have encountered self-sacrifice and deep religious devotion on the part of people who have never had contact with the gospel. These cases seem to show that non-Christians not only can but at times have responded positively to God's influence on their lives.

What the salvation of non-Christians means

The evidence both from the Bible and human experience thus supports the view that non-Christians can be saved even without having heard the gospel. Saying this, however, requires us to state clearly just what this position does not involve. As we said above, it does not involve the idea that God has some other means of saving people outside Christ. It simply means that in certain cases God can save individuals who do not have an explicit knowledge of Jesus. We should not say that such people are saved by "living up to all the light they have." This suggests that they are saved on the basis of their works, and no one can be saved by personal performance, with or without a knowledge of the gospel. Salvation is entirely a matter of divine grace.

The difference the gospel makes

In addition, the idea that non-Christians can be saved does not imply that Christian mission is superfluous, or unnecessary. There are two reasons for this. First, the fact that some non-Christians may be able to respond positively to God without having heard the gospel for themselves does not mean that all of them can. There may very well be people who do not respond to God without the gospel who might if they had a chance to hear it. Hearing the gospel will certainly enhance a person's perception of God and improve the chances that he will respond favorably to the offer of salvation.

Hearing the gospel also makes an important contribution to those who may have accepted salvation without it. An explicit knowledge of the gospel enriches our experience of God immeasurably. People who have known of Christ all their lives tend to forget this fact. It is easy to take for granted the portrait of God that Christianity provides and suppose that everyone thinks of him as loving and compassionate. Life without the gospel, however, is frequently a life of fear and insecurity. The gospel alone brings the complete assurance that we are accepted by God. So there is every reason to spread the gospel, even with the belief that some may be saved without having heard it.

The question of the salvation of non-Christians raises the further question of the status of non-Christian religions. This question is unavoidable in today's world. During this century the non-Christian portion of the world's population has increased. Our "shrinking planet" brings us into contact with other peoples and cultures. Many non-Christian religions have also become potent missionary forces themselves, even in such "Christian" countries as the United States of America.

Understanding non-Christian religions

We cannot give this question the attention it deserves here, but we can note several things that should characterize a Christian's attitude toward non-Christian religions. First of all, we need to study and understand other faiths. We cannot hope to present the gospel effectively to people without appreciating their own religious background.

We also need to recognize that non-Christian religions are not all alike. At their best, they reflect the highest of human aspirations and offer profound insights into the nature of reality. At their worst, they are demonic, keeping their adherents in ignorance and fear. But each religion deserves to be taken seriously and regarded in its best light. We should examine the highest expressions of other religions, and not concentrate on distorted forms they may assume in certain people's lives.

As we seek to understand other religions, we should not approach them with an attitude of smugness, or self-congratulation. Our confidence in the truth of Christianity justifies a sense of security, but not one of superiority. With the right attitude, we can engage in a real dialogue with members of other faiths. We can listen as well as speak. Various passages in Acts suggest that we point to elements of continuity between Christianity and non-Christian religions, as well as presenting their differences (Ac 17:22–31). The gospel incorporates the best of human insight, although it goes far beyond it with truth that requires special revelation.

THE SHAPE OF CHRISTIAN MISSION

We have considered the purpose and scope of Christian mission, and we have discussed a couple of important questions these topics raise. Now we must direct our attention to the form and content of the church's mission. We need to examine what happens as the church extends its community in the world. "Contextualization" is a helpful word for describing the shape of the church's mission.[3]

Contextualizing the Christian message

Contextualization involves two things. First, it implies that the presentation of the gospel should take into account the situation of the people to whom it is addressed. The witness a Christian bears to a university professor, for example, will be different from the one he bears to a migrant farm worker. The essential content of the message is the same, but the manner of presentation, the shape of the message, will vary depending on the audience. This is especially important in communicating the gospel from one culture to another. Certain forms of communication are effective in one society which another would consider outrageous, just as certain methods of evangelism may be effective in one period of American history and totally ineffective in another.

As we have described it, the mission of the church is to extend the reign of God in the world. It establishes a community of people who acknowledge God's authority and a situation where his will for human beings is enacted—where healing and love occur, where there is restoration and reconciliation. From the biblical concept that God created human beings in his image, we also learn that God's reign is not deterministic or totalitarian. God shares his sovereignty with us. He allows us to participate in his work. This suggests that there are aspects of the community the gospel creates that God does not establish by fiat. He allows us to participate in shaping the life of the church. This brings us to the second aspect of contextualization.

3. For a helpful discussion of contextualization, see C. Norman Kraus, *The Authentic Witness: Credibility and Authority* (Grand Rapids, Mich.: William B. Eerdmans Publishing Co., 1979), pp. 51–72. Chapter 2 of this book is entitled, "Contextualizing the Witness—The Discerning Community."

To contextualize the church in its mission is to adapt the shape of the community to the circumstances of the people. It requires us to recognize and respect the differences between cultures.

Stated in the negative, contextualizing the church's mission means refusing to impose the cultural forms of one society on people of another. Becoming a Christian, for example, does not necessarily mean learning to eat with a knife and fork, or wearing white shirts and ties, or building meeting places out of concrete blocks instead of wood and thatch.

The church's failure to contextualize its mission accounts in large measure for the bad name that Christian mission sometimes acquires. Mission work often went hand in hand with colonialism. In fact, some colonists regarded the missionary as a helpful ally in achieving their goals. His work often made it easier to subject people to economic exploitation. It is little wonder that certain leaders in developing countries today have little use for Christianity. They see it as an unpleasant reminder of their colonial past.

On the positive side, contextualization means allowing people to determine for themselves the shape of the Christian community in their culture. Unity in Christ does not require uniformity in Christian practice. More likely, it leads to a certain degree of diversity. From one culture to another, attitudes among church members may vary toward such things as religious music and appropriate dress. On a more substantive level, attitudes may even vary on such matters of policy as polygamy and the role of women in church leadership.

Contextualizing the Christian community

There is a solid biblical basis for contextualization in Christian mission. The doctrine of the incarnation provides the most important principle. To communicate God's love to the world, the Son assumed human nature. He came to human beings in their own form, submitting to the conditions of their existence and facing the same challenges and difficulties. The mission of the church requires a similar incarnation. The Christian community must assume cultural forms appropriate to the different peoples of the world.

The New Testament contains an interesting example of contextualization. At the church council described in Acts 15, early Christian leaders apparently agreed to ask Gentile converts to the church to refrain from eating meat that had been offered to idols (Ac 15:20). Yet in writing to the Christian church at Corinth some time later, Paul discussed the matter without any reference to the council's decision. He left the decision up to individual conscience (1 Cor 8). Here we have an instance where a matter of general church policy was revised in light of local circumstances.

Reasons for contextualization

THE RATIONALE FOR CHURCH ORGANIZATION

The historical reality of the church

The question of contextualization presupposes that the church should take an identifiable form in the world. The church is a spiritual reality. It owes its origin to God, and the presence of the Spirit determines the inner quality of its life. He creates an invisible bond of fellowship among its members. But the church is also a visible community. It is a social and historical reality as well as a spiritual one, and for this reason the church must have an organization, or structure.

The church needs organization for other reasons, too. The most important of these is its mission. To communicate the gospel, the church must depend on the cooperative efforts of all its members. Organization helps them to coordinate their efforts for maximum effectiveness. In fact, order should characterize everything the church does (1 Cor 14:40).

Different spiritual gifts

The church also needs organization because of the different gifts, or abilities, of its members (1 Cor 12). To allow every person the opportunity to manifest his gift, and to prevent church members from working at cross purposes with each other, organization is necessary. The apostles needed assistance in administering the financial affairs of the church to enable them to devote themselves to the ministry of the Word. For that purpose the office of deacon was created (Ac 6:1–6).

Church discipline

The occasional need for discipline within the church also calls for organization. According to the first Gospel, Jesus prescribed a rather well-defined pattern for dealing with a member who persisted in sin (Mt 18:15–17). Paul encouraged the Christians in Corinth to settle disputes among themselves, rather than taking them to courts of law (1 Cor 6:1–2), and he admonished the same congregation to expel a member whose scandalous sexual behavior threatened to bring reproach on the church (1 Cor 5:1–2). Such proceedings require organization.

The church's place in society

The church needs organization for external, as well as internal, reasons. As a social institution, the church exists in society alongside other institutions. Society contains economic, political, educational, judicial, and military organizations or structures, to name a few. In order to define its purpose over against those of other institutions, the church needs to be organized. It needs an identifiable form in the world.

There is no doubt that the church needs to be organized, but just how it should be organized is a much more difficult question. There are several factors that bear on the appropriate form of church organization. They do not define a precise structure, but they do point in a certain direction, and away from some unfortunate tendencies in church organization.

The lordship of Christ over the church should mold its organizational structure. As head of the church, which is his body, Christ is the supreme authority for the church. No organizational form should eclipse his sovereignty over his people. This excludes any view of church leadership which elevates human authority figures to unwarranted heights.

The priesthood of all believers is another idea that relates to church organization. This was one of the important concerns of the Reformation. It consists in the recognition that every church member has a spiritual ministry to perform. The clergy, or the ordained ministry, does not engage in a more privileged form of service than other members of the church, but merely a different one. All the members have spiritual gifts, and they all have an important contribution to make to the life of the church.

The same concept is a reminder that each individual has direct access to the mercy of God. Church organization is important, but not because the church controls our eternal destiny. The church is not a mediator between God and man. It does not dispense salvation to individuals. Recognizing this will prevent us from attaching too much importance to any particular structure for the church.

The importance of the church's mission also has implications for organization. It reminds us of the purpose of church organization. The church does not exist in order to perpetuate a certain structure; instead, the church is organized in order to facilitate its work. Every aspect of a church's organization must therefore be evaluated in light of its contribution to the overall mission of the church. This may lead to occasional revisions in its organization.

Sin is another theological concept that bears on church organization. Self-interest typically influences our behavior, even when we're convinced that our motives are the best. There is an unavoidable tendency to confuse our own desires with the welfare of the community as a whole. Consequently, we need to distribute power among a significant number of people in order to minimize its abuse.[4]

4. Reinhold Niebuhr makes this important point in these memorable words: "Man's capacity for justice makes democracy possible; but man's inclination to injustice makes democracy necessary" (*The Children of Light and the Children of*

THE FORMS OF CHURCH ORGANIZATION

The Christian church has taken many different forms of organization during its long history. Virtually all of them embody one, or a combination, of two fundamental types. One is the hierarchical type, and the other is the democratic type.[5]

Hierarchy

A hierarchical church structure concentrates power at the top level of church organization. Authority flows down at the discretion of its highest leaders. There is a lot of emphasis on structural continuity with the past, and a preoccupation with maintaining unity in the church. Typically, members of the clergy direct the affairs of the church.

The Roman Catholic Church provides a familiar example of hierarchical church organization. The pope is the single most powerful individual in the church. Catholics place him in a direct line of succession from Peter, whom they regard as the first bishop of Rome. They give the pope supreme authority in matters of doctrine, as well as administration.

Democracy

In a democratic form of church organization, authority resides with the general membership and flows from there upward to higher levels of organization. Church leaders are typically elected, rather than appointed, and there is strong emphasis on accountability. Laypersons usually take an active role in church leadership.

Many Protestant churches exhibit a congregational, or democratic, church structure. The basic organizational unit is the local church, which governs its own affairs. It selects and employs its own pastor, and it decides whether or not to join with other congregations to form larger organizational units, such as conferences or synods.

Each type of church structure has its advantages and disadvantages. Hierarchical church organizations insure a strong sense of unity and cohesiveness within the church. But they tend to emphasize the importance of the ordained ministry at the expense of the rest of the membership, and there tends to be a lack of accountability on the part of church leaders.

Darkness: A Vindication of Democracy and a Critique of Its Traditional Defense [New York: Charles Scribner's Sons, 1960], p. xiii).

5. Ron Walden describes these two organizational types in "How Hierarchical Views of the Church Emerge" (*Spectrum*, vol. 9, no. 2, pp. 20–21).

For their part, democratic church organizations encourage a sense of general responsibility among the membership and allow for considerable diversity within the church. But they often have difficulty cultivating a large-scale sense of unity, and they sometimes make it hard for ministers to exercise pastoral authority over the congregation.

The Seventh-day Adventist Church incorporates features from both types of church organization. The local church, or congregation, is the basic unit. A number of churches in a territory form a conference, and several conferences make up a union. The unions in one part of the world form a division, one part of the General Conference, which oversees the worldwide affairs of the church.

SDA Church organization

In the local church, the general members elect all the church officers with the exception of the pastor, who is appointed by the executive committee of the local conference and paid directly by the conference office. There are constituency meetings which elect church officers from the conference level up, the best-known of which is the General Conference session, which now meets every five years. Its delegates elect the president of the General Conference, along with its other officers.

On the local level, and to some extent on that of the conference, Seventh-day Adventist church organization exhibits features of a democratic church organization. From the conference level up, however, it takes on a more hierarchical form. This gives unity to the worldwide activity of the church and accounts, in large measure, for the vigorous mission program for which Seventh-day Adventists are known. This organizational pattern, however, tends to remove church officials from accountability to the general membership. The general membership participates actively in the affairs of the local church, but the proportion of laypersons to clergy steadily decreases with each step up the organizational ladder.

THE GOSPEL MINISTRY

The most important distinction in the structure of the church today is between the ministry and the general membership, or between the clergy and the laity, as they are often called. We need to consider what an ordained ministry means and what it does not mean. For the most part, Seventh-day Adventists share the perspective of Protestant Christians in general on this question.

Ministerial responsibilities

The work of the gospel ministry includes several components. The most important of these is the proclamation of the Word, or preaching. In fact, the word "preacher" is often synonymous with "minister." The basic task of the minister is to interpret the contents of the Bible and assist people in applying them to their lives. A closely related task is leadership in worship. This goes hand in hand with preaching, since the sermon is ordinarily the major component of the Protestant worship service.

Another important part of the minister's work is the "cure of souls," to use a traditional expression. This consists in ministering to people on a personal basis, particularly as they face important turning points in their lives. It often involves helping individuals resolve personal difficulties.

Administrative responsibilities tend to occupy more and more of a minister's time today. The typical pastor now devotes most of his time to directing the various activities of the church. In the Adventist church, the pastor is an ex officio leader in every organization, from the church board to the Pathfinder Club. He is often evaluated by the breadth of his interests and his enthusiasm for every aspect of church life.

The meaning of ministry

There is no biblical figure that corresponds precisely to the contemporary Protestant minister, but there are New Testament precedents for the role he fulfills. The earliest are Jesus' disciples. He sent them on missionary activities and directed them to serve others (Jn 21:15–17). Among the gifts of the Spirit to the church, Paul mentions prophets, evangelists, pastors, and teachers (Eph 4:11), and his letters also mention the leaders in local congregations. They distinguish between bishops and elders on the one hand, and deacons on the other (1 Tim 3:1–13; Tit 1:5–9). It is not exactly clear whether "bishops" and "elders" were the same in the New Testament, although evidence seems to support this view, but it was not until later that bishops had authority over an entire congregation.[6]

The presence of a professional ministry in the church means several things. It indicates that the church as a whole values the activities that ministers perform enough to support those who engage in them full time. But the primary reason for the ministry is theological. The ministry is important because what a church believes is important.

6. Kenneth A. Strand discusses this development in church history in "The Rise of the Monarchical Episcopate" (*Spectrum,* vol. 4 [1966], pp. 65–88). This article is reprinted as chapter 1 in *Three Essays on Early Church History with Emphasis on the Roman Province of Asia* (Ann Arbor, Mich.: Braun-Brumfield, 1967).

The primary task of the ministry is to interpret and apply the church's beliefs for the benefit of its members.

The work of the ministry is essential to the church's life. But this does not make the minister superior to other people, nor does the minister stand as an intermediary between God and man. Unlike a priest, the minister does not dispense the means of grace to a worshiping congregation. Each individual must develop a personal relationship to God. Finally, as the word itself implies, the basic purpose of the ministry is service; it is to render assistance to others. Mission, or evangelism, is the task of the whole people of God, not just of the clergy. Accordingly, when a congregation and its minister labor together, they are not helping him do his work; he is helping them do theirs.

This view of the ministry has implications for two important elements in the minister's experience. These are the "call" to the ministry and ordination to the ministry. Neither elevates a person to higher spiritual status, but each one underscores the importance of the ministry to the life of the Christian community.

The call to the ministry

In the thinking of some people, a "call" is synonymous with "a call to the ministry." They believe that ministers are different from everyone else because their work is more important than any other, and because God is less interested, or certainly less involved, in helping other people decide what to do with their lives. According to this concept, ministers, and only ministers, are divinely summoned to their work. Moreover, this summons usually arrives dramatically, not unlike the way biblical prophets were called (cf. Isa 6:8–10; Jer 1:4–10; Ezek 2:1–4).

In contrast to this popular view, the New Testament indicates that all Christians are "called." Indeed, to be "called" is part of what it means to be a Christian (e.g., Rom 8:28, 30; 1 Cor 1:9). Those who are called accept salvation and enter a new life in Christ, and they demonstrate their calling in daily life. This means that all of us are divinely called. God intends for us to represent him whatever we do for a living, and every line of work can be a means for serving the Lord. Negatively, then, a divine call is not essentially a dramatic summons extended only to those God wants to enter church work as a profession.

Positively, a specific call to the ministry involves four things.[7] First, it includes the call to be a Christian, which the minister shares

7. H. Richard Niebuhr describes these aspects of the ministerial call in *The Purpose of the Church and Its Ministry: Reflections on the Aims of Theological Education* (New York: Harper & Row, Publishers, 1956), p. 64.

with all members of the church. Second, there is a person's secret call, or the inner conviction by the Holy Spirit that God intends for him to devote his life to the gospel ministry. This, too, is similar to what others experience. Ideally, each Christian will feel that his occupation fulfills God's plan for his life.

Although many people will identify this secret call as *the* call to the ministry, the latter includes two more elements. Both involve a person's relationship to other people. One is the "providential" call. This is the possession of the abilities needed for success in the ministry. God does not call people to tasks for which they are unsuited. Or, to put it another way, God does not call someone to a certain work without giving him the qualifications to fulfill it and the opportunities to prepare for it adequately.

Finally, there is the "ecclesiastical" call. This is the recognition by the Christian community that a person has received a call from God to the gospel ministry. It is important not to over- or underestimate the importance of the ecclesiastical call. The call of the church does not replace the other dimensions of the ministerial call. As we have noticed, it does not confer superior spiritual status on someone. It simply acknowledges qualities and experiences that are already present. On the other hand, the ecclesiastical call is not incidental or inconsequential. When God calls a person to the ministry, he also leads members of the community to acknowledge this fact. So the response of other Christians to a person's sense of ministerial calling plays an important role in confirming or disproving its validity.

Ordination is the formal confirmation of a person's call to the ministry by the Christian community.[8] In many denominations, it follows a period of theological education, usually at a seminary or divinity school, and in the case of the Seventh-day Adventist Church it typically follows several years of ministerial experience, too.

Arguments for women's ordination

In recent years no aspect of church life has generated more discussion among various Christian communities than the question of women's ordination.[9] Among Seventh-day Adventists, too, opinion on the issue is sharply divided.

8. Raoul Dederen develops a Seventh-day Adventist perspective on the topic in "A Theology of Ordination," *Ministry,* vol. 52, no. 2 (February 1978), pp. 24K–24P.

9. For divergent approaches to this question by Seventh-day Adventists, see Willmore Eva, "Should Our Church Ordain Women? Yes," and Bernard E. Seton, "Should Our Church Ordain Women? No," as well as accompanying editorials in *Ministry,* vol. 58, no. 3 (March 1985), pp. 14–25.

People on both sides find support for their position in the Bible. Those in favor of ordaining women point out that both the biblical doctrines of creation and salvation affirm the equality of women. The first chapter of the Bible summarizes the creation of human beings with these words: "So God created man in his own image, in the image of God he created him; male and female he created them" (Gen 1:27). An important passage in Paul's writings describes the effects of salvation on conventional human distinctions: "For as many of you as were baptized into Christ have put on Christ. There is neither Jew nor Greek, there is neither slave nor free, there is neither male nor female; for you are all one in Christ Jesus" (Gal 3:27–28).

Besides affirming the fundamental equality of the sexes, the Bible also records the important role that women played in the history of Israel, the life of Jesus, and the experience of the early Christian community. Miriam, for example, took her place alongside Moses and Aaron as one of Israel's most significant leaders (Gen 15:20–2l; Mic 6:4), and Deborah was one of the "judges" of Israel (Jdg 4:4–6). The Gospels mention the significant role of women in Jesus' life. Evidently a number of women accompanied Jesus during his ministry (Mk 15: 40–41), and women were the first witnesses to his resurrection (Mt 28:1–10; Mk 16:1–8; Lk 24:1–12; Jn 20:11–18). Paul describes Priscilla and her husband Aquila as "my fellow workers" (Rom 16:3), and according to Acts, she helped instruct Apollos (18:26). Paul also identifies Phoebe as "a deaconness of the church at Cenchreae" (Rom 16:1), using the very same Greek word applied elsewhere to one of the orders of Christian ministry (Ac 6:1–6; 1 Tim 3:8–13).

Women have also played a prominent role in the Seventh-day Adventist community. Ellen G. White is indisputably the single most important figure in the history of the church, but other women have made significant contributions, too, in a variety of ministerial roles, including evangelism, pastoral ministry, and religious education. Indeed, it seems to many that women have already been called to the ministry in every sense mentioned above except the ecclesiastical one, and the church should recognize the fact by extending ordination to them as well.

Seventh-day Adventists who oppose the ordination of women also appeal to the Bible to support their position. They observe that there is no biblical command to ordain women, nor any record in the New Testament that women were ever ordained. In addition, there are several passages that seem to indicate that women are intended to occupy a place in human affairs that is distinct from, if not inferior to, that of men. After the fall, God assigned different responsibilities to

Arguments against women's ordination

Adam and Eve, and this suggests that men and women have different roles to play (Gen 3:16–19; cf. 1 Cor 11:3–9). The priesthood of Israel was exclusively a male province (Ex 28:1, 41), and the people Jesus himself ordained to lead the early church were all men (Mk 3:14; Jn 15:16). In addition, Paul counsels against permitting women to teach in public, or exercise authority over men (1 Tim 2:11–15).

Another argument used against the ordination of women is the necessity for uniform church order. Various cultures exclude women from positions of authority, so it would be impossible to ordain women in certain parts of the world without creating a scandal and threatening the work of the church. In order to maintain church unity, therefore, Seventh-day Adventists should not ordain women anywhere in the world, according to this reasoning.[10]

Besides giving different answers to the question of women's ordination, Seventh-day Adventists also have different opinions as to the importance of the issue. To some, it involves an incidental feature of church polity, and it must not distract church members from fulfilling their basic mission in the world. To others, it relates to the very heart of that mission. As they see it, the issue is ultimately whether or not the church will put into practice its theological commitment to the gospel, which affirms the equality and dignity of all human beings. Clearly, the issue of women's ordination presents the church today with a tremendous challenge, both socially and theologically. The church's response to this question will have far-reaching consequences of great importance.[11]

THE QUESTION OF THE TRUE CHURCH

Divisions in Christianity

The mission of the church led us to consider the visible structure, or organization, of the church, but we have said nothing so far about the most obvious feature of Christianity today. This is the fact that it exhibits an enormous variety of forms. There are the great divisions

10. The 1974 Annual Council of the General Conference of Seventh-day Adventists voted "To record our opinion that because the Seventh-day Adventist Church is a world church which includes in its fellowship peoples of all nations and cultures, and because a survey of its world divisions reveals that the time is not ripe nor opportune, therefore, in the interest of the world unity of the church, no move be made in the direction of ordaining women to the gospel ministry" (quoted in Dederen, "A Theology of Ordination," p. 240).

11. At the time of this writing, the General Conference of Seventh-day Adventists is scheduled to express a decision on this issue at its meeting in the summer of 1985.

among Eastern Orthodoxy, Roman Catholicism, and Protestantism, and there are further divisions within Protestantism. The Lutheran and Reformed streams diverge on many different points, and numerous organizations have developed still further from the roots of the Reformation. There are also a number of religious groups whose status as Christian is debatable. Usually referred to as "cults," they bear only marginal resemblance to other Christian bodies and typically value their independence very highly.[12]

The divisions within Christianity have occasioned great concern among Christians in recent years. The ecumenical movement arises from the conviction that these divisions are a reproach to the name of Christ, and its goal is to achieve the unity for which Jesus prayed among his disciples (Jn 17:21). Ecumenists promote dialogue among religious groups and encourage different organizations to consolidate. Other Christians resist such efforts; they feel that the inevitable price of such unity will be doctrinal compromise and a loss of spiritual vitality. They value their distinctive points of faith and practice too highly to downplay their significance. Smaller organizations, in particular, fear that their identity would be lost in such unions.

Attitudes toward Christian diversity

The diversity of Christian organizations raises the perplexing question of the one true church. There are two contrasting ways of answering this. One is to relativize the significance of organizational diversity; the other is to absolutize it. According to the first, all Christian groups are equally valid as expressions of the one true church. None of them embodies it exclusively. It doesn't really matter, then, which church you belong to, as long as you participate in the congregational life of some Christian community.

The alternative approach identifies the one true church with a specific Christian organization. One visible entity serves as Christ's official representative in the world and is the primary means through which salvation becomes available to human beings. Naturally, in this view, which church you belong to is a matter of extreme importance. Salvation may be theoretically possible for people not connected with the right church, but they cannot hope to enjoy all the benefits of full-fledged members. A further consequence of this view is the judgment that other Christian groups are "false" churches. If any of their

12. Anthony A. Hoekema describes the distinctive traits of the cult in *The Four Major Cults* (Grand Rapids, Mich.: William B. Eerdmans Publishing Co., 1963), pp. 377–88. The four religious groups Hoekema discusses are Mormonism, Seventh-day Adventism, Christian Science, and Jehovah's Witnesses. He recognizes that his description of Seventh-day Adventism as a cult is controversial (pp. 388–403).

members are saved, it will be in spite of their teachings, not because of them.

For the most part, these two positions represent extremes in the thinking of Christians today. In most minds, existing Christian organizations represent the one true church with varying degrees of adequacy. Some are closer to the ideal than others, and some may be aberrations of genuine Christianity. But, they feel, no one organization can claim to be the "true church." It even sounds arrogant to suggest the idea.

Christian unity in the New Testament

The kind of division facing us today was not a problem in the time of the New Testament. Rival organizations did not yet exist, so we do not find in the Bible a clearly stated answer to our particular question. Nonetheless, Christian unity was a matter of great concern to the apostles, and there are numerous passages which deal with it.

Paul's letters emphasize two aspects of unity in the church. One is the identity which members share by virtue of their common experience of salvation in Christ. This is the dominant theme in the first part of his letter to the Ephesians, for example, where he argues that Christ has broken down the dividing wall between Jews and Gentiles (Eph 2:14–16). He makes the same point in Galatians, where we find the ringing statement, "There is neither Jew nor Greek, there is neither slave nor free, there is neither male nor female; for you are all one in Christ Jesus" (Gal 3:28).

The second aspect of Christian unity is a consequence of the first; it is the attitude of fellowship and love toward other members of the church (Eph 4:2–3). In the great hymn of 1 Corinthians 13, Paul presents love as the solution to discord within the church. Earlier in the same letter he bemoans the rivalry between different Christian factions, or parties, in the same congregation (1 Cor 1:10–13; 3:3–7).

For Paul, the things that unite Christians are much more fundamental than the differences among them: "There is one body and one Spirit, just as you were called to the one hope . . . one Lord, one faith, one baptism, one God and Father of us all" (Eph 4:4–6).

The church visible and invisible

A prevalent way of responding to the problem of Christian division is to employ the venerable distinction between the visible and the invisible church.[13] The invisible church includes all who are truly

13. According to John Calvin, for example, "the church includes not only the saints presently living on earth, but all the elect from the beginning of the world. Often, however, the name 'church' designates the whole multitude of men spread over the

dedicated to Christ, as opposed to the merely "nominal" members of the church. The visible church is a "sign" of the invisible church, but it is by no means identical to it. Although affiliation with the visible church is important, membership in the invisible church is what really counts.

This distinction is helpful because it prevents us from exaggerating the significance of any specific organization or structure, but it tends to obscure the importance of several things. One is active participation in a concrete fellowship of believers. Another is doctrinal correctness. A third is the concrete embodiment of authentic Christian community. All of these are essential components in the life of a Christian, and minimizing their significance detracts from Christian experience.

Many of these considerations play a role in the approach of Seventh-day Adventists to the question of the true church. In general, we can characterize the Adventist position as one which affirms the distinctiveness of Seventh-day Adventism within Christianity, but does not absolutize it. Seventh-day Adventists claim to have a specific role to fulfill in the plan of salvation, but they do not believe that this excludes non-Adventists from salvation. They see elements of continuity, as well as discontinuity, in their relation to other Christian groups.

Seventh-day Adventists have always described themselves as Protestants. They consider themselves to be part of the great stream within Christianity which began four hundred years ago in the attempt to recover the essential message of the New Testament. Indeed, they view their particular task as a continuation of the work of reform that began at that time. The Reformers insisted on the Bible alone as the rule of faith and practice. Seventh-day Adventists agree. Their insistence on observing the seventh-day sabbath, for example, is an application of this principle to the question of the appropriate day for Christian worship. Seventh-day Adventists affirm many of the concerns of other Christians and share almost all of their beliefs with members of other Christian groups. They see, in the general history of Christianity, the record of God's saving activity for human salvation.

Seventh-day Adventists and other Christian groups

---

earth who profess to worship one God and Christ. . . . In this church are mingled many hypocrites who have nothing of Christ but the name and outward appearance" (*Institutes of the Christian Religion,* IV.i.7, trans. Ford Lewis Battles [Philadelphia: The Westminster Press, 1960)], p. 1021). A. T. Hanson presents a brief discussion of the distinction in his article, "Invisible Church, Visible Church" (Alan Richardson, ed., *A Dictionary of Christian Theology* [Philadelphia: The Westminster Press, 1969], pp. 173–175).

Seventh-day Adventists also approve of the missionary activity of other Christian organizations. In the words of one official document, they "recognize every agency that lifts up Christ before men as a part of the divine plan for the evangelization of the world."[14] Thus they see themselves as part of a larger divine plan for worldwide evangelism.

But these elements of continuity have not led Seventh-day Adventists to seek organizational consolidation with other Christians; in fact, they are generally suspicious of the ecumenical movement. This is due to the discontinuity created by a strong sense of uniqueness. Adventists believe that they are the "remnant" destined to bear God's final message to the world before the return of Christ.

The remnant

The remnant is an important biblical concept. In one sense, it refers to the Israelites who survived national catastrophe; in another sense, it refers to a group who will receive the promises of God to his people (Jer 23:3; 31:7). Paul applies the term to those who believe in Christ (Rom 11:5). Revelation describes the remnant of the woman's seed—that is, the church—as those who keep the commandments of God and have the testimony of Jesus Christ (Rev 12:17).

Seventh-day Adventists believe that they are the remnant referred to in Revelation because of the circumstances of their origin and their distinguishing doctrinal features. The prophecies of the Bible indicate that Adventism has come into existence during the final phase of human history. Adventists' concern for the sabbath displays a special commitment to the commandments of God, and the presence of the spirit of prophecy in their midst in the form of Ellen White's ministry is a manifestation of the testimony of Jesus mentioned in Revelation (12:17; cf. 19:10; 22:8–9).

Three angels' messages

Seventh-day Adventists also believe that they have something of utmost importance to communicate to the world. This proclamation embodies the messages of the three angels recorded in Revelation 14:6–12, so it includes a call to worship God the creator in view of the fact that the judgment has begun. It also includes a call to turn from the practices of a corrupt religious system and avoid the punishment of those who oppose God. Adventists believe that this constitutes God's final warning to a world that has largely rejected his

14. *Constitution, Bylaws, and Working Policy of the General Conference of Seventh-day Adventists,* rev. ed., October 1970, p. 185; quoted in Gottfried Oosterwal, *Mission Possible: The Challenge of Mission Today* (Nashville, Tenn.: Southern Publishing Association, 1972), p. 82.

grace. It directly precedes Christ's return to save his people from the earth.

In recent discussions certain Adventists argue that the biblical concept of "remnant" includes more than doctrinal purity. It also involves a deep sense of social responsibility. Consequently, they maintain that Seventh-day Adventists must take a more aggressive position on important social issues in order to fulfill the role of the remnant.[15]

Supporters of this view cite the strong appeals for justice we find in the prophets (Am 5:24), along with their promises that God will eventually relieve the suffering of the poor and oppressed (Isa 61:1–3). They note that Jesus applied such prophecies to his own ministry (cf. Lk 4:16–21) and displayed a remarkable concern for the downtrodden people of his day (Lk 15:1–2). And they observe that the book of Revelation protests the corrupt and intolerant institutions that persecute God's people (Rev 12–13). This line of thought enlarges the conventional view of the work of the remnant church. It calls Seventh-day Adventists to bear a witness in the world that takes into account all the dimensions of human existence—social and even political, as well as doctrinal and personal.

Their special sense of mission characteristically leads Seventh-day Adventists to emphasize their differences, rather than their similarities, to other Christian organizations. Recently there have been attempts to find more positive ways to express this relationship. One suggestion is to think of the Seventh-day Adventist Church as a prophetic minority within the larger Christian community.[16]

A prophet is a member of a community who bears a message from God, a message often critical of the community and typically calling for drastic changes in its thought and life. But although he plays a distinctive role, the status of the prophet is one of service rather than privilege. The content of his mission, negative though it is at times, expresses God's concern for all his people. It indicates that he has not rejected them, but still hopes for their salvation.

Prophetic ministry

Taking this as a model for the work of the Adventist church supports a strong sense of mission while also affirming God's interest in all his people—indeed, for all the people of the world. Seventh-day Adventists, therefore, have no basis for indulging in self-congratulation or excluding themselves from other people. To the contrary, they should

15. Charles Scriven, "The 'Remnant' and the Church: A Reconsideration" (unpublished paper; April 1985).

16. This is Jack Provonsha's approach in "The Church as a Prophetic Minority," *Spectrum,* vol. 12, no. 1, pp. 18–23.

cultivate a sense of fellowship with members of other churches. Moreover, some suggest, recalling the central concerns of the biblical prophets may arouse Adventists to bear a more vigorous witness against the evils of society. This type of witness may involve a departure from traditional political conservativism.

There are ways for Seventh-day Adventists to conceive their role in history which affirm their distinctive sense of mission, but manage to avoid the unfortunate and unproductive tendency to exclusiveness.

STUDY HELPS

Questions for review

1. What is the nature and purpose of the church's mission?

2. What are the arguments for and against the idea that non-Christians can be saved?

3. What does it mean for the church to "contextualize" its mission?

4. Why should the church be organized and what major forms does church organization take?

5. What is the role of Christian ministers?

6. What does it mean to describe the Seventh-day Adventist Church as a "remnant" and as a "prophetic minority"?

Questions for discussion

1. A famous Indian once said, "I have too much respect for the teachings of Christ to be a Christian." Conditions in the church often contradict the teachings of the Bible. When should this lead Christians to break with the established church(es) and set up a new organization?

2. When should a church member be disfellowshipped? Is behavior or belief a more pressing reason for such action? Who should decide when a person no longer belongs in the church: church administrators, local church members, or the individual involved?

3. Evaluate the evangelistic potential of the following means (along with others you may think of): motion pictures, television programs (series and specials); videotapes; athletic organizations (e.g., Athletes in Action); musical groups; radio and television commercials; newspaper and magazine advertisements; direct mailing;

Christian entertainers and political leaders speaking out about their beliefs.

4. The membership of the Seventh-day Adventist Church in North America is growing much more rapidly among black and Hispanic than among white portions of the population. Why is this the case?

5. Traditionally the leaders of the Seventh-day Adventist Church on the General Conference level have been predominantly North American (as well as male and white). Now over eighty percent of the church's membership lives outside North America, while members in North America provide most of the church's financial support. Should the makeup of the church's world leadership reflect the distribution of its membership or of its financial resources?

6. There are those who believe that the election of SDA church officers above the local church level should involve more of the general church membership. Some even suggest having more than one candidate for each office to create a genuine choice. Assess the potential advantages and disadvantages of such developments.

7. How should Seventh-day Adventists relate to members of other Christian churches who have a strong relationship with God? How should they relate to such people who belong to non-Christian religions?

1. Outline the steps church discipline should follow, according to Matthew 18:15–17.

Suggestions for Bible study

2. Paul's sermon in Athens is often described as an evangelistic failure because it resulted in few conversions and because he left for Corinth determined to know nothing "except Jesus Christ and him crucified" (1 Corinthians 2:2). From your study of Acts 17:22–34 and the knowledge you may have of ancient Greece, what do you think of this view?

3. Make a study of the word "bishop," using Bible commentaries and dictionaries, along with books on church history. What does this word mean when it appears in Philippians 1:1, 1 Timothy 3:1–2, and Titus 1:7? How was it used in the later Christian church?

4. The New Testament books of 1 and 2 Timothy and Titus are known as the "Pastoral Epistles" because they present Paul's counsel to

two of his proteges who became important church leaders. These letters give us valuable insights into the conditions and concerns of early Christians. What do we learn about the following topics from the designated portions of these letters?

    a. The responsibilities of ministers (1 Timothy 1:3–5; 2:1–2; 4:6–5:2; 5:19–22; 2 Timothy 1:13–14; 2:14–16; 4:1–5; Titus 1:5, 13; 2:1–10; 3:8–11)

    b. The qualifications of local church leaders (1 Timothy 3:1–13; 5:17–22; Titus 1:5–9)

    c. The welfare program of the church (1 Timothy 3:3–15; cf. Acts 4:32; 6:1)

5. According to the following biblical passages, what is the significance of ordination? Mark 3:14–15; Acts 6:6; 13:2–3; 14:23; 1 Tim 4:14 (cf. 2 Timothy 1:6); 1 Timothy 5:22

6. Early Christians were obliged to make a number of important decisions. How did they resolve the issue at hand in each of the following passages?

    a. Acts 1:15–26

    b. Acts 6:1–6

    c. Acts 15:1–29

7. What do we learn about the work of evangelism from the "Missionary Discourse," as it is sometimes called, which Jesus delivered to his disciples (Matthew 10:5–42)? Who is responsible for it? What are their duties, privileges, and liabilities?

SUGGESTIONS FOR FURTHER READING

From Adventist writers

In a sense, all that Ellen G. White wrote is related to the church. Her longest work, for example, is a collection of writings entitled *Testimonies for the Church,* whose nine volumes in one way or another deal with virtually every facet of this doctrine. The books *Evangelism, Gospel Workers,* and *Testimonies to Ministers* are shorter compilations of her writings devoted to the life, work, and organization of the church. In more general terms, she discusses the mission and ministry of the church in the following passages: *Desire of Ages,* pp. 818–828; *Acts of the Apostles,* pp. 17–34.

    Gottfried Oosterwal's book *Mission Possible: The Challenge of Mission Today* (Nashville, Tenn.: Southern Publishing Association, 1972) is the single most important Adventist book on this important topic. A special section of *Spectrum,* vol. 12, no. 3 (pp. 2–31), contains articles discussing various aspects of the contemporary task of Christian mission. Russell Staples' article "Must Polygamists Divorce?" (*Spectrum,* vol. 13, no. 1, pp. 44–53) raises the question of contextualization in the mission work of the Seventh-day Adventist Church.

Raoul Dederen presents "A Theology of Ordination" in a supplement to *Ministry,* vol. 52, no. 2 (February 1978), pp. 24K–24P. A discussion of "The Ministry of Women," including a description of the 1974 Annual Council action on the role of women in the church, follows this piece. Janice Eiseman Daffern deals with the urgent question of the ordination of women to the ministry in "How Long Must Women Wait? Prospects for Adventist Church Leadership," *Spectrum,* vol. 12, no. 4, pp. 39–43.

Seventh-day Adventists have devoted increasing attention in recent years to questions of church organization and polity. The *Church Manual,* issued by the General Conference of Seventh-day Adventists and periodically revised, contains the basic description of Seventh-day Adventist church organization and government. Ron Walden examines recent developments in church polity in light of hierarchical and congregational models of church organization in "How Hierarchical Views of the Church Emerge" (*Spectrum,* vol. 9, no. 2, pp. 16–22). Within the space of a year and a half, *Spectrum* devoted special sections in two issues to questions of church government: "Reshaping the North American Division" (vol. 13, no. 1, pp. 2–35), and "A Call for an Open Church" (vol. 14, no. 4, pp. 14–53).

Jack W. Provonsha proposes a model for relating the Seventh-day Adventist Church to other Christian groups in "The Church as a Prophetic Minority," *Spectrum,* vol. 12, no. 1, pp. 18–23.

Gerhard F. Hasel analyzes the biblical concept of the remnant in *The Remnant: The History and Theology of the Remnant Idea from Genesis to Isaiah* (3d ed.; Berrien Springs, Mich.: Andrews University Press, 1980).

From other writers

A particularly readable analysis of the relation between Christianity and other religions is Norman Anderson, *Christianity and World Religions* (Downers Grove, Ill.: Inter-Varsity Press, 1984), which concludes that Christianity is decisively unque among the world's great religions. Hendrik Kraemer presents a similar thesis in *Why Christianity of All Religions?* trans. Hubert Hoskins (Philadelphia: The Westminster Press, 1962). Different answers to the question of Christianity's uniqueness appear in E. L. Allen, *Christianity Among the Religions* (Boston: Beacon Press, 1960), and J. H. Bavinck, *The Church Between the Temple and the Mosque: A Study of the Relationship Between the Christian Faith and Other Religions* (Grand Rapids, Mich.: William B. Eerdmans Publishing Co., n.d.).

Two challenging but readable books by H. Richard Niebuhr have become classics in the area of church and society. *Christ and Culture* (New York: Harper & Row, Publishers, 1951) explores five different models for conceiving the relations between Christianity and civilization. *The Social Sources of*

Denominationalism (New York: The World Publishing Company, 1957) applies the famous categories of Ernst Troeltsch and Max Weber—sect, church, and denomination—to the various forms Christianity has taken in America.

11

MEMBERS OF THE CHRISTIAN CHURCH: THEIR SPIRITUAL STATUS

Biblical basis

"Jesus answered him, 'Truly, truly, I say to you, unless one is born anew, he cannot see the kingdom of God' " (John 3:3, 5).

"For by grace you have been saved through faith; and this is not your own doing, it is the gift of God—not because of works, lest any man should boast" (Ephesians 2:8–9).

"No one born of God commits sin; for God's nature abides in him, and he cannot sin because he is born of God" (1 John 3:9).

Genesis 15:6	1 Corinthians 1:29–31
Psalm 32:1–5	1 Corinthians 6:11
Psalm 51	Galatians 3–5
Psalm 130	Ephesians 2–3
Isaiah 55:6–7	1 Thessalonians 5:22–23
Ezekiel 33:10–16	Hebrews 10:26–31
Luke 18:9–14	James 2:14–26
John 3:1–8	2 Peter 1:3–11
John 8:31–36	1 John 1:5–2:17; 3
Romans 3:21–8:39	

In chapter 9, we examined two of the important symbols for the church in the New Testament. We saw that the "people of God" points to the church's role in the history of salvation, and the "body of Christ" illuminates the relationship between Christ and the church as well as the relationships among church members themselves.

Symbols for salvation

The New Testament also employs a number of symbols to identify or characterize the members of the church. They indicate in different ways what happens to those who experience salvation and help us to understand what it is that makes Christians unique.

Some of these symbols describe the experience of salvation as a change in our basic relationship to God. This is true of expressions like "justification" and "adoption." Another group points to a transformation that takes place within a person, a change in attitude or orientation. Some of these focus on God's activity, such as "new birth," "recreation," and "resurrection," and some of them focus on the human role, such as "repentance," and "faith." Others, like "conversion," simply refer to the experience of change as a whole. In addition, there are descriptions of salvation as a change in behavior, or lifestyle. Among them are "life in the Spirit" and "life in Christ."

We cannot do justice to these rich and varied descriptions here, but a few of them have become virtually synonymous with different aspects of the experience of salvation and require careful consideration. Three of these are "new birth," "justification," and "sanctification."

We typically associate these expressions with different experiences, or with different phases in the overall experience of salvation. But this is not entirely accurate, for the experience of salvation is a unity. Even though it has distinguishable facets, it is one comprehensive experience, rather than a series of different experiences. So it would be more accurate to think of these different terms as descriptions of salvation as a whole, rather than as references to different parts of it. A similar situation exists with the biblical descriptions of human beings. As we noticed in an earlier chapter, the Bible employs different terms to describe man, such as "soul" and "body." But each expression refers to the person as a whole, not just to part of him. Similarly, the descriptions of salvation each refer to the entire experience, rather than to part of it. Although they view it from different perspectives, they point to the experience as a whole.

THE NEW BIRTH

The expression "born again" appears in John's account of Jesus' conversation with the Jewish leader Nicodemus (3:3, 5). On that occasion Jesus used the term to emphasize the dramatic change required for entrance into the kingdom of God. It suggests that the experience of salvation involves a total transformation, nothing less than a completely new start in life, a totally new identity. The expression also points to the fact that this experience is the result of divine activity. The Greek for "born again" can also be translated, "born from above." Jesus also said that one must be born "of the Spirit" to enter the kingdom of God. The term thus reminds us of God's initiative in the work of salvation.

Jesus further described the new birth by invoking the symbol of the wind. We can hear and feel the wind, but we don't know "whence it comes or whither it goes" (Jn 3:8). This points to the mysterious nature of the new birth experience. Its beginnings may be imperceptible, but it is still real; and, like the wind, it has tangible consequences. Similarly, a person who has been born again may not be able to pinpoint the moment the experience occurred, but the evidence of his life will show that it has taken place.

In some respects, the new birth experience is like falling in love. There may be such a thing as "love at first sight," but for most people, coming to love someone is a gradual process that takes place over a period of time. Typically, a person becomes aware that the experience has already happened. He knows he is in love, but he doesn't know exactly how or when it started.

JUSTIFICATION: SALVATION BY FAITH

None of the New Testament decriptions of salvation has generated more discussion in the history of the church than "justification." For many people it is not a symbol of salvation; it is a precise description of the experience. The term figures prominently in Paul's doctrinal discussions, particularly in Romans and Galatians. If you know what Paul means by "justification," you have grasped the central element in his understanding of salvation, and, in the opinion of many, you know what the gospel is all about.

The word itself is a legal term, conjuring up images of courts and judges. If you have ever been to court yourself, you probably found the experience a sobering one. Important issues are settled in court. What happens there often determines the course of a person's entire life.

As Paul uses the term, "justification" is a judicial act. It is what a judge does in a court of law when he renders a verdict of "not guilty." He declares a person innocent of the charges against him. Justification is the opposite of condemnation (cf. Rom 8:33–34).

The central question in the book of Romans is how a person can obtain a verdict of "not guilty" when he stands before God, the judge of the universe. In other words, how can we obtain justification?

The thesis of Paul's position is that justification, or righteousness, is entirely the gift of God. By grace he makes it available to us in Jesus Christ, and we receive it by faith—that is, by trusting him. To use his own words, "By grace you have been saved through faith; and this is not your own doing, it is the gift of God" (Eph 2:8). Paul makes the same point in two of the important summary statements in Romans: "Therefore, since we are justified by faith, we have peace with God through our Lord Jesus Christ" (5:1); "There is therefore now no condemnation for those who are in Christ Jesus" (8:1).

Each element in this description deserves further attention. "Grace" is the divine characteristic which motivates God to extend salvation to sinners. It is often defined as "unmerited favor." This quality about God becomes particularly evident in his treatment of the unworthy: he is generous toward those who are utterly undeserving of his favor. In fact, grace abounds in response to sin (Rom 5:20).

Justification as a gift

The idea of "gift" is closely related to grace. The content of God's gift is Jesus Christ and all the things that he makes available. His death is the means of our salvation (Rom 3:25; 5:9). He is "our wisdom, our righteousness and sanctification and redemption" (1 Cor 1:30). He is the source of various gifts to the church (Eph 4:11–12), and he is the one from whom the Spirit comes to us.

"Gift" may be the single most important word in helping us grasp Paul's understanding of salvation. The bestowal of a gift depends entirely on the attitude of the giver. A gift is not earned; it is not payment for work well done. If you agree to paint someone's house for a certain price and he pays you for the job, you don't view the money as a gift. After all, you are entitled to it. You earned it.

A gift is not a reward, either. You may not earn a reward, in the strict sense of the word, but you typically do something that merits special attention. Suppose you return a lost wallet containing a sizable amount of cash. The owner may give you fifty dollars out of gratitude for your consideration and honesty. You didn't really earn the money, but to some extent you deserved it. You did something to make him feel grateful to you.

A gift is different from both payment and reward because the recipient does nothing to deserve it. Only the giver's generosity explains it. In fact, anything the receiver does to offset the expense of the gift or contribute to its purchase destroys the quality of the transaction, reducing it to the level of a financial exchange and altering the relationship it establishes. Such a response may even suggest a lack of gratitude on the part of the recipient.

Suppose you need open heart surgery and don't have a dime to your name. A wealthy friend learns of your plight and takes care of all the expenses. He makes it clear that there are no strings attached; he just wants to see you alive and well. How would he feel if you sent him twenty dollars as "your part of the cost"? Would he appreciate it? Not likely. This paltry sum is nothing compared to the magnitude of his gift, and your sending it would only indicate that you don't understand the value of what he did for you. Only one response is appropriate: sheer gratitude. Any effort on your part to defray the expense would only insult the giver.

For Paul, salvation is entirely the gift of God; there is nothing about us that deserves it. The only appropriate response is to accept it with a full and grateful heart. The word "faith" describes our part in the experience of salvation. As Paul uses it, the word means "trust"— trust in God to give us salvation, since we could never obtain it on our own.

"Faith" is one of the most important terms in Christian theology. **The meaning** It lies at the heart of Paul's doctrine of salvation, and it is often iden- **of faith** tified as the essential condition, or the one indispensable requirement, for salvation. To comprehend the nature of salvation, we need a clear understanding of the meaning of faith.

To begin with, faith in a Christian sense is always directed toward a specific object. It is never merely faith; it is faith *in* something—or, better, faith in some*one.* The validity of faith depends on the trustworthiness of its object. According to the New Testament, saving faith is faith in God, or faith in Jesus Christ. Everything depends on trusting the right person.

In the second place, faith is always receptive in character. It is not a virtue we develop on our own and offer to God; it is a response to God's gracious offer of salvation to us. He takes the initiative.

Third, faith is an intelligent decision, involving both the mind and the will. Faith is based on evidence. It is not a blind leap in the dark, but an intelligent response to the many indications that God deserves our trust. Faith is trust in God because he deserves to be trusted.

At the same time, faith goes beyond the available evidence, because it involves total commitment—unconditional trust in its object. The evidence on which faith is based is never compelling; it never forces us to decide one way or another. It simply makes possible an intelligent decision. This limitation is important, because it preserves our freedom to choose. If the evidence were overwhelming, there would be no room for choice; our response to God would be totally determined. As it is, the evidence is sufficient for an intelligent decision, but not enough to eliminate freedom of choice.

We can summarize this brief analysis of faith with the following statement: We receive salvation by trusting God freely and completely in response to evidence that is sufficient but not coercive.

LEGALISM: SALVATION BY WORKS

Paul develops his understanding of salvation in direct and deliberate contrast to a drastically different approach. Instead of accepting righteousness as a divine gift, many people regard it as a human achievement and try to work for it. If terms like "grace," "gift," "Jesus Christ," and "faith" describe the way of salvation that God makes available, expressions like "works," "law," "boasting," and "our own righteousness" describe its great rival in the experience of many human beings.

"Legalism" is the well-known name for this other approach to salvation. It consists in the attempt to gain righteousness by successfully keeping the law. These efforts lead to "our own righteousness" (Rom 10:3; Phil 3:9), and provide a basis for "boasting" (Rom 3:27). Works-righteousness, then, is the great antithesis to righteousness by faith.

According to Paul, legalism and righteousness by faith are completely opposed to each other. He insists that we receive righteousness as a divine gift, independent of the law: "For we hold that a man is justified by faith apart from works of law" (Rom 3:28); "For no human being will be justified in his sight by works of law" (3:20); "But now the righteousness of God has been manifested apart from law" (3:21); "For God has done what the law, weakened by the flesh, could not do" (8:3); "not by works of the law, because by works of the law shall no one be justified" (Gal 2:16).

The defects of legalism

Not only does the law provide no basis for salvation, but any reliance on the law destroys the righteousness that comes as a gift from God: "If justification were through the law, then Christ died to no purpose" (Gal 2:21). Legalism and righteousness by faith are mutually exclusive. They won't mix in any proportion. Like the attempt to pay for a gift, the slightest reliance on works destroys a saving relationship with God. Faith alone is the means of receiving salvation.

In addition to arguing that legalism doesn't work and that salvation is entirely a gift, Paul goes on to show the true situation of the legalist. For one thing, legalism is incredibly naive; it drastically underestimates the effects of sin on human beings. Sin utterly destroys our ability to keep the law and places all of us under condemnation (Rom 3:9; 5:12). In our morally weakened condition, none of us can keep the law (8:3). In fact, all the law can do now is condemn us. It provides no basis for salvation.

But legalism is more than naive; it is downright sinful. It arises from the proud assumption that fallen human beings can do something on their own to merit divine favor, when nothing could be farther from the truth. Indeed, for Paul, legalism is the outstanding example of the effects of sin. Nothing demonstrates the pathetic predicament of fallen humanity more vividly than the person who thinks he can gain righteousness by his own efforts (cf. Rom 7:13–25).

Besides all this, what makes the plight of the legalist truly desperate is the fact that he doesn't realize the seriousness of his predicament. He thinks everything is going well, when in fact he is headed for disaster. During his own experience as a legalist, Paul felt enormously successful. He had as much reason for confidence in his own efforts as anyone could (Phil 3:4), and as to righteousness under the law, he was blameless (3:6). In light of the righteousness of Christ, however, he saw that all his supposed accomplishments were so much garbage (3:8). Instead of heading for life, the thing he intended, he was actualy headed for certain destruction (Rom 7:15–20). The legalist is like a person with a fatal disease who doesn't have an inkling that he is sick.

Justification and the reign of God

The central concern of righteousness by faith clearly reflects our guiding theme of the reign of God. Paul's doctrine of justification emphasizes the sovereignty of God in the experience of salvation. In harmony with the biblical concept of reconciliation, it views salvation as his work from first to last. Here, as always, our great temptation is to take God's place, to try to do what only he can do. In the final analysis, this is the fundamental problem with legalism. It is an affront to the sovereignty of God. It denies our true situation of utter dependence on him. The only solution to the problem of sin is the one that God alone provides.

We need to remember the priority of God's activity as we consider the opposition between faith and works, because it is he, not faith, that saves us. The heart of the doctrine of righteousness by faith is not that we are saved by faith and not by works, but that we are saved by God, not by man.

SALVATION AND THE LAW OF GOD

Paul's vigorous critique of legalism raises a couple of important questions about the law of God. First, since the law does not provide a basis for salvation, some may conclude that God doesn't really care about our behavior. Second, because it condemns us to death, the law may also appear to be something evil. Both of these views are mistaken.

Paul and James on faith and works

There seems to be a contradiction in the New Testament about the relation between faith and works. As we have seen, Paul asserts that "a man is justified by faith apart from works of law" (Rom 3:28), but according to James, "A man is justified by works and not by faith alone" (Jas 2:24). Are works essential to salvation, then, or not? The apostles seem to disagree.

We can resolve this apparent conflict by analyzing the terms involved and by taking note of the author's specific concern in each passage. For Paul, "faith" is trust, or commitment; it is complete dependence on God for salvation. "Works" are works of law—acts of obedience motivated by the desire to gain righteousness. With these connotations the terms "faith" and "works" are obviously opposed to each other.

James uses "faith" to refer to a person's religious profession. It may be genuine, or "living," or it may be "dead"—a mere profession and nothing more (2:14–26). The "works" of which James speaks are the outward manifestation of a genuine commitment; they show that a person's profession of religion reflects what he truly is. With these connotations, the terms "faith" and "works" are fully compatible.

It is clear that the apostles have two different issues in mind in the passages referred to. Paul's question is the basis of salvation. Is it a human achievement or a divine gift? James's concern is the effect of salvation. What sort of behavior does it produce? Accordingly, the points they make are also different. Paul insists that works do not provide a basis for our salvation, and James asserts that salvation will lead to responsible, ethical behavior.

Both apostles are concerned with the misuse of the law. For Paul, the problem is "legalism," using law as a means of salvation. But for James, the problem is "antinomianism," the practice of disregarding the law entirely, feeling that how we live is irrelevant to our ultimate salvation.

In light of these considerations, there is really no conflict between the two apostles on the question of faith and works. In fact, Paul is fully in harmony with James when it comes to the effects of salvation. He, too, insists that salvation leads to responsible, loving behavior. In his best-known passage on the subject, he refers to these results as the "fruit of the Spirit" (Gal 5:22), but elsewhere he speaks of "faith working through love" (Gal 5:6), and of "good works" as the product of salvation (Eph 2:10; cf. Rom 8:4).

The nature of the law

Paul recognizes that his rejection of legalism may appear to be an attack on the law, so he is careful to emphasize that the cause of our difficulties is sin, not the law. In itself, the law is something entirely good: "So the law is holy, and the commandment is holy and just and good" (Rom 7:12). The law does not bring us death; rather, "it was sin, working death in me through what is good" (7:13). To avoid making the mistake that concerns Paul here, it will be helpful to examine briefly the nature and function of the law in human history.

As used in the Bible, the word "law" has a variety of meanings. It can refer to all the legal material in the Old Testament, or more specifically to the ten commandments (Ex 20:3–17). It can also refer simply to the idea of law, rather than any particular law. It can even refer to a principle, or characteristic pattern of human behavior—what we might call a law of human nature.[1]

In relation to sin and salvation, the law functions in several different ways. Most fundamentally, the law expresses God's unchanging will for human life. It is a statement of the ideal, and it therefore provides a permanent standard for human conduct. This means that the law is something good and helpful. It is a guide for life and a source of joy. We find this attitude in many of the psalms, where the law is described as a "delight" (1:2), a source of wisdom (19:7–10), and an object of love (119:97).

As a permanent guide for human behavior the law is a condition of the covenant. To enjoy God's continued blessings, his people must meet his requirements. "Obey and live, disobey and die" (cf. Dt 11:26–28); these words succinctly state the relation between the covenant and the law. In order for human beings to enjoy God's favor, the requirements of the law must be met.

Sin and the law

It is especially important to note what the law does and does not do as a result of sin. As the unchanging standard of righteousness,

1. W. Gutbrod, "Nomos," Theological Dictionary of the New Testament, ed. G. Kittel and G. Friedrich, trans. G. W. Bromiley, vol. 4 (Grand Rapids, Mich.: William B. Eerdmans Publishing Co., l967), pp. 1070–72.

the law defines and condemns sin. Without the law, we wouldn't know what sin was (Rom 7:7, 13; cf. I Jn 3:4). It is the law that makes sin, sin. But by revealing the character of sin, the law also condemns the sinner; it shows that he deserves to die. Ironically, then, what is originally and basically a source of life becomes an instrument of death in the hands of sin. As Paul says, "The very commandment which promised life proved to be death to me" (Rom 7:10).

Because sin destroys the ability to keep the law, the law does not provide the sinner with a means of becoming righteous. It reveals that there is a serious problem, but it offers no solution (Rom 3:20). It simply leaves us with a death sentence hanging over our heads. This explains why Paul got so upset when people turned to the law in an effort to gain salvation (cf. Gal 3:1–3). They were looking to be saved by something that could only condemn them (cf. 1 Cor 15:56). Salvation has to come from some source other than the law. And it does. In Jesus Christ, the righteousness of God is manifested "apart from law" (Rom 3:21).

Salvation and the law

We have already discussed Paul's doctrine of justification, so now we need to note the major effects of salvation on the law. To begin with, salvation upholds the law as the standard of righteousness. It neither removes nor changes its contents. The law remains as the expression of God's will for human life. As a matter of fact, the whole plan of salvation is a standing testimony to the unchangeability of the law (Mt 5:17–18), for if the law could change, the problem of sin would simply dissolve.

Salvation doesn't change the law, but it does change our relation to the law. It delivers us from the law's condemnation (Rom 8:1). Through Jesus Christ, God makes the righteousness which the law requires available to us as a gift. The "just requirement of the law" is fulfilled in those who are in Christ (Rom 8:4). They are free from sin and the penalty of death (Rom 6:18, 23).

The plan of salvation also reveals how futile it is to view the law as a means of gaining righteousness. It would be foolish of God to go to all the trouble to provide a way of salvation "apart from law," if the law itself could save.

Besides delivering us from the condemnation of the law, salvation provides us with a powerful incentive to keep it. Indeed, by freeing us *from* the law, Christ frees us *for* the law. The law remains for Christians as a guide for life.[2] We are able to appreciate its value, if

2. In the words of John Calvin, "The third and principal use [of the law], which pertains more closely to the proper purpose of the law, finds its place among believers

anything, more fully, because we are no longer depending on it for salvation. Out of gratitude for what God has done for us, we are delighted to do what is pleasing to him. Forgiveness, therefore, does not do away with the law, but provides the deepest reason for keeping it.[3]

Salvation puts us in a new situation, as far as the law is concerned. We can describe this transition with reference to the old and new covenants. The law is related to both. But human effort was the basis of obedience in the old covenant experience, so it was doomed to fail. The new covenant, in contrast, is based on "better promises" (Heb 8:6). It leads to obedience to the law that arises from the heart (Jer 31:33), the only sort of obedience that pleases God.

SANCTIFICATION

Justification is certainly one of the most important terms the New Testament uses to describe the condition of those within the Christian church, but it is not by any means the only one. The apostolic writings often refer to members of the church as "the saints," and "the sanctified" (Ac 9:32; 1 Cor 14:33; Eph 2:19). This description, too, deserves careful consideration.

The English word "sanctification" comes from the Latin word *sanctus,* meaning "holy." The basic idea of the holy is that of something separate, or radically different from the ordinary. The holy stands in contrast to everything profane, or secular. In the Old Testament, the word "holy" applies primarily to God; secondarily it applies to things related to God, such as the temple, the priests, and even the nation of Israel.

The meanings of "sanctification"

When the New Testament describes church members as holy, or as saints, it refers to their unique relation to God. As saints they

---

in whose hearts the Spirit of God already lives and reigns." According to Calvin, believers profit from the law in two ways: it teaches them the nature of God's will and helps them to avoid transgression (*Institutes of the Christian Religion,* II.vii.12, ed. John T. McNeill, trans. Ford Lewis Battles [Philadelphia: The Westminster Press, 1960], pp. 360–61).

3. B. A. Gerrish makes this point in "Grace Demanding," *Criterion,* Spring 1980, p. 8.

are people set apart for a special purpose, and, like the priests and sacrifices in Hebrew worship, they must be pure and innocent. Their lives must be unblemished. This is why the New Testament insists on personal purity and godly living among the followers of Christ.

As it is used by most people today, the word "sanctification" has a somewhat different meaning. It generally refers to growth in grace, or character development. It is the progress in Christian living that naturally follows a person's commitment to Christ as Savior.

In this sense, sanctification is significantly different from justification. Justification is the change in status that takes place as soon as a person accepts Christ. It is a fundamental change in our relationship to God, and it is complete at once. A person is totally justified in a moment. In contrast, sanctification begins at conversion and continues throughout life; it is never finished. Such comparisons give these two dimensions of salvation a complementary quality. In a familiar statement, Ellen White describes justification as our title to heaven, and sanctification as our fitness for it.[4]

The New Testament never puts the two concepts together this neatly, nor do we find any description of sanctification comparable to the extensive treatment of justification by Paul. But the concept of Christian growth certainly appears in the New Testament, and several passages mention the importance of acquiring positive traits of character (e.g., 2 Pet 1:5–9). Our conventional concept of sanctification does have a biblical basis.

Salvation and sanctification

In order to understand sanctification correctly, we need to keep several points in mind. The first is that sanctification is essential to salvation. People sometimes equate salvation with justification and treat sanctification as something secondary, or subordinate, but it is not. It belongs to the experience of salvation, too; in fact, it is inseparable from justification. According to Paul, God made Christ Jesus "our wisdom, our righteousness and sanctification and redemption" (1 Cor 1:30). In the words of John Calvin, "Christ justifies no one whom he does not at the same time sanctify."[5]

The same thing is true of all the aspects of salvation, as we have seen. They aren't separate experiences, occurring at different times;

---

4. "The righteousness by which we are justified is imputed; the righteousness by which we are sanctified is imparted. The first is our title to heaven, the second is our fitness for heaven" (*Review and Herald*, June 4, 1895; reprinted in *Messages to Young People*, p. 35).

5. John Calvin, *Institutes of the Christian Religion*, III.xvi.1, ed. John T. McNeill, trans. Ford Lewis Battles (Philadelphia: The Westminster Press, 1960), p. 798.

they are facets of the same experience. The justified *are* the sanctified. They aren't two different groups, or even the same group at different times. When God justifies a person, as Calvin says, he sanctifies him, too; he sets him apart for a special work in the world. To emphasize this we are treating the experience of salvation within the doctrine of the church, because a person doesn't receive salvation and then decide whether to join the church. Entering the Christian community is part of what it means to be saved. Fellowship with others is essential to the experience.

Another characteristic of sanctification deserves special attention also. This is the fact that sanctification is a divine activity. Occasionally people get the idea that justification is God's work and sanctification is our work, as if he took care of our past sins and left it up to us to live a good life from then on. But the New Testament doesn't support this notion. It gives God responsibility for both justification and sanctification. "It is God who justifies," Paul says in Romans (8:33), and in another letter he writes, "May the God of peace himself sanctify you wholly" (1 Thess 5:23).

Sanctification as the work of God

One reason people separate the two may be the role that human effort plays in sanctification. Because works contribute nothing to justification, it is clearly God's work throughout. But since sanctification includes human effort, it appears that works do make a contribution, and sanctification turns out to be a combination of human and divine activities.

Although human effort plays a role in sanctification, it is not correct to think of this as a contribution to the experience, or to view sanctification as partly God's work and partly our own. One of Paul's statements helps us to understand the true relationship between God's activity and ours: "Work out your own salvation with fear and trembling," he says, "for God is at work in you, both to will and to work for his good pleasure" (Phil 2:12–13).

From the first part of the statement salvation appears to be our responsibility; we have to expend effort in order to be saved. But the second part reveals that God is intimately involved in our activity—so much so, in fact, that what appears at first to be solely human effort turns out to be God's work, too, when we examine it closely enough. Consequently, there is nothing in the experience of sanctification that a person can point to as his contribution, or his personal achievement. Even our own efforts are the result of God's activity. Boasting is excluded from sanctification, as well as from justification.

The role of human effort in sanctification is similar to the role of faith in justification. Faith is a condition of justification; God does not justify a person against his will. But this doesn't make justification a cooperative achievement. It is not partly God's work and partly man's. In the same way, human effort is a condition of sanctification, but this doesn't make sanctification in part a human achievement. God's activity always has priority. Sanctification, too, displays the reign of God.

SALVATION AND HUMAN FREEDOM

Predestination

This is a good place to consider the role of human freedom in the experience of salvation. At times in the history of the Christian church, people have maintained that God decided who would be saved and lost ahead of time, all by himself. Human choice had nothing to do with it. This was the position of the Protestant Reformers, in fact. They wanted to remove any possible basis for human beings to congratulate themselves, so they attributed everything involved in salvation entirely to God. This resulted in the doctrine of "double predestination," which exerted a strong influence in the Calvinist branches of Protestant thought. This is the idea that God has foreordained some human beings to eternal life and others to eternal damnation.[6]

Hardly anyone subscribes to the notion of double predestination today, and there are good reasons for rejecting it. For one, it is not a biblical doctrine. The Bible never speaks of God rejecting people from all eternity. It does refer to predestination and election, but it characteristically uses these terms in a positive sense, and their primary application is to groups, such as Israel or the church, rather than to individuals.

Human responsibility

In addition, many biblical passages appeal to human choice, and many blame human beings for rejecting salvation. We think of Joshua's demand, "Choose this day whom you will serve" (Josh 24:15); and of Elijah's challenge, "If the Lord is God follow him; but if Baal, then follow him" (1 Kgs 18:21); and of Ezekiel's pleading appeal,

---

6. In the words of John Calvin, its most famous proponent, "We call predestination God's eternal decree, by which he compacted with himself what he willed to become of each man. For all are not created in equal condition; rather, eternal life is foreordained for some, eternal damnation for others" (*Institutes of the Christian Religion,* III.xxi.5, ed. John T. McNeill, trans. Ford Lewis Battles [Philadelphia: The Westminster Press, 1960], p. 926.

"Turn back, turn back from your evil ways" (Ezek 33:11). Among the texts that give human beings responsibility for the consequences of sin are: "The soul that sins shall die" (Ezek 18:4); and Jesus' statement, "This is the judgment, that the light has come into the world, and men loved darkness rather than light, because their deeds were evil" (Jn 3:19). It doesn't make sense for God to hold human beings responsible for rejecting him unless they are free to do otherwise.

Because human beings are free, their salvation depends upon their continued acceptance of it. This excludes the popular idea of "once saved, always saved." Some people believe that a person who accepts salvation, or makes a commitment to Christ, will ultimately be saved, no matter how he lives or what he decides later. The one decision guarantees it. Such an idea is erroneous. God gives us freedom to reject him; he won't force salvation on anyone who decides he doesn't want it, even if this reverses a former decision.

The Bible, moreover, frequently warns Christians about the danger of falling away from salvation. This is a prominent theme in Hebrews (6:4–6; 10:26–39; 12:25), and Peter insists that those who return to their sinful ways after knowing Christ are worse off than before (2 Pet 2:20). Such statements make it clear that the experience of salvation is not irreversible. People won't be saved regardless of their choice.

At the same time, it is important to emphasize the human basis of this condition. "Once saved, always saved" is true of God's intentions. As far as he is concerned, once a person accepts salvation, the matter is settled for eternity. He will never change his mind, unless the person turns away. The truth is that God never rejects anyone. But he allows us to reject him, and he will respect this decision.

Assurance of salvation

Our assurance of salvation lies totally in the character of God and in what he has accomplished in Jesus Christ. It is his eager and unchanging desire to save fallen human beings (1 Tim 2:4; 2 Pet 3:9). He will go to any lengths to achieve this goal (Jn 3:16; Rom 8:32). Because of what Christ has done, "He is able for all time to save those who draw near to God through him" (Heb 7:25). We can be absolutely confident that God accepts us and that his plans for us will eventually be fulfilled. But this is a confidence based on what *he* has done, not on anything *we* have done—not even on our own decision to follow him.

Human freedom, then, makes our experience of salvation voluntary; it means that God never saves a person against his will. But it doesn't mean that accepting salvation is something we get "credit" for. In fact, we can't point to any part of the experience as something we do by ourselves. All we can say is that God saves us from beginning to end. The work is entirely his, but he never violates our freedom in the process.

CHRISTIAN PERFECTION

We mentioned above that sanctification is generally understood as progress in the Christian life. It signifies improvement, and it is often synonymous with personal growth, or character development. This progressive quality in sanctification raises the perplexing question of perfection. If sanctification is a process that takes time, it is natural to ask where this process is headed and when it is complete.

Process or goal?   The question of perfection is complicated by the fact that the word is used in several different ways. Sometimes it applies to the entire process of Christian growth, so we hear of growth *in* perfection. A person may be perfect in each stage of his development—as an infant, a toddler, a child, an adolescent, and an adult. Similarly, a Christian may be perfect in each stage of his development—from his first knowledge of God to complete maturity.

At other times, perfection refers to the goal of the sanctification process, so we hear of growth *toward* perfection. The idea that perfection is a goal raises further questions. Is the goal attainable? If so, when will we reach it? As we think about these questions, it is helpful to remember that the word "goal" can function in two rather different ways.

A goal is always something you aim at or move toward, but in some cases it refers to an ideal objective and in other cases to a practical one. Suppose, for example, that you are sailing off the coast of southern California. If it's a clear night, you may steer the boat toward a particular star. You make it your goal. You don't expect to reach the star, naturally, but aiming for it keeps you on the right course. If your destination is Catalina Island, however, you might steer toward the lights of Avalon. In this case, you actually expect to reach your goal.

The question is whether Christian perfection is more like the star or the harbor in our illustration. Is it an ideal we aim toward to keep us on the right course? Or is it something we should actually expect to reach at some point in our experience?

The answer depends on just what we mean by perfection, because people define it in different ways. One is to equate it with sinlessness. In this view, perfection is total conformity to the law of God; it means behavior that is utterly devoid of transgression.

A somewhat broader definition identifies perfection as Christian maturity. This, too, can have different meanings, but it generally refers to a deep commitment to God and the presence of positive traits of character. In this sense, the perfect Christian is one who would never betray his loyalty to God and whose life is filled with love to God and other human beings. This definition of perfection focuses on attitudes rather than behavior, and allows for the possibility of incidental or accidental departures from the law of God.

John Wesley, for one, held this second view of perfection. He defined it as "the loving God with all our heart, mind, soul, and strength." He avoided the expression "sinless perfection" because, in his words, "a man may be filled with pure love, and still be liable to mistake." Wesley didn't expect freedom from actual mistakes until we reach heaven.[7]

Only perfection in the sense of Christian maturity is a realistic goal for us in this life. Sinlessness may be an ideal worth keeping in mind, but we can hardly expect to attain it until we are glorified when Christ returns.

There are several reasons for this conclusion. One is the Greek word for perfection, which is *telos,* meaning "complete," or "mature." It does not suggest the idea of sinlessness. In addition, instead of claiming sinlessness, some of the most outstanding figures in the Bible insisted that they had a long way to go before they reached it. Paul, for example, denied that he was perfect, and said he intended to "press on toward the goal" (Phil 2:12–14). John insisted that we only deceive ourselves if we claim to be without sin (1 Jn 1:8).

Sinlessness or maturity?

"Perfectionism" is the view that we can reach sinlessness in this life. This idea has several unfortunate consequences. One is the tendency to think of perfection in negative rather than positive terms. Instead of the presence of positive traits of character, perfection in this view consists of avoiding certain undesirable forms of behavior. A second difficulty with perfectionism is its emphasis on character development as the central concern of salvation. This is certainly a part of salvation, but it is not necessarily the most

Problems with perfectionism

7. John Wesley, *A Plain Account of Christian Perfection* (London: The Epworth Press, 1952), pp. 42–45.

important part. What Christ does *in* us must not obscure what Christ does *for* us.

Third, perfectionism often leads to an unhealthy preoccupation with oneself. It is certainly appropriate for us to be concerned about our spiritual condition. The Bible often emphasizes the importance of self-examination (1 Cor 10:12), but this is not the central interest in a Christian's life.

By all standards, Jesus was the perfect man. His behavior was sinless, the Bible asserts. But the most attractive part of his life was not his moral heroism, impressive as that was; rather it was his self-forgetful service to others. He was the one man in history whose first concern in every situation was the welfare of other people. A person whose central concern is his own moral attainments will not be able to think unselfishly of others.

There is a sense in which perfectionism is really a moot point, for even perfectionists agree that no one should ever claim to be sinless. In fact, a truly sinless person wouldn't even be aware of the fact. There are good reasons, therefore, not to insist that we should expect to reach sinlessness in this life.

STUDY HELPS

Questions for review

1. What symbols does the New Testament use to describe the experience of salvation?

2. What is Paul's understanding of justification? Why does it exclude legalism?

3. How should we interpret the contrasting statements of Paul and James about the relation of faith and works?

4. What are the various functions of the law in relation to sin and salvation?

5. What do "sanctification" and "perfection" mean?

6. What is "perfectionism," and what are some of the difficulties it involves?

Questions for discussion

1. How much information must a person have in order to exercise faith in God?

2. At what age is a person first capable of religious conversion? How may social and psychological factors affect the experience?

3. Some people suffer from low self-esteem. Others have an inflated opinion of themselves. How can the concept of righteousness by faith help to solve both of these personal problems?

4. Why does sanctification take time? Why doesn't God give us perfect characters the moment we accept Christ?

5. Some equate salvation with justification, and view sanctification as its aftermath. For others, salvation is essentially sanctification, and justification is merely a prelude to it. How will these contrasting views affect a person's religious experience?

Suggestions for Bible study

1. What do the following parables of Jesus teach about righteousness by faith?
   a. The hidden treasure and the pearl of great value (Matthew 13:44–46)
   b. The unforgiving servant (Matthew 18:23–35) and the two debtors (Luke 7:41–43)
   c. The great banquet (Matthew 22:1–14; cf. Luke 14:15–24)
   d. The lost sheep, the lost coin, and the lost son (Luke 15:1–32)
   e. The Pharisee and the tax collector (Luke 18:9–14)
   f. The laborers in a vineyard (Matthew 20:1–16)

2. The struggle with the law Paul describes in Romans 7:14–25 is one of the most widely debated passages in his writings. Is Paul describing his own experience, or the experience of people generally? Is the struggle something that happens before conversion, or after conversion? What do you think?

3. According to many scholars and theologians, the law serves a variety of functions. John Calvin, for example, discusses three different uses of the law (*Institutes of the Christian Religion,* III.vii.6–12). What functions of the law of God do the following passages describe?
   a. Psalm 19:7–11; Deuteronomy 28:13–15; Matthew 5:17–20; Luke 10:25–28
   b. Romans 3:20; 4:15; 5:20; 7:7; 1 Corinthians 15:56
   c. 1 Timothy 1:9–10; Galatians 3:24
   d. Romans 13:8–10; James 1:22–25; 2:8–13

4. The experiences of guilt and forgiveness figure prominently in Hebrew religion. Study the elements of Hebrew worship described in Leviticus 4:1–6:7 and 16:2–34. What knowledge, or information, did they communicate to the worshipers? What emotional impact did they have?

5. Examine the words "call" and "predestine" (or their cognates) as they appear in the following verses. Do they support the Calvinist view that God decides the eternal destiny of each human being? If not, what do they mean?

   Matthew 22:14; Romans 8:28–30; 1 Corinthians 1:2; Galatians 1:6; 5:13; Ephesians 1:4–5; 1 Thessalonians 2:12; 2 Timothy 1:9; Hebrews 9:15; 1 Peter 1:2

6. How does the freedom Jesus describes in John 8:31–36 relate to the kinds of freedom that typically concern people who are young, politically oppressed, or economically disadvantaged?

7. Study the biblical use of the word "perfect," along with its synonyms "blameless" and "mature." Is the notion of "sinless perfection" biblical? Be sure to include the following verses in your study:

   Genesis 6:9 (cf. 9:21–25); 1 Kings 15:14 (cf. 15:11–15); Job 1:1 (cf. 42:6); Matthew 5:48; 19:21; Ephesians 4:12–13; Philippians 3:12, 15; Colossians 4:12; James 1:4

SUGGESTIONS FOR FURTHER READING

From Adventist writers

Questions concerning the experience of salvation have generated lively discussion within the Adventist church for years. Occasionally, differences of opinion have erupted in heated debate and, once in a while, unfortunately, in bitter disagreement.

Ellen G. White's writings contain many statements on the topic. A number of them appear in the compilation *Selected Messages,* vol. 1 (pp. 211–241; 345–398).

E. J. Waggoner, *Christ and His Righteousness* (Oakland, Calif.: Pacific Press Publishing Co., 1890 [reprinted Nashville, Tenn.: Southern Publishing Association, 1972]) presents the influential views of one of the earliest Adventists to consider the topic at length. Waggoner, along with A. T. Jones, presented an important series of messages at the 1888 General Conference. The following works all contain a review of these messages and their impact on the Adventist church: Arthur G. Daniells, *Christ Our Righteousness*

(Washington, D.C.: Review and Herald Publishing Association, 1941); LeRoy Edwin Froom, *Movement of Destiny* (Washington, D.C.: Review and Herald Publishing Association, 1971); A. V. Olson, *Through Crisis to Victory: 1888–1901* (Washington, D.C.: Review and Herald Publishing Association, 1966); and Norval F. Pease, *By Faith Alone* (Mountain View, Calif.: Pacific Press Publishing Association, 1962).

More recent discussions of the experience of salvation include Edward Heppenstall, *Salvation Unlimited: Perspectives in Righteousness by Faith* (Washington, D.C.: Review and Herald Publishing Association, 1974); Hans K. LaRondelle, *Christ Our Salvation: What God Does for Us and in Us* (Mountain View, Calif.: Pacific Press Publishing Association, 1980); and Edward W. H. Vick, *Is Salvation Really Free?* (Washington, D.C.: Review and Herald Publishing Association, 1983). Though serious, these books are all readable.

V. Bailey Gillespie explores the psychological dynamics of conversion in *Religious Conversion and Personal Identity: How and Why People Change* (Birmingham, Ala.: Religious Education Press, 1979).

On the question of perfection, scholars will appreciate Hans K. LaRondelle, *Perfection and Perfectionism: A Dogmatic-Ethical Study of Biblical Perfection and Phenomenal Perfectionism,* (2d ed.; Berrien Springs, Mich.: Andrews University Press, 1975).

For general readers, *Perfection: The Impossible Possibility* (Nashville, Tenn.: Southern Publishing Association, 1975) presents the contrasting views of four contemporary Adventist scholars: Herbert E. Douglass, Edward Heppenstall, Hans K. LaRondelle, and C. Mervyn Maxwell.

For a further statement of this writer's views see Richard Rice, "Sanctification and Perfection: Another Look," *Ministry*, June 1984 (pp. 6–8, 15).

From other writers

Traditional and contemporary systematic theologies, particularly those by conservative authors, will include sections on the experience of salvation.

Two brief, and readable, accounts of this doctrine are Gerharde O. Forde, *Justification by Faith—A Matter of Death and Life* (Philadelphia: Fortress Press, 1982), and H. D. McDonald, *Forgiveness and Atonement* (Grand Rapids, Mich.: Baker Book House, 1984).

G. C. Berkouwer offers sustained treatments of individual facets of the doctrine in *Divine Election,* trans. Hugo Bekker (Grand Rapids, Mich.: William B. Eerdmans Publishing Co., 1960); *Faith and Justification,* trans. Lewis B. Smedes (Eerdmans, 1954); and *Faith and Sanctification,* trans. John Vriend (Eerdmans, 1952). The determined reader can learn much from Berkouwer, though he gives a lot of attention to Dutch theology.

Students who want a succinct review of one of the greatest confrontations in the history of Protestant thought in this area will value Alan P. F. Sell, *The Great Debate: Calvinism, Arminianism, and Salvation* (Grand Rapids, Mich.: Baker Book House, 1983).

Geoffrey J. Paxton critically analyzes the development of the doctrine of salvation by faith in Seventh-day Adventist thought in *The Shaking of Adventism* (Wilmington, Del.: Zenith Publishers, Inc., 1977).

A true classic on the question, John Wesley, *A Plain Account of Christian Perfection* (London: The Epworth Press, 1952), deserves careful reading.

12

MEMBERS OF THE CHRISTIAN CHURCH: THEIR WAY OF LIFE

"You shall love the Lord your God with all your heart, and with all your soul, and with all your mind. This is the great and first commandment. And a second is like it, You shall love your neighbor as yourself. On these two commandments depend all the law and the prophets" (Matthew 22:37–40).

"Love is the fulfilling of the law" (Romans 13:10).

"Lead a life worthy of the calling to which you have been called" (Ephesians 4:1).

Biblical basis

Exodus 20:1–17	Acts 5:27–29
Leviticus 19:9–10	Romans 6:12–19
Psalm 1	Romans 12–13
Psalm 112	Galatians 5:13–6:10
Proverbs 3:1–2, 5–7	Ephesians 4:17–6:20
Isaiah 58:6–9	Philippians 2:12–13
Amos 5:21–24	Philippians 4:8
Micah 6:6–8	Colossians 3:1–4:6
Malachi 3:6–12	Hebrews 11–13
Matthew 5–7	James 1:19–2:17
Matthew 18:15–20	1 Peter 2:11–3:12
John 15:12–17	1 John 4:7–21

In chapter 10 we said that the church fulfills its mission through proclamation and demonstration. It not only recounts the gospel, but also displays the effects of responding to it, providing a "theater of grace," where the world can see what happens when the reign of God becomes a reality in human lives.[1] We have said a number of things about the church's proclamation of the gospel, but we need to say more about its demonstration of it. This requires us to consider what is often referred to as "the Christian life."

It is challenging to understand Christianity. It is much more challenging to live it. Just to survey what the Christian life involves would require a book at least as long as this one. We can only introduce the subject here, and reflect on a few of its most important aspects. We will limit ourselves to four basic concerns: (1) the relation between salvation and the Christian life; (2) the inner dynamic of the Christian life; (3) some guiding principles for Christian behavior; and (4) the various spheres of Christian responsibility.

CHRISTIAN IDENTITY AND CHRISTIAN BEHAVIOR

As we have seen, salvation involves a fundamental change in personal identity. Those who receive salvation are "born again," "justified," and "sanctified;" indeed, they have already begun "eternal life" (1 Jn 3:14). Their situation is completely transformed, and they stand in a totally new relationship to God. Moreover, this transformation is entirely the gift of God. Human beings do nothing to deserve it or contribute to it; all they do is accept it.

By itself, this would be plenty of cause for rejoicing, but it is only part of the good news. Salvation involves a transformation in concrete human life, as well as a change of identity, and affects what we do, as well as what we are. Indeed, it is impossible to be a Christian and not have it show in the way you live. This is the point of James's letter, as we discovered earlier.

To understand the Christian life, we need to grasp the basic relationship between Christian identity and Christian behavior. To put it briefly, what a Christian does is a consequence of what he is, not a condition of it. A Christian leads a praiseworthy life because God *has*

---

1. Ellen G. White uses this memorable image to describe the church: "Enfeebled and defective as it may appear, the church is the one object upon which God bestows in a special sense His supreme regard. It is the theater of His grace, in which He delights to reveal His power to transform hearts" (*Acts of the Apostles,* p. 12).

saved him, not because he hopes God *will* save him. What he is, is basic, or prior, to anything he does.

We see this in the use Paul makes of indicative and imperative forms of speech. As you may recall from studying grammar, indicative sentences make statements; they tell you what is the case. Imperative sentences give commands; they tell you to do something. In Paul's letters, the imperative material typically follows the indicative material, as an effect follows its cause. He usually begins by reminding his readers of all that God has done for them. Then he tells them how they ought to live, as a consequence of the fact. In Romans, for example, he discusses justification by faith in Christ as a gift from God in the first five chapters. Then he urges his readers to live lives free of sin: "Let not sin therefore reign in your mortal bodies, to make you obey their passions" (Rom 6:12). Resistance to sin results from the new status sinners acquire before God.

We see the same pattern in his other letters. When Paul discusses the way Christians should behave, he describes it as a consequence of their new situation: "I therefore . . . beg you to lead a life worthy of the calling to which you have been called" (Eph 4:1; cf. Gal 5:13–14; Col 3:1–16). In short, Paul's message on practical Christian living is this: "Become what you are!" "Now that you are God's children, live like it."[2]

Indicative and imperative

LIFE IN THE SPIRIT

Besides urging Christians to live a certain way, Paul also identifies the inner dynamic that enables them to do so. For Paul, the Christian life is "life in the Spirit." The presence of the Holy Spirit in our lives is both a sign of salvation and a motivating power. The Spirit assures us of our salvation; we know that we are God's children because of the Spirit he has given us (Rom 5:5; 8:14, 16; 2 Cor 1:22; cf. 1 Jn 3:24; 4:13). In

---

2. In a stimulating discussion of the doctrine of justification, Gerhard O. Forde argues for combining the death-life metaphor found in Paul's writings with the familiar moral or legal metaphor of justification in order to achieve a more adequate view of salvation (*Justification—A Matter of Death and Life* [Philadelphia: Fortress Press, 1982], p. 3). According to Forde, the death-life metaphor puts a new construction on the role of works in the Christian life. In answer to the perennial question, "We have to do something, don't we?" Forde replies, "NO! In fact that is no longer the question. Now the question becomes, 'What *are* you going to do now that you don't *have* to do anything?' " (ibid., p. 33; italics his).

addition, the presence of the Spirit yields a rich harvest of fruit: love, joy, peace, patience, kindness, goodness, faithfulness, gentleness, self-control (Gal 5:22). Therefore, all the good a Christian does is the effect of the Spirit's presence in his life.

Human effort in the Christian life

Since divine power makes it possible for us to live godly lives, some people conclude that human effort has no role to play. They believe that the only thing we can do is let God control our activities. Once we have surrendered completely to him, good works will automatically appear in our lives, totally as the effect of his power. In fact, if we do put forth effort, one argument goes, it only reveals our failure to trust God completely, and the works that result are not really ''good works'' at all. According to this view, then, there is no place for human endeavor. Divine power and human effort are mutually exclusive.

Instead of the ''either-or'' of this position, the Bible supports a ''both-and'' view of the relation between divine and human effort in the Christian life. We see this in the frequent use of the imperative in the Bible, especially in the New Testament. Christians are plainly commanded to behave a certain way; they are told to do some things and to abstain from doing others. In one letter, for example, Paul addresses husbands, wives, children, slaves, and masters, along with his Christian readers in general. In each case, he gives specific directions as to how they should act (Eph 5:21–6:20). The natural conclusion is that Christian living involves personal endeavor, putting forth effort and trying to accomplish certain things.

We also find testimonies of strong personal effort on the part of the biblical writers themselves. Again, Paul's letters contain some striking statements. ''Straining forward to what lies ahead,'' he states in one passage, ''I press on toward the goal for the prize of the upward call of God in Christ Jesus'' (Phil 3:13–14). He even compares his exertion to that of an athlete: ''I do not run aimlessly, I do not box as one beating the air; but I pommel my body and subdue it, lest after preaching to others I myself should be disqualified'' (1 Cor 9:27). From verses like these it appears that personal effort played an important role in Paul's own experience.

The paradox of grace

But although the Bible urges Christians to put forth effort, it never describes the results as their own accomplishments. Good works never provide a basis for self-congratulation, because these very works, on closer inspection, are nothing other than the product of divine power. The best text on this point, again from Paul, is this: ''Work out your own salvation with fear and trembling; for God is at work in you, both to will and to work for his good pleasure'' (Phil

2:12–13). There is a mysterious coincidence between human effort and divine activity in Christian experience.

Some people refer to this phenomenon as "the paradox of grace." What appears at first to be the result of human effort turns out on closer inspection to be the product of divine power.[3] When Paul compared his efforts to those of other apostles, he said, "I worked harder than any of them, though it was not I but the grace of God which is with me" (1 Cor 15:10). This was not false modesty on Paul's part. He really believed that God was responsible for his success.

Similar expressions emerge in the lives of other men of God. Augustine wrote, "Even if men do good things which pertain to God's service, it is he himself that brings it about that they do what he commanded."[4] His famous prayer describes obedience as divine gift as well as command: "Give what thou commandest, and command what thou wilt."[5] In the same vein, Anselm prayed, "Whatsoever our heart rightly willeth, it is of thy gift."[6] Ellen White makes a number of similar statements, including this one: "All his biddings are enablings" (*Christ's Object Lessons,* p. 333).

This, then, is the central paradox of the Christian life. We are responsible for our behavior. We have work to do, and we must put forth serious effort. But in the final analysis, we claim nothing for ourselves. God's power accounts for all our accomplishments.

This may seem to be more complicated than the view that we should "let go and let God," but in fact it is much easier to live with. It allows us to go ahead and strive to fulfill our responsibilities without undue concern about our motives and attitudes. In particular, it protects us from the frustration of having to try hard not to try at all.

There are several reasons why a Christian's efforts don't lead to boasting or pride. One is the fact that the very ability to strive comes

Christian humility

3. According to D. M. Baillie, the essence of this paradox "lies in the conviction which a Christian man possesses, that everything good in him, every good thing he does, is somehow not wrought by himself but by God. This is a highly paradoxical conviction, for in ascribing all to God it does not abrogate human personality nor disclaim personal responsibility. Never is human action more truly and fully personal, never does the agent feel more perfectly free, than in those moments of which he can say as a Christian that whatever good was in him was not his but God's" (*God Was in Christ: An Essay on Incarnation and Atonement* [New York: Charles Scribner's Sons, 1948], p. 114).

4. Augustine, *De Praedestinatione Sanctorum,* c. 19, quoted in Baillie, *God Was in Christ,* p. 114.

5. Augustine, *Confessions,* x, 29, quoted in Baillie, *God Was in Christ,* p. 115.

6. Quoted in Baillie, *God Was in Christ,* p. 115.

ultimately from God; it isn't something we are responsible for. Another is the motivating, enabling presence of the Spirit, which we noticed above. A third is the recognition that the good results of our work are far out of proportion to the amount of our effort. They must be due to the magnifying, multiplying power of God; we can't take credit for them.

The hiddenness of godliness

This last point is closely related to a theme that figures prominently in Jesus' teachings. Some describe it as the "hiddenness of godliness."[7] It is a fact that those who do the most to serve God are characteristically the least impressed with their accomplishments. In the parable of the sheep and goats, the ones blessed by the king for their deeds of mercy are strangely unaware of what they have done. "Lord," they ask, "when did we see thee hungry and feed thee, or thirsty and give thee drink?" (Mt 25:37). They can no doubt remember having done such things, but they are not aware of having done them for the king. That is, they are not aware of the full significance of their behavior. They are preoccupied with those who need their help—the hungry, the thirsty, the lonely—not with their own activity.

Jesus makes the same point in the Sermon on the Mount. Toward the beginning he says, "Let your light so shine before men, that they may see your good works and give glory to your Father who is in heaven" (Mt 5:14). But later on he states, "Beware of practicing your piety before men in order to be seen by them; for then you will have no reward from your Father who is in heaven" (Mt 6:1).

What does Jesus mean to say? Should the goodness of his followers be public, as his first statement indicates, or private, according to the second? We have an answer to this question if we think about who sees this goodness and who doesn't. The good works of the righteous are obvious to others, for they glorify God as a result. But they are hidden from the righteous themselves. They are not impressed with the importance of their actions, because their own behavior is not the center of their concern. They are eager to give God the glory for anything they accomplish.

The mistake of attempting to exclude effort from the Christian life results from misapplying a sound theological principle. Effort has no part in establishing our identity as the people of God; it makes no contribution to the new status we acquire as the result of salvation. God does this without our effort. This is the essential point of righteousness by faith.

7. Cf. Dietrich Bonhoeffer, "The Hidden Righteousness," in *The Cost of Discipleship*, trans. R. H. Fuller (rev. ed.; New York: The Macmillan Company, 1963), pp. 172–179.

However, the fact that human effort does not establish our relationship to God does not mean that it has no role to play within this relationship. Indeed, there is every reason to believe otherwise, for instead of excluding effort from the Christian life, the knowledge that we are justified by faith inspires it. Recall the line of thought in Paul's letters. Knowing that we are now the children of God, totally because of God's love and grace, provides a powerful incentive to live like his children. As we have just seen, to the extent that we succeed, we will give him all the glory.

The Spirit in community

We have spoken of the Christian life, or "life in the Spirit," as if it were essentially an individual matter, and this is how we typically think of it. As the New Testament describes it, however, life in the Spirit is primarily a corporate, or social, phenomenon. It is something that happens to a concrete group of people, not privately to individuals. It operates in the particular kind of community that only the power of the Spirit creates.

We mentioned this as we approached the doctrine of the church, but it bears repeating here. The primary manifestation of the power of the Spirit in this world is the presence of genuine Christian community. We see the Spirit at work where people exhibit in their relationships to others, both inside and outside the community, the life of love and service exemplified by Jesus Christ.

This means that the principle sphere of the Spirit's activity is what happens between people, rather than within them. Life in the Spirit does involve certain personal attitudes and behavior, of course; it affects the way people live on an individual basis. But more fundamentally it affects human beings in their togetherness. This is why the New Testament places such emphasis on what believers have in common. It describes them as a family, and it speaks of "one body and one Spirit . . . one Lord, one faith, one baptism, one God and Father of us all . . ." (Eph 4:4–6).

The widespread failure to recognize the social or corporate dimension of the Spirit's work accounts for the preoccupation with individual religious experience that is characteristic of conservative Christianity. It can also lead to excessive emphasis on certain other human groups, such as the family or the nation.

We have analyzed the relation between salvation and behavior, and we have explored the inner dynamic of the Christian life. Now we will examine the principles by which Christians live. After that, we will review the various areas where these principles apply.

THE MEANING OF LOVE

Faith, hope, and love describe the basic structure of the Christian life (1 Cor 13:13). Faith is an essential aspect of our relationship to God. As we have seen, it consists of unreserved trust and commitment. Hope characterizes our relationship to the future. As we shall see in our study of eschatology, it involves an affirmative view of time and history. Love characterizes our personal relationships and is the single most important principle in the Christian life.[8] In fact, it would be accurate to say that love is the most important concept in all of Christian thought, for the person who understands love knows what God is like and what being a Christian is all about (1 Jn 4:7–12).

Important as it is, love is extremely difficult to describe. It is at once a means and an end, both a gift and a command. While setting us free, it makes us responsible. It fulfills the law, but it also transcends the law. Theologians have pondered the meaning of love for centuries, but, like many great ideas, it is easier to illustrate than to define. We can identify its central character by looking to God, since he is love personified (1 Jn 4:8).

Love is self-forgetful

We find the clearest display of love in the central act of salvation history. The Father gives his Son to save the world from sin (Jn 3:16; 1 Jn 4:9), and the Son gives his life (Jn 15:13). From this twofold gift we learn that love consists in self-sacrificing service to others. It places supreme value on persons, and it seeks what is best for them without counting the cost or calculating the consequences.

We mentioned that love applies to our relationships to God and to other human beings. It lies at the heart of the two commands that summarize the law: "You shall love the Lord your God with all your heart, and with all your soul, and with all your mind" (Mt 22:37; cf. Dt 6:5); and, "You shall love your neighbor as yourself" (Mt 22:39; cf. Lev 19:18). Paul says the same thing when he states that love is the fulfilling of the law (Rom 13:8, 10).

To love God is to value God supremely for his own sake. It means that we love God because he is supremely worthy of love, not because we expect a reward for loving him. Those who serve God in hopes that

---

8. In the words of Anders Nygren, "The idea of love occupies a—not to say the—central place in Christianity, both from a religious and an ethical point of view" (*Agape and Eros:* Part I: A Study of the Christian Idea of Love; Part II: The History of the Christian Idea of Love; trans. Philips S. Watson [New York and Evanston: Harper & Row, Publishers, 1969], p. 27). According to Nygren, "The Christian idea of love . . . involves a revolution in ethical outlook without parallel in the history of ethics . . ." (ibid., p. 28).

he will serve them do not really love him. Their devotion is based on the desire to gain something for themselves. Genuine love does not ask, "What's in it for me?" It is not motivated by the desire for a reward. Overemphasizing the rewards awaiting those who are faithful to God makes a travesty of religion. The Bible describes the glories in store for the redeemed in order to communicate the depth of God's commitment to human beings, to tell us how God feels toward us. Knowing this should awaken an answering love in our hearts. But to transfer our affection from the Giver to the gift is to misconstrue the whole relationship. Our love for God is genuine only if we love him for who and what he is, not for what we expect to gain from the relationship.

In terms of our guiding theme, to love God means to welcome his sovereignty in every area of life. On the individual level, this involves accepting his authority in everything we do. Love leads to a life of complete openness to the reign of God. Every personal resource is made available to him. Every aspect of life, every detail of behavior, is subjected to his will.

Love and the reign of God

To love God not only means to accept his sovereignty over ourselves, it also means to view everything else in light of his sovereignty, too. This is why love for God naturally results in love for others. Knowing the value that God places on people will lead us to respect them, too, for if we love God, we will share his values and regard other people in light of his attitude toward them.

This was the point of Jesus' command to love one's enemies; it means to pattern our activity after God's own. In Jesus' words, God "makes his sun rise on the evil and the good, and sends rain on the just and on the unjust" (Mt 5:45). God's treatment of human beings is not based on what they deserve. He does not reserve his blessings for those who return his affection. Neither should we. If we are perfect as he is perfect (Mt 5:48), we will not base our treatment of others on the way they treat us.

Besides patterning our actions after God's own, loving others also involves extending God's sovereignty in the world. It means working to bring about a state of affairs that resembles the way things are in the kingdom of God. This involves striving to relieve human suffering wherever we find it. It means opposing oppression and working for freedom and justice in human affairs.

Because love is unconditional, it is also unrestricted; its scope is all-inclusive. This, too, is suggested by Jesus' command to love our enemies, which shows that no one is excluded from genuine love. The second great command, "Love your neighbor," is universal and concrete at the same time. My neighbor is not some vague generality, or an abstraction. My neighbor is a concrete reality, a specific person. My neighbors are the people I meet in the day-to-day course of life. At the same time, my neighbor might be anyone. As the parable of the good Samaritan shows (Lk 10:29–37), our neighbor is the person who needs our help, regardless of race, religion, or social status. The word "neighbor" applies to every human being.

LOVE AND LAW

Love is action

We mentioned that love to God and man summarizes the law. To understand love, it will be helpful to explore its relation to the law a bit further. To begin with, it is important to note that love is commanded. Remembering this prevents us from confusing love in the Christian sense with some sort of affection. Love is something you do, not something you feel. We all know that feelings come and go. We have limited control of our emotions. It would be frustrating indeed to find ourselves commanded to feel a certain way.

Instead, the command to love relates to action. It does not require us to entertain a certain emotion in the process. As a result, we are free to love people even if we don't particularly like them. We can value them and act in their best interest whether or not we have feelings of personal affection for them.

The last words of the command, "You shall love your neighbor as yourself," are instructive here. It is possible to love yourself even when you are very unhappy with yourself. You may be displeased with your recent behavior. Perhaps you made a complete fool of yourself, and you know it. In this case, you don't like yourself. But you can go on loving yourself anyway. You can still take care of yourself. Similarly, we love others when we act in their interest, whether or not we feel a particular way about them.

Love fulfills the law

The essential relation between law and love is one of form and content. As the summary of the law, love identifies the essence of the law's requirements. Love is what the law is really all about. In Paul's words, "Love is the fulfilling of the law" (Rom 13:10). Consequently, the person who genuinely loves, who acts with the welfare of others uppermost in mind, will fulfill the law. The right attitude leads to the kind of behavior that the law prescribes.

While love is the content of the law, the law describes the form of love. It provides a pattern for the appropriate expression of love. This can be extremely helpful, because the proper attitude alone does not guarantee beneficial behavior. A well-intentioned person can sometimes make mistakes. The law gives us much-needed guidance for expressing love in helpful ways.

The law also serves as a constant reminder that genuine love involves action as well as attitude. Without the concrete commands of the law, we might be tempted to think that good intentions are enough. There is the danger that love could degenerate into a vague sentiment, or an empty expression of concern (cf. Jas 2:15–16). The law prevents this. Because of the law, we can be sure that there is no love wherever the needs of human beings are disregarded.

On the other hand, as we have seen, obedience to the law is worthless in the absence of love, for without love, commandment keeping degenerates into sterile legalism. The essential purpose is gone. This is why God got so upset at times with the religious ceremonies of his people (cf. Amos 5:21–23). What he really wants is genuine devotion and a concern for human life (Ps 51:16–17; Amos 5:24). Sacrifices are worthless if these are missing.

Love prevents us from legalism because it never comes to an end. There will always be a need for love. When we realize that love is the heart of the law, we cannot congratulate ourselves for keeping it, for we can never say that we have loved enough.

Love not only fulfills the law; it transcends it. Genuine love goes beyond anything a legal code could possibly require. The most a law can demand is fairness, or equality. The command, "Love your neighbor as yourself," is a good example. It reminds us that our neighbor has rights equal to our own, but it thus presupposes that we have rights, too. The law is satisfied when people have the same rights and privileges. Love is not. Love is willing to sacrifice its own interests for the benefit of others.

Love transcends the law

This is why the life of Jesus provides the supreme example of love. He constantly denied his own needs and abandoned his own rights for the welfare of other people. In the end, he gave up life itself. "Greater love has no man than this, that a man lay down his life for his friends" (Jn 15:13). His self-denial and self-sacrifice provide the permanent model for Christian behavior (cf. Phil 2:4–8; 1 Pet 2:21–24). Our ideal surpasses any legal code.

Love is the ideal for Christian behavior. But we live in a world that is less than ideal, and this complicates the whole enterprise of Christian living. Christians are committed to the ideal of love in every circumstance, but they must also be aware of the total situation in which

Love in a fallen world

we live. In this regard we need to take into account several different factors.

The doctrine of creation affirms the essential goodness of life and of all that exists. This justifies the pursuit of useful, constructive activity and prevents us from becoming pessimistic about life. The doctrine of the fall accounts for the brokenness of the world as we find it. It reminds us that things are not the way God meant them to be. It also reminds us that even our best actions will be tainted with self-interest.[9] The biblical doctrine of sin prevents us from expecting simple solutions to the problems we face.

The doctrine of salvation affirms the presence of a restorative power in the world. God has not left the world alone to suffer the consequences of sin; he is at work to mitigate the effects of the fall and ultimately achieve his purposes. Finally, the doctrine of last things reminds us that the present situation is temporary. The ideal is yet to come. We can never reach it here.

These basic doctrinal themes support a rather complicated attitude toward the Christian life. We might describe it as an optimism that is not naive and a realism that is not cynical.[10] These beliefs prevent us from assuming that life in this world can ever be ideal. Christians cannot expect good behavior to have only pleasant consequences. It is always risky to love; in certain situations it may even appear foolish. At the same time, we cannot abandon the world. Love requires us to pursue a life of service, and the doctrines of creation, salvation, and last things affirm the ultimate value of such a life.

The position of Christians in the world, then, is ambiguous. They are in the world, but not of the world (cf. Jn 17:15–16). They commit their lives to loving others because this is what it means to follow Christ, and because they believe this is worthwhile in the scale of ultimate values, but they do not expect it to make sense in our present situation.

We can express this ambiguity in light of our guiding theme. The reign of God is a present reality, but it will not be fully realized until the future. As a result, we cannot identify the kingdom of God with any achievable state of affairs in the present, but we cannot relegate it

9. As Reinhold Niebuhr put it, "No virtuous act is quite as virtuous from the standpoint of our friend or foe as it is from our standpoint . . ." (*The Irony of American History* [New York: Charles Scribner's Sons, 1952], p. 63).

10. These are essentially the words Langdon Gilkey uses to describe his outlook during a time when he found he was strongly influenced by Reinhold Niebuhr's thought: "It was now possible for me to face the war [World War II] with a realism that was not cynical and an idealism that was not naive" (*Shantung Compound: The Story of Men and Women Under Pressure* [New York: Harper & Row, Publishers, 1966], p. 73).

entirely to the future, either. God is at work in the present, in spite of appearances. And he uses human actions to accomplish his work, although we may not be aware of it, so we can never abandon the attempt to live as citizens of the kingdom here and now.

LOVE FOR GOD

With this basic description of the Christian life in mind, we can reflect on the major spheres of responsibility that Christians face, and reflect on a few representative obligations within them. As we do so, some familiar Adventist concerns will arise. We cannot deal with them at length, but we can try to show what their place is in an overall concern for Christian living.

Our most comprehensive responsibility is to God. As God's children, we accept his authority over every area of life and give his claims on us priority over all others. This is the essential meaning of the first commandment: "You shall have no other gods before me" (Ex 20:3). Nothing rivals God's authority.

This also means that all our obligations have a spiritual dimension; everything expected of us is part of the one fundamental responsibility to love God with our entire being. Knowing this prevents us from feeling overwhelmed by the hundreds of requirements in the Bible. What God really wants is our complete allegiance. This matters more to him than punctilious attention to details.

Because our obligation to God is comprehensive, he has a claim on all of our personal resources. There is no possession or ability that does not belong to him. Viewed in this light, our basic role is that of servants, or stewards, accountable to God for the use we make of our lives. The memorable parables in Jesus' great sermon on last things (Mt 24–25) emphasize this aspect of the Christian life. In particular, the parable of the talents indicates that human beings will be judged by their behavior. They will be asked to account for the use they make of the resources God places in their care.

The practice of tithing expresses a sense of stewardship to God and acknowledges God's sovereignty over our financial resources. To tithe is to give a tenth of our income. Abraham honored Melchizedek with tithe (Gen 14:20), and Jacob promised to tithe in response to God's assurance of care for him (Gen 28:22). The people of Israel were commanded to pay tithes, which were used to support the Levites, the religious leaders of the nation (Num 18:24). The tithe was

Financial resources

their inheritance, since they received no land when Palestine was divided among the Hebrew tribes. Following this precedent, Seventh-day Adventists use tithe funds to support church employees engaged in the work of gospel ministry (cf. 1 Cor 9:13–14).

God attaches special significance to the tithe, but he requests other offerings, too. The purpose of these practices is to encourage a spirit of constant gratitude for everything we have (cf. Dt 8:18). Giving does more than acknowledge God's right to what is given; it acknowledges his ownership of everything we have. It reminds us that there is nothing that we have not received (1 Cor 4:7), for it all belongs to God (Ps 24:1). Recognizing God's generosity can have tremendous blessings (Mal 3:6–12). It assures us that he will always care for our needs (Phil 4:19; Ps 37:25), and it protects us from the danger of overestimating the value of material prosperity (Lk 12:13–21; 1 Tim 6:10).

Physical resources

Seventh-day Adventists also emphasize the stewardship of our physical resources. Adventists are widely known for a commitment to healthful living. This leads them to abstain from the use of harmful substances such as alcohol, tobacco, and various drugs. Adventists typically refrain from eating the flesh of animals the Bible identifies as "unclean" (Lev 11; cf. Gen 7:2), and many follow a vegetarian diet. In recent years Adventists have shown an active interest in other aspects of healthful living, including physical fitness.

There are several reasons for this concern for physical health. One is a wholistic view of human nature. Adventists believe that human beings are physical, as well as spiritual, and that the various dimensions of human life are interrelated. Our physical condition thus has an effect on our mental and spiritual condition. Another reason is the desire to witness against the evils of society, which explains our position against the use of alcohol better than health principles alone. The Adventist commitment to abstinence arose from the great temperance movement in America during the last century. It appropriately expresses a sense of outrage at the terrible cost in human suffering that the misuse of alcohol has produced in our society.

A third reason for this interest in health is the conviction that our bodies are the temple of the Holy Spirit (1 Cor 6:19), so we should glorify God physically, as well as in other ways. This also justifies a concern for personal appearance.

Because human beings bear the image of God, everything about them should be representative of their Maker. Christians will therefore seek to dress in a way that contributes to a positive portrayal of him. This excludes attire that is ostentatious or immodest (1 Tim 2:9; 1 Pet 3:3), or undignified or inappropriate. It also excludes a preoccupation with personal appearance. How we look is a part of life, but it is only a part. It should not receive more attention than it deserves.

LOVE FOR OTHERS

Next to our responsibility to God, our most comprehensive sphere of responsibility is to other human beings. The second great command describes this sphere: "You shall love your neighbor as yourself." As we noticed above, this command is both universal and concrete. It requires a commitment to the well-being of every other human being. It calls for a concern, not just for humanity in the abstract, but for each person affected by our action. Our "neighbor" includes everyone reached by our influence.

The word which best describes the Christian's role within this sphere of responsibility is "servant." Following Christ's example, the Christian is servant of all (Jn 13:3–15). As a child of God, he is secure enough to deny himself and even abandon his own rights in order to benefit others.

The word "neighbor" in the second great command refers to individual human beings, but the command involves responsibilities to different human groups as well. Human beings do not live as separate, isolated units. They live in relationships with others. Our overarching obligation to others, then, includes several spheres of responsibility within it which correspond to the different groups in which we participate.

FAMILY RESPONSIBILITIES

Children

The most basic, and obvious, social unit is the family. Within the family, Christians have obligations as children, spouses, and parents. The fifth of the ten commandments is the first to mention our responsibilities to human beings. It directs us to honor our fathers and mothers (Ex 20:12). Paul also urges children to obey their parents (Eph 6:1; Col 3:20), and at least one passage suggests that reconciliation between parents and children is one of the effects of salvation (Mal 4:6).

This sphere of obligation involves more than mere obedience. It also involves living in a way that brings honor to one's parents, and caring for them as the need arises.

It is possible to exaggerate and distort this responsibility, important as it is. In one letter Paul qualifies the extent of filial obligation by saying, "Children, obey your parents in the Lord" (Eph 6:1). In a sinful world, it is possible for different obligations to conflict. When this happens our prior responsibility is always to God. We cannot obey our parents if what they request of us conflicts with our duty to him.

We also fail to honor our parents if we submit to an unwarranted extension of their authority over us. It is possible for parents to so dominate their children that they prevent them from becoming fully developed human beings in their own right. A person who realizes this is happening to him has a responsibility to resist parental control. Naturally, this measure is a last resort, and no one should take such a course without prayerful reflection and the mature counsel of others.

Husbands and wives

Husbands and wives have responsibilities to each other, too. Sexual fidelity is basic (Ex 20:14). Marriage cannot survive betrayal on this fundamental level of physical and emotional commitment. Sexual responsibility also includes a willingness of spouses to express their affection physically. Paul advises married couples not to refrain from normal sexual relations (1 Cor 7:5).

There is much more to marriage than sexual activity, of course. Paul directs husbands to love their wives, and wives to be subject to their husbands (Eph 5:22, 25; Col 3:18–19). This advice has generated a lot of discussion. Some people believe that this establishes the husband's superior authority as a divine ideal. Others maintain that it is a necessary consequence of sin to have one spouse superior to another. Still others attribute Paul's statement to the cultural circumstances of his day, when women were decidedly inferior to men both socially and politically. The precise relationship between husbands and wives will probably always reflect the prevailing culture to some extent, but it is important to remember that the biblical account of creation places men and women on the level of complete equality (Gen 1:27; 2:20–24), and that the gospel transcends any barrier of a sexual nature (Gal 3:28).

Parents

A third aspect of the familial sphere of obligation is the responsibility of parents to children. According to the Bible this extends far beyond providing for their physical needs. It includes the work of training children for a useful life (Prov 22:6); it requires sensitivity to their emotional needs (Col 3:21); and most important, it involves religious instruction (Dt 6:7). By precept and example, parents determine the religious orientation of their children. No other factor affects a child's relationship to God as do parents.

Family relationships provide some of the most powerful symbols in the Christian religion. The New Testament speaks of God as our Father. It compares Christ's care for the church to a husband's love for his wife (Eph 5:25), and it refers to church members as brothers and sisters. This not only tells us something about the religious realities referred to, it also tells us something about the quality these human relationships should exhibit. Our love for the members of our families should reflect the commitment and the tenderness that characterize God's own love for human beings.

This sphere of human obligation suffers from widespread neglect today. Sexual standards are generally declining, and there is an increasing loss of commitment to the family as the framework for an ideal lifestyle. As a result, the family is a topic of enormous concern to contemporary Christians. Affirming our commitment to the family can be an important part of the church's current witness to the world.

But it is not faithful to the Bible to elevate the family as the single most important human community. According to the Bible, it is not; the church is. The distinctions on which families are based are transcended in the body of Christ (cf. Gal 3:28), and the bonds that unite its members are stronger than those of any other relationship.

In addition, overemphasizing the religious importance of the family can have unfortunate consequences. It creates the impression that one can live a complete Christian life only within a family situation. This leaves those who are unmarried, for whatever reasons, feeling as if they were spiritually substandard. An adequate view of the Christian community would prevent this mistake.

CHURCH RESPONSIBILITIES

In the New Testament, the church, the community of the Spirit, constitutes the most important corporate entity in this world. The church is a new social reality, created by the Spirit, and its members enjoy a fellowship which is not possible in any other human relationship (1 Jn 1:3). The community in which they participate reflects the perfect harmony that characterizes the reign of God.

The New Testament also indicates that the church represents the sphere of our greatest interpersonal responsibility. We have obligations to fellow Christians that surpass those we have to members of any other group. Many of these obligations are spiritual. According to the New Testament, members of the church should pray for each other (Eph 6:18; Jas 5:16); sympathize with each other (Gal 6:2);

confess their sins to each other (Jas 5:16); forgive each other (Col 3:13); counsel and advise each other (Gal 6:1); and love each other (1 Pet 4:8). In all ways Christians should serve one another, putting the interests of others ahead of their own, just as Christ did (Phil 2:3–5).

According to the New Testament, a Christian's service to other members of the church also includes financial support when needed. After Pentecost, believers sold their property and gave the funds to the church, and the church took responsibility for supporting its poorer members. Later on, Paul collected funds as he traveled among different congregations to assist the Christians in Jerusalem (2 Cor 9:1). From the beginning, then, the church supported its members in need.

But the mechanics of distributing aid have never been smooth. Deacons were appointed in the early church because the apostles found the task so demanding that it interfered with their special responsibility to preach the gospel (Ac 6:1–5). Paul had to give Timothy some lengthy advice about who was eligible for assistance from the church (1 Tim 5:3–16). We cannot expect this aspect of our church responsibilities to be easy to fulfill, but it is important, nonetheless.

An often-neglected part of our obligation to the church is the responsibility of leadership, or holding church office. The New Testament describes such work as a tremendous privilege and carefully discusses the qualifications of elders and deacons (1 Tim 3:1–13). Many Christians today, however, are reluctant to assume such responsibilities. This is tragic. Given the challenge it faces, the church needs dedicated, qualified leadership in every area of its operation.

SOCIAL RESPONSIBILITIES

A larger sphere of Christian responsibility is the obligation to society in general. The Bible never suggests that we should limit our association to members of the church (1 Cor 6:9–10; Rom 12:18), or that our spiritual identity should lead us to withdraw from the world (Jn 17:5). Instead, we are part of the world and its institutions. We participate in society, and we have social obligations.

At a minimum these include avoiding offensive or unlawful behavior (1 Pet 4:15), and attempting to live peaceably with other people (Rom 12:18). Beyond that, Christians should be productive, useful members of society, known for their good behavior (2 Cor 8:21; Eph 4:28; 1 Pet 2:12). They should also benefit others by their actions (Gal 6:10), even when they have suffered mistreatment themselves (Rom 12:17).

The Reformation doctrine of vocation did a lot to clarify the role of the Christian in the world. It was a reaction to the monastic ideal that led people to withdraw from society in order to lead a fully religious life. The Reformers insisted that a Christian's place was in society, pursuing his calling or "vocation" for the good of others. They affirmed the goodness and the religious significance of useful activity. For them, the religious life was an active, productive life, not a passive, withdrawing one.[11]

The Protestant ethic

The "Protestant ethic," as it is often called, developed from this doctrine of vocation. Some scholars believe that the vigorous economy that developed in the countries of central and northern Europe and eventually in North America during the centuries after the Reformation arose from this affirmation of the value of work. In this view, religious commitment is fully compatible with financial success; in fact, it even promotes it.[12]

Seventh-day Adventists typically reflect the Protestant ethic. They encourage their members to work, and they support a large private school system designed, in part, to prepare its graduates to assume useful roles in society.

Christians have an obligation to live as productive members of society, but they cannot give prevailing social and economic structures unqualified approval. Christians are in the world, but they are not of it. They do not share its values, and they cannot support social structures that violate the dignity of human beings. There are times when Christians must criticize the society in which they live.

Christian social criticism

Christian social criticism can take two forms—implicit and explicit. Christians implicitly criticize society when they follow standards of behavior that are higher than what society expects. Christians who refuse to engage in dishonest or exploitative practices that are generally tolerated implicitly criticize the financial standards of society. They also bear a critical witness when they refuse to allow prevalent

11. In the words of B. A. Gerrish, "Three beliefs are particularly associated with the Protestant movement: the authority of the Word, justification by faith alone, and the priesthood of all believers. . . . We may perhaps add a fourth idea of great religious and even social consequence: vocation—that the good works required of the justified man are not so much special religious acts as the thankful performance of his calling for the good of his neighbor" ("Reformation," in *The Encyclopedia of Philosophy,* ed. Paul Edwards [New York: Macmillan Publishing Co., Inc., and The Free Press, 1967], 7:100).

12. Max Weber examines the relationship mentioned here in his classic study, *The Protestant Ethic and the Spirit of Capitalism,* trans. Talcott Parsons (New York: Charles Scribner's Sons, 1958).

social structures to interfere with their fellowship in the church. New Testament Christians accepted slaves as full-fledged members of the church (cf. Eph 6:5–9), and Paul urged Philemon to welcome back his escaped slave Onesimus as a brother in the Lord (Phlm 16). By its treatment of slaves, the early Christian community rejected an institution that was basic to the social and economic life of ancient times.

There is a widespread conviction among conservative Christians today that this is as far as Christian social criticism should go. In the opinion of many, we should be content to witness against the evils of society by living lives that are above reproach and influencing others by our example.

But there is a place for explicit as well as implicit criticism. There are times when Christians have the obligation to speak out on social issues and attempt to influence social policy and change social conditions. The biblical prophets set a precedent for such activity by denouncing the social ills of their day (e.g., Amos, Micah). Christians in the nineteenth century recognized this responsibility when they sought the abolition of slavery and the prohibition of alcoholic beverages.[13]

When should the church explicitly criticize society? This question is not easy to answer. Christians need to keep at least two things in mind as they address it. First, the church must be an influential factor in society to make explicit witness effective. This may be one reason why the church of the nineteenth century bore an explicit witness against slavery, while the witness of the apostolic church was implicit. At the beginning, the Christian church had a negligible impact on society; it was struggling just to survive. In nineteenth-century Europe and North America, however, Christians were a powerful social force.

A second factor bearing on this question concerns the central purpose of Christian mission. The church must not allow its social concerns to preempt the proclamation of the gospel. The experience of some Christian groups reveals that a preoccupation with social

---

13. Seventh-day Adventists were among those who agitated for these reforms. Ellen G. White strongly supported both abolition and prohibition. She asserted, "The institution of slavery does away with [moral agency] and permits man to exercise over his fellow man a power which God has never granted him, and which belongs alone to God" (*Testimonies for the Church,* vol. 1, p. 358). She counseled Seventh-day Adventists not to obey "the law of our land requiring us to deliver a slave to his master" (ibid., p. 202).

She also urged that "laws be enacted and rigidly enforced prohibiting the sale and the use of ardent spirits as a beverage" (*Review & Herald,* November 8, 1881). "Let the voice of the nation demand of its lawmakers that a stop be put to this infamous traffic" (*Ministry of Healing,* p. 346). She told Adventists at the Iowa campmeeting of 1881 that they should not only support but get out and vote for prohibition (*Temperance,* p. 255).

transformation can obscure the importance of the message the church has to communicate. In certain countries, for example, powerful social movements have co-opted the human resources of the church and left it with no distinctive voice.[14]

The solution is not to abandon our responsibilities to society, but to find the proper relationship between these concerns. The idea of the Kingdom of God, which figures prominently in Jesus' preaching, suggests that social change is part of the good news of salvation. It is not in competition with it. The message of the church to the world consists primarily of the announcement of what God has done in Jesus Christ, but it also includes a call for changes in human society. Neither element should obscure the other.

The basis for this claim lies in our guiding theme. God's reign is not merely spiritual. It extends to every aspect of human life, including the physical and social dimensions of our existence. This is clearly evident in the writings of the prophets. Religious observances are worthless, they insisted, unless the worshipers are also concerned with justice and human welfare. Indeed, if this quality is missing from the lives of his people, God finds their acts of devotion downright repulsive (Amos 5:21-24).

POLITICAL RESPONSIBILITIES

The final sphere of obligation we shall consider is the Christian's responsibility to the state. It is customary to equate the state with society, but the two are not identical. It is important to keep them distinct, and to remember that a Christian's responsibilities to them are different.

Society is basic to human life. We exist only in relation to others, and we participate in society as an essential condition of our existence. Our society embodies the larger circle of human beings in which we live. Differences in language and culture, and sometimes in race, distinguish societies from each other. The church transcends societal boundaries (Gal 3:28), but Christians cannot avoid participating in the specific societies which surround them. In fact, we have just argued, they have a responsibility to do so.

14. This is the opinion of Luis Zurita concerning Marxist movements in certain Latin American countries ("Typology of Church Response to Social Change in Latin America," an address at Loma Linda University, Riverside, California, May 28, 1981).

A state is the prevailing political, or legal, structure in a society, the organ of government. It preserves social order by wielding power; this is its primary function. It may or may not reflect the will of the society in general, depending on the nature of its political system. Democratic states seek to involve citizens in the processes of politics and government, while totalitarian states, in contrast, impose their decisions upon their citizens.

Christian cooperation with government

Christians cannot avoid the responsibilities of citizenship, nor should they attempt to do so (Rom 13:1; 1 Pet 2:13). Jesus advised Jews to pay the taxes required by Rome (Mk 12:17). Paul echoes this advice in his letter to the Romans (Rom 13:6–7). Those who enjoy the benefits of government can expect to contribute to its support.

The New Testament affirms the importance of the government's role in maintaining social order. It specifically mentions punishment of wrongdoers and the fear of punishment it inspires (Rom 13:3–4; 1 Pet 2:14). Paul even describes human institutions as the means by which God exercises sovereignty in the world: "For there is no authority except from God, and those that exist have been instituted by God" (Rom 13:1). In honor to God, then, Christians should honor the state. They should respect its officials (Rom 13:7; 1 Pet 2:17) and keep its laws, and they should comply with its demands for support. In short, Christians should be good citizens.

Christian resistance to government

At the same time, there are definite limits to a Christian's obligation to the state. The requirements of the state may conflict with God's requirements. When that happens, "We must obey God rather than men" (Ac 5:29), to use the words of Peter. The state has a legitimate claim on our allegiance, but we cannot submit to its authority when this violates our duty to God.

Our primary loyalty to God may lead us into civil disobedience. If that happens, it should not surprise us to meet the unpleasant consequences. The New Testament speaks of persecution as a fact of life for Christians in this world. It encourages us to face the prospect bravely, and rejoice when we can share the sufferings of Christ (1 Pet 3:13, 17; 4:12–13).

States tend to make claims for themselves which Christians cannot honor. The books of Daniel and Revelation vividly portray this characteristic by depicting different nations as ravenous beasts which oppose God's power and threaten his people (cf. Dan 7; Rev 13). Obviously, Christians cannot give their allegiance to such centers of power. The authority of the state is never supreme for the Christian. This authority is legitimate to the extent that it comes from God and reflects the nature of his own sovereignty, but when it encroaches on God's supremacy, its claims must be resisted.

One of the most difficult tasks Christians face is that of determining just when the laws of the land conflict with the laws of God. To what extent can we comply with the state without violating our obligations to God? Occasionally, the issues are clear-cut. We cannot, obviously, worship something less than God, or violate one of his direct commands (cf. Dan 3:16–18). In other cases, however, the questions are much more complicated.

Problems: Legalized injustice

What should a Christian do, for example, if a law perpetuates social injustice, such as racial segregation? Should he keep the law in deference to the authority of the state? Should he keep the letter of the law but ignore the spirit by personally treating people of other races with kindness and generosity? Should he seek to change the law through accepted political practices, such as seeking public office or placing an initiative on the ballot? Or should he openly, visibly defy such a law? In the name of conscience, Christians have pursued all these courses of action.

War

A most perplexing question concerns a Christian's participation in war. Some Christians are convinced that they have a duty to go to war whenever the government requires it. They feel that the government, not they, becomes responsible for any lives they might take. Other Christians object to any form of military service under any circumstances.[15] Some even object to the very act of registering for the draft. There are mediating positions between these extremes.

Some Christians believe that certain wars are justified, but not others.[16] They would be willing to defend their country against a clear threat to its survival, for example, but they are unwilling to go to war in some distant part of the world to implement a questionable foreign policy. There are also Christians who will participate in military service short of bearing arms and threatening human life. Many Seventh-day

15. Quakers, or members of the Society of Friends, are foremost among those who espouse Christian pacificism (cf. Sydney E. Ahlstrom, *A Religious History of the American People* [New Haven and London: Yale University Press, 1972], p. 645).

16. The so-called "just war theory" has a long tradition in the Roman Catholic Church. In brief, it consists in the view that Christians are justified in engaging in warfare provided certain conditions obtain: (1) an injustice persists; (2) all peaceful means for settling the dispute have been exhausted; (3) the damage caused by the war will be no greater than the injustice; (4) there is a good chance they will win (Rene Coste, "War," in *Encyclopedia of Theology: The Concise Sacramentum Mundi,* ed. Karl Rahner [New York: The Seabury Press, 1975], p. 1811).

Adventists in the armed forces of the United States have served in noncombatant capacities, as medics, for example.[17] But the military organizations of many countries do not provide this option to their personnel.

Military support   A related question is a Christian's involvement in any form of military endeavor. Can a Christian manufacture combat boots? conduct research pertaining to biological warfare? construct a nuclear bomb? Can a Christian pay the taxes that support these enterprises?

Beyond encouraging church members in the United States to register as noncombatants, Seventh-day Adventists have devoted relatively little attention to such perplexing questions. We have a lot of work to do in thinking through our responsibilities as citizens in light of our fundamental identity as children of God.[18]

Our examination of the Christian life has concentrated on the fundamental obligation of love and the various spheres of responsibility it entails. This should not obscure the fact that the dominant note of the Christian life is joy rather than duty. Ideally, all that a Christian does flows from a profound sense of gratitude to God for the gift of salvation, as we saw in our analysis of the relation between Christian identiy and Christian behavior. Such gratitude makes the Christian life primarily one of celebration. Christians celebrate what God has done in all they do. They celebrate his sovereignty over every area of life, and they seek to extend his reign in the world. But their celebration finds specific focus in the distinctive activities of worship, which is the topic of our next chapter.

17. For a brief discussion of Seventh-day Adventists and noncombatancy, see "Noncombatancy," in *Seventh-day Adventist Encyclopedia,* ed. Don F. Neufeld (Washington, D.C.: Review and Herald Publishing Association, 1966), pp. 871–872.

18. Efforts in this direction include the "Conscience Project," a seminar sponsored by the General Conference of Seventh-day Adventists, designed to assist high-school students in deciding their relation to military service. Participants are assured that the church will stand behind any conscientious decision. Scholarly reassessments of the church's traditional position include articles in a special section of *Spectrum,* vol. 1, no. I, entitled, "The Christian and War": Chuck Scriven, "The Case for Selective Nonpacifism"; Donald R. McAdams, "A Defense of the Adventist Position"; Emanuel G. Fenz, "The Case for Conscientious Objection"; and more recently, James N. Coffin, "Second Thoughts on Adventists in the Military," *Spectrum,* vol. 15, no. 1, pp. 29–33.

STUDY HELPS

1. What is the relation between Christian identity and Christian behavior?

2. What is the appropriate role of human effort in Christian experience?

3. What are the essential characteristics of Christian love?

4. What is the relation between love and the law of God?

5. What are the comprehensive objects of Christian responsibility?

6. What are a Christian's responsibilities in the areas of family, church, society, and politics?

1. Christian experience includes knowledge, emotion, and behavior. How is behavior related to these other dimensions?

2. What should a Christian do when different responsibilities conflict? Suppose, for example, that telling the truth would endanger someone's life, or that a person can survive only if he steals.

3. What right or responsibility does a church have for the behavior of its members? Should it require certain forms of behavior, provide general guidelines, or just leave ethical decisions up to the individual? What approach should a church-related school or college take toward its students?

4. The Seventh-day Adventist Church requires its members to adhere to certain standards of behavior. Marital fidelity and abstinence from alcohol and tobacco, for example, are "tests of fellowship." The Church strongly encourages other types of behavior, such as tithe-paying and a vegetarian diet, but does not make them a requirement for membership. And finally, the Church leaves certain decisions, such as whether or not to have an abortion, up to individual judgment. How does, and how should, a religious community decide which issues belong in each category?

5. How can young people achieve moral and ethical maturity in an environment like a strong Christian home or a church-related school, where many important decisions are, in effect, made for them?

6. In the nineteenth century Seventh-day Adventists in the United States supported efforts to pass laws prohibiting the sale and use

of alcoholic beverages (cf. *Gospel Workers,* pp. 387–88), while they resisted efforts to legalize Sunday observance. Is this consistent? When is it appropriate for Christians to legally enforce practices based on their religious beliefs? When is it not appropriate? Consider issues like legalizing prayer in public schools and outlawing the practice of abortion.

7. How are religion and morality related? Can they be separated? Can a person be moral without being religious?

Suggestions for Bible study

1. The Bible contains hundreds of commandments, covering virtually every aspect of human activity. Study the examples listed below. Which sort of commandments are permanently valid, and which have temporary or limited application? How can you tell the difference?

   a. Exodus 20:3–17
   b. Exodus 22:25; Deuteronomy 23:19
   c. Leviticus 11:7 – 8 (cf. 11:46–47)
   d. Leviticus 19:9–10; Deuteronomy 24:19–21
   e. Ephesians 6:5–9
   f. 1 Timothy 2:11–15; 1 Corinthians 11:5
   g. John 15:12

2. With two exceptions, the Ten Commandments are formulated in negative terms—"thou shalt not." Study Exodus 20:3–17. How would you express the content of each commandment in a positive way?

3. In a number of instances in the Bible, people have God's approval to do something that appears to violate one of his commandments. How do you account for the following "violations" of the law? (The relevant commandments are indicated in parentheses.)

   a. Genesis 22:2 (cf. Exodus 20:13; Leviticus 20:2)
   b. Deuteronomy 25:5–6 (cf. Leviticus 18:16)
   c. 1 Samuel 15:1–3 (cf. Exodus 20:13; Matthew 5:44)
   d. 1 Samuel 21:6 (cf. Leviticus 24:9)
   e. Mark 2:23 (cf. Exodus 20:8)

4. How did Jesus distinguish between more and less important requirements in the law? See Matthew 22:35–40; 23:23.

5. Jesus' Sermon on the Mount is the Bible's most important description of the Christian life. Read Matthew 5–7. Outline the major

sections of the sermon. Is the life Jesus describes here a realistic possibility in this world?

6. Paul's most famous description of the heart of Christian living is 1 Corinthians 13. Analyze the essential qualities of love as Paul identifies them in this chapter. How does love transcend legalistic requirements on the one hand (see John 8:1–11) and the prerogatives of personal liberty on the other (see 1 Corinthians 8)?

SUGGESTIONS FOR FURTHER READING

This chapter touches on two areas whose literature is nearly as vast as that of Christian theology as such, namely Christian spirituality and Christian ethics. The following suggestions barely hint at the material available.

From Adventist writers

Many, if not most, of Ellen G. White's writings concern some aspect of the Christian life. Her lengthy *Testimonies for the Church* for the most part applies Christian principles to practical problems, as do her various "Counsels to . . ." books and other books such as *Messages to Young People* and *Christian Service.*

Ellen G. White's writings on the spiritual life are unsurpassed. The best example is *Steps to Christ,* probably the most widely read of her books. Others include *My Life Today, The Sanctified Life, Sons and Daughters of God,* and *Thoughts from the Mount of Blessing,* as well as many portions of her "Conflict of the Ages" series, especially *Desire of Ages.* These writings are among the greatest resources of the Seventh-day Adventist Church.

In addition, there are hundreds of devotional books and pamphlets on various aspects of Christian living by Adventist authors. Such material constitutes most of the items available at Adventist Book Centers.

The area of ethics and decision-making has attracted increasing attention from Adventist writers in recent years. Two examples are John Brunt, *Decisions: How to Use Biblical Guidelines When Making Decisions* (Nashville, Tenn.: Southern Publishing Association, 1979), and Morris L. Venden, *Salvation by Faith and Your Will* (Nashville, Tenn.: Southern Publishing Association, 1978).

Related works include Gordon Kainer, *Faith, Hope and Clarity: A Look at Situation Ethics and Biblical Ethics* (Mountain View, Calif.: Pacific Press Publishing Association, 1977), and James Londis' interpretation of the ten commandments, *God's Finger Wrote Freedom* (Washington, D.C.: Review and Herald Publishing Association, 1978).

A special section of *Spectrum* (vol. 12, no. 2), entitled "Making Ethical Decisions," contains the following articles: James Walters, "Toward an

Adventist Ethic''; Gerald Winslow, ''Adventists and Abortion: A Principled Approach''; and David R. Larson, ''Four Ways of Making Ethical Decisions.''

From other writers

Two descriptions of the Christian life, notable for their clarity and inspiration, are Dietrich Bonhoeffer, *The Cost of Discipleship,* trans. R. H. Fuller (rev. ed.; New York: The Macmillan Company, 1963), and C. S. Lewis, *Mere Christianity,* especially Book 3 (New York: The Macmillan Company, 1960).

A good place to begin reading about theological ethics is Lewis B. Smedes, *Mere Morality: What God Expects from Ordinary People* (Grand Rapids, Mich.: William B. Eerdmans Publishing Co., 1983). Smedes reflects on the last six of the ten commandments as norms for personal life. The following suggestions may be helpful to those who wish to explore this area further.

There are several important works in Christian ethics whose authors are known primarily as theologians and whose ethical reflection arises from fundamental theological concerns and commitments. These include Karl Barth, *Ethics,* ed. Dietrich Braun, trans. Geoffrey W. Bromiley (New York: The Seabury Press, 1981); Dietrich Bonhoeffer, *Ethics,* ed. Eberhard Bethge, trans. Neville Horton Smith (New York: The Macmillan Company, 1955); Emil Brunner, *The Divine Imperative: A Study in Christian Ethics,* trans. Olive Wyon (Philadelphia: The Westminster Press, 1947); and Helmut Thielicke, *Theological Ethics:* Vol. 1: Foundations, ed. William H. Lazareth (Philadelphia: Fortress Press, 1966); Vol. 2: Politics, ed. William H. Lazareth (Philadelphia: Fortress Press, 1969); Vol. 3: Sex, trans. John W. Doberstein (Grand Rapids, Mich.: William B. Eerdmans Publishing Co., 1964).

There are also important works in Christian ethics by authors whose primary concerns are ethical but whose basic resource is the Christian faith. These include H. Richard Niebuhr, *The Responsible Self: An Essay in Christian Moral Philosophy* (New York: Harper & Row, Publishers, 1963); Reinhold Niebuhr, *An Interpretation of Christian Ethics* (New York: The Seabury Press, 1979); and the following works by James Gustafson: *Christ and the Moral Life* (New York: Harper & Row, Publishers, 1968), *Can Ethics Be Christian?* (Chicago: University of Chicago Press, 1975), and *Ethics from a Theocentric Perspective,* Vol. 1: Theology and Ethics (Chicago: University of Chicago Press, 1981).

J. Philip Wogaman examines the way in which Christian beliefs and commitments enter into the process of making decisions in *A Christian Method of Moral Judgment* (Philadelphia: The Westminster Press, 1976).

Christian ethics is social as well as individual, of course. The numerous books in this area include E. Clinton Gardner, *Biblical Faith and Social Ethics* (New York: Harper & Row, Publishers, 1960), and Stephen Charles Mott, *Biblical Ethics and Social Change* (New York: Oxford University Press, 1982). For a ''radical'' approach to Christian social ethics by a Mennonite theologian, see John Howard Yoder, *The Politics of Jesus* (Grand Rapids, Mich.: William B. Eerdmans Publishing Co., 1972).

Liberation Theology is an important development in contemporary Christian thought. Its proponents maintain that the application of Christian principles and beliefs to concrete social and political problems is central, not peripheral, to the task of theology. A good description of liberation theology is Robert McAfee Brown, *Theology in a New Key: Responding to Liberation Themes* (Philadelphia: The Westminster Press, 1978).

A recent development in Christian ethics is to approach ethics primarily as a matter of character development within community rather than a decision-making process concerned with resolving moral dilemmas. This theme apears in these works by Stanley Hauerwas: *A Community of Character: Toward a Constructive Christian Social Ethic* (Notre Dame: University of Notre Dame Press, 1981); *Vision and Virtue: Essays in Christian Ethical Reflection* (Notre Dame: University of Notre Dame Press, 1981).

13

THE MEANING
OF CHRISTIAN WORSHIP

**Biblical
basis**

"O come, let us worship and bow down, let us kneel before the Lord, our Maker!" (Psalm 95:6).

"Go therefore and make disciples of all nations, baptizing them in the name of the Father and of the Son and of the Holy Spirit" (Matthew 28:19).

"For as often as you eat this bread and drink the cup, you proclaim the Lord's death until he comes" (1 Corinthians 11:26).

Exodus 3:1–6
Exodus 25:8
1 Kings 8
Psalm 84, 95–100
Isaiah 6:1–8
Matthew 6:5–13
Matthew 26:26–29
Mark 1:9
Mark 11:15–18
John 3:22–23
John 4:19–24

John 6:25–59
John 13:1–15
Acts 2:38
Acts 8:35–39
Romans 6:3–4
1 Corinthians 11:23–26
Colossians 2:12
Hebrews 10:25
Revelation 4–5
Revelation 7:9–17

Worship is the most important activity of the Christian church—not because Christians are the only ones who worship, but because their worship identifies them as a distinct group. Christian worship consists in the periodic gathering of church members to celebrate the origin and destiny of their community and to strengthen the bonds of their common life in Christ. To understand worship, we need to consider the essential characteristics of this experience and examine some of the activities which it includes.

THE MEANING OF WORSHIP

According to an influential work, worship of whatever kind is "the response of the creature to the Eternal."[1] It is what a person does when he finds himself in the presence of God. This definition implies certain things about both the subject (human beings) and the object (God) of the experience.

The object of worship

Worship obviously presupposes that God exists, but it also implies that he has certain qualities, or characteristics. The most impressive of these is superior power, or majesty. Worship arises from the apprehension of God as something infinitely greater than we are, and more than that, as something qualitatively different. It is not just that God has some of our admirable traits to a much greater degree than we do. He is "wholly other," drastically different from us. Before him, we feel our contrasting finiteness; we sense the frailty, the tenuousness, the dependency of our own existence. In some instances worshipers are overwhelmed by the majesty of God. They feel empty and insignificant in comparison to what they experience (e.g., Isa 6:5). When God spoke directly to the Israelites from Mount Sinai, for example, they were afraid they would die, and they asked Moses to speak to them instead (Ex 20:19).

The attitudes of worship

A realization of God's infinite greatness evokes a sense of awe, or reverence, on our part. It gives us profound respect for his power and majesty. This is not the only attitude involved in worship, but without it, the experience loses its transcendent dimension. It ceases to relate us to anything beyond ourselves.

Another important attitude in worship is adoration. This arises from the recognition that God is worthy of supreme devotion. We can, and should, commit ourselves totally to him. Adoration takes us beyond mere awe, because God is more than sheer power, or overwhelming majesty. Our worship is prompted by the sense that we are

1. Evelyn Underhill, *Worship* (New York: Harper & Brothers, 1936), p. 3.

grasped by a love beyond our comprehension—a love that values us beyond anything else we know. We are commanded to love God with all the powers of our being (Dt 6:4), but this command rests on God's prior love for us (1 Jn 4:10, 19).

Besides reverence and adoration, worship also involves an attitude of celebration, a sense of joy and thanksgiving. God not only presents us with his majesty and goodness; he has acted on our behalf, and he invites us into his fellowship. Worship celebrates what God has done for us, and Christian worship focuses specifically on what God has done for his people in Jesus Christ.

Because worship involves the attitudes of reverence, adoration, and joy, it can take place anytime; it can provide a background for all of our activities. Medieval monks used to say, *Laborare est orare,* "To work is to pray." In a sense we can worship as we work, study, and play. Worship can be part of everything we do.

But that is not enough. Worship involves certain attitudes, but it also involves activities. Specific acts of worship are important because there is an interaction between religious commitment and its expression. Commitment gives rise to expression, but expression also deepens commitment. Worship is not only the outgrowth of our ongoing experience with God, it also stimulates this experience. So in order to provide a background for the rest of life, there must be times when worship occupies the foreground, too.

DIMENSIONS OF THE WORSHIP EXPERIENCE

The various acts of worship should form a cohesive whole, for worship is a single experience, not many different experiences. This comprehensive experience ideally includes several different qualities, or dimensions.

Beauty

We might call one the "aesthetic" dimension. Order and beauty should characterize our acts of worship. This was one of Paul's concerns when he counseled the church in Corinth about the unruly display of spiritual gifts during their meetings (1 Cor 14). A lack of order detracted from the meaning of their services and threatened to give Christian worship a bad name. We tend to associate the aesthetic dimension closely with the role of music in worship, but it applies to other acts of worship, too. Nothing in a worship service should distract the participants from concentrating on what is taking place.

Important as this dimension is, worship is not merely an aesthetic experience. We can't equate worship with what happens at a fine musical performance, for example. Worship contains other dimensions as well. One of these is the inspirational, or motivational, dimension. If the aesthetic dimension speaks to our senses, this dimension addresses our emotions.

Ideally, worship deepens our religious commitment and renews our dedication to God's service. We should leave a worship service with increased enthusiasm for Christianity. This does not mean that worship is merely a means to an end. It does not imply that the center of Christianity lies elsewhere, say, in service to others, or in meeting the challenges of everyday life with confidence in God. Worship is an end in itself. It is its own reason for being. But genuine worship will enrich the rest of life, too.

A third dimension of worship is its informative, or cognitive, character. Worship stimulates the mind, as well as the senses and the emotions. We naturally think of the sermon in this connection. A good sermon will give you something to think about, in addition to motivating you to action. You should leave a worship service knowing more than when you entered. But each act of worship, not just the sermon, deserves concentration. Worship at its best draws on all our mental powers and requires us to focus our complete attention on what is taking place.

The corporate dimension of worship is important, too. Private devotions are essential to Christian life, but they cannot replace the experience of worshiping with others. Meeting together keeps us in touch with each other and enables us to encourage one another (Heb 10:25). More important, something unique happens when a group of people with common religious commitment engage in worship together. A new dynamic is created. Jesus promised his presence to as few as two or three gathered in his name (Mt 18:20). This doesn't mean that he isn't with us individually as well, but it suggests that we can experience his presence in a special way in concert with other people.

The participatory dimension of worship is closely related to its corporate dimension. It presupposes that a number of people are involved in worship, and it emphasizes that worship is something that all of them do. We must avoid confusing worship with a performance, as if those on the platform worshiped while the rest of the people watch. Actually, there are no spectators at a worship service, only

Inspiration

Education

Community

Participation

participants. For this reason, a good order of service will provide opportunities for all the people to express their devotion together. The hymns and the offering are familiar possibilities. Others include responsive scripture readings and the regular use of the Lord's Prayer.

Incarnation

The idea of the incarnation provides a helpful theme for understanding Christian worship. As a christological doctrine, this is the belief that God assumed human nature in the person of Jesus. On a broader level, this central act in the history of salvation suggests an intimate relationship between finite and infinite, time and eternity, creation and creator, matter and spirit, and the visible and the invisible—to use several characterizations. It suggests an interaction between these two aspects of reality. The physical can serve as a receptacle for the spiritual, and the spiritual can infuse material things with transcendent significance. As a result, physical things can serve as pointers to spiritual things.

Distortions of worship

Keeping these various dimensions in mind will protect our worship experience from several distortions. Some form of idolatry results when we lose sight of the incarnational character of Christian worship. Idolatry is devotion to some feature of the creaturely world, instead of the Creator. In its cruder manifestations, it involves a physical object, or artifact, but it occurs whenever we allow the means of religious devotion to obscure its true object. We are guilty of idolatry, for example, if the choir's performance becomes an end in itself and fails to direct us to God, or if the sermon is merely an exercise in public speaking.

Formalism, or ritualism, is another distortion of worship. It occurs whenever we engage in acts of worship mechanically, with little concern for their meaning. A preoccupation with the aesthetic dimension of worship can lead to formalism. It is important for our worship to be dignified, but a precise order of service alone does not ensure genuine worship.

The opposite distortion is too much informality. In the attempt to avoid formalism people sometimes err in the other direction and take an almost casual attitude toward worship. Their acts of worship become haphazard and disjointed. Such an approach is inadequate to express profound commitment. Ultimately it trivializes religion and threatens to reduce it to a form of entertainment.

Public and private worship

We have emphasized the corporate dimension of worship in this section, but worship includes acts of private devotion, as well as services involving a group or congregation of believers. This is one of several ways in which Christian experience reflects the "principle of alternation," as one scholar calls it.[2] This refers to the fact that the Christian life contains a balance of contrasting factors. It includes both work and rest, for example. After Jesus ministered to the multitudes, he communicated with God in solitude (cf. Mk 6:46). And after their successful missionary journey, Jesus invited the disciples to come to a lonely place and rest a while (Mk 6:31).

The life of the Christian community alternates between gathering and scattering. Church members meet together to celebrate their common heritage as God's children and provide each other encouragement. Then they return to their homes and occupations to fulfill their mission in the world. Accordingly, worship is both public and private. Public worship strengthens Christians for their individual encounters with the world, and private worship gives integrity to their public expressions of devotion.

PRAYER

No act of worship, public or private, is more basic or more important than prayer. Prayer is universal to human experience. On the most rudimentary level, it arises from a deep sense of need. Throughout the world and throughout history, human beings have realized their dependence on a higher power and sought its help. We instinctively pray when we find ourselves in a desperate situation. As the saying goes, there are no atheists in foxholes.

Beyond this universal sense of dependence, prayer assumes many different forms. This is because the way people pray inevitably reflects their understanding of God. In one of the great religious confrontations described in the Bible, Elijah challenged the priests of Baal to a showdown on Mount Carmel (1 Kgs 18:20–40). The purpose was to establish once and for all who deserved the worship of the Israelites. None of the contrasts between Elijah and his opponents is more striking than the difference between their prayers. Instead of repetitious ranting, Elijah called on God with quiet confidence (vss. 36–37).

The Bible records many prayers. In fact, the longest book in the Bible is a collection of prayers. The Psalms, or the Psalter, as the book is sometimes called, played a prominent role in Hebrew worship. They

Prayer in the Bible

---

2. The expression is W. E. Hocking's; quoted in *The Interpreter's Bible*, ed. George Arthur Buttrick (12 vols.; New York and Nashville: Abingdon Press, 1951–1957), 7:743.

contain some of the most magnificent poetry ever written (e.g., Psalm 23). They are theologically profound. And because they express the full range of human experience, from joy to despair, and from ecstasy to abject misery, they speak with power to every generation.

Jesus' life and work reflect the close relation between a person's prayers and his concept of God. According to the Gospels, Jesus himself spent many hours in prayer, and his teachings on prayer were among the most important things he said (Mt 6:5–13). Jesus often prayed alone, sometimes early in the morning (Mk 1:35), sometimes after a long day's work (Mk 6:46). He also prayed with others. The "Lord's Prayer," of course, he prayed with his disciples and gave them as a model (Lk 11:1–4; cf. Mt 6:9–13). The longest recorded prayer of Jesus is the moving "high priestly" prayer he offered for his disciples the night before he died (Jn 17). His prayers often exuded confidence in God (e.g., Jn 11:41–42), but at times they were filled with anguish, accompanied with "loud cries and tears" (Heb 5:7).

One of the distinctive features of Jesus' prayers was the way he addressed God. He used the Aramaic word *Abba,* which is similar in some ways to the English expressions "Daddy" and "Papa."[3] It suggests that we can approach God confidently, and regard him with the same sort of affection we feel toward our parents. Jesus assured his listeners that God is just as willing to give his children good things as human parents are (Mt 7:9–11).

The attitudes of prayer

From the prayers of the Bible and from the Bible's teaching about prayer, we learn about the basic attitudes and the essential elements of this act of worship. Two important attitudes that should characterize prayer are honesty and trust. One of the striking things about the psalms is their emotional candor. They often express sentiments that are less than praiseworthy—self-pity, for example (Ps 22:6), or a desire for revenge (Ps 137:7–9)—yet they belong to the great songs of Israel. Honesty is the antidote to prayers that fall into hackneyed formulas or stale patterns. When we pray we should tell God what is really on our minds, not what we think he wants to hear.

The Bible also indicates that trust is basic to prayer (Jas 1:6–8). The confidence that God wants the very best for us, that he never holds out on us or keeps us at arm's length, is the only attitude in harmony with the biblical portrait of God. Without the conviction that God

---

3. Gerhard Kittel, *"Abba," Theological Dictionary of the New Testament,* ed. Gerhard Kittle, ed. and trans. Geoffrey W. Bromiley (10 vols.; Grand Rapids, Mich.: William B. Eerdmans Publishing Co., 1964–1976), 1:5–6.

is on our side, our prayers will always be tentative, if we bother to pray at all.

The prayers of the Bible contain four or five essential elements. The first is adoration and praise to God. the Hebrew name of the book of Psalms means "the book of praises," or simply, "praises."[4] The fundamental purpose of prayer is to praise God. The reason for praising God is the simple fact that he deserves it. God is the only appropriate object of adoration. He alone deserves to be worshiped (Ex 20:3). The sequence of phrases in the Lord's Prayer emphasizes the priority of God and his glory to the things we expect him to do for us. Prayer at its best is God-centered, not self-centered.

The elements of prayer: praise

Thanksgiving is closely related to adoration, or praise. It arises from the recognition that all that makes life worth living originates with God. We appropriately sing of God as the one "from whom all blessings flow." Indeed, he is the source of life itself (Ac 17:25). This element in prayer brings into focus the dominant theme of the Christian life. As we have seen, service and obedience flow from the experience of salvation. They are the result, not the basis, of a new relationship with God. Consequently, Christians live out of a profound sense of gratitude (cf. 1 Thess 5:18).

Thanksgiving

The element of confession expresses the inevitable feeling of need and unworthiness that accompanies an awareness of God's greatness. When Isaiah saw the Lord "sitting upon a throne, high and lifted up," he said, "Woe is me! For I am lost; for I am a man of unclean lips" (Isa 6:1, 5). We cannot experience the presence of God without sensing our creatureliness and our sinfulness.

Confession

The psalms give eloquent expression to human fallenness (e.g., Ps 103:10–14), and the Lord's Prayer includes a request for divine forgiveness (Mt 6:12). In addition to a general sense of unworthiness, prayer often expresses remorse for specific sins. This is the concern of the so-called "penitential psalms," of which Psalm 51 is probably the best known. Its forthright acknowledgment of personal guilt and its poignant longing for restoration to God's favor make it a model for all who seek forgiveness.

The most familiar element in prayer is petition. In fact, "to pray" is often synonymous with "to ask" or "to request." We should never

Petition

---

4. Edward J. Young, *An Introduction to the Old Testament* (rev. ed.; Grand Rapids, Mich.: William B. Eerdmans Publishing Co., 1964), p. 297.

feel reluctant to present our requests to God. As we have noted, he is more eager to give his children good things than human parents are. At the same time, however, God is more interested in what we need than in what we want. Like a loving and responsible parent, he sometimes withholds from us things that would not benefit us. This is one explanation for the perplexing phenomenon of unanswered prayer.

People often find it hard to understand why God doesn't give us many of the things we ask for, especially when they seem important. It is possible that God sees that the supposed blessing would not be a blessing at all, so instead of what we want, he gives us something better. This is not the only reason why petitions go unfulfilled, of course. In certain cases there are conditions to be met, such as placing oneself in harmony with God's will, and considering the welfare of others, as well as our own. It is selfish for us to ask God for something we want, if it would deprive other people of something they need. In other cases, a request may involve asking God to do something that would violate his way of working in the world. As a parent, I pray that God will help my children to resist temptation, but I recognize that he cannot force them to be faithful to him. The fulfillment of this prayer depends in large measure on their response to God's influence.

The attitude of trust may be more important when it comes to our petitions than with any other aspect of our prayers. Prayer is not some sort of magic that places God's power at our disposal. It is not a device for getting God to perform on command, like the genie in Aladdin's lamp. Along with worship in general, prayer is fundamentally a personal encounter. Jesus emphasized this when he described God as "spirit," and said, "Those who worship him must worship him in spirit and truth" (Jn 4:24). We must respect God's right to respond to our petitions in his own way, whether it coincides with our preferences or not. It is important to remember that the essential purpose of prayer is not to make God willing to give us what we need; it is to help us become willing to receive what we need.

Intercession

Intercessory prayers are petitions that involve other people. The Bible clearly encourages such prayers (e.g., 2 Thess 3:1; Jas 5:14–16), but people have often questioned their purpose. According to the Bible, God knows all things, he desires the salvation of all human beings, and he bestows blessings on good and evil alike. Consequently, we have to wonder what value intercessory prayer could have. God doesn't need our prayers to acquire information about other people, nor do our prayers make him more willing to bless them. He already knows everything about them and loves them far more than we do.

One answer to this question is that prayer has an important effect on the person who prays, whether or not it directly affects the people he prays for. Praying for others can change our attitudes and make us more inclined to regard them with love and respect. Moreover, if the people we pray for somehow learn of our prayers and our concern, this knowledge may have a positive influence on them, too. Besides praying together with his disciples (Jn 17), for example, Jesus also told his disciples that he was praying for them (Lk 22:32).

These results of intercessory prayer are valuable, but they don't seem to apply in cases where people are inaccessible to us and unaware of our prayers for them. Just how do our prayers affect people in these circumstances? The Bible does not address this specific question, and Christians have never agreed on an answer to it, but this does not mean that intercessory prayer is ineffective, or that it only benefits the person who prays. Our intercessory prayers express a sense of solidarity with other human beings. We are embedded in the great fabric of humanity. What happens to others inevitably involves us, and what we do affects them, too. Furthermore, God has ways of working in the world that we cannot understand.

The strongest evidence of the power of intercessory prayer comes from the life of Jesus. According to the Gospels, Jesus healed a number of people in direct response to the faith of others. These include the centurion's servant (Mt 8:5–13), the daughter of the Syrophoenician woman (Mk 7:24–30), and the epileptic boy (Mk 9:14–29). Such instances confirm the encouraging statement that "the prayer of a righteous man has great power in its effects" (Jas 5:16).

Public prayer

Besides certain basic attitudes and several essential elements, prayer also takes different forms. Both public and private prayer have their specific functions. Alone with God, we can give free rein to our thoughts and feelings. We can talk to him without inhibitions, as we would to our closest friend. In contrast, public prayer seeks to express the thoughts and desires of a group of people, rather than those of a single person. It is not simply private prayer offered in the hearing of other people. Because of its distinctive purpose, public prayer requires a different approach. In general, the most effective public prayers are developed in advance. They are not necessarily read or memorized, but they are carefully prepared. It takes time to identify the thoughts that truly reflect the needs of a community and find the words to give them adequate expression.

Unceasing prayer

Prayer is not limited to specific acts of worship, important as these are. In another mode, prayer represents an attitude that permeates the Christian's life. Paul urged the readers of his earliest letter to "pray constantly" (1 Thess 5:17). He evidently meant that they should pray nonstop, so to speak—that is, maintain uninterrupted communion with God. This is possible because God is always available to us. He does not require us to go to a specific place or assume a distinctive posture in order to reach out to him. He offers us his companionship in every circumstance of life.

BAPTISM

A lack of space prevents us from analyzing each act of worship independently, but we cannot overlook the most distinctively Christian acts of worship—baptism and the Lord's Supper. When properly appreciated, these services promote our worship experience to the highest possible level. When unappreciated, however, they degenerate into mere routine; in fact, for some people they are almost a nuisance. In general, Seventh-day Adventists do not place a high value on these rites. We justify observing them by appealing to Christ's commands in the New Testament, but they figure infrequently in our worship services and relatively little is written or said about their meaning.

Questions about baptism

When it comes to baptism, there are two major issues that concern us—its mode and its meaning. The two are closely related. One of the most vigorously discussed questions among Protestant Christians is the age when a person should be baptized. Some Protestants practice infant baptism, as do Catholics. They believe that we should think of a person as part of the Christian community from birth. For them, baptism expresses the commitment of family and church to bring children up in the fear of the Lord. Others insist on "believer's baptism." They maintain that a person should choose to be baptized, and they view baptism as the expression of a person's own decision to respond to the gospel.

A somewhat related issue is the appropriate manner for administering baptism. Some churches baptize by sprinkling, others by immersion. Infants are typically sprinkled, and churches that support believer's baptism typically practice immersion.

There is no explicit biblical command on either of these points. The overall evidence, however, supports the concept of believer's baptism and the practice of baptism by immersion.

Believer's baptism

The New Testament usually connects the command to baptize with other activities which only a reasonably mature person could do.

At the end of the first Gospel, the command to baptize stands between the commands to make disciples of all nations and to teach them to observe Christ's commandments (Mt 28:19–20). At the conclusion of his sermon at Pentecost, Peter urged his listeners, "Repent, and be baptized" (Ac 2:38). The Ethiopian was baptized after Philip explained the gospel to him (Ac 8:26–28), and many people in Corinth were baptized after hearing and believing the preaching of Paul (Ac 18:8). Such passages indicate that baptism is part of a personal response to the gospel and expresses the conviction of someone who knows what he is doing.

Baptism by immersion

Evidence supporting the practice of baptism by immersion is of three types: linguistic, historical, and theological. The English word "baptize" comes from the Greek word *baptizo,* but it is really a transliteration, not a translation. That is to say, it gives us the word in the letters of our alphabet, but it does not express the actual meaning of the Greek in English. One authoritative Greek-English dictionary gives the meaning of *baptizo* as "dip, immerse, plunge, sink, drench, overwhelm."[5] This translation clearly suggests baptism by immersion rather than by sprinkling or pouring.

The New Testament descriptions of baptism also support the practice of immersion. John baptized at a certain place, "because there was much water there" (Jn 3:23). After Jesus was baptized, he "came up out of the water" (Mk 1:10). And when Philip baptized the Ethiopian, they both "went down into the water" and "came up out of the water" (Ac 8:38–39). These expressions give us the picture of baptism by immersion in biblical times. In addition, there is evidence from ancient architecture that people practiced baptism by immersion well into the Christian era. Many early Christian buildings contain baptistries clearly designed to accommodate immersion.

There is also theological evidence for immersion. According to the apostle Paul, baptism commemorates the death, burial, and resurrection of Jesus (Rom 6:4; Col 2:12). It expresses a person's sense of identity with the climactic events of his mission, and it represents the transition from the old life of sin to the new life of the Spirit. Immersion, which literally buries a person in water, serves as a more fitting symbol of this transition than sprinkling. It more vividly recalls Jesus' own experience.

5. William F. Arndt and F. Wilbur Gingrich, *A Greek-English Lexicon of the New Testament and Other Early Christian Literature* (Chicago: The University of Chicago Press, 1957), p. 131.

**The meaning
of baptism**

This brings us to the meaning of baptism, which, of course, is more important than its practice, although the two aspects are related. Unless baptism means something, unless it points to something beyond itself, it really serves no purpose.

To begin with, baptism is a "rite of passage" signifying entrance into the Christian church. As a result, the experience of baptism somehow embodies everything it means to be a Christian. On the objective side, our baptism establishes our relation to Christ. We become part of the community which Jesus founded, and more than this, we acquire a new identity in relation to Christ. Baptism shows that the life of Jesus is decisive for our life. In particular, his death, burial, and resurrection have personal significance for us. They determine what we are.

On the subjective side, baptism signifies a new orientation in a person's life. With baptism, we are no longer in bondage to sin; we have the freedom of life in the Spirit. The repentance which accompanies baptism involves turning away from earlier values and behavior patterns and acquiring a new style of life. In Paul's words, "You also must consider yourselves dead to sin and alive to God in Christ Jesus. Let not sin therefore reign in your mortal bodies, to make you obey their passions" (Rom 6:11–12).

Washing or cleansing is a prominent religious symbol, and it figures in the meaning of baptism, too. Sin is almost universally felt as a source of defilement, or uncleanness. It leaves a stain on us, and we need purification. Accordingly, to be baptized is to be cleansed from past sins. Its waters wash away the guilt and remove the stains. In part, the ceremonial cleansings of Hebrew worship lie behind this understanding of baptism.

Along with all this, and perhaps basic to it, baptism is a sign of discipleship (Mt 28:19). It indicates a person's pledge to follow Jesus and continue the work he did; it expresses commitment to a life of service. In fact, this may be the only thing that Jesus' baptism has in common with ours. Certainly he needed no cleansing from sin. But the first three Gospels all portray his baptism as the definite transition between the years of preparation and his public ministry.

THE LORD'S SUPPER

The Lord's Supper is the other most distinctive part of Christian worship. According to the New Testament, Jesus instituted it while observing the Passover with his disciples on the night before he died (Mt

26:26–29; Mk 14:22–25; Lk 22:14–19; 1 Cor 11:23–25). A person usually receives baptism only once in his life, to express the great transition which salvation involves. But a Christian celebrates the Lord's Supper repeatedly. It plays a different role in his experience.

Questions about the Lord's Supper

Christians refer to this service by several different names. "Eucharist," which means "thanksgiving," is one of the oldest. "The Lord's Supper" is the common title among Protestants, who also speak of "Communion." Roman Catholics call it the "Mass."

Christians have also interpreted the service in many different ways. The most controversial issue is the nature of Christ's presence at the service. According to the Catholic doctrine of transubstantiation, Christ is physically present in the elements. With the words of the priest, the essential reality of bread and wine changes into that of the body and blood of Christ, although their outward form remains the same. Accordingly, the mass is regarded as a sacrifice, and partaking of the elements is a means of receiving grace.

The Protestant Reformers rejected this concept, but they did not agree on an alternative. For Protestants in general, Christ is spiritually present at the celebration of the Lord's Supper, but he is not somehow identical with the elements employed. Partaking of them is not conceived as a means of obtaining divine grace.

Feet washing

A few religious groups, including Seventh-day Adventists, practice feet-washing in connection with this symbolic meal. They base this on an incident recorded in John 13. Before the evening Passover meal, Jesus washed his disciples' feet, a task ordinarily performed by a servant. When he finished, Jesus told his disciples, "If I then, your Lord and Teacher, have washed your feet, you also ought to wash one another's feet. For I have given you an example, that you also should do as I have done to you" (Jn 13:14–15). Adventists often refer to this as the "ordinance of service" because it expresses willingness to serve others, especially fellow members of the body of Christ. The act of washing with water also recalls the cleansing from sin we noticed in connection with baptism.

The Lord's Supper is celebrated in a variety of different forms, but the service is basically very simple. It consists of eating bread, usually unleavened, and drinking wine, or grape juice, in company with other Christians. Participants usually repeat Jesus' words at the institution of the service and offer prayers of thanks for his love and sacrifice.

The Meaning of the Lord's Supper

The Lord's Supper has played an important part in the Christian community from the very beginning, mostly because it is rich with experiential and theological significance. We shall consider four dimensions of the experience here.

Memory

The most obvious dimension of the Lord's Supper is memory. According to the tradition recorded by Paul, Jesus said, "Do this in remembrance of me," twice during the service—once as he broke the bread and again as he passed the wine. The Lord's Supper vividly reminds us of Jesus, focusing our attention specifically on his death. He said, "This is my body," as he broke the bread, and he described the wine as "my blood of the covenant, which is poured out for many for the forgiveness of sins" (Mt 26:28; cf. Mk 14:24). The Lord's Supper puts Jesus' death in a sacrificial perspective. It was something he went through on our behalf, the means by which salvation becomes available to us. Partaking of the elements reinforces our awareness that what happened then affects us here and now.

Anticipation

Another dimension of this important service is anticipation. The Lord's Supper directs our attention to the future, as well as to the past. All four passages recording the institution of the first service refer to the future. According to the first Gospel, Jesus said, "I tell you I shall not drink again of this fruit of the vine until that day when I drink it new with you in my Father's kingdom" (Mt 26:29). Paul concludes his summary of the Lord's Supper with the statement, "For as often as you eat this bread and drink the cup, you proclaim the Lord's death until he comes" (1 Cor 11:26). The concept of a messianic banquet figured prominently in Jewish thought at Jesus' time (cf. Lk 14:15). Jesus himself used a banquet theme in two of his parables (Mt 22:1–14; Lk 14:16–24). The Lord's Supper reminds us of the joy of personal fellowship with Christ that awaits us when the kingdom of God is fully established. It intensifies our desire to participate in that experience.

Dependence on Christ

The Lord's Supper also awakens a sense of dependence on Jesus here and now. The fourth Gospel does not record the institution of the Lord's Supper, but we find there a more highly developed "theology of the Eucharist" than anywhere else in the New Testament. In the "Bread of Life Discourse," recorded in John 6, Jesus speaks of his flesh and blood as the source of eternal life: "Unless you eat the flesh of the Son of man and drink his blood, you have no life in you; he who eats my flesh and drinks my blood abides in me, and I in him'' (Jn 6:53–56).

The purpose of these striking statements is to emphasize our utter dependence on Jesus Christ. The symbolism of the communion service suggests that we are as dependent on Christ for spiritual life as we are on food and drink for physical life. The acts of eating and drinking during the Lord's Supper make us vitally aware of this fact. They help us to realize the importance of a deep and abiding connection with Jesus.

Fellowship

The word ''communion'' focuses on a fourth dimension of this experience. The Lord's Supper promotes a sense of fellowship among members of the church. It is a communal meal, something we all share together. One of the achievements of the Reformation was to return the cup to the laity, the general membership of the church. The elements of the Lord's Supper belong to every Christian. Our mutual partaking of the bread and wine and our gathering around a common table, so to speak, strengthen the bonds of affection that hold us together in the church. They remind us of the profound unity of need and fulfillment that we all share in the body of Christ.

THE FUNCTION OF RELIGIOUS SYMBOLS

The prosaic outlook of the secularistic world we live in threatens the vitality of religious services like baptism and the Lord's Supper. Many people participate in them by rote, out of a sense of duty, with little attention to their meaning. It will help us to appreciate the importance of these aspects of Christian worship if we reflect briefly on the nature of religious symbols.

Suppose someone points to the bread on the communion table and asks, ''What is it?'' What would it take to answer his question? We could say, ''Something to eat,'' but that would not be adequate. True, the bread is food, and we do eat it, but its real purpose is not to satisfy hunger. For most people, the Lord's Supper does not replace a meal. To answer the question, we have to explain what the bread means, because it directs our attention to something else.

Symbols indicate

This is the first characteristic of religious symbols. They point to something beyond themselves; their significance lies in something else. Signs do this, too. If you see a flashing red light ahead of you on the highway, you instinctively slow down. It indicates the presence of something that could threaten your safety. In itself, the light isn't that important. Chances are you don't time the length of the flashes or pause to admire that particular shade of red. What makes the light important is what it signifies. Similarly, the purpose of baptism is not hygienic, and the purpose of the Lord's Supper is not nutritional. Their meaning lies in the spiritual realities to which they direct our attention.

For symbols to serve as effective indicators, they need to be transparent to their object. They must be means, not ends in themselves. It helps if a symbol is relatively simple, for this makes it easier for us to see through it, or beyond it. A symbol that is too elaborate, or too overwhelming, can arrest our attention and make it impossible for us to think about anything else. The beauty of the central symbols of Christian worship is their simplicity. Bread, wine, and water are common materials, and eating, drinking, and bathing are ordinary activities. They are the sort of thing we do every day. As a result, we can easily see beyond them to the spiritual realities which they represent.

If this were the only function of symbols, it would be natural to wonder if we could just as well do away with them. Once you understand, for example, that baptism signifies "commitment to Christ," "cleansing from sin," and so forth, why not just think about those things and forget about the water? Two things prevent us from concluding that symbols are dispensable. One is the nature of symbols themselves, and the other is the nature of human beings.

Symbols participate

Symbols, like signs, point beyond themselves, as we have seen. Unlike signs, however, symbols are intimately related to their objects, or referents. In the well-known words of theologian Paul Tillich, a symbol "participates in that to which it points."[6] The connection between a symbol and its object is not entirely arbitrary. Powerful religious symbols "fit" their objects in a special way; their very content is uniquely appropriate to the reality they represent. Bread and wine, for example, are certainly common things, but they are enormously important. Such staples are indispensable for life, so they fittingly express our utter dependence on Christ. Similarly, baptism by immersion vividly recalls the death, burial, and resurrection of Jesus.

This characteristic of symbols is closely related to the incarnational theme in Christian worship we mentioned earlier. There is an intimate relation between the spiritual and the material aspects of reality. Physical objects and activities can serve as vehicles for grasping spiritual realities, and certain things provide more effective vehicles

6. Paul Tillich, *Dynamics of Faith* (New York: Harper & Row, Publishers, 1957), p. 42.

than others. This is why the particular symbols of Christian worship cannot be exchanged for others.

For the same reason, religious symbols have the capacity to illuminate all of experience in a remarkable way. Because a symbol participates in the reality to which it points, it never remains merely what it was before; it becomes something "more." Because bread serves as a symbol of Christ's sacrifice, it is never merely a means of nutrition. It acquires a new significance. Every meal we eat can remind us of our dependence on God for all that makes life possible and worthwhile.[7] Here again, the incarnational theme emerges, for on every hand we can find indicators that there is more to reality than meets the eye. We are embedded in the physical, but we are surrounded by the spiritual, too.

Symbols illuminate

Another thing that makes symbols so important is their capacity to speak to all levels of human being. We are not merely intellectual beings. We do more than just think. We are creatures with senses, emotions, and imagination, and a complete worship experience, as well as a complete religious experience, involves all of these. The powerful symbols of Christian worship awaken all the aspects of our nature.

Symbols stimulate

An additional characteristic of human existence contributes to the importance of symbols. This is the interaction between thought and behavior, between attitude and action. We generally think of our behavior as the product or expression of our attitudes. We feel a certain way, so we act a certain way. But the influence flows in the other direction, too. Our behavior can affect the way we feel. Most of us have discovered, for example, that we begin to feel friendly toward other people if we make an effort to speak and act in a friendly way. Doing certain things can lead to certain attitudes.

The importance of this for religious symbols is obvious. In one sense, symbols serve as expressions of religious devotion; they arise from a religious commitment. But in another sense, they awaken religious commitment. Religious symbols both invite and intensify a sense of devotion to Christ. There is nothing that can take their place.

---

7. In the words of Ellen G. White, "To the death of Christ we owe even this earthly life. The bread we eat is the purchase of His broken body. The water we drink is bought by His spilled blood. . . . The light shining from that Communion Service in the upper chamber makes sacred the provisions for our daily life. The family board becomes as the table of the Lord, and every meal a sacrament" (*Desire of Ages,* p. 660).

This brings to a close our examination of the doctrine of the church. As developed here, it is the most comprehensive aspect of Christian theology and involves more of the day-to-day concerns of Christians than any other doctrine. It deserves much more consideration than it usually receives. We now turn to the two doctrinal concerns for which Seventh-day Adventists are best known and for which the denomination is named. These are the return of Christ and the seventh-day Sabbath.

STUDY HELPS

Questions for review

1. What are the basic attitudes involved in worship?

2. What are the essential dimensions of the worship experience?

3. What are some of the prevalent distortions of the worship experience?

4. What does baptism signify? What evidence supports the practice of immersion?

5. What is the meaning of the Lord's Supper?

6. What are the essential characteristics of religious symbols? Why are they important?

Questions for discussion

1. What are the major differences between public worship and private devotional experiences? Why are both important?

2. At times entertainment assumes the characteristics of worship. Some people seem to display religious fervor at athletic contests and rock concerts. What are the consequences of investing entertainment with religious significance?

3. Conversely, people often expect worship to be entertaining. For example, some "religious" tunes are indistinguishable from popular ones. What are the consequences of looking to worship for entertainment?

4. The sermon is the most prominent element in most Adventist worship services, as in Protestant services in general. How do you evaluate the sermons you hear? What makes a sermon good, as far as you are concerned? Should it amuse, inform, inspire, or what?

5. The Bible does not specify how often Christians should celebrate the Lord's Supper. What factors should determine the frequency?

6. What constitutes a good public prayer? Are the most effective public prayers prepared ahead of time, or offered impromptu?

7. How does the place of worship affect the experience? In what ways should a church's structure and interior design reflect the beliefs of its congregation?

1. Isaiah 6 records a dramatic encounter with God. Study it as a model worship experience. What did Isaiah see and hear, and what was his response? How did the experience begin, and how did it end? Accordingly, what should our worship consist of? **Suggestions for Bible study**

2. The book of Psalms is the Bible's most extensive collection of worship material. Page through the psalms. Make a list of the different emotions they express. How can our worship experiences enable us to express these emotions?

3. Theology and prayer are closely related. According to one theologian, "Theology . . . has its basis in the . . . experience of prayer" (Heinrich Ott, *God,* trans. Ian and Ute Nicol [Richmond, Va.: John Knox Press, 1974], p. 95). Study the most prominent prayers of Jesus recorded in the Gospels: Matthew 7:9–13 and John 17:1–26. What understanding do they express of God, man, salvation, church, and last things?

4. One of Jesus' most specific discussions of worship appears in John 4:20–23. Study these verses carefully. What concepts and attitudes characterize worship at its best?

5. Study Hebrews 8–10. According to these chapters, how does the work of Christ transform the worship experience of people familiar with the services of the Old Testament?

6. The book of Revelation contains a number of scenes depicting the worship of God in a heavenly setting. What do they indicate as to the nature and purpose of worship in eternity? See Revelation 4–5; 7:13–17; 14:1–5; 15:1–4; 19:1–8.

7. According to the following passages, when is worship unacceptable to God?

   a. Leviticus 10:1–3; 1 Samuel 2:12–17
   b. 1 Samuel 15:17–23

    c. Amos 5:21–24; Micah 6:6–8; Psalm 51:16–17
    d. Matthew 21:12–16; Mark 11:15–17; Luke 19:45–46; John 2:13–17

SUGGESTIONS FOR FURTHER READING

From Adventist writers

Ellen G. White comments on different aspects of worship in many places in her writings. Some of the more sustained treatments are "Behavior in the House of God" (*Testimonies for the Church,* vol. 5, pp. 491–500) and two chapters in *Desire of Ages,* "A Servant of Servants" and "In Remembrance of Me" (*Desire of Ages,* pp. 642–661). She also has a great deal to say about prayer. One of her best-known discussions is "The Privilege of Prayer" in *Steps to Christ* (pp. 93–104).

There are many articles on worship by Adventist writers. Most of them appear in *Ministry,* the church's publication for clergy. Over the years a few books on various aspects of worship have appeared. The most comprehensive is Norval F. Pease, *And Worship Him* (Nashville, Tenn.: Southern Publishing Association, 1967), which touches on the theology and history of Christian worship and examines the specific form and content of the Adventist worship service.

William G. Johnsson explores the significance of baptism in *Clean! The Meaning of Christian Baptism* (Nashville, Tenn.: Southern Publishing Association, 1969).

Harold Byron Hannum encourages the pursuit of excellence in religious music in *Music and Worship* (Nashville, Tenn.: Southern Publishing Association, 1969).

From other writers

The general Christian literature on worship is voluminous. It ranges from examinations of the fundamental experience of worship through discussions of the precise meaning of the sacraments to manuals on how to conduct more stimulating religious services.

One of the standard works in the field is Evelyn Underhill, *Worship* (New York: Harper & Brothers, 1936). This challenging book analyzes the essential experience of worship, and surveys the different forms worship takes in a variety of Christian communities.

For a number of years "liturgical renewal" has been a topic of considerable interest among Protestants, as well as Roman Catholics. Two readable books on this topic are Kenneth G. Phifer, *A Protestant Case for Liturgical Renewal* (Philadelphia: The Westminster Press, 1965), and Massey Hamilton Shepherd, Jr. (ed.), *The Eucharist and Liturgical Renewal* (New York: Oxford University Press, 1960).

Reformed theologian Alasdair I. C. Heron investigates the development of the Eucharist, or the Lord's Supper, for serious students in *Table and Tradition: Toward Ecumenical Understanding of the Eucharist* (Philadelphia: The Westminster Press, 1984).

Liturgical Experience of Faith, ed. Herman Schmit and David Power (New York: Herder and Herder, 1973), contains a series of rather technical articles on the different elements of worship.

Much can be learned about the theology of church music from a book like Albert Edward Bailey, *The Gospel in Hymns: Background and Interpretations* (New York: Charles Scribner's Sons, 1950).

Two well-known books on the topic of prayer are George Arthur Buttrick, *Prayer* (New York and Nashville: Abingdon-Cokesbury Press, 1942), and Harry Emmerson Fosdick, *The Meaning of Prayer* (Chicago: Follett Publishing Company, 1949, 1962). John Baillie presents a beautiful collection of morning and evening prayers for personal devotions in *A Diary of Private Prayer* (New York: Charles Scribner's Sons, 1949).

14

THE DOCTRINE OF LAST THINGS:
THE ROOTS OF ADVENTIST ESCHATOLOGY

"Unto two thousand and three hundred days; then shall the sanctuary be cleansed" (Daniel 8:14, KJV).

"I am sure that he who began a good work in you will bring it to completion at the day of Jesus Christ" (Philippians 1:6).

"He is able for all time to save those who draw near to God through him, since he always lives to make intercession for them" (Hebrews 7:25).

Exodus 20:5–6
Leviticus 16
Daniel 2
Daniel 7–9
Amos 5:18–20; 8:9–10
Joel
Luke 4:16–21

Acts 2:14–36
Romans 13:11–12
Hebrews 2:17–18; 4:14–16
Hebrews 8–9
James 5:8
1 Peter 4:7
Revelation 6, 8–10

THE TIMELINESS OF CHRISTIAN ESCHATOLOGY

Where is history going? What will life be like in ten, twenty, or fifty years? What will people eat? What will they wear? How will they work? What will they do for entertainment? How many children will the average family have? Will there even be an "average family"? How long will people live? What will they die from? Will the nations of the world achieve peace? Or will human beings annihilate themselves?

The questions go on and on, and they interest us enormously. One reason for our fascination with the future is the realization that there may not be a future at all—at least, as far as human beings are concerned. The world's great military powers have enough explosives to blow us all away many times over, and they persist in adding to their stockpiles. In the effort to guarantee national security, the nations of the world have made themselves less secure than ever.

If we are spared a nuclear holocaust, we face the equally un-attractive prospects of starving to death or poisoning ourselves with pollution. World population is rapidly increasing, while natural resources are dwindling. It doesn't take a genius to see that more and more of us will have less and less to share, until finally we all have nothing.

Time was when only religious people talked about the "end of the world," but now it is a concern of every thinking person. The more we think about it, the more sobering it becomes. Hope springs eternal in the human heart, but there is little basis for optimism about the future of humanity. Human beings have made great strides in many areas, but getting along with each other is not one of them. Neither is taking proper care of the environment. Technology has brought us many good things, but it has also pushed us to the brink of disaster.

These depressing facts are worth considering here for two rea-sons. First, they show that we need something more than human means to solve our present problems. Unless we get "outside help," nothing can save us from destruction. Second, this sobering reality establishes the lively relevance of Christian eschatology today. What Christians have been saying about the end for centuries takes on new meaning as we look around us now. The doctrine of last things doesn't deal with the far-off future. It speaks directly to the present. It is as timely as the morning paper and the hourly newscast.

Threats to the future

Like many theological terms, "eschatology" has Greek roots. The Greek adjective *eschatos* means "last," and the familiar suffix *-ology* is usually translated "theory of," or "doctrine of." So "escha-tology" simply means "doctrine of last things."

In the traditional arrangement of Christian theology, eschatology comes at the end, after the doctrine of the church, but this doesn't mean it is just a footnote to the central concerns of Christian faith. Eschatology is not an afterthought. It is the climax to which all the rest leads, the ringing conclusion of all that Christians have to say.[1]

The meaning of Christian eschatology

---

1. According to many recent scholars, eschatology applies not just to part of what Christians believe, but to all of it. They maintain that Christian faith is eschatological

At the same time, this aspect of Christian faith has generated a wide diversity of theological views. In fact, nowhere in Christian thought do we find a more bewildering variety of biblical interpretations and doctrinal formulations. Controversy surrounds almost every aspect of this doctrine—from the time of Christ's return and the ultimate fate of the wicked, to the identity of the antichrist and the location of Armageddon. The list of eschatological questions is much too long to answer here, so we will limit our inquiry to the most basic elements in the doctrine.

Many people equate eschatology with a description of last-day events. The word sometimes conjures up visions of prophetic charts and tables designed to pinpoint our location in the march of time and predict in detail the course of the future. It is true that eschatology includes an understanding of how history will end, and we will examine the sequence of events that Seventh-day Adventists anticipate. But Christian faith interprets human history as a whole, not just its final segment. It views all of history in light of God's saving activity, and it sees the end of history as the climax of the process. History will conclude, Christians believe, with the full and final realization of the reign of God in human affairs. Only when the reign of God is fully established will the real meaning of history be clear.[2]

As a result, history's final events mean nothing by themselves; they have to be related to the process that precedes them. For this reason, it is more important to understand the meaning of history's final events than to know the precise nature or sequence of their occurrence.

Our investigation of eschatology begins with a look at the Christian view of time and concludes with an analysis of the meaning of the future for life in the present. Along the way, we shall examine the origin and content of the distinctive eschatological concerns of the Seventh-day Adventist Church.

---

through and through. In the words of a well-known British theologian, "all statements about the End . . . are fundamentally affirmations about God," and "every statement about God is *ipso facto* an assertion about the end, a truth about eschatology" (John T. Robinson, *In the End God* [New York: Harper & Row, Publishers, 1968], pp. 22, 47).

2. See Wolfhart Pannenberg's concept of a "final future." With the final future, Pannenberg argues, reality will at last become a totality, and the meaning of the entire course of history will become evident (*Basic Questions in Theology: Collected Essays*, trans. George H. Kehm [Philadelphia: Fortress Press, 1971], 2:62).

THE BIBLICAL VIEW OF TIME

The roots of Christian eschatology reach deep into the soil of Hebrew thought, so we must begin our analysis by turning to the Old Testament. The heart of Hebrew religion was the belief that God had acted in history for the salvation of his people. The events recorded in the book of Exodus—the call of the fathers, the deliverance from slavery, the covenant at Sinai, and the conquest of Canaan (cf. Dt 26:5–10a)— lay at the center of the Hebrew faith.[3]

History and salvation

Convinced that God had been active in their past, the Israelites believed that God would continue to act in their behalf in the future. He would bring the work of salvation he had begun to its final consummation. Accordingly, their attitude toward the future was based on a confidence in God established by his previous activity. Their concept of the future was essentially an extension of God's actions in their past (cf. Isa 48:20–21; 51:10–11). In the Old Testament, therefore, the "eschaton" is that part of salvation-history which is still to come and which presses for its realization. The future is not like a distant destination we are slowly making progress toward; it is threatening to break in on us.

The main event in the Old Testament is the coming of God to his people. This event involves both salvation and judgment. It spells disaster for the enemies of God, but it brings restoration and deliverance to the remnant who are faithful to him. In the Old Testament, judgment and salvation are not two contrasting divine activities, but two aspects of a single unit (cf. Ex 20:5–6).

The coming of God

Hebrew writers often referred to God's coming as "the day of the Lord," and they were careful to describe the event in its negative as well as its positive aspects. Amos portrayed the day of the Lord as a day of darkness and gloom (5:20), and Zephaniah described it as a day of wrath, a day of distress and anguish, a day of ruin and devastation (1:15). In the day of the Lord, the enemies of God will finally be reckoned with and the faithful remnant will be delivered to enjoy the personal presence of their Savior.

Apocalyptic literature—the kind of writing we find in Daniel— also describes the end of history.[4] Apocalyptic literature typically

Apocalyptic

3. For a readable account of the historical nature of biblical faith, see G. Ernest Wright and Reginald H. Fuller, *The Book of the Acts of God: Contemporary Scholarship Interprets the Bible* (Garden City, N.Y.: Doubleday & Company, Inc., 1960).

4. According to G. Ernest Wright and Reginald H. Fuller, apocalypticism is

arises during periods of persecution. It reaffirms God's promises to his people in the face of difficult circumstances. There is no clear progression from the difficulties of the present to the fulfillment of God's promises. The end will come with a dramatic conflict in which God defeats the evil powers that dominate the present era. In its distinctive way, then, apocalyptic literature expresses the essential content of Old Testament eschatology, that history will reach its climax with the completion of God's saving activity. At last his people will enjoy his presence, untroubled by any disruptive influence.

The uniqueness of the biblical view of time

The biblical view of history contrasts sharply with other concepts of time. According to the Greek view of life and the world, history repeats itself; everything that happens is just like what has already happened. Since the past determines the future, nothing really new can ever occur. The Greek view allows no room for a unique, incomparable event.

According to the Bible, it is not the past that gives history its essential character, but the future, the goal toward which it moves. Moreover, history is the sphere of personal activity, not of impersonal natural law. What ultimately determines the course of history isn't an indelible pattern stamped on the scheme of things; it is the will of a personal God who acts to accomplish his purposes.[5]

The biblical view of history also differs sharply from the primitive, or archaic, view of time.[6] Primitive peoples try to escape the terror of history, or the irreversibility of time. By using myths and rituals, they seek to return periodically to a "golden age" that existed at the beginning of things.

We find no such flight in the Bible, of course. The Bible affirms the value of history, because it regards history as a series of divine activities, or revelations. Since God reveals himself in history, the unique, unrepeatable events of history have intrinsic value. The biblical view of time and history is like a line, rather than a

---

"characterized by the view that the current world is meaningless, evil, wicked. God has given it over to destruction and in due time he will intervene and bring in the end of this age while inaugurating his kingdom" (*The Book of the Acts of God: Contemporary Scholarship Interprets the Bible* [Garden City, N.Y.: Doubleday & Company, Inc., 1960], p. 145).

5. For a succinct comparison of Greek and biblical attitudes toward history, see Karl Lowith, *Meaning in History* (Chicago: University of Chicago Press, 1949), pp. 4–9.

6. Mircea Eliade compares the archaic view of time with that of Christian faith in *The Myth of the Eternal Return, or, Cosmos and History,* trans. Willard R. Trask (Princeton, N.J.: Princeton University Press, 1971), especially the last chapter.

circle. History is going somewhere. It has a goal; it does not repeat itself.[7]

We can see that the biblical view of history is determined by the biblical concept of God. The Israelites believed that history was meaningful because God was directing the course of events to a definite conclusion. They looked forward to the future because of their confidence in God.

JESUS AND THE END OF HISTORY

What the New Testament says about Jesus makes sense only in light of this Hebrew concept of history. Its central claim is that God was acting for the salvation of all men in the life, death, and resurrection of Jesus (Ac 2:22–24, 31–32; cf. 1 Cor 15:3–5). In relation to the Old Testament view of history, this means that the climax of history arrived with Jesus; he fulfills the meaning of history. In other words, the end has arrived. We are now living in the last days.

The end has arrived

Alongside this "even now" of present realization, we also find in the New Testament the "not yet" of anticipation. There are numerous

The end is near

7. This is not to say that history exhibits no pattern. Similar circumstances lead to similar consequences, on the large scale of history as well as on the smaller scale of individual human existence. Indeed, this is one implication of the doctrine of providence, with its affirmation of God's sovereignty in human affairs. Over the long haul, for example, social justice provides for greater national security than do discrimination and oppression.

The denial that history repeats itself arises from the biblical concept that history will eventually end with the fulfillment of God's purposes for humankind and the Christian affirmation that God was present in the historical life of Jesus in a unique, unprecedented, and unsurpassable way.

Many writers have commented on the relation between the linear concept of time expressed in the Bible and the unique significance attributed to certain historical events by Christian faith. According to Edward W. H. Vick, "The doctrine of the incarnation means that the divine appears within the temporal order, that is to say that the temporal order is 'substantial' enough to receive it. But such an outlook was possible only because the view of history held by Biblical writers was linear, as opposed to the cyclical view of the Greeks" (*Let Me Assure You* [Mountain View, Calif.: Pacific Press Publishing Association, 1968], p. 173). Langdon Gilkey credits Augustine with the definitive expression of this view of history: "With Augustine the Western, and so the modern sense of temporal passage comes to definitive and formative expression: historical time is a linear sequence, each of whose moments contains the possibility of ultimate significance, whose events form a pattern related to that ultimate significance, and so whose course as a whole possesses an intelligible and coherent unity relevant to the gaining of final salvation" (*Reaping the Whirlwind: A Christian Interpretation of History* [New York: Seabury, 1976], pp. 162–63).

texts which look forward to the return of Christ in the very near future. Indeed, the entire New Testament, from Matthew to Revelation, breathes the spirit of fervent expectancy: ''For salvation is nearer to us now than when we first believed; the night is far gone, the day is at hand'' (Rom 13:11–12); ''The Lord is at hand'' (Phil 4:5); ''We who are alive, who are left, shall be caught up . . . to meet the Lord in the air'' (1 Thess 4:15–17); ''The coming of the Lord is at hand'' (Jas 5:8); ''The end of all things is at hand'' (1 Pet 4:7); ''Children, it is the last hour'' (1 Jn 2:18); ''I am coming soon'' (Rev 22:6, 12, 20).

The New Testament uses several expressions to refer to the return of Christ. The best-known is *parousia,* or ''coming,'' which refers to the official visit of a ruler (Mt 24:3, 27, 39). We also find the favorite expression of the Old Testament, ''the day of the Lord,'' which carries the theme of judgment (2 Pet 3:10, 12). Another description is ''apocalypse,'' the revealing of something hidden (1 Cor 1:7); and a fourth is ''epiphany,'' or ''appearing,'' by which the Greeks referred to the appearance of gods among men (2 Thess 2:8; cf. Ac 14:11–12).

The end is delayed

There was a strong sense in the apostolic church that Christ's return was near, but early Christians were also aware that it had not occurred as soon as they had expected. Several texts indicate that a series of events would have to take place before the Lord could return (Ac 20:29; 2 Thess 2:3; 2 Tim 4:3ff). At least one notable passage deals explicitly with the delay as a problem facing the Christian community. Peter attributes the apparent delay to God's forbearance—his unwillingness that any should perish (2 Pet 3:9).

Early Christians, then, believed that the decisive act of salvation had already taken place. With Jesus, the end of history had arrived, but the full realization of salvation was yet to come. They looked for Jesus to return and complete the process. Thus they saw themselves living ''between the times.'' The climax of history was past, but its conclusion was still to come.

We can illustrate their situation with imagery from World War II. After D-Day, the great invasion at Normandy, it became clear that the Allied forces would win. The final outcome of the war was assured. But there was still a lot of mopping up to do before Germany surrendered, and it was several months until V-Day, when hostilities finally ceased. Similarly, Christians find themselves living between the D-Day of Christ's victory over the powers of darkness and the V-Day of Christ's return in glory.[8]

8. Oscar Cullman uses this striking illustration in *Christ and Time: The Primitive Christian Conception of Time and History,* trans. Floyd V. Filson (rev. ed.; London: SCM

PROPHECY AND HISTORY

As years passed, it was evident that a considerable amount of time would elapse between the earthly ministry of Jesus and his glorious return, and Christians were forced to examine the question of its meaning. What is the significance of the historical period that lies between these two climactic events?

For many Christians, the prophecies of the Bible provide an answer to this question. They believe that prophecy enables us to see the religious significance of different developments in the course of history.

Joachim

A twelfth-century churchman, Joachim of Floris, did much to stimulate thought along these lines.[9] He believed that the various symbols of prophecy corresponded to actual historical persons and events. By interpreting these symbols, we can plot the course of history through its various stages, and we can also see where we are at present in the overall stream of events.

On the basis of this concept, the passage of time since Christ was on earth ceases to be an embarrassment to the church. Prophecy shows that God is still active in the world. He is currently working in human affairs, bringing the plan of salvation to a conclusion.

Schools of prophetic interpretation

All who regard prophecy as a forecast of historical events are indebted to Joachim's ideas, even if their specific interpretations differ from his. In a sense, he was the pioneer of all three major schools of prophetic interpretation—preterist, historicist, and futurist. Preterism sees the historical events of which prophecy speaks as lying in the past. Futurism regards these events as yet to take place. Historicism applies the prophecies to successive phases of world history up to and including the present, and extending to the end of time. All of them relate prophecy to world history in a manner similar to Joachim.

Press Ltd., 1962), p. 84.

9. LeRoy Edwin Froom discusses the work of Joachim in *The Prophetic Faith of Our Fathers: The Historical Development of Prophetic Interpretation* (4 vols.; Washington, D.C.: Review and Herald Publishing Association, 1950–54), 1:683–716. Froom states, "With Joachim of Floris . . . we reach the most outstanding figure among the medieval expositors of prophecy. With him we definitely come to a turning point. . . . He is important not only contemporarily, for the new era that he introduced, but for his far-reaching influence upon exposition for centuries to come" (ibid., p. 683). Another discussion of Joachim's views appears in Karl Lowith, *Meaning in History* (Chicago and London: The University of Chicago Press, 1949), pp. 145–159.

To summarize, Christians believe that history is meaningful because God is working in historical events for human salvation. The climax of his saving actions was the life, death, and resurrection of Jesus. This work will conclude with the return of Christ and the complete establishment of God's reign over human beings.

The basic posture of Christians in the world is therefore one of confidence in the past and eager anticipation for the future. Because of what God has already done, they look forward to what he has yet to do.

In addition, many Christians believe that biblical prophecy describes the relation between human history and the work of salvation. By interpreting the prophetic symbols accurately, we can see the spiritual significance of different historical developments, and we can understand our own role in the scheme of things. Seventh-day Adventists are among those who hold this view of prophecy.

ADVENTISM AND THE ADVENT MOVEMENT

Traditionally there have been several things that distinguish Seventh-day Adventist eschatology from the approaches of other Christians to the doctrine of last things. One of the earliest was the conviction that the return of Christ is very near. Another is a certain understanding of the various events which surround this momentous occasion. A third is the importance of eschatology to the self-understanding of Adventists as a people. As their denominational name indicates, Seventh-day Adventists wish to be known as those who await the advent, or coming, of Christ. The church traces its beginnings to the great advent movement that radiated from the northeastern United States in the middle of the nineteenth century. To capture the spirit of Adventism in this crucial doctrinal area, it will help to take a brief look at its originating impulse.

William Miller   The central figure in the advent movement of the last century was William Miller (1782–1849).[10] Born in Massachusetts and raised in upstate New York, Miller was an avid reader as a child, often sitting by the fireplace after the chores were done. As a young man, he

---

10. An account of William Miller's personal and public religious life appears in the opening chapters of Francis D. Nichol, *The Midnight Cry* (Washington, D.C.: Review and Herald Publishing Association, 1954). The historical data in this and the following chapters of the text are drawn from this book.

frequented the library and joined a literary society in the Vermont town where he settled with his wife. With a number of his friends he espoused deism, the view that God does not take an active interest in human affairs. Miller served in the state militia and in the United States Army in the War of 1812. His experiences in the service left him disillusioned with human behavior, and he suffered periods of deep despondency.

In 1816 he was converted to Christ, and for two years he studied the Bible intensely to learn more of his Savior. His method was to examine one verse at a time, going only as fast as he could grasp the meaning of the text. Whenever he ran into something he couldn't understand, he used a concordance to locate other passages on the same topic, studying them until he found answers. In this way he allowed the Bible to explain itself.

Miller reached his most startling conclusions from studying the prophetic portions of the Bible. He believed that these prophecies pointed to literal historical events, and concluded that the personal return of Christ to earth lay in the near future, only twenty-five years away. The most important text in this calculation was Daniel 8:14: "Unto two thousand and three hundred days; then shall the sanctuary be cleansed" (KJV). This verse mentions both a time period and an event. Miller believed that days in prophetic time corresponded to literal years (cf. Num 14:34; Ezek 4:6), and he believed that the 2300 days of Daniel 8 started simultaneously with the seventy weeks of years in Daniel 9, which began with Artaxerxes' decree in 457 B.C.

Miller interpreted the event mentioned in Daniel 8:14, the "cleansing of the sanctuary," as a reference to the purification of the earth that would accompany the return of Christ. Putting these factors together, he came to his momentous conclusion. In his own words, "I was thus brought, in 1818, at the close of my two years' study of the Scriptures, to the solemn conclusion, that in about twenty-five years from that time all the affairs of our present state would be wound up."[11]

The advent movement

Miller reviewed his position for the next five years and became more and more convinced it was correct. During the 1830s he presented his views to small groups around New England, but his work became a full-fledged movement in 1840, due in large measure to the promotional efforts of Joshua V. Himes, a pastor in Boston. *The Signs of the Times* began publication in 1840; *The Midnight Cry* followed two

---

11. William Miller, *Apology and Defense* (Boston: Joshua V. Himes, August 1845), pp. 11–12 (quoted in Nichol, *The Midnight Cry*, p. 35).

years later. There was a series of "General Conferences of Christians Expecting the Advent," and Miller's followers began holding camp-meetings in 1842.

Although all who belonged to the movement believed that Christ's return was near, not all of them were committed to a specific time. This changed in the summer of 1844. With the passage of 1843, it was clear to Miller and his followers that they had miscalculated. A closer look at chronology revealed that the 2300 days of Daniel 8:14 extended into 1844, since there is no "zero" year in historical time.

In addition, certain Millerites began to teach that the cleansing of the sanctuary referred to in Daniel 8:14 would fulfill the Hebrew Day of Atonement service described in Leviticus 16. They further believed that this antitypical cleansing would occur when the Day of Atonement was scheduled—that is, on the tenth day of the seventh month in the current Jewish year. According to the calendar of one Jewish sect, this corresponded to October 22. Those who argued for this date were known as the "Seventh-Month Movement."

Not all of Miller's followers accepted the view that Christ would return on October 22, 1844. Miller and Himes did not take this position themselves until early in the month. But on the morning of October 22, thousands met in groups here and there throughout New England, confident that they would meet their Lord before the day was over.

The Great Disappointment and its aftermath

Their later reference to the experience as the "Great Disappointment" reflects the emotional blow that fell when their hopes were not fulfilled. Those who went through it said their grief defied description.

The impact of the Great Disappointment understandably fragmented the Millerite movement. Daniel 8:14 received further examination, and the two most important reactions held contrary interpretations of its contents. The majority of Millerites, including Miller himself, continued to believe that the text pointed to the return of Christ, but they felt that something was wrong with their calculation of the time and that the 2300 days did not, as they had thought, end on October 22, 1844.

Others were convinced that their interpretation of the time period was correct. They believed that the 2300 days of Daniel 8:14 did come to an end on October 22, 1844. This group included many of the principal figures in what became the Seventh-day Adventist Church. These early Adventists looked back on their experience of waiting for Christ to come on this specific date and recalled it as the happiest part of their entire lives. To reject the calculations responsible for this experience, they felt, would be to deny that God had led them. This they could not do, so they turned their attention to the other element in

Daniel 8:14 and came to a new interpretation of the cleansing of the sanctuary.

CHRIST IN THE HEAVENLY SANCTUARY

To summarize developments that occurred over some thirteen years, these early Adventists concluded that the sanctuary of Daniel 8:14 was in heaven, not the earth. Hebrews, for example, speaks of Christ ministering in the "heavenly sanctuary" (Heb 8:15). They came to believe that on October 22, 1844, Christ entered the most holy place of the heavenly sanctuary rather than leaving it to come to this world. The cleansing of which Daniel 8:14 speaks means blotting out the sins recorded against God's people in the books of heaven. It requires a work of judgment, or investigation, to determine which sins should be expunged.[12] The "cleansing of the sanctuary," then, refers to the results of an investigative judgment which takes place in heaven just before the return of Christ to earth.

The investigative judgment

For Seventh-day Adventists, Christ's work in the heavenly sanctuary thus includes two distinct activities which began at different times. Since his ascension to heaven, Christ has mediated the benefits of his atoning sacrifice for human beings. His work as our high priest consists of forgiving sins, providing human beings direct access to God, and directing the work of the church on earth. In 1844, Christ began the investigative judgment. In this phase of his high priestly ministry, Christ examine the life records of his professed followers throughout human history. At its conclusion he blots out the sins of those whose lives were/are consistent with their profession. The investigative judgment directly prepares for the return of Christ to deliver his people from the earth.

12. Ellen G. White describes the cleansing of the heavenly sanctuary in these words: 'As anciently the sins of the people were by faith placed upon the sin offering and through its blood transferred, in figure, to the earthly sanctuary, so in the new covenant the sins of the repentant are by faith placed upon Christ and transferred, in fact, to the heavenly sanctuary. And as the typical cleansing of the earthly was accomplished by the removal of the sins by which it had been polluted, so the actual cleansing of the heavenly is to be accomplished by the removal, or blotting out, of the sins which are there recorded. But before this can be accomplished, there must be an examination of the books of record to determine who, through repentance of sin and faith in Christ, are entitled to the benefits of His atonement. The cleansing of the sanctuary therefore involves a work of investigation—a work of judgment" (*The Great Controversy*, pp. 421–22).

Questions about the investigative judgment

Over the years, this doctrine has raised a number of questions, inside as well as outside the church.[13] There are questions about the word translated "cleansed" in the King James Version of Daniel 8:14. It occurs only once in the Bible in that form, and its meaning is not entirely clear. There are also questions about the use of Leviticus 16 to interpret Daniel 8. In the one case, the sins of God's people are removed from the sanctuary; in the other, God removes the defilement caused by his enemies. In addition, Hebrews 8 and 9 pose problems for the view that Christ did not enter the most holy place of the heavenly sanctuary until 1844. These chapters seem to indicate that the Day of Atonement services, when the high priest entered the most holy place of the Hebrew sanctuary, were fulfilled at Jesus' ascension.

There are other questions about prophecy in general. Some wonder about the year-day relationship as a principle of prophetic interpretation. Extending the 2300 days of Daniel 8:14 to the middle of the nineteenth century seems to conflict with many New Testament passages which proclaim the nearness of Christ's return to those who lived in the first century.

The concept of the investigative judgment also raises questions of a predominantly theological nature. For some, it detracts from the sufficiency of Christ's atoning sacrifice as the basis of human salvation. If during his earthly ministry Jesus accomplished everything necessary to save us from sin, what is the point of an investigative judgment?

Moreover, the idea that our sins are not blotted out until an end-time judgment threatens to deprive us of the assurance of salvation. We may accept Christ and believe that we are forgiven, but our sins stand against us in the heavenly record until some indefinite future time when they are finally removed.

The doctrine of the heavenly sanctuary is important to Adventists' sense of denominational identity, and questions like these have received a lot of attention, spoken and written, in recent years. We cannot review this extensive discussion here, but it will help us keep the doctrine in proper theological perspective to do at least two things.

13. Fifteen of the forty-eight questions discussed in *Seventh-day Adventists Answer Questions on Doctrine: An Explanation of Certain Major Aspects of Seventh-day Adventist Belief* (Washington, D.C.: Review and Herald Publishing Association, 1957) deal with the interpretation of Daniel 8 and 9 and the subject of Christ's ministry in the heavenly sanctuary. More recently, several Adventist periodicals devoted issues to questions related to the sanctuary doctrine raised by Desmond Ford and discussed at a conference which met at Glacier View, Colorado, in 1980: *Adventist Review,* September 4, 1980; *Ministry,* October 1980; *Spectrum,* vol. 11, no. 2.

One is to view the doctrine of the sanctuary as part of God's overall work of salvation. Judgment is positive, not merely negative, in the Bible; it is something God does *for* his people. In the case of justification, which is a judicial act, for example, God establishes the identity of his people and places them in a positive relationship to himself. The doctrine of the sanctuary reaffirms the great themes that God is on our side and that he seeks our fellowship (cf. Ex 34:7). There is nothing about the heavenly sanctuary that should make us feel insecure or unloved.

We also need to keep in mind the basic purpose of the investigative judgment. According to one interpretation, it concerns the eternal status of individual human beings. Specifically, it deals with the records of all who at some point in time have responded to God's offer of salvation. But it is also possible to view the investigative judgment in relation to our comprehensive theme of the reign of God. From this perspective, the investigative judgment examines the ultimate effectiveness of God's activity in human history.[14] The suffering and distress that are part of human experience raise questions about the nature and value of God's sovereignty. By reviewing the cumulative impact of what God has done in human affairs, the investigative judgment demonstrates that God's ways are right. It shows that he is the supreme source of all that is good in the world and that evil is no fault of his.

Such a review cannot take place until the end of history, because every human action and every historical event continues to exert an influence until the end of time. The investigative judgment, then, is a comprehensive review of the overall effect of God's saving activity on human lives. It establishes for all eternity the conclusion that God fully deserves to be God.

It also keeps the doctrine of the sanctuary in proper perspective to remember its relation to the original impulse of Seventh-day Adventism. The doctrine of the sanctuary enabled early Advnetists to affirm the validity of their "Adventist experience." It supported them in the conviction that God had been leading in the events preceding the Great Disapointment and that they were not merely victims of a prophetic miscalculation.[15]

Interpreting the investigative judgment

The sanctuary and the Adventist experience

14. For a more extended development of the position suggested here, see Richard Rice, "The Relevance of the Investigative Judgment," *Spectrum,* vol. 14, no. 1, pp. 32–38.

15. Ellen G. White remarked of that experience, "We were firm in the belief that the preaching of definite time was of God. It was this that led men to search the Bible

This confidence enabled them to maintain the Advent at the center of their experience. Early Adventists reinterpreted the key text of the Millerite movement, but they regarded themselves primarily as Adventists, nonetheless. They eventually called themselves "Seventh-day *Adventists*," not "Seventh-day Believers in the Heavenly Sanctuary," or something similar. Their central object of interest continued to be the Lord's return, and they perpetuated an attitude of expectancy.

By explaining why Christ did not come as soon as anticipated, the doctrine of the sanctuary made it possible for Adventists to continue to hope for his appearing, but it also indicates that his coming cannot be very far away. The investigative judgment is an aspect of the last judgment, so it is itself an eschatological idea. It supports the expectation that Christ's return is near. Because the final phase of Christ's work as our high priest has begun, Adventists can say, we know that it cannot be long until he returns to this earth.

To keep the doctrine of the sanctuary in proper perspective, then, we need to remember its eschatological focus. For Seventh-day Adventists, it has always been closely related to the great theme of the return of Christ.

STUDY HELPS

Questions for review

1. What is the biblical view of time, and how does it differ from the Greek view and the archaic view?

---

diligently, discovering truths they had not before perceived" (*Life Sketches,* p. 62; cf. *The Great Controversy,* p. 457). The following doctrinal development confirmed early Adventists in this belief: "Mr. Miller and those who were in union with him supposed that the cleansing of the sanctuary spoken of in Daniel 8:14 meant the purifying of the earth by fire prior to its becoming the abode of the saints. This was to take place at the second advent of Christ; therefore we looked for that event at the end of the 2300 days, or years. But after our disappointment the Scriptures were carefully searched, with prayer and earnest thought; and after a period of suspense, light poured in upon our darkness; doubt and uncertainty were swept away. Instead of the prophecy of Daniel 8:14 referring to the purifying of the earth, it was now plain that it pointed to the closing work of our High Priest in Heaven, the finishing of the atonement, and the preparing of the people to abide the day of His coming" (*Life Sketches,* p. 63). Indeed, one effect of Ellen G. White's first vision was to assure early Adventists after the Great Disappointment that God had been guiding them through the experience: "On this path the Advent people were traveling to the city, which was at the farther end of the path. They had a bright light set up behind them at the beginning of the path, which an angel told me was the midnight cry" (*Early Writings,* p. 14).

2. What are the characteristics of "apocalyptic" literature?

3. What biblical expressions refer to the return of Christ?

4. What are the principal schools of prophetic interpretation?

5. What led William Miller to believe that Christ would return around 1843?

6. What is the significance of October 22, 1844?

7. What is the "investigative judgment," and what questions does this concept raise?

1. Does Christian faith require that history eventually come to an end? Why could it not go on and on indefinitely? **Questions for discussion**

2. Why is the prospect of nuclear annihilation more frightening than, say, that of death in a traffic accident? Or is it?

3. Does Christian eschatology exclude the possibility of a global nuclear war? Why, or why not?

4. The popularity of certain motion pictures indicates that people are fascinated by the possibility of "extra-terrestrial" life. How do you explain this? Does it reflect a deep-seated conviction that human salvation must ultimately come from beyond this world?

5. Although the Bible contradicts the old adage that "history repeats itself," to a certain extent the saying is true. In what ways *does* history repeat itself? Why is this so?

6. Marxists interpret history in economic terms. An unavoidable class struggle, they believe, will lead to an ideal society with no private property and no social ills. Compare this concept to biblical eschatology.

7. "America, America, God shed his grace on thee," a familiar song proclaims. How has a belief in divine providence shaped America's understanding of itself?

8. Certain thinkers insist that history is not self-explanatory. We need a principle derived from beyond history, they argue, in order to make sense of things. Do you agree? What principles for interpreting history does the Bible provide? How does biblical prophecy help us to understand the world in which we live?

Suggestions for Bible study

1. Study Matthew 24:36. The Millerites were surely aware of this text. Why do you suppose they nevertheless calculated the precise date of Christ's return?

2. Study Daniel 8:9–14. What happens to the sanctuary after 2300 evenings and mornings? What translations do different versions of the Bible give? What activities precede this event?

3. How is the time period mentioned in Daniel 8:14 related to those mentioned in the following verses: Daniel 9:24–27; Revelation 12:6, 14; 11:2; 13:5. You may find it helpful to consult the *Seventh-day Adventist Bible Commentary,* along with other commentaries.

4. Study Leviticus 16. What aspects of the Day of Atonement services prefigure the end of human history?

5. Seventh-day Adventists are sometimes criticized for regarding Satan as a sin bearer, because of their interpretation of Leviticus 16:8, 10, 20–22. Analyze these verses. What is the relation of the people of Israel to the scapegoat (Azazel)? How does the scapegoat prefigure the ultimate fate of the devil?

6. The first six chapters of Daniel are largely narrative or biographical in content. The last six are prophetic. What themes do these two sections of the book have in common? (Look for important conflicts and their resolutions.)

7. In the aftermath of the Great Disappointment, Millerites drew encouragement from the example of various biblical figures who had similar experiences. How were people disappointed according to the following passages? What was the result? Exodus 14:10–31; Jonah 3–4; Matthew 20:11, 19.

SUGGESTIONS FOR FURTHER READING

From Adventist writers

Ellen G. White's writings, of course, contain the definitive expression of Adventist eschatology, especially the last half of *The Great Controversy,* which discusses the Millerite movement, the doctrine of the heavenly sanctuary, and a long series of events leading up to the return of Christ and extending to the restoration of the earth.

Seventh-day Adventists have always had a keen interest in the interpretation of Daniel and Revelation. The denomination's most influential book on the subject is Uriah Smith, *The Prophecies of Daniel and the Revelation* (originally published as separate books in 1867 and 1873). Recent studies include Desmond Ford, *Daniel* (Nashville, Tenn.: Southern Publishing Association, 1978); C. Mervyn Maxwell, *God Cares: The Message of Daniel for You and Your Family* (vol. 1; Mountain View, Calif.: Pacific Press Publishing Association, 1981); Kenneth A. Strand, *Perspectives in the Book of Revelation* (Worthington, Ohio: Ann Arbor Publishers, 1975; reprint ed., 1978); Roy Allan Anderson, *Unfolding the Revelation* (rev. ed.; Mountain View, Calif.: Pacific Press Publishing Association, 1974). The classic Adventist study on prophetic interpretation is LeRoy Edwin Froom, *The Prophetic Faith of Our Fathers: The Historical Development of Prophetic Interpretation* (4 vols.; Washington, D.C.: Review and Herald Publishing Association, 1950–54). A more recent treatment of prophetic interpretation is Hans K. LaRondelle, *The Israel of God in Prophecy: Principles of Prophetic Interpretation* (Berrien Springs, Mich.: Andrews University Press, 1983).

Adventists have also written a great many books on the sanctuary, its structure, its various services, and their theological significance. Two older works in this area are Stephen N. Haskell, *The Cross and Its Shadow* (South Lancaster, Mass.: The Bible Training School, 1914; facsimile reproduction, Nashville, Tenn.: Southern Publishing Association, 1970); and M. L. Andreasen, *The Sanctuary Service* (Washington, D.C.: Review and Herald Publishing Association, 1937). Roy Adams presents the results of a scholarly investigation of different formulations of the sanctuary doctrine in *The Sanctuary Doctrine: Three Approaches in the Seventh-day Adventist Church* (Berrien Springs, Mich.: Andrews University Press, 1981).

Donald F. Neufeld traces the early development of the sanctuary doctrine in a series of articles entitled "How SDA's Adopted the Sanctuary Doctrine" (*Review and Herald,* January 3–February 28, 1980).

In 1980, two Adventist periodicals devoted entire issues to Desmond Ford's analysis of the sanctuary doctrine and the church's reaction to it: *Ministry,* October 1980; and *Spectrum,* vol. 11, no. 2.

In the past several years, Seventh-day Adventists have also explored the contemporary meaning of the sanctuary doctrine. Articles on this theme include William G. Johnsson, "What the Sanctuary Doctrine Means Today," parts 1–6, *Adventist Review,* May 14–July 23, 1981; Fritz Guy, "Confidence in Salvation: The Meaning of the Sanctuary," *Spectrum,* vol. 11, no. 2; and contributions by Richard Rice, Fritz Guy, and Jon Dybdahl to a special section entitled, "The Sanctuary Revisited" in *Spectrum,* vol. 13, no. 1.

The authoritative account of the Millerite movement is Francis D. Nichol, *The Midnight Cry* (Washington, D.C.: Review and Herald Publishing Association, 1944). Nichol's work lays to rest some prevalent misconceptions as to what William Miller and his followers believed and practiced.

Two Adventist historians have examined the question of the meaning of history from the perspective of Christian faith. They are George Edgar Shankel, *God and Man in History: A Study in the Christian Understanding of*

History (Nashville, Tenn.: Southern Publishing Association, 1967); and Siegfried J. Schwantes, *The Biblical Meaning of History* (Mountain View, Calif.: Pacific Press Publishing Association, 1970).

From other writers

Most reading in eschatology and the philosophy of history is rather difficult. At the same time, many interesting works are available in these areas. The motivated student will find some of the following titles stimulating.

Philosophies of history include Karl Lowith, *Meaning in History* (Chicago: University of Chicago Press, 1949), which examines the theological implications of the philosophy of history; and *The Philosophy of History in Our Times,* ed. Hans Meyerhoff (Garden City, N.Y.: Doubleday Anchor Books, 1959). An important anthology containing various contemporary Christian views of history is *God, History, and Historians: An Anthology of Modern Christian Views of History,* ed. C. T. McIntire (New York: Oxford University Press, 1977). Herbert Butterfield, *Christianity and History* (New York: Charles Scribner's Sons, 1949), is a highly readable and influential essay in the area. Mircea Eliade describes the primitive, or archaic, view of time and contrasts it with the biblical view in *The Myth of the Eternal Return, or, Cosmos and History,* trans. Willard Trask (Princeton, N.J.: Princeton University Press, 1971).

Two of this century's most influential New Testament scholars offer contrasting interpretations of biblical eschatology. Rudolf Bultmann, *History and Eschatology: The Presence of Eternity* (New York: Harper Torchbooks, 1957), expresses an existentialist point of view. Oscar Cullmann argues for the theological significance of human history since Christ in *Christ and Time: The Primitive Christian Conception of Time and History,* trans. Floyd V. Filson (rev. ed.; London: SCM Press Ltd., 1962), and *Salvation in History,* trans. Sidney G. Sowers, et al. (New York: Harper & Row, Publishers, 1967).

Two works which generated widespread interest in eschatology several years ago are Jurgen Moltmann, *Theology of Hope: On the Ground and the Implications of a Christian Eschatology,* trans. James W. Leitch (New York: Harper & Row, Publishers, 1967), and Wolfhart Pannenberg, *Theology and the Kingdom of God* (Philadelphia: The Westminster Press, 1969).

Besides the many religious works in this area, a number of other attempts to anticipate the future of human society have appeared over the past several years. Among the most widely discussed are Robert L. Heilbroner, *An Inquiry into the Human Prospect* (New York: W. W. Norton & Company, Inc., 1975); Alvin Toffler, *Future Shock* (New York: Random House, 1970), and *The Third Wave* (New York: William Morrow and Company, Inc., 1980).

15

THE DOCTRINE OF LAST THINGS: THE CONTENT AND MEANING OF HUMAN DESTINY

Biblical basis

"The Lord himself will descend from heaven with a cry of command, with the archangel's call, and with the sound of the trumpet of God" (1 Thessalonians 4:16).

"According to his promise we wait for new heavens and a new earth in which righteousness dwells" (2 Peter 3:13).

"Behold, I am coming soon, bringing my recompense, to repay every one for what he has done" (Revelation 22:12).

Isaiah 35
Isaiah 65:17–25; 66:18–23
Jeremiah 4:23–28
Daniel 12:1–3
Matthew 24–25
John 5:28–29
John 14:1–3
Acts 17:30–31
Romans 14:9–12

1 Thessalonians 4:13–5:11
2 Thessalonians 2:1–11
1 Timothy 4:1–3
2 Timothy 4:3–4
Titus 2:13
2 Peter 3
Revelation 1:4–7
Revelation 16
Revelation 19:11–22:5

There are four basic elements in Christian eschatology— the return of Christ, the resurrection of the dead, the judgment, and the restoration of the earth—and there are vast differences in their interpretation. Christians disagree about the way in which these events will be realized, and some question the extent to which they point to the literal future.

The perspective of Adventist eschatology

Seventh-day Adventists look forward to the personal return of Christ to earth. Along with other conservative Christians, they regard the resurrection, the judgment, and the restoration of the earth as literal, too. The sequence of future events which Adventists anticipate has some unique features, however, and displays several distinctive theological concerns.

Seventh-day Adventists are pre-millennialists. This means that they believe that Christ will return before the thousand-year period mentioned in Revelation 20. But unlike many pre-millennialists, they are not pre-tribulationists. They do not believe that the church will be delivered, or raptured, from the earth before the time of suffering that precedes Christ's coming.

With this initial characterization in mind, we will briefly sketch the concluding events in earth's history from a Seventh-day Adventist perspective.

AN ADVENTIST OUTLINE OF FINAL EVENTS

The end of time

As pre-millennialists, Seventh-day Adventists regard Christ's return as an interruption in the period of human history that precedes it. They do not believe that the situation here on earth will gradually improve until history eventually merges into the kingdom of God. Instead, the quality of religious, moral, and social life will progressively decline, and the human condition will finally reach a point of unprecedented decay (1 Tim 4:1; 2 Tim 4:3–4).

At the same time, the work of salvation reaches its final stages. The investigative judgment takes place in heaven, and the church fulfills its mission by carrying the gospel to all the world (Mt 24:14). Seventh-day Adventists have a special role to play in this task. They announce the arrival of the judgment and warn people to escape the punishment that the enemies of God will soon receive (Rev 14:6–12).

As the moral state of human beings deteriorates, the difference between those who accept God's sovereignty and those who reject it becomes increasingly vivid. A knowledge of salvation is universally available, and oppressive political and social conditions oblige everyone to make a decision for or against God. Finally, every human being makes his decision for eternity and the polarization of the righteous and the wicked is complete.

The close of probation

When that takes place, to use Adventist terminology, "probation" closes; there is no further opportunity to repent. Christ ceases his high-priestly ministry, and the status of every human being is fixed forever (cf. Rev 22:11). This is an ominous prospect, to be sure, but it is not an arbitrary act on God's part. The close of probation is not like a door slamming shut, regardless of who is on the outside. Instead, it is God's recognition of the status that human beings have chosen for themselves.

The sobering aspect of the close of probation is not the possibility that someone will decide to accept God's offer of salvation five or ten minutes too late. It is the recognition that we are fixing our eternal destiny every day of our lives. By our actions and attitudes we decide whether God has our ultimate loyalty or not. The decision need not be a clear-cut, sharply focused experience, but we make it nevertheless. The close of probation simply acknowledges that these choices are irreversible. Our eternal destiny is something we ourselves determine.

The time of trouble

After the close of probation and just before the return of Christ, the earth experiences a tremendous upheaval and its inhabitants suffer enormously. This is the "time of trouble" or the "tribulation" of which the Bible speaks (cf. Dan 12:1). The seven last plagues fall, inflicting widespread destruction (Rev 16).

The Bible describes these plagues as a manifestation of the wrath of God (Rev 16:1), which makes us wonder about their purpose. Why are these plagues necessary? Since probation has closed, they do not lead anyone to repentance. It seems out of character for God to impose purely vindictive or retributive punishment. The Bible tells us that getting even doesn't interest God (Ezek 18:32); this motive never explains his actions.

Our guiding theme may provide an answer to this question. According to the biblical descriptions of the end of history, just before Christ returns God's sovereignty is rejected by humanity in general. He no longer exerts an influence in human affairs. The scene prior to Christ's return illustrates what happens when God is no longer sovereign. Human beings are at the mercy of the elements; the earth becomes uninhabitable; and the forces of darkness have free reign to torment and destroy.

During this time God's people suffer intensely. God cares for their physical needs (Isa 33:16), but the cause of their anguish is primarily spiritual. Their experience is like that of Jacob on the eve of his meeting with his estranged brother Esau (Jer 30:7; Gen 32:11–30). They know that they must face God very soon, and they wonder if they are ready. They search their lives to see if they have surrendered completely to him.

**The return
of Christ**

These dark scenes come to an end with the return of Christ to earth. According to the New Testament, his return is glorious and univerally visible (1 Thess 4:16; Rev 1:7; Mt 24:27). It brings great rejoicing to those who are waiting for him (Isa 25:9), but it causes the wicked to mourn (Mt 24:30). They seek to escape from his presence (Rev 6:15–17), but are destroyed by the brightness of his coming (2 Thess 2:8).

Reunion is the dominant note of Christ's return. It brings together at last all those who have accepted the gift of salvation. The dead in Christ come to life, clothed with immortality, to see their Lord (1 Thess 4:16; 1 Cor 15:51–53), and the living saints, instantly transformed from mortal to immortal, imperishable forms, rise to meet Christ with them (1 Thess 4:17; 1 Cor 15:51–53). From this point on through eternity, they are never again to be separated from Christ (1 Thess 4:17).

It is no wonder that Christ's return is the great hope of the church. It fulfills the promise Jesus gave his disciples centuries ago: "I will come again . . . that where I am you may be also" (Jn 14:3). According to Paul, his return is the "blessed hope" (Tit 2:13), and those who belong to him "love his appearing" (2 Tim 4:8). It climaxes the plan of salvation. God's objective from the beginning of sin was to restore human beings to fellowship with him, and now that goal is finally reached.

Although the plan of salvation reaches a conclusion with the return of Christ, it is not entirely complete. It is still necessary to remove the consequences of sin from the universe, and there needs to be a final reckoning with those who have rejected God. According to Seventh-day Adventist eschatology, these events take us through the millennium to the final destruction of the wicked and the restoration of the earth.

The millennium

With other pre-millenialists, Adventists believe that the thousand-year reign of Christ begins with his return to earth (Rev 20:4), but they are unique in locating this reign, not on earth, but in heaven. After rescuing his people from the earth, Christ returns with them to heaven, where they enter the glorious places he has prepared for them (Jn 14:1–3).

Meanwhile, the scene on earth is one of utter desolation, reminiscent of its chaotic state at the beginning of creation (Jer 4:23–26). There are no human inhabitants. This is where Satan is bound (Rev 20:2–3). For a thousand years, with no one to tempt or torment, he is left to contemplate the bleak consequences of his rebellion against God.

We know little of the activity of the saved during this period of time, but there is a suggestion of what they might be doing. At one place in his letters, Paul tells Christian believers that they will judge the world, indeed, that they will judge angels (1 Cor 6:2–3). It is possible that the redeemed will examine God's dealings with those who are lost and will have an opportunity to find answers to any questions about the fairness of God's decisions.

At the end of the millennium the New Jerusalem, containing the redeemed, descends to earth (Rev 21:2), and the resurrection of the wicked takes place. Jesus stated that all the dead would come to life again (Jn 5:28–29). The book of Revelation says that the resurrection of the righteous and the resurrection of the wicked take place a thousand years apart (20:5). At the same time, Satan is loosed from "the bottomless pit" (Rev 20:3). Surrounded by those who have rejected God, he makes one last, desperate attempt to overthrow God's sovereignty by leading a massive assault on the New Jerusalem (Rev 20:7–9).

The final judgment

The maneuver is interrupted, however, when God appears on a great white throne and calls the assembled multitudes to judgment (Rev 20:11–13). He reviews the record of each life, and condemns the wicked to eternal death. The fire which then purifies the earth destroys those who have rejected God's authority (Rev 20:9–10, 14–15; 2 Pet 3:10), consuming them along with Satan and his angels (Mt 25:41).

The final scene in biblical eschatology is the restoration of the earth. After the destruction of the wicked, God re-creates the earth in its primeval splendor (Rev 21:1; 2 Pet 3:13; cf. Isa 35). All traces of sin are removed from the environment, and the new earth becomes the home of the redeemed throughout eternity.

The restoration of the earth

As beautiful as the new earth is, its most outstanding feature is the personal presence of God (Rev 21:22). This is what brings the work of salvation to its fulfillment. Human beings are restored to intimate fellowship with their creator. The obstacles that sin imposes are completely removed, the consequences of sin are reversed, and the reign of God is realized in human life without distortion.

THE ULTIMATE FATE OF THE WICKED

The biblical portrayal of the destruction of the wicked raises a number of questions. It leads us to ask about the time, the length, the nature, and the purpose of their suffering.

**When the
wicked suffer**

According to popular religious belief, the wicked enter "hell" as soon as they die and suffer there through all eternity. However, the Bible offers abundant evidence that the punishment of the wicked does not begin until the final judgment. According to the biblical view of human nature, the dead are not conscious, so they are incapable of suffering. They are brought back to life to meet the judgment, as we saw in the passages just cited. According to other passages, Christ brings his reward with him when he comes (Rev 22:12); therefore the punishment of the wicked does not occur before the end of the world.

As for the length of their punishment, the Bible indicates that their actual suffering is temporary; it comes to an end. According to one text, the wicked will be burned up, reduced to ashes (Mal 4:1–3). In other words, they are utterly annihilated. Texts that speak of them as burning with "eternal fire" or burning "forever" need to be carefully interpreted. They do not indicate a fire that never stops (cf. 2 Pet 2:6 and Jude 7), but a fire with permanent consequences. "Forever" does not always mean without ending; it often means as long as whatever it refers to lasts (cf. 1 Sam 1:22, 28).

There are also theological factors that exclude the concept of unending torment. Such an idea is certainly incompatible with that of the perfect happiness of the saved. How could anyone's happiness be complete with the knowledge that others are suffering unspeakable torment? Even in a scheme of retributive justice, the idea is unfair. Eventually, it seems, everyone would have suffered in proportion to his sins, and further punishment would be excessive.

**How the
wicked suffer**

What causes the wicked to suffer? Their suffering certainly includes a physical aspect, but there is reason to believe that this is not the real cause of their anguish. What distresses them most is the awareness that their loss is the result of their own perversity. All that the redeemed enjoy might have been theirs. It was freely offered to them, too, but they chose to reject it. The final judgment consists in their having to face the full consequences of their choice.

The essence of their suffering, then, is spiritual or mental, rather than physical, and it is nothing other than the natural consequence of the course they have chosen for themselves. The vivid biblical portrayals of the fate of the wicked should not lead us to conclude that eternal death is something God arbitrarily imposes. It follows from their own choice. To reject God is to turn away from life, because life comes only from him. Annihilation, or extinction, then, is not something God adds to sin, to somehow compensate for it in the scheme of things. It is the inevitable consequence of sin. Those who reject God choose death (Prov 8:36).

But why does God bring the wicked back to life to look these consequences full in the face? Since they are already dead, why not leave them that way? What is the point of the second resurrection and the last judgment?

Why the wicked suffer

Once again, we must exclude the idea that God enjoys seeing people suffer, even if they get what they deserve. He finds no pleasure in the death of the wicked, so we can rule out the notion that God is gratified to see the wicked "get theirs" at last. Instead, we can view the final judgment as a manifestation of God's care for his creatures, even the ones who have rejected him. God pays them the compliment of telling them the truth. He gives even his enemies the opportunity to see that his dealings with them have been fair. In the final analysis, the strange act of punishment, apparently so out of character for God, is a manifestation of his love.

There are some who find the love of God so impressive that they believe everyone will eventually respond to it. Sometimes called "universalism," this is the view that everyone will ultimately be saved. A love as vast and tender as God's, it asserts, finally overcomes all obstacles and breaks down all resistance. No one can resist it forever.

The problem with universalism is not just that it contradicts the biblical portrayals of the fate of the wicked. It also conflicts with the biblical teaching that people settle their eternal destiny in this life (Lk 16:19–31), and it overlooks an important aspect of love, rather than carrying the idea to its logical conclusion.

There is no greater manifestation of love than to allow others the freedom to accept or reject it, and then to respect the choices they make. So the final destruction of the wicked does not conflict with the love of God; instead, it testifies to it. It shows that God loves enough to allow others to decide for themselves whether to accept him or not. When that choice is final, God respects it; he will not force a change in loyalty.

THE MEANING OF ETERNAL LIFE

Our brief review of Adventist eschatology will leave many people unsatisfied. For some, it is much too sketchy; it omits many of the "last-day events" that people are fond of discussing. It also offers nothing in the way of a precise chronology; it doesn't say how soon these things will happen and/or how long they will take.

Reactions to last-day chronologies

Others will find this review too elaborate. For them, the Christian hope loses meaning with attempts to give it precise content. In their view, we trivialize our ultimate destiny by trying to provide concrete pictures of what it will involve. We honor the future more, they believe, by maintaining a respectful silence about its details.

There is something to be said for both reactions. Certainly, they can help us to avoid two undesirable extremes in our eschatology. One is to lose sight of the future entirely; the other is to forget its central point in a preoccupation with details.

In spite of its vivid imagery, the Bible does not give us a literalistic account of human destiny. Its descriptions do not provide a basis for extensive speculation; in fact, its central dynamic prevents such activity. The primary impact of biblical eschatology is on our attitude toward the present. It returns us to our day-to-day activities with a new sense of their significance. At the same time, however, Christian hope does lead us to anticipate a real, literal future, and it gives us a basic idea of what this future involves. Consequently, before turning to the meaning of Christian eschatology for our present existence, it will be helpful for us to reflect further on its portrayal of human destiny.

Eternal life: present and future

As it occurs in the Bible, especially in the writings of John, the expression "eternal life" is rich with meaning. It refers fundamentally to a certain quality of life, one made possible only by Christ, and one we can experience here and now. As the apostle said, "He who has the Son has life," present tense (1 Jn 5:12).

The Johannine concept also includes the more conventional sense of "eternal life"—namely, the idea of endless life, or immortality—and this is an important element in Christian hope. Christians deny that death has the last word about human existence. As we have seen, they look forward to a future beyond death, where human life will continue in a perfect environment and realize its full potential.

There was a time when the concept of immortality enjoyed widespread acceptance. The major question in people's minds was how to achieve it; they took its existence for granted. This is no longer the case. Along with many other aspects of Christianity, belief in immortality is widely challenged. A mature faith cannot ignore the questions it raises in today's world, so let us consider some of the prevalent objections to this important idea.[1]

1. The American philosopher Charles Hartshorne objects to the conventional concept of immortality—"subjective immortality" in his terms—in various places throughout his writings. Instead, he argues for "objective immortality." For a comparison of these two ideas see his recent book *Omnipotence and Other Theological Mistakes* (Albany: State University of New York Press, 1984), pp. 32–37. John Hick also treats many objections to the concept of immortality in his comprehensive study, *Death and Eternal Life* (New York: Harper & Row, Publishers, 1976), especially pp. 97–109, 147–152.

To begin with, there are those who object to the concept of eternal life on religious grounds. They observe that the attribute of immortality is divine rather than human (cf. 1 Tim 6:16). Consequently, the very idea of human immortality is a manifestation of arrogance, expressing an unwillingness to accept our proper place in the scheme of things. God, not man, is meant to live forever.

Objections to immortality: "Arrogant"

Furthermore, the kind of future many people anticipate is totally self-centered. The materialistic pleasures they associate with heaven, or paradise, have nothing to do with genuine religion.

Others respond to the idea of human immortality by arguing that it is unnecessary to a sense of meaning in life. We do not have to insist on endless existence in order for life to be worthwhile; there are other ways of establishing personal significance. Among contemporary philosophers, existentialists, for example, maintain that we realize the meaning of life on a momentary basis. With each act of authentic decision, life's ultimate purpose is fulfilled. Because meaning is a matter of quality, not quantity, how long we live has nothing essential to do with it.

"Unnecessary"

Still others believe that our lives have abiding significance, not because *we* live forever, but because *God* lives forever. Our experiences make a permanent contribution to his experience, and he preserves their value forever. In this way, too, our lives make a permanent difference in the scheme of things, regardless of how long they last, and that is all we really need.

Some even argue that immortality would be undesirable. They believe that eternal life would be nothing short of misery. After all, human beings typically lose interest in life as the years go by. Once the novelty of different experiences wears off, there is less and less to live for. The natural thing is to expect life to come to an end, they say; no enlightened person would want it to go on indefinitely.

"Undesirable"

One of the most powerful critiques of eternal life arises from moral considerations. Many people think of eternal life as a reward for good behavior, so the prospect of living forever gives them a strong incentive to do good in this life. But critics object that it is anything *but* moral to do good in order to be rewarded. To be moral, they argue, is to do the right because it is right, not because we hope to gain something for doing it or because we fear the negative consequences if we don't. Instead of leading to moral behavior, they assert, the desire for eternal life empties one's actions of any real moral value.

"Immoral"

Furthermore, the objection continues, the idea of immortality makes no sense as a reward for good behavior if a "reward" is something you deserve. It doesn't make sense to repay a few years of even the very best behavior with an eternity of indescribable delights. Such a reward is way out of proportion to what anyone deserves.

"Unrealistic"

Yet another objection to the idea of eternal life is that it distracts us from the responsibilities and opportunities of this life. In this vein, Karl Marx described religion as the "opium of the people."[2] The prospect of a future life where all our dreams come true sometimes makes people willing to submit to oppression and injustice instead of working to eliminate them.

"Inconceivable"

Finally, there are those who object to the notion of eternal life because it is inconceivable. They find no coherent concept of a future beyond death in any of those suggested. Reincarnation, the belief that the soul inhabits one body after another in a succession of earthly lives, fails to provide an adequate account of personal identity from one life to the next. The idea that the soul is inherently immortal ignores the importance of the physical dimension of human existence. And, as we have seen, the idea of the resurrection of the dead at some future time faces the challenge of accounting for the personal identity of those who are raised with those who have died. In short, there are many different concepts of the future life, and questions surround them all.

Eternal life reinterpreted as:

It is clear from these objections that our concept of eternal life must rest on solid religious and conceptual grounds. We need more than an optimism based on personal desire, or a sentimentality fueled by gospel songs and pictures of the Holy City. We need a carefully formulated theology of human destiny. Most of the objections mentioned presuppose an inaccurate or inadequate understanding of what Christians really hope for, so, in an effort to respond to them, we will identify some of the central elements in a valid Christian concept of eternal life.

A gift of God

Christian hope assumes that our personal identity can be recovered or preserved beyond death, but it does not attribute this to

---

2. "Toward a Critique of Hegel's Philosophy of Right," in Lewis S. Feuer, ed., *Basic Writings on Politics and Philosophy: Karl Marx and Friedrich Engels* (Garden City, N.Y.: Doubleday Anchor Books, 1949), pp. 262–63; quoted in *Readings on Religion from Inside and Outside*, ed. Robert S. Ellwood, Jr., (Englewood Cliffs, N.J.: Prentice-Hall, Inc., 1978), pp. 83–84.

some inherent or innate quality in us. It is due entirely to the creative and re-creative power of God. We find a close association of these two functions in Romans 4:17, which describes God as the one "who gives life to the dead and calls into existence the things that do not exist." Trust in God, then, is the basis of Christian hope.

Recognizing the importance of God to Christian hope helps us to identify what it really is that Christians hope for. It is true that many distort the content of Christian hope by overemphasizing its secondary aspects. There are people who glorify the material features of the New Jerusalem, for example, as if it were a never-never land of childish delights, a religious version of the Big Rock Candy Mountain. Others view the future as a compensation for the trials and deprivations of this life. It is a place where we can lay down our burdens and leave all our worries and cares behind. Still others see the future as a way of having all their dreams come true. They count on doing then all the things they lack the time or ability to do now.

Fellowship with God

There is an element of truth in all these notions, of course, but the central concern of Christian hope is missing. The heart of Christian hope is not self-gratification; it is the prospect of personal fellowship with God. Only his presence makes the future worth hoping for.

One of Jesus' best-known parables suggests this interpretation. In the parable of the talents, a man divided his sizable estate among three trusted servants and took a journey. Sometime later, he returned and asked them to account for their service in his absence. Those who had faithfuly met their responsibilities received the following commendation: "Well done, good and faithful servant; you have been faithful over a little, I will set you over much; enter into the joy of your master" (Mt 25:21).

These last words give us the clue we are looking for. It is the fellowship of the master, sharing his joy, rejoicing in the fulfillment of his purposes, that constitutes the true reward of faithful service. For the committed Christian, fellowship with God is the major thing that makes eternal life attractive.

Service

The master's commendation in this parable suggests a second element in a valid Christian concept of human destiny: the prospect of future service. From this parable we learn that the reward for faithful service is not the end of all responsibility; it is not the chance to relax and let others serve us. It is the opportunity for further service and greater responsibility.

Placing these two elements at the center of Christian hope makes it possible for us to respond to many of the objections to eternal life we noted above. For one thing, it gives us a clearly God-centered, rather than self-centered, view of human destiny. It directs us away from the gratification of personal desires and provides us with a truly religious view of the future.

This concept of human destiny also eliminates self-indulgence by its emphasis on service. Eternal life is other-oriented, not self-oriented. It seeks the glory of God and the welfare of one's fellows. Even when hope reaches its fulfillment, there is a place for love, as Paul's great hymn reminds us (1 Cor 13:13). Indeed, only when hope is fulfilled can love be realized to its fullest extent.

ETERNAL LIFE AS RESTORATION

There is another aspect of Christian hope that deserves attention here, and that is the theme of restoration and fulfillment. As the Bible portrays eternal life, all traces of sin and fallenness are removed. Human beings will finally be able to live as life was meant to be. Eternal life involves the recovery of all dimensions of human existence.

Physical and spiritual restoration

On the most fundamental level, this includes the restoration of physical or bodily existence. There will be changes in our constitution, as Paul's description of the resurrection body indicates (1 Cor 15:42--50), but our existence will have a corporeal basis. The biblical concept of resurrection is that of the re-creation of the entire person, including a physical form.

Eternal life also includes spiritual restoration. For Christians, the central attraction of the future is the prospect of intimate fellowship with God, as we just observed. The loss of God's presence was one of the consequences of sin, and the goal of biblical religion is to reunite God with his people. This was the purpose of the various forms of Hebrew worship (Ex 34:7), and it was the principal effect of the incarnation, which brought God to human beings in the form of humanity itself. Eternal life restores human beings to the presence of God.

Social restoration

Eternal life fulfills the social, along with the spiritual, dimension of human existence. It restores genuine human fellowship. Sin alienates us from each other as well as from God, making it impossible for us to trust and share to the fullest. To an extent, the church restores genuine human society. In the community of the Spirit, there is a strong sense of unity among the members and a willingness to put the interests of others ahead of one's own. But the achievement of community in the church is provisional at best. Selfish tendencies and feelings of rivalry always interfere with true fellowship.

In the life to come, human beings will finally enjoy genuine community. Our relationships with each other will not be inhibited by feelings of insecurity or a lack of trust. We can be completely open with each other and devote ourselves completely to service.

The social fulfillment of human existence is probably the most neglected aspect of eternal life. Popular concepts of the life to come typically concentrate on its prospects for individuals. We often allow ourselves to imagine the magnificent dwellings we expect to inhabit and all the personal interests we will pursue. We seldom think of what the future entails for God's people as a group.

But the biblical portrayals of human destiny are emphatically social; they consistently describe the redeemed as a group, a community, rather than as separate individuals. For example, in the book of Revelation, the city, the New Jerusalem, becomes the principal symbol for the future life. This suggests that human destiny involves vast numbers of people living together in complete harmony. Incidentally, the word for the "mansions" in the King James Version of John 14:2 is more accurately translated as "rooms." Taken this way, Jesus' assurance, "In my Father's house are many rooms," suggests a single home large enough to accommodate all God's children, not a series of colonial estates. Heaven may be more like apartment living than life in rural or suburban America.

Another well-known corporate metaphor in the book of Revelation is the figure of the 144,000 (Rev 7:4). The nature and identity of this group are widely discussed among students of biblical prophecy. Some believe that it refers to exactly 144,000 individuals—no more, no less. Others believe that the number is symbolic, since it includes 12,000 representatives from each of the twelve tribes of Israel (Rev 7:5–8). Either way, the figure suggests that God will have a complete people at the end of time. The human beings awaiting Christ's return will constitute a single, well-defined group, not a scattering of individuals essentially unrelated to each other.

As we have seen, the biblical portrayal of the resurrection also emphasizes the corporate, or social, aspects of humanity's future. The righteous, living and dead, receive immortality together (1 Thess 4:15). One group does not precede the other, nor do individuals enter eternal life one at a time, as popular religion often conceives it. It is as a group, as one vast community, that human beings are restored to immortal life.

People sometimes wonder about the possibility of service in an ideal situation. If we identify serving others primarily with meeting needs or compensating for deficiencies, then it is difficult to think of it as part of the life to come. But if genuine service is essentially to enrich and upbuild the lives of other people, to be devoted to bringing them happiness, then it makes sense to include it in our concept of human destiny.

In fact, there is a sense in which real service only begins with the future life. In our present situation, it requires a lot of time and effort just to survive. Consider what it takes to meet the bare necessities of life; think of the time and money we spend obtaining food and shelter and maintaining our physical health. Most service in this life consists in helping others to meet their basic needs, too. But in the future we will have much more to give than we do now, and instead of making up for deficiencies we can enrich and enhance the lives of others. Our service can be totally positive.

The spirit of service permeates the life to come; in fact, it is its very essence. This illuminates the nature of the reign of God and helps to explain why the wicked are annihilated. They would be miserable living with those whose lives are motivated by love, just as they would resent the constant companionship of the God they have rejected. It is in their own interest that those who have rebelled against God cease to exist.

Environmental restoration

Eternal life also involves a restoration of our environment. Human beings are terrestrial creatures. This earth was our original home, and it will be our final home. Our ultimate destiny is inseparably linked to that of this planet, so the complete fulfillment of human existence has ecological dimensions, too. This is why the last book of the Bible speaks of a new heaven and a new earth (Rev 21:1).

We need to beware of the tendency to speculate about the precise features of the new earth. We know there will be no death and nothing to harm us, but we know next to nothing about its geography or the forms of life that will inhabit it. Nor do we know much about our own physical constitution. But these things need not concern us. We can be sure that God will make every provision for our happiness, and we can leave the future in his hands. A preoccupation with its details can distract us from the more important aspects of the future—our relation to God and to other human beings. These are the things that deserve our primary attention.

THE RELATION OF THE FUTURE TO THE PRESENT

We have examined the future which Christian hope anticipates, as Seventh-day Adventists understand it. We have also explored some of the basic dimensions of human destiny, under the theme of restoration. We began our study of this doctrine by asserting that Christian hope includes more than a concept of the future. Besides predicting the end of history, we observed, Christian faith interprets the entire course of history. With this in mind, we need to do two more things to bring our eschatology to a close. We need to see how the end of history relates to the present course of history, and we need to explore the impact of the future on our life here and now.

Between the end of history and the process that precedes it there is a threefold relationship of revelation, fulfillment, and transformation. First of all, the future reveals the true meaning of history; it discloses its inner nature. For one thing, it shows that history is the arena of God's activity and that, in spite of all appearances, God has been at work throughout the course of history to accomplish his purposes.

Revelation

Apocalyptic literature portrays human history as the stage on which superhuman forces of good and evil are struggling to dominate our lives. The nature of this drama—its central plot, we might say—becomes clear to all at the end of history.

The end of history also reveals the true identity of human beings. The final judgment indicates the precise role of every person in the drama that lies at the center of history. Whether a person is really good or evil finally becomes apparent. In fact, the effects of all our actions will then be seen for the first time. So much of what we do and say now seems lost forever. At times we find this frustrating, watching our best efforts come to nothing, as far as we can tell; at other times we take comfort in the thought that our misdeeds will be quietly forgotten. But the end of history will reveal the ultimate impact of everything we do. For better or worse, it will bring to light the cumulative influence of every word and act ever said or done. This is the significance of the biblical references to the books of record that are consulted in the last judgment (Ecc 12:14; Mt 12:36; 25:31–46; Rev 20:12).

Something else that emerges at the end of history is the true scale of values. In the present scheme of things, wealth, power, and beauty are much more important than such qualities as compassion, honesty, and generosity. Superior intelligence, for example, will usually attract more attention than, say, personal integrity. But the future will reveal that these less conspicuous things are ultimately more important. At present, the good are often victims of the shrewd, and it seems foolish at times to do right. But in the future, the wisdom of such qualities will be plain to see. Those who pursue them are the ones who have been in touch with the "real" world all along.

Fulfillment

Besides revealing the true meaning of history, the future also brings history to a conclusion. The word "end" not only means the termination, or cessation, of something; it can also mean "goal," or "purpose." The end which Christian hope anticipates is not merely the termination of history. It is the goal to which history moves. What goes on now reaches its culmination then.

The future will complete, or fulfill, the present in several different ways. As we have seen, the work of salvation reaches its conclusion with the great reunion of God with his people, and the restoration which begins in human life now is then fully achieved. On the other hand, the destruction which results from sin is also fully realized. In the last judgment, those who have rejected God receive the consequences of their choice. The separation and destruction that begin here will be final then.

Transformation

The end of history not only reveals and completes its meaning; it also transforms it. There will be discontinuities, as well as continuities, between the present and the future. As we have seen, the essential dimensions of human life continue. Human existence will still be physical, spiritual, and social, and our personal identities will be preserved. But our lives will also be dramatically transformed. We will be capable of experiences that we cannot imagine now. We will enjoy unprecedented closeness to God, and our fellowship with other human beings will be more intimate than anything we presently experience. The future will transcend and surpass the present.

Knowing that the future will transform the present prevents us from unrealistic expectations in this life. It is true that salvation brings a restorative, renewing power into our lives, but it does not completely remove us from the effects of sin. We still exist in a condition of fallenness, and we still suffer the consequences of man's rebellion against God. As the biblical record vividly shows, those who accept God's gift of salvation are not immune from misfortune, illness, bereavement, or death. There is a sense in which eternal life begins now, as we have seen, but we will not enjoy it in its fullness until Christ returns.

We sometimes speak of the future which hope anticipates as the "end of history," and so it is, but it is also a new beginning. Sin interrupted the fulfillment of God's original plans for human beings, but with the end of this historical epoch we will at last be free to pursue our destiny, unencumbered by sin's negative effects. We can finally become everything we were meant to be.

People often think of this life as concrete reality and the future as a shadow of it, but in fact the reverse is true. The present is but a faint intimation of what God has in store for his children. Only then will we enjoy life at its very fullest. The joys of eternity lie beyond our powers of imagination. "No eye has seen, no ear has heard, no mind has conceived what God has prepared for those who love him" (1 Cor 2:9).[3]

THE MEANING OF THE FUTURE FOR THE PRESENT

With its understanding of history and the end of history, Christian faith presents us with a distinctive view of life here and now. In fact, there are many who believe that this is the most important part of the doctrine of last things. What Christian faith says about the present, they maintain, is even more significant than what it tells us about the future.[4] We can determine the Christian's position in the present world by exploring the meaning of hope.

Hope is the most elusive of the three cardinal virtues. We hear a great deal about faith and love, but we find no comparable concern for hope, though it is just as basic to the structure of the Christian life. Hope is an experience, or a quality of experience, which includes two essential elements. One is a certain concept of the future; the other is a specific attitude toward the future. Without some concept of what to expect, there is nothing to give substance to our hope, nothing to hope *for*. But without the proper attitude toward the future, all our concepts of the future are valueless, however detailed and well-argued they may be. We have examined the concept of the future which Christian faith presents. Now we need to concentrate on the attitude it prescribes.

The structure of hope

To begin with, hope never views the future with calm detachment. The hoped-for future is never just something that hasn't happened yet. Hope makes a personal investment in the future; it views that future in distinctly personal terms. When I hope, I see *the* future as *my* future.

In the second place, hope involves a strong desire for the realization of its object. Those who really hope for the coming of Christ, in

---

3. These words are often applied to the future life, as they are here, but they are only secondarily eschatological. Primarily they refer to the glories we can experience here and now as a result of the salvation God offers us in Jesus.

4. In his interpretation of "The Meaning of the Second Advent," for example, Adventist theologian Sakae Kubo discusses "The Advent and the Present Life," before addressing "The Advent and Future Events" (*God Meets Man: A Theology of the Sabbath and Second Advent* [Nashville, Tenn.: Southern Publishing Association, 1978]).

Paul's words, are those who love his appearing (2 Tim 4:8). They long for his return. It is what they live for, the goal of their existence. For this reason, hope leads to a certain detachment from the present.

If the future is the ultimate object of life, then we cannot make an unreserved, unqualified commitment to the present order of things. The future which Christians anticipate will transform and surpass the present, so the enterprises of the present, however important they are, can never occupy all our attention. Our health, our careers, our families, our society—all these are legitimate objects of Christian concern, but they do not, singly or collectively, exhaust our interest. Hope directs us beyond the present order to something superior that is yet to come. It underlines the *not yet* that is essential to Christian life.

Hope emphasizes the priority of the future, but it also leads us to appreciate the present and commit ourselves to living constructively now. This is because hope sees the future in direct relation to the present. In hope, the end of history and the "last things" are never far away, at some distant point in time. They are always near, at hand, "even at the doors." For hope, then, the future impinges on the present; it threatens to break in at any time.

Watchfulness

The attitude of "watchfulness" expresses this dimension of hope. It presupposes a direct connection between the present and the future. As we have seen, Christian eschatology views the end of history in continuity with what precedes it. The future will complete, or fulfill, the process of history as a whole. But its relation is particularly close to the period of history that directly precedes it. In Adventist eschatology, for example, the return of Christ resembles a dramatic rescue, delivering God's people from a world that is falling apart. Just before the end arrives, there will be indications that it is near. The Bible refers to these as "signs of the times" (Mt 16:3).

The Bible describes a variety of things as signs of the end. There are catastrophic natural phenomena (Mt 24:29) and deteriorating social and political conditions (Mt 24:15–22). The religious situation is distressing (Mt 24:24). But the signs are not restricted to dramatic events; they include relatively unspectacular things, too. The most important sign of all, the supreme sign, is the fulfillment of the church's mission—the proclamation of the gospel to all the world (Mt 24:14). Ultimately, anything that gives evidence of the lordship of Christ over history, and anything that resists Christ's lordship over history, can represent a sign.

The signs are not signs to just anyone, however. One has to see them from the proper perspective in order to grasp their true meaning. We need faith to see that the end is near. Signs are not the basis of faith, and it is wrong to demand signs as a condition for believing (Mt 16:4). After all, there may be false signs (cf. Mt 24:24). But the signs do corroborate and strengthen faith as well as bolster confidence that the end will come soon.

Because they know that the end is near, Christians have a special responsibility to prepare for it. This, too, assumes a degree of continuity between present and future. Our situation at the end of history depends on our decisions and actions now. Several of the parables in Jesus' great sermon on last things (Matthew 24–25) emphasize the importance of preparing for the future by fulfilling our present responsibilities. In the parable of the talents, for example, the servants who were ready for their master's return were faithfully doing the work he had given them when he left. Similarly, in another parable, the watchful servant was the faithful servant, the one hard at work when the master finally came home (Mt 24:46).

Although the signs indicate that Christ's return is near, they do not pinpoint his arrival. Since we never know just when he will come, we need to be ready at all times (Mt 24:36, 44). This lends a note of urgency to our preparation for the future.

The Christian's attitude toward the future, then, includes a confidence that does not harden into smugness or presumption and a sense of urgency that does not deteriorate into frenzy. It manifests itself in the faithful fulfillment of present responsibilities.

The delay of Christ's return

Besides confidence and urgency, being ready for the future also requires a good deal of patience. This is particularly important in view of the fact that the Lord has not returned as soon as expected. The "delay of the parousia," as it is often called, has posed a challenge to Christian hope from the very beginning, as we noticed in the previous chapter. The evidence in the New Testament itself indicates that the early church moved through several stages in its attitude toward the Lord's return. Although they initially expected that his coming was very near (cf. 1 Thess 4:17), early Christians eventually concluded that he had been delayed (2 Pet 3).

Seventh-day Adventists face a similar problem today. The church has proclaimed the soon return of Christ for well over one hundred years. Several generations have grown up in the belief that they would meet Jesus, only to mature, age, and finally die without seeing their hopes fulfilled. It is not easy to maintain a spirit of expectancy over a long period of time. There is the constant danger of becoming disillusioned.

There are two ways to respond to the delay of the parousia. Some believe that there is no delay, as far as Christ himself is concerned. In their view God has set the time of Christ's return, and when that time arrives he will come. His purposes know no haste or delay; there only appears to be a delay because our perspective is limited. Supporters of this view remind us that God's experience of time is different from ours. With him, "One day is as a thousand years, and a thousand years as one day" (2 Pet 3:8). In addition, they often appeal to the concept of absolute foreknowledge. If God knows the future in all its detail, then he knows exactly when Christ will return. It really doesn't make sense to speak of the second coming as delayed; it will happen when God foresees it will happen.

The alternative view maintains that there has indeed been a delay. Christ intended to come earlier, but circumstances in this world have prevented him from doing so. In particular, he is unwilling to return when so many are unprepared to meet him. In his mercy, God does not wish "that any should perish, but that all should reach repentance" (2 Pet 3:9). This view makes human beings responsible for the delay, so it encourages us to hasten Christ's return by preparing ourselves for it and influencing others to do the same (cf. 2 Pet 3:12).

People occasionally respond to Christ's failure to come when expected by "time-setting." In order to generate a sense of urgency and enthusiasm, they predict Christ's return on or by a specific date and devote their energies to preparing for it. Such measures are counterproductive, however. They not only disregard the clear biblical statement that the time of Christ's return is unknown (Mt 24:36), but they inevitably lead to disappointment and despair. An artificial enthusiasm that arises from such measures is not the sort of readiness that the Bible describes.

The objections to time-setting also apply to attempts to construct elaborate chronologies of last-day events. They too can be a form of time-setting. They seek to establish the precise relationship of Christ's return to current events in order to heighten our anticipation. Ironically, their actual effect is often the opposite. By setting down a sequence of developments that will precede the second coming, these schemes unwittingly encourage people to believe that Christ cannot come until certain things have taken place, and this leads them to relax their efforts to prepare for it.

The meaning of hope

To conclude, there are several things that hope involves and several things it doesn't. On the negative side, hope does not require us to know exactly when Christ will come. In fact, an exhaustive account of the future would remove hope's essential element of uncertainty, or unexpectedness. Hope does not even require us to believe that Christ's return is immediate. Jesus discouraged his disciples from jumping to conclusions about the nearness of his coming (cf. Mt 24:6). This does not mean we can postpone it indefinitely, but we cannot make our hope dependent on a certain time frame or some specific sequence of events.[5]

In addition, hope does not require us to place eschatology at the center of our faith, in spite of its importance. For Christians, the most important part of human history lies behind us. In the climactic events of Jesus' life, death, and resurrection, God acted to secure our salvation for all time. The future is simply the outworking of what was decisively accomplished then, so our expectations have their only basis in what God has already done.

On the positive side, hope embraces four essential qualities. First, of course, it includes believing that Christ will return. Those who hope are confident that "the coming one shall come and shall not tarry" (Heb 10:37), so they face the future with optimism. We lose hope, obviously, when we doubt the promise of his coming or give way to despair. Second, hope includes wanting Christ to come. It means living for his return as the ultimate object of life. We live without hope if we live entirely for the present, if we allow the concerns of the moment to consume our attention and energy.

Third, hope involves watchfulness. It means knowing that Christ may come at any time, and recognizing the unique opportunities of our present situation. We lose hope when we relegate the Lord's return to the remote and irrelevant future, when we view it as having no more immediate significance than, say, the eventual cooling of the sun.

Finally, hope includes preparation. It means fulfilling our present responsibilities with enthusiasm and dependability. As the parable of the servants indicates, we lose hope if we presume upon the delay of Christ's return to neglect our duties and indulge our appetites. The wicked servant did not deny that the master would eventually come home, but he felt no sense of urgency to prepare for the event (Mt 24: 45–51).

In a word, to live in hope is to live for the future in the present out of confidence in the past.

---

5. This is not to say that it is either impossible or undesirable to develop a general outline of the end of history, only that we must avoid emphasizing the chronological aspect of eschatology at the expense of the personal content of Christian hope—the reunion of Christ with his people.

STUDY HELPS

Questions for review

1. According to SDA eschatology, what activities and events precede Christ's return?

2. What happens when Christ returns?

3. What takes place during and after the millennium?

4. What is the ultimate fate of the wicked?

5. What is the meaning of eternal life and how have people questioned the concept?

6. How does Christian hope regard the future? How does it regard the present?

7. What are the biblical "signs of the times" and what do they mean?

8. How do different people respond to the fact that Christ has not yet returned?

Questions for discussion

1. This chapter lists a number of objections people have raised to the idea of eternal life. How would you answer each of them?

2. How important is the hope of a future life to a sense of meaning in this life? Would a Christian commitment make sense if there were no life after death?

3. To what extent have descriptions of heaven in pictures and music influenced your concept of human destiny? Has this effect been positive or negative?

4. The concept of the "great controversy" figures prominently in Adventist thought. How will the end of history resolve the major issues in this conflict?

5. What makes it especially difficult to wait for something when you don't know just when it will happen? How was the experience of the Millerites before the Great Disappointment different from that of Christians awaiting the return of Christ today?

6. How do you explain the extensive involvement of Seventh-day Adventists in medical and educational work when they believe that the return of Christ is near?

7. Can you think of a particular time when you really looked forward to

Jesus' coming? What makes the event a source of joy rather than fear?

Suggestions for Bible study

1. The Old Testament typically describes human destiny with reference to a person's life on earth and its effects on his descendants (see Exodus 20:5–6, 12; Genesis 15:5; Psalm 91:16). But what basis does the concept of the resurrection of the dead have in the following Old Testament passages? Hosea 6:1–2; Isaiah 25:8; 26:19; Daniel 12:1–3; Ezekiel 37:13.

2. Revelation 21–22 contains what are probably the best-known descriptions of the earth made new. How does the account in these chapters compare with the descriptions found in the following Old Testament passages? Isaiah 35; 55:12–13; 60; 65:17–25; 66:12–14, 22–23; Zechariah 14:6–9; Amos 9:9–15.

3. The concept of a secret rapture of the church before the time of tribulation that precedes the visible return of Christ is prevalent among conservative Christians. Some of the biblical texts used to support this view are Matthew 24:40–41; 1 Thessalonians 4:17; 5:2. What is your response to this idea? What texts support the contrary view that God's people remain on the earth until Christ returns in glory?

4. Study the great parables of Jesus recorded in Matthew 25. What themes do they have in common? Taken together, what do these parables tell us about the return of Christ?

5. People often wonder about the nature of human relationships in the life to come. Many of the questions concern marriage and the family. What do the following passages indicate or imply as to the future of these relationships? Matthew 22:23–33; Mark 12:18–27; Luke 20:27–38; Isaiah 61:9; 65:23.

SUGGESTIONS FOR FURTHER READING

From Adventist writers

Besides the writings of Ellen G. White, there are numerous books by Adventist authors on the end of history. Indeed, there is probably no topic on which Adventists have written as much. A familiar approach is to outline history's closing events and indicate how near we are to the end of time. Examples are Fernando Chaij, *Preparation for the Final Crisis* (Mountain View, Calif.: Pacific Press Publishing Association, 1966); Robert H. Pierson, *Good-bye, Planet*

Earth (Mountain View, Calif.: Pacific Press Publishing Association, 1976); and George McCready Price, *The Time of the End* (Nashville, Tenn.: Southern Publishing Association, 1967).

Along with works of this nature, there are those which examine the meaning as well as the content of the end of history. This is Sakae Kubo's approach in *God Meets Man: A Theology of the Sabbath and Second Advent* (Nashville, Tenn.: Southern Publishing Association, 1978).

The delay of Christ's return is a topic of considerable interest to Seventh-day Adventists. Herbert E. Douglass maintains that God expects a higher level of character development among his people in the last days in *Why Jesus Waits* (Washington, D.C.: Review and Herald Publishing Association, 1976), and *The End: The Unique Voice of Adventists About the Return of Jesus* (Mountain View, Calif.: Pacific Press Publishing Association, 1979).

Other works that focus on the experience of God's special people at the end of history include Beveridge R. Spear, *Cry Aloud* (Washington, D.C.: Review and Herald Publishing Association, 1973); and Morris L. Venden, *The Return of Elijah* (Mountain View, Calif.: Pacific Press Publishing Association, 1982).

There are also books that emphasize the special preparation needed for the trying times ahead, such as Fernando Chaij, *The Key to Victory* (Nashville, Tenn.: Southern Publishing Association, 1979); and DeWitt S. Osgood, *Preparing for the Latter Rain* (Nashville, Tenn.: Southern Publishing Association, 1973).

In ominous tones, Lewis R. Walton describes the momentous forces he sees lurking within the Adventist church in *Omega* (Washington, D.C.: Review and Herald Publishing Association, 1981) and *Decision at the Jordan* (Washington, D.C.: Review and Herald Publishing Association, 1982).

Articles by Jonathan Butler, Roy Branson, Richard Coffen, and Tom Dybdahl in a *Spectrum* issue featuring eschatology (vol. 8, no. 1) suggest that the present is meaningful and deserves our constructive attention even though it will end with Christ's return. Charles Scriven argues for an affirmation of life in this world while we prepare for the next in "Two Kinds of Hope," *Adventist Review,* May 31, 1984.

In his much-discussed article "The World of E. G. White and the End of the World," *Spectrum,* vol. 10, no. 2, Jonathan Butler examines the cultural and historical context in which *The Great Controversy* was written.

From other writers

There is an enormous diversity among Christian thinkers as to what the end of history involves. Some construct elaborate scenarios while others insist that we should emphasize its basic meaning and avoid attempts to spell it out. The style of works in this area is similarly diverse. Many are book-rack paperbacks intended for popular consumption, while others are weighty scholarly tomes for the dedicated academician. Only one generalization is possible:

Whatever your level of interest, there is surely something in the area of eschatology that will hold your attention.

Popular for many years, Hal Lindsey, *The Late Great Planet Earth* (Grand Rapids, Mich.: Zondervan Publishing House, 1970), presents a breathless account of earth's last years from a "dispensationalist" point of view. Readers who like a sensationalist approach to religious issues will enjoy this.

In *The Last Things: An Eschatology for Laymen* (Grand Rapids, Mich.: William B. Eerdmans Publishing Co., 1978), George Eldon Ladd refutes dispensationalist eschatology with a careful analysis of relevant New Testament passages. This book is particularly effective, since Ladd grew up accepting the dispensationalist perspective.

G. C. Berkouwer, *The Return of Christ,* trans. James Van Oosterom, ed. Marlin J. Van Elderen (Grand Rapids, Mich.: William B. Eerdmans Publishing Co., 1972), thoroughly discusses the major issues of Christian eschatology. Berkouwer's perspective is conservative, and he is conversant with the full range of contemporary scholarship.

Paul S. Minear, *Christian Hope and the Second Coming* (Philadelphia: The Westminster Press, 1954), explores the meaning of the principal biblical symbols associated with the theme of Christ's return.

One of the best works available on human destiny is John Hick, *Death and Eternal Life* (New York: Harper & Row, Publishers, 1976). Its wide-ranging survey of religious and philosophical interpretations of death and afterlife are readable and highly informative, although its concluding attempts to formulate a constructive synthesis are far less helpful. Another analysis of eschatological issues is Hans Schwarz, *On the Way to the Future: A Christian View of Eschatology in the Light of Current Trends in Religion, Philosophy, and Science* (Minneapolis: Augsburg Publishing House, 1972).

The implications of the future for life in the present have interested many Christian thinkers. Two responses to this question in the past several years are Carl E. Braaten, *Eschatology and Ethics: Essays on the Theology and Ethics of the Kingdom of God* (Minneapolis: Augsburg Publishing House, 1974), and Ted Peters, *Futures—Human and Divine* (Atlanta: John Knox Press, 1978).

16

THE DOCTRINE
OF THE SABBATH

**Biblical
basis**

"Remember the sabbath day to keep it holy" (Exodus 20:8).

"Blessed is the man . . . who keeps the sabbath" (Isaiah 56:2).

"The sabbath was made for man, not man for the sabbath; so the Son of man is lord even of the sabbath" (Mark 2:27–28).

Genesis 2:1–3	Luke 4:16
Exodus 20:8–11	Luke 23:56
Exodus 31:12–17	John 5:1–16
Deuteronomy 5:12–15	Colossians 2:16–17
Deuteronomy 10:1–5	Hebrews 4:3–10
Isaiah 58:13–14	Revelation 7:1–4
Mark 2:23–3:6	Revelation 14:9–11

INTRODUCTION

Last is never least in Christian theology. Our discussion of the sabbath appears here, not as an afterthought, but as the climax of our review of the major contents of Christian faith. We give the doctrine of the sabbath a place of its own, not because it has no essential relation to any of the other doctrines we have examined, but because it relates to all of them in a special way.

Seventh-day Adventists are probably best known by people in general for the religious significance they attach to the seventh day of the week. They are not the only Christians to do this, nor were they the first, but Adventists are the largest Christian denomination to observe the seventh day.

The doctrine of the sabbath has an interesting history in the Adventist church. Early Adventists accepted the sabbath under the influence of Seventh Day Baptists and more or less adopted their approach to the doctrine.[1] They regarded sabbath observance as the appropriate response to a divine command that has never been changed.

The sabbath in Adventist history

The sabbath acquired additional significance for Seventh-day Adventists within their unique eschatological perspective. Returning to the biblical sabbath, they believed, was the final phase in the long work of recovering the pure faith of biblical Christianity. Furthermore, its observance is the identifying mark of God's people at the end of time. Early Adventists believed that the sabbath established their identity as the remnant church which keeps the commandments of God— all of them (Rev 12:17). Indeed, they held, the sabbath represents the "seal of God" mentioned in the book of Revelation (7:2–3). It indicates complete loyalty to God and acceptance by him. As a result, the contrasting religious practice, Sunday observance, signifies a rejection of God's authority.

During the past few years, Adventist scholars and theologians have begun to take a new look at the sabbath. Instead of concentrating on the origin and identity of the biblical sabbath or on its dramatic eschatological significance, Adventists are now exploring its larger meaning. They are seeking to relate the sabbath to some of the major themes of the Christian faith and are exploring the potential value of the sabbath experience for human life in general. We could say that Seventh-day Adventists are in the process of moving from a doctrine of the sabbath to a more comprehensive theology of the sabbath.

The sabbath today

In order to give this aspect of Adventist belief the treatment it deserves here, we need to do several different things. In keeping with the traditional concerns of Adventism, we need to review the biblical evidence for Christian sabbath observance. This will lead us to survey the biblical treatment of the sabbath, as well as the "first-day" texts in the New Testament. We must also deal briefly with the

1. Raymond F. Cottrell describes the indebtedness of Seventh-day Adventists to Seventh Day Baptists for their understanding of the Sabbath in "Seventh Day Baptists and Adventists: A Common Heritage," *Spectrum,* vol. 9, no. 1, pp. 3–5.

change from sabbath to Sunday as the generally accepted day of Christian worship and examine the religious significance of this historical development.

Then we will explore the meaning of the sabbath in the context of Christian faith as a whole. We will try to show how it relates to the principal themes we have already examined—the doctrines of God, man, salvation, church, and last things. Our discussion will conclude with a consideration of appropriate sabbath observance.

If our efforts are successful, the sabbath will emerge as something more than one among several Seventh-day Adventists beliefs, and much more than just a peculiar religious practice. We will appreciate it as one of the most important theological and experiential resources that Adventists have. Properly understood, the sabbath is the capstone of Adventist theology and potentially its most valuable contribution to the larger Christian world.

THE SABBATH IN THE BIBLE

Sabbath in the Old Testament

The Bible first mentions the seventh day of the week in the story of creation. Having made the world and its inhabitants in six days, the Lord rested on the seventh day, which he blessed and hallowed (Gen 2:1–3). Later, one of the ten commandments identifies the seventh day of the week as ''sabbath'' and requires its observance (Ex 20:8–11; Deut 5:12–15). This indicates that sabbath keeping is one of the primary responsibilities of human beings. Both the Exodus and the Deuteronomy versions of the decalogue command us to abstain from work in honor of God's activity, but the two versions refer to different divine actions.

In Exodus 20, the reason given for sabbath observance is God's creative activity. Our sabbath rest commemorates his original rest at the conclusion of creation (Ex 20:11). In Deuteronomy 5, however, the reason given for sabbath observance is God's deliverance of the Israelites from Egyptian bondage (Dt 5:15). This suggests that the sabbath commemorates salvation as well as creation.

Besides these important references to the sabbath, the Old Testament contains many others. A number of them describe the sabbath as a reminder of the special relationship that exists between God and his chosen people. According to Exodus 31:12–17, for example, the sabbath is a sign of sanctification and is meant to be kept forever. According to Isaiah 58:14, God intends for the sabbath to be a delight to his people.

Exodus 16 recounts the miraculous way God fed the Israelites in the wilderness. Each morning the ground was covered with a mysterious substance they could eat. But there was no manna on the sabbath, and the manna kept from the previous day remained fresh—the only time in the week this happened. This story is significant, in part, because it refers to sabbath observance prior to the dramatic proclamation of the law from Mount Sinai, thus refuting the idea that the sabbath was not kept before the ten commandments were given.

The New Testament also contains many references to the sabbath. We do not find a direct command to keep the day holy, but its sacred significance is clearly assumed. Proper sabbath observance was a point of contention between Jesus and the Pharisee. In what is probably the most famous New Testament passage on the sabbath, Jesus defended his disciples against the charge of sabbath breaking because they happened to pluck and eat a few grains of wheat. He insisted that the sabbath was made for man, not man for the sabbath (Mk 2:27–28). His point was that the sabbath was meant to be a blessing to human beings, rather than a burden.

Jesus and the sabbath

The true purpose of the sabbath also emerges from the numerous accounts of Jesus' sabbath miracles. According to the Gospels, Jesus healed people on the sabbath no fewer than seven times during his ministry. These stories indicate that the relation between the sabbath and healing is more than coincidental; Jesus was trying to demonstrate what the sabbath is all about. His actions portray the sabbath as a day of healing, or salvation, a day meant to restore people to the fullness of life that God intends for all of us. The New Testament puts the sabbath in a very positive perspective.

People sometimes interpret Paul's polemic against legalism as a rejection of the sabbath, but the apostle's specific concern was the misuse of the law as a means of gaining salvation. He never taught people to ignore its basic precepts. Colossians 2:16 contains Paul's most controversial reference to the sabbath: "Therefore let no one pass judgment on you in questions of food and drink or with regard to a festival or a new moon or a sabbath."

Paul and the sabbath

Many believe that this text justifies disregarding the sabbath, but the historical context of the letter to Colossae supports a different conclusion. It suggests that Paul objected to a mistaken motive for sabbath observance, rather than to sabbath keeping itself. A complicated heresy apparently threatened the faith of those early Christians. Besides sabbath observance, it included, among other things, the worship of angels and various ascetic practices (cf. Col 2:18, 21). When

Paul mentioned the sabbath, he had in mind the kind of sabbath observance involved in this false religious system, not sabbath observance as such.[2]

Implicit evidence for sabbath

The New Testament does not state in so many words that early Christians worshiped regularly on the sabbath, but there are indications that this was the case. Paul regularly attended synagogue services, as Jesus had done during his earthly life (Lk 4:16). During his missionary travels he typically began proclaiming the gospel in each town by visiting the local synagogue, whenever there was one (Ac 13:14, 44; 14:1; 17:1–2; 18:4, 19). It is natural to assume that those who accepted Jesus as the Messiah continued to worship on the seventh day of the week.

At least twenty years after Jesus' crucifixion, Luke wrote that the women who prepared his body for burial rested on the sabbath ''according to the commandment'' (Lk 23:56). This reference suggests that the sabbath needed no introduction to Luke's readers; they were familiar with its observance.

Perhaps the strongest indication that members of the apostolic church kept sabbath is the silence of the New Testament on the subject. We know that early Christians worshiped regularly (cf. Heb 10:25), and we know that many of them were Jews, with a lifetime of sabbath keeping behind them. If becoming Christians led them to worship on another day of the week, this would have been a drastic departure from their tradition. It would surely have been a source of controversy, just as the question of circumcision was. It could hardly have escaped mention in the apostolic writings.

The ''first day'' in the New Testament

The New Testament not only says nothing to indicate that early Christians disregarded the sabbath, but it also attaches no religious significance to the first day of the week. There are eight references to the first day in the King James Version of the New Testament. One of them, Mark 16:9, was probably not a part of the original Gospel. Four pertain to visits to Jesus' tomb early on the morning of his resurrection (Mt 28:1; Mk 16:2; Lk 24:1; Jn 20:1). The context of one of them, Luke

---

2. Samuele Bacchiocchi makes the point in these words: ''We conclude therefore that Paul in Colossians 2:16 is not condemning abstinence from food and drink or the use of sacred days such as the Sabbath, but the wrong motive involved in their observance. What Paul attacks is the promotion of these practices as auxiliary aids to salvation, and as means to gain protection from the 'elements of the universe' '' (*From Sabbath to Sunday: A Historical Investigation of the Rise of Sunday Observance in Early Christianity* [Rome: The Pontifical Gregorian University Press, 1977], p. 358).

24:1, suggests that the women visited the tomb on the first day of the week precisely because it was not considered sacred.

John 20:19 describes Jesus appearing to his disciples on the evening of the first day of the week, hours after his resurrection. They were gathered behind shut doors out of fear of the authorities, not in order to hold a religious service.

In 1 Corinthians 16:2 Paul encourages his readers to put something aside on the first day of every week so he can take a contribution to the Christians in Jerusalem. He doesn't want to solicit funds during his coming visit. Some people conclude that the believers in Corinth were worshiping on Sunday. But this is advice to Paul's readers as individuals ("each of you"), not a call for collections during their worship services. In fact, the text says nothing at all about a religious service.

The only text in the New Testament to mention a religious service on the first day of the week is Acts 20:7. It describes Paul's eventful meeting with Christians at Troas, as he traveled toward Jerusalem to complete his third missionary journey. Several things prevent us from concluding that this verse describes a regular first-day service.

One is the fact that Paul planned to leave "on the morrow," after a week in Troas. The meeting was a farewell occasioned by Paul's departure, not a regular weekly occurrence. Second, the meeting occurred in all likelihood on Saturday night, as the New English Bible indicates, so it may have been a continuation of sabbath services that Paul and his fellow believers held together. Third, the fact that Paul resumed his journey on the next day implies that the first day of the week did not hold particular religious significance for him. In fact, it may be that he waited to start traveling until the sabbath was over, because he wanted to keep it holy. This text therefore does not describe a regular religious service among Christians on the first day of the week.

Many people believe that Revelation 1:10, "I was in the Spirit on the Lord's day," indicates that the apostolic church held Sunday to be sacred. It is true that in time the expression "the Lord's day" came to refer to the first day of the week,[3] but there is nothing to suggest that this was its meaning in the book of Revelation.

---

3. The *Seventh-day Adventist Bible Commentary* makes this point in discussing Revelation 1:10: "Although this term ['Lord's day'] occurs frequently in the Church Fathers with the meaning of Sunday, the first conclusive evidence of such use does not appear until the latter part of the 2d century in the Apocryphal Gospel According to Peter (9, 12; *ANF*, vol. 9, p. 8), where the day of Christ's resurrection is termed the 'Lord's day.' Since this document was written at least three-quarters of a century after John wrote the Revelation, it cannot be presented as a proof that the phrase 'Lord's day' in John's time refers to Sunday" (Washington, D.C.: Review and Herald Publishing

**The uniqueness
of the sabbath**

Those who maintain that Christians have no obligation to observe the sabbath often argue that it was part of the Hebrew system of worship which the ministry of Jesus superseded. Like such things as animal sacrifices and circumcision, they believe, it once had a role to play in the lives of God's people, but it is no longer important. However, there are several things about the seventh-day sabbath that distinguish it among the various aspects of Old Testament religion.

One is the nature of the event which the sabbath commemorates. Unlike the Passover, for example, which celebrates an important event in Hebrew history, the sabbath is a memorial of creation. It celebrates the origin of the world, rather than national deliverance, so it has univeral significance. It is potentially important for every human being.

Another thing that makes the seventh-day sabbath unique is its relationship to the weekly cycle. The Hebrews observed other sabbaths and holy days, but all of them are identified by the calendar. They are determined by days, months, and years. The Day of Atonement, for example, was the tenth day of the seventh month. Not only does the sabbath come more often than any other holy day, but its occurrence does not correspond to any natural phenomenon. Months, of course, are related to the behavior of the moon, and the year is related to the cycle of the seasons. But there is nothing in the realm of nature that establishes the seven-day week, and with it, the weekly sabbath.[4]

Some people question whether the days of our week now are continuous with the weekly cycle of biblical times. They wonder if changes in the calendar have affected the identity of the sabbath. There is no indication that the seven-day weekly cycle has been interrupted since apostolic times. Calendar changes have involved the day of the month, intending to bring the date into harmony with the season

---

Association, 1957, 7:735). For a scholarly discussion of the expression "Lord's day" in early Christian literature, see Samuele Bacchiocchi, *From Sabbath to Sunday: A Historical Investigation of the Rise of Sunday Observance in Early Christianity* (Rome: Pontifical Gregorian University Press, 1977); Fritz Guy, " 'The Lord's Day' in the Letter of Ignatius to the Magnesians," *Andrews University Seminary Studies* 6 (1968):46–59; William H. Shea, "The Sabbath in the Epistle of Barnabas," *Andrews University Seminary Studies* 4 (1966):149–175.

4. There have been attempts to associate the weekly sabbath with the different phases of the moon, but the results are not convincing (see Niels-Erik A. Andreasen, *The Christian Use of Time* [Nashville, Tenn.: Abingdon, 1978], p. 23; and *The Old Testament Sabbath* [Missoula, Mont.: Society of Biblical Literature Dissertation Series, 1972], pp. 3–5, 94–101).

of the year, but they did not affect the days of the week.[5] As a matter of fact, we now make an adjustment in the calendar every four years in order to account for the actual time of the earth's rotation around the sun. Leap year contains 366 days, instead of the usual 365. Adding a day to the month of February, however, does not affect the weekly cycle. If February 28 comes on a Monday, the next day is always Tuesday, whether it is February 29 or March 1.

The sabbath and the ten commandments

The most distinctive feature of the sabbath in the Old Testament is its inclusion in the ten commandments, which are often referred to as the "moral law," because they embody universal human obligations. There is nothing temporary or restricted in their scope; they apply to human beings in every situation, in every period of history. And there, right in the middle of these timeless precepts, is the command, "Remember the sabbath day, to keep it holy" (Ex 20:8). Its location implies that it is just as important as any of the others.

In fact, even within the Decalogue the sabbath is distinctive. The fourth commandment is the only one that specifically identifies the giver of the law. It states that he is the creator of the world, which establishes his authority over human beings. He has the right to impose obligations and require obedience.

Second, the fourth commandment has a somewhat arbitrary, or gratuitous, character. Unlike the other nine, it does not follow as a logical consequence of recognizing that we have obligations to God and to other human beings. Every other command makes sense, if you think carefully about what the human situation requires. But there is no reason to honor a day except for the fact that God asks us to, and there is no reason to keep the *seventh* day holy apart from the fact that God set this particular day aside and endowed it with unique significance. This is one reason why sabbath observance serves as a special indication of loyalty to God. It expresses the allegiance of people who need no other reason for doing something than the fact that God asks them to.

Several things indicate that the ten commandments, or the moral law, occupied a special place among the many regulations that governed Hebrew life and worship (cf. Dt 10:1–5). According to the

---

5. The famous change from the Julian calendar to the Gregorian calendar in 1582 involved "dropping" ten days, so that October 4 was followed directly by October 15. But the weekly cycle was not affected. October 4, 1582, was Wednesday, and the next day, October 15 according to the new reckoning, was Thursday (William Markowitz, "calendar," *Academic American Encyclopedia* [21 vols.; Danbury, Conn.: Grolier Incorporated, 1984], 4:28).

biblical account, God himself spoke the ten commandments from Mount Sinai to the entire congregation of Israel, not long after he delivered them from Egypt (Ex 20:1). The law stated the basic conditions of God's covenant with the children of Israel as his chosen people. They were so overwhelmed to hear the voice of the Lord, however, that they begged Moses to intercede for them. Consequently, God communicated his other instructions to Moses, who wrote them down and taught the people (Dt 31:9).

According to the biblical narrative, God himself also inscribed the ten commandments on two stone tablets. They were the only commands to receive such direct divine attention, and they were the only commandments to be placed within the ark of the testimony, which occupied the most holy place in the Hebrew sanctuary (Ex 25:21).

It is clear, then, that the ten commandments in general, and the sabbath commandment in particular, were not just a few of many ritual requirements that came to an end with the death of Christ. The evidence indicates that they embody God's expectations of human beings in every time and place. By definition, moral obligations are permanent; they can never be done away with, or "fulfilled" in this sense of the word (cf. Mt 5:17–18). As a result of sin, of course, the ten commandments do not represent a means of gaining righteousness, but this doesn't mean we can ignore them. They continue to set the standard for human behavior, and they provide a guide for life.[6]

To summarize, the Bible upholds the importance of the sabbath in both the Old and New Testaments. The sabbath began with creation, and it occupies a place in the ten commandments. It signified God's special relationship with the people of Israel, but its meaning applies to all other human beings, as well. Jesus honored the Sabbath and illuminated its true significance. There is no indication in the New Testament that early Christians disregarded the sabbath or transferred its significance to another day of the week.

FROM SABBATH TO SUNDAY

How the change occurred

Today the vast majority of Christians worship on the first day of the week. Since there is no biblical evidence to support the practice, it is natural to wonder when and why it began. There is no simple answer to this question; in fact, it is one of the most complicated problems in early Christian history. We cannot review the extensive discussion of

---

6. Recall the discussion of salvation and the law of God in chapter 11 above.

this important question here, but we can sketch some of the major factors involved in the change.[7]

The transition from sabbath to Sunday observance by the majority of Christians was a gradual development. It began very early in the history of the church, and it took place over a long period of time. People sometimes say that the Roman emperor Constantine changed the day of worship with the Sunday law he decreed in the early fourth century, but there is evidence that some Christians worshiped on Sunday from as early as the middle of the second century—that is, within fifty years of the death of the apostles. On the other hand, there is evidence that most Christians attached special significance to the sabbath down into the fourth and fifth centuries. Such evidence indicates that the change was not the effect of any single decision, but rather was the result of a long process.

The writings of early Christians give several reasons to support their Sunday observance. The one most frequently mentioned is Jesus' resurrection from the dead on that day of the week.[8] Another is the fact that creation began on that day.[9] This is ironic, of course, since the Bible describes the seventh-day sabbath as a celebration of creation, and the New Testament indicates that Christian baptism recalls the resurrection of Jesus (Rom 6:3, 4).

It is significant that no early Christian writer supports Sunday observance by appealing to the Bible. In fact, one important theologian named Tertullian, who lived in northern Africa about A.D. 200, openly admitted that there is no scriptural support for the practice. But, he argued, "You can vindicate the keeping of even unwritten tradition established by custom."[10] In other words, in his view the general practice of the church is enough to establish something, even if there is no biblical evidence for it.

Another factor contributing to the change from sabbath to Sunday was the growth of anti-Jewish feelings within the church. The Romans officially recognized the Jewish religion, and in the beginning, Christians profited from the close relationship between Christianity and Judaism. But as Christianity grew in size and influence, this

---

7. For a recent account of this important development, see Samuele Bacchiocchi, *From Sabbath to Sunday: A Historical Investigation of the Rise of Sunday Observance in Early Christianity* (Rome: Pontifical Gregorian University, 1977).

8. For example, *Epistle of Barnabas* 15, in *The Apostolic Fathers,* trans. and ed. J. B. Lightfoot (London: Macmillan and Company, 1891; reprint, Grand Rapids, Mich.: Baker Book House, 1962), p. 152.

9. Justin, I Apology 67, in *Early Christian Fathers,* trans. and ed. Cyril C. Richardson (London: The Macmillan Company, 1970), p. 287.

10. *The Chaplet* 4, in *The Ante-Nicene Fathers,* 3:95.

association became a liability, and Christians wanted to distinguish themselves from Jews. One way to do this was to disregard sabbath keeping, since this was a conspicuous Jewish practice. Consequently, we find early Christian statements discouraging sabbath observance along with those encouraging the observance of Sunday.

An early second-century letter of "Barnabas" from Alexandria, Egypt, for example, states that it is impossible for anyone to keep the seventh day holy.[11] It goes on to say that Christians celebrate Sunday, the day Jesus rose from the dead. Toward the end of the same century, Irenaeus, an important church leader in southern France, took the opposite tack. He said that Christians should not keep idle one day of rest, because they are constantly keeping sabbath by giving homage to God.[12] Once Sunday keeping was fairly well established, some writers argued that Christians didn't need sabbath because they had Sunday to observe.[13]

The growing support for Sunday observance reached a climax in the fourth century with two important developments. The Roman emperor Constantine issued the first Sunday law in A.D. 321. It read, "On the venerable Day of the Sun let the magistrates and people residing in cities rest, and let all workshops be closed."[14] This law carried civil authority. A number of years later, a church council held in Laodicea, a city in Asia Minor, issued the first Sunday law to carry religious authority. It said, "Christians shall not Judaize and be idle on Saturday but shall work on that day; but the Lord's day [an obvious reference to Sunday] they shall especially honor, and, as being Christians, shall, if possible, do no work on that day."[15]

Sabbath keeping had not died out among Christians at this time, however. There is evidence from the third, fourth, and fifth centuries that Christians had a special regard for the sabbath as well as Sunday. They celebrated the Lord's Supper on both days.[16]

11. *Barnabas* 15.

12. Irenaeus, *Proof of the Apostolic Preaching* 96; trans. Joseph P. Smith, S.J., "Ancient Christian Writers," vol. 16 (Westminster, Md.: The Newman Press, 1952), p. 104.

13. Tertullian, *On Idolatry* 14, *The Ante-Nicene Fathers,* 3:69.

14. *Codex Justinianus,* lib. 3, tit. 12, 3; trans. in Philip Schaff, *History of the Christian Church,* vol. 3 (5th ed.; New York: Scribner, 1902), p. 380, note 1; quoted in *Seventh-day Adventist Bible Students' Source Book,* ed. Don F. Neufeld and Julia Neuffer (Washington, D.C.: Review and Herald Publishing Association, 1962), p. 999.

15. Council of Laodicea, canon 29, trans. in Charles Joseph Hefele, *A History of the Christian Councils,* vol. 2, trans. and ed. H. N. Oxenham (Edinburgh: T. and T. Clark, 1896), p. 316; quoted in *Seventh-day Adventist Bible Students' Source Book,* p. 885.

16. *Apostolic Constitutions,* vii. 23 VII, chapter 23, in *The Ante-Nicene Fathers,* 7:495; Socrates, *Ecclesiastical History,* V, chapter 22, in *The Nicene and Post Nicene Fathers,* 2d series, 2:132.

Because there is no biblical support for the practice, Seventh-day Adventists regard Christian Sunday observance as a departure from the apostolic faith of the church. In more dramatic terms, they interpret it as one of the most important parts of an extensive apostasy that has afflicted Christianity for centuries. Besides a counterfeit day of worship, this religious system included the papacy, with its extravagant claims for the visible head of the church, and such unbiblical practices as infant baptism, prayers for the dead, the celibacy of the clergy, and the sacrifice of the mass.

Seventh-day Adventists believe that this development in the history of the church fulfills various biblical prophecies.[17] The book of Daniel describes the attempts of God's enemies to change the law (7:25). At one point in his ministry Paul predicted that fierce doctrinal conflict would follow his departure (Ac 20:29–30), and John indicated that religious errors were entering the church even during the days of the apostles (1 Jn 4:3). The fact that Sunday observance began early in the history of the church is therefore no proof that it is a part of genuine Christianity.

Historically, Seventh-day Adventists have interpreted their work as a continuation of the Protestant Reformation, which began the process of returning to the faith of the Bible. They believe that their specific task is to complete this work of reform by recovering the biblical sabbath during the closing days of human history. Sabbath observance thus has important eschatological significance for Adventists.

This is particularly evident in the description of the sabbath as the "seal of God." Several biblical passages describe God's people receiving a seal, or mark, in the forehead (Ezek 9:4, 6; Rev 7:3; 14:1). A seal is an instrument that leaves a distinctive mark, or impression. Official documents, for example, used to bear the seal of their author. Even the stone in front of Jesus' tomb bore a seal (Mt 27:66). A seal can be a stamp of approval, like the "Good Housekeeping Seal of Approval," or it can be a mark of identification which signifies ownership. In the relevant biblical passages, those who receive the seal of God enjoy a special relationship with him. They are completely loyal to God, and he protects them from the judgments that fall on the wicked.

Seventh-day Adventists believe that sabbath observance represents the "seal of God."[18] As we have mentioned, the fourth

17. See, for example, the discussion of Daniel 7:7–8, 19–25 in *The Seventh-day Adventist Bible Commentary* (7 vols.; Washington, D.C.: Review and Herald Publishing Association, 1953–57); 4:823–28, 830–38.

18. Ellen G. White makes this identification in several of her writings. For example, ". . . [T]he sabbath of the fourth commandment is the seal of God" (*The Great*

commandment alone identifies God, the giver of the law, as the sovereign of the universe, so it bears his mark, so to speak, in a special way. In addition, the "arbitrary" character of the fourth commandment makes keeping it a matter of personal loyalty to God. Sabbath observance, then, distinguishes certain people as God's very own.

Adventists believe that the sabbath acquires this special significance just before Christ returns, when religious and social conditions on earth reach an all-time low. A public expression of loyalty to God will then make people very conspicuous and invite persecution. Divine protection will become very important.

Besides the seal of God, the book of Revelation also speaks of the "mark of the beast" (14:9). This is something that identifies those who give their loyalty to God's enemies. It signifies that a person has abandoned all allegiance to God. Since observing the sabbath, the day of worship God established, is the seal of God, the mark of the beast logically represents a rival or counterfeit day of worship. We have seen that Sunday observance has no biblical support, so it is a likely candidate for the mark of the beast. Seventh-day Adventists believe that the time will come when keeping Sunday will indicate that a person has removed his loyalty from God and given it to the powers that oppose him.

This is perhaps the darkest, least attractive aspect of Adventist theology. It seems to label all who do not share certain convictions about the sabbath as avowed enemies of God. To many, such a belief appears arrogant and self-serving; it sounds as if Adventists believe their interest in the sabbath makes them God's favorites. To avoid giving this impression, several things need to be done.

One is to emphasize that the sabbath is God's gift to all human beings. Adventists should work to make this gift available to others, rather than congratulate themselves on possessing it. Seventh-day Adventists also need to avoid the legalistic spirit that many people associate with sabbath keeping. No one is saved by keeping the law, not even the fourth commandment. We need to remove legalistic connotations from the sabbath, both as we think of it ourselves and as we present it to others.

Third, and perhaps most important, Adventists need to remember that sabbath and Sunday observance acquire such dramatic significance only within a certain historical situation. Sunday keeping

Controversy, p. 640). "The Sabbath is a sign of the relationship existing between God and His people, a sign that they honor his law" (Testimonies for the Church, vol. 6, pp. 349–350).

becomes the "mark of the beast" only when people have a clear understanding of the issues involved in selecting a day of worship. That time has not yet come, so it is theologically inaccurate and personally irresponsible to speak of anyone as having the mark of the beast now.[19]

THE MEANING OF THE SABBATH

Traditionally Seventh-day Adventists tend to view the sabbath as a distinguishing feature of their church. The reference to the sabbath in the denominational name reflects the desire to let people know that Adventists are different from the majority of Christians. But the sabbath is more than a mark of distinction, and its theological impact extends beyond eschatology. It has an important bearing on every aspect of Christian faith. To appreciate more fully the significance of the sabbath, we need to explore its relation to the major themes of Christian faith reviewed in the preceding sections of this book.

The sabbath and God

The sabbath is a powerful testimony to the sovereignty of God. Only he can create, and only he can make something holy. This is why Adventists object so strongly to the change from sabbath to Sunday as the Christian day of rest and worship. Without a clear divine mandate, such a development is nothing less than an affront to God. As the source of reality, God is radically different from everything else. The sabbath calls attention to the qualitative distinction between God and the world, so it excludes idolatry. It is impossible to represent the creator adequately by means of any creaturely object; instead, the sabbath symbolizes God's presence by means of time rather than space.

The sabbath not only emphasizes the infinite distance between God and the world; it also calls attention to God's closeness to the

---

19. Ellen G. White is emphatic on this point: ". . . [T]here are now true Christians in every church, not excepting the Roman Catholic communion, who honestly believe that Sunday is the Sabbath of divine appointment. God accepts their sincerity of purpose and their integrity before Him. But when Sunday observance shall be enforced by law, and the world shall be enlightened concerning the obligation of the true Sabbath, then whoever shall transgress the command of God . . . is worshiping the beast and his image. . . . And it is not until the issue is thus plainly set before the people, and they are brought to choose between the commandments of God and the commandments of men, that those who continue in transgression will receive 'the mark of the beast'" (*The Great Controversy,* p. 449).

world. God did not create the world and lose interest in it or leave it to run on its own. The world continues to exist only because his power sustains it. He is deeply concerned with everything that happens in it, and the sabbath expresses his commitment to the world he made.

The sabbath also reveals that creation is not a casual activity on God's part; rather, it expresses the very essence of his divinity. God affirms the value of creation at each stage in the process. In the first chapter of Genesis we find the repeated expression, ''God saw that it was good.'' This shows that God appreciated what he made, and the sabbath shows that God values the world enough to celebrate its existence.

In the same way, the sabbath demonstrates that God is a personal being. It proves that God is not a blind force, or an unconscious cosmic power which creates because it has no alternative. God creates out of personal freedom; it is something he chooses to do, not something he is compelled to do. The sabbath expresses God's creative freedom by showing that he creates when he chooses and refrains from creating when it pleases him.

The sabbath further demonstrates God's personness by showing that he seeks personal relationships. God not only enjoys and values what he creates; he also seeks fellowship with his creatures. He invites us to share the joy that he experienced with the completion of his creative work. The Bible speaks of the sabbath as ''entering God's rest'' (cf. Heb 4:3–10), suggesting that the sabbath is God's gift to us, not something he imposes on human beings to lord it over them or exact submission from them. The sabbath is an opportunity to share a joyous experience with God himself.

The sabbath, then, gives us a rather well-developed portrait of God. It calls to mind his essential qualities of immanence, transcendence, power, and personness. It reminds us, too, of his basic attitude toward the world. He is not only conscious of it and interested in it; he is generous and loving toward it, as well.

The sabbath and creation

If we look at the God-world relationship from the other side, the sabbath also tells us some important things about creation. Precisely as a created entity, the world is finite and contingent; it has its limits. It is less than supremely powerful, and it is less than supremely important. Nothing in the world deserves our ultimate loyalty.

For all its limitations, however, the world is nevertheless something good. It is not divine, but this does not make it evil. The sabbath affirms the dignity and value of what God has made. According to the fourth commandment, sabbath rest extends even to beasts of burden. The earth and its creatures are important because God made them and cares about them; their value does not depend on their potential usefulness to human beings. Refraining from labor on the sabbath permits us to look at our environment from a fresh perspective, seeing it as something beautiful rather than merely useful. The sabbath presents the world to us as a work of art, not as a warehouse.

Because it establishes the dignity and value of creation, the sabbath affirms all the dimensions of creaturely existence. God created the world of space and time, and he pronounced it "good." To be physical is nothing to be ashamed of, then, and time is something positive rather than negative.

People often think of temporal reality as inferior, or even evil. A traditional view of God, for example, places him beyond time in a static realm of "eternity," as if temporality would compromise his perfection. But the sabbath upholds the value, the goodness, of time. For one thing, it calls our attention to time as the primary mode of divine revelation. According to the Bible generally, God reveals himself predominantly in events, in history, rather than in things. The sabbath also suggests that God himself experiences time, since it points to a transition from creating to resting on God's part. In addition, the sabbath implies that everything that happens in time has value. In sanctifying a part of time, God shows that all of time is important; the other six days of the week, and the activities that fill them, are also significant. So the sabbath has something to say about life in general and reality as a whole, as well as about their divine source.

The sabbath also has much to say about human beings. It describes our relationships to God, to each other, and to the rest of creation. In each relationship there are contrasting dynamics of distance and proximity.

The sabbath and human life

To begin with, the sabbath reminds us that we are finite and dependent; we are creatures, subject to the sovereignty of our creator. In view of God's infinite superiority, we owe him praise and adoration. In fact, this is our first responsibility—to love God with all the powers of our being (Dt 6:5). It takes priority over all other obligations—to family, friends, and society. Sabbath observance acknowledges our recognition of God's claims on our lives, but it does more than that. It celebrates his lordship. We rejoice in the knowledge that he is ultimately in charge of things.

The sabbath not only emphasizes the vast distance between human beings and God; it also points to the close relationship between them. Created in God's image, human beings have a unique capacity for fellowship with him. In his company, we can enjoy the fruits of his creative activity. The sabbath gives us an opportunity to celebrate our heritage as God's representatives in the world he has made.

The sabbath also addresses our relationship with other human beings, and here, too, we find the dynamics of distance and proximity. The sabbath is a day of freedom, and freedom from labor means freedom from bondage to other people. According to the fourth commandment, servants are not to work on the sabbath. Since no one is subordinate to another on sabbath, each person stands before God in his individual identity and dignity. On the sabbath we step out of the various stations we occupy during the week. This reminds those who work for others of their basic liberty as children of God, and it reminds those who direct others during the week that they too are under the sovereignty of God.

By setting us free from labor, the sabbath reminds us of our true significance. We have a tendency to look to our occupations, or our income, for assurance that our lives are worthwhile. But the sabbath tells us that we are important because we matter to God. He loves us as his children, quite apart from what other people think of us. The sabbath reminds students that academic accomplishments do not exhaust their significance as human beings. It reminds others that their status within the organization that employs them, or the profession they have trained for, is not the most important thing about them.

The sabbath is a day of freedom *for,* as well as freedom *from.* Because it frees us from the things that separate us during the week, the sabbath gives us unique opportunities for fellowship. On the sabbath, differences of occupation and education lose their significance. We realize that what we have in common before the Lord is more important than the various structures that distinguish us during the week, so we can associate with each other as equals and enjoy each other's company as brothers and sisters in Christ.

For these reasons, the sabbath has important social implications. It attaches such value to human beings that no person can ever be merely the property of another. A real appreciation for the sabbath would therefore make slavery impossible. The sabbath speaks against every practice that deprives human beings of their sense of worth and dignity. Oppressive economic and social structures, which make it impossible for people to provide for themselves, contradict the message of the sabbath. Those who appreciate the meaning of the sabbath will seek to eliminate such things.

The sabbath also illuminates the relationship between human beings and the rest of creation. By reminding us of our creatureliness, the sabbath makes us aware of our unity with the natural world. In light of the sabbath, we see our dependence on the environment to supply our needs, and we sense our common destiny with the earth.

We also become aware of what distinguishes us from the other forms of creaturely existence, and this sense of distance from creation does two things. On the one hand, it allows us to see the world as something valuable and significant in its own right. It does not exist merely for us; it exists for God. He made it and pronounced it good. The sabbath, then, permits us to enjoy the world for its own sake and prevents us from viewing everything in light of its potential to meet our needs.

This sense of distance from the rest of creation also encourages a sense of stewardship on man's part. The ability to step back and look at the world as something worthy in itself, and not merely valuable to us, is the same ability that enables us to have such influence on it. We have a responsibility to care for the world, not merely to enjoy it. We do not need to apologize for using the resources of the earth to meet our needs, but we must exercise this ability responsibly. We might say that the sabbath provides the basis for a theological ecology; it calls for respect for our environment.

As a day of worship, the sabbath reminds us of our uniqueness in the scheme of things. Of all earth's creatures, only human beings are not exhaustively defined by their place within the natural cycles of this planet. We can look beyond the specific space-time continuum in which we live. Because it elevates us above the daily round of activity that meets our physical needs, the sabbath calls attention to the needs of the spirit and reminds us that our source and destiny lie beyond the realm of material things. In the words of Jewish theologian Abraham Joshua Heschel, ''The seventh day is a reminder that God is our father, that time is life and the spirit our mate.''[20] The sabbath, therefore, is an opportunity for self-realization, a day on which we can realize most fully our human potential.

In addition to its important connections with the doctrines of God and man, the sabbath also relates to the doctrine of salvation. To begin with, the sabbath commemorates God's saving activity as well as his creative activity. As we noticed earlier, the reason given for sabbath observance in Deuteronomy 5 is God's deliverance of Israel. This was the primary example of salvation in the Old Testament. Some New Testament scholars see a parallel between creation week and passion week, the momentous climax of Jesus' life that began with his

The sabbath and salvation

20. *The Sabbath: Its Meaning for Modern Man* (New York: The Noonday Press, 1975), p. 76.

cleansing of the temple and ended with his crucifixion on the sixth day.[21] Just as God rested when the work of creation was complete, so Jesus rested in the tomb when the work of redemption was complete. We can celebrate both accomplishments each sabbath.

The sabbath is an appropriate symbol of the nature of salvation, too, reminding us that our salvation is the work of God, not a human achievement. On sabbath we cease from our own works in the world to contemplate the works of God. In their light we realize the relative insignificance of anything we can accomplish, and we sense our utter dependence on God. We are aware that of ourselves we can do nothing. All of this resembles our situation in the experience of salvation. Salvation, too, is entirely the gift of God. We do nothing to contribute to it; we can only accept what God has done for us. To receive salvation, we have to give up all self-reliance and trust completely in him.

The sabbath further illuminates the experience of salvation with its emphasis on divine-human fellowship. The purpose of salvation is to reconcile human beings to God, and the sabbath symbolizes this experience. Because the sabbath is also a sign of sanctification, according to the Bible, it directs our attention to that aspect of salvation, too, reminding us of God's desire to work within us to transform our lives after his likeness.

In an earlier chapter, we observed that a symbol not only points to something beyond itself; it also participates in that to which it points. This is true of the sabbath. As a symbol of salvation, the sabbath does not merely direct our attention to certain features of the experience; it promotes the experience. Effective sabbath observance can help us experience salvation more fully.

The clearest indication of this is the sabbath miracles of Jesus.[22] It was no coincidence that Jesus healed so often on the sabbath. His purpose was not just to show that the prevalent concept of the sabbath was mistaken; he wanted to do more than prove that the sabbath was not meant to be a burden. He wanted to demonstrate what the sabbath was for, so he healed people to get the point across.

The message of these miracles is that the sabbath is a day for wholeness and restoration. The Greek word for "healing," remember,

---

21. This is the view of L. S. Thornton, *The Dominion of Christ* (London: Dacre Press, 1952). David H. Kelsey discusses Thornton's analysis of the typologies at work in the gospel in *The Uses of Scripture in Recent Theology* (Philadelphia: Fortress Press, 1975), pp. 57–64.

22. See John C. Brunt, *A Day for Healing: The Meaning of Jesus' Sabbath Miracles* (Washington, D.C.: Review and Herald Publishing Association, 1981).

also means "salvation." Jesus intended his dramatic actions to awaken people to the fact that sabbath could be an experience of salvation for all of them. The sabbath is a day for wholeness, an opportunity for life in all its fullness. When we realize the saving significance of the sabbath, sabbath keeping can enhance and contribute to the experience of salvation.

The sabbath also bears on the corporate dimension of salvation. In other words, it has implications for the doctrine of the church. First of all, it reminds us that the community of the Spirit is the creation of God. There are scholars who believe that the outstanding example of God's creative power in the Old Testament was the origin of Israel. God created Israel out of nothing, so to speak, and made of her a nation. Similarly, the Christian church owes its existence entirely to the power of God; it is not the product of human activity.

The sabbath and the church

We have already explored the interpersonal significance of the sabbath. It frees human beings from various forms of bondage to each other, and in so doing, it frees them for new and richer fellowship. Certainly this has a bearing on the life of the church. The sabbath reminds us that every member is essential to the body of Christ, and it provides us with opportunities to enjoy the company of other Christians. This makes the sabbath the appropriate day for public worship.

Finally, the sabbath has important eschatological significance. We noticed earlier that Seventh-day Adventists believe that it will become a decisive religious issue just before Christ returns, but it has eschatological meaning for other reasons, too.

The sabbath and the future

One is the way the sabbath directs us beyond the things of this world. By calling us apart from the ordinary activities of life, the sabbath reminds us that our present situation is not permanent. The things that occupy our time and attention during the other six days of the week do not deserve our ultimate concern, because we are on our way to something better. We must not allow the joys and sorrows of life here, however worthy of our interest, to distract us from it.

At the same time, the sabbath gives us a foretaste of the life to come by making available to us in a promissory way the ultimate reward of God's people. The work of salvation will reach its goal when God makes his eternal home with men in the new earth, but the sabbath anticipates that situation by providing an opportunity for intimate relationship with God here. The experience of eternity can begin now in the lives of those who appreciate the meaning of the sabbath and experience salvation to the fullest.

The sabbath also directs us to the future with its assurance that God has not abandoned the earth. He instituted the sabbath as an expression of his commitment to creation. In spite of all that sin has done to destroy the beauty of this planet, it is still God's world, and he promises to restore it to its former splendor. More than that, he intends to fulfill his purposes for all his creatures, particularly human beings. The sabbath assures us that we will eventually become everything that we were originally meant to be.

There are indications that the sabbath, too, will play a role in human destiny. One prophetic portrait of the future life describes the inhabitants of the new earth coming to worship God from sabbath to sabbath (Isa 66:23). Even in this ideal situation, it seems, human beings will enjoy periods of rest and worship.

The sabbath, then, is a powerful symbol for the entire experience of salvation. It illuminates all its dimensions—personal, social, and historical—just as it sheds extensive light on the fundamental doctrines of God and man. From all this it is clear that the sabbath has enormous theological importance. It is far more than a curious religious practice by a relatively small segment of Christianity. It adds significance to the entire range of Christian beliefs and provides a means of uniting them into a cohesive, coherent body of faith.

The sabbath and the reign of God

Let us conclude this exploration of the sabbath's meaning with a reference to the reign of God. The sabbath is closely related to the reign of God, and the importance of the sabbath to Adventist life and thought is one reason for taking this idea as the guiding theme of this review of Adventist theology.

The sabbath reminds us that God is the origin and destiny of creation. Human history began with the reign of God, and it will end in the same way. To an extent, sin interrupted God's reign in human affairs, but it did not remove it. The sabbath indicates that God has been at work to restore his sovereignty ever since. It also shows that God does not reign by simply imposing superior power; he typically works in and through the things he has made. The creator unites with the creature to accomplish his purposes. We see this most clearly in the person of Jesus—a human being in whom God was personally present. We also see it in the mission of the church, in which human activity is infused with divine power. The sabbath, then, celebrates the reign of God in all its aspects.

THE SABBATH EXPERIENCE

The sabbath is an experience as well as a doctrine, and this deserves careful attention, too. As a symbol, the sabbath participates in that to which it points, and it opens up dimensions of personal experience not otherwise available to us. Perhaps here more than anywhere we see the interplay between belief and practice. A deeper understanding of what the sabbath means can make our experience of the sabbath richer. On the other hand, the appropriate celebration of the sabbath can help us to grasp its meaning more fully.

The first step toward a rewarding sabbath experience is to recognize what a challenge real sabbath keeping is. Several things make sabbath observance difficult. For one, the presupposition of the sabbath flies in the face of our modern secular consciousness. People today, for the most part, have no sense of the sacred. From a purely analytical viewpoint, all words are simply sounds, and all places are pieces of real estate. There are no sacred names, no holy places, and there is no such thing as holy time. As measured by clocks and calendars, all days are alike; one moment is identical to every other. The sabbath, however, presupposes that all time is not the same. Time can be holy. Certain hours have a unique capacity for the manifestation of God's presence.

The challenge of sabbath keeping

Another obstacle to rewarding sabbath keeping is our culture's attitude toward the weekend. In the Western world in general, and in the United States in particular, the weekend is leisure time. Just think of all the television commercials urging you to take it easy when the work of the week is over. There is a tendency to regard the sabbath as just a part of the weekend, and to view the day as a chance for self-gratification. But if this is all we expect from the sabbath, we have not begun to appreciate what it means, and our sabbath experience is bound to be inadequate.

The tendency to think of sabbath keeping in negative terms also interferes with a meaningful sabbath experience. People often begin questions about sabbath observance with the words, ''What's wrong with . . . ?'' If we are determined to draw a fine line between right and wrong sabbath activities, or to find out how much we can get away with and not actually break the commandment, then we're not even close to understanding what the sabbath is all about.

This brings us to the basic principle of effective sabbath keeping, which is to think of sabbath observance in positive, rather than negative, terms. Our basic concern should not be to avoid what's

The opportunity of sabbath keeping

wrong on the sabbath. Rather, it should be to discover what we can do that will help us realize the meaning of the sabbath to the fullest. We need to approach the sabbath as a glorious opportunity, not as a tedious obligation. We need to remember the basic purpose of the sabbath—to realize our true identity in relationship to God, to other human beings, and to the world we live in. The sabbath experience is life at its best.

Another suggestion for developing a meaningful sabbath experience is to do everything possible to reinforce a sense of the day's uniqueness. This will lead us to put some obvious restrictions on our activities. Hard manual labor and blatantly commercial enterprises are obviously inappropriate; they can't help but interfere with the spirit of the sabbath. But we may need to consider other limitations, depending on our situation. A graduate student in religion, for example, may choose to put aside his theological books on the sabbath, not because there is something "wrong" with reading such things on sabbath, but because this is his work. It is the sort of thing he does throughout the week. To continue the same activity right through the sabbath would rob the day of its special quality and make the sabbath just another day. For the same reason a pastor I knew made it a practice to complete his sermon preparation before the sabbath began. He wanted to reserve the sacred hours for fellowship with his family.

Celebrating the sabbath with special activities or ceremonies can also encourage a sense of its uniqueness. Family traditions can make an important contribution here. Many people find it helpful to mark the beginning and the end of the sabbath with a distinctive worship service. Special meals and out-of-the-ordinary activities can also contribute to this goal.

Worship and fellowship have an important role to play in the sabbath experience. This is a day to enjoy God's companionship and to celebrate his goodness. Our religious attitudes should be those of adoration and praise, rather than a concern for whatever needs we might have, spiritual or otherwise. The sabbath is a day for others. It is not meant to be spent in solitude, as a general rule. It provides a golden opportunity for families and friends to enjoy each other and to befriend those who are lonely.

Effective sabbath keeping doesn't just happen; it requires careful preparation. For our sabbaths to be meaningful, we need to give careful attention to them ahead of time. We will try to do everything possible in advance, so nothing distracts us from the central purpose of the day. The most meaningful experiences in life are often those that we look forward to the most. Hours of planning go into events like graduations and weddings. One of the things that makes such occasions significant is the fact that we expect them to mean a lot to us; we approach them with great anticipation.

Anticipation plays an important role in making the sabbath meaningful, too. The first word of the fourth commandment is "remember." This suggests that sabbath observance involves more than twenty-four hours out of the week; it applies to the week as a whole. In fact, it refers to a way of life. When we realize the profound experience that the sabbath represents, it becomes the high point of living. All of life becomes a pilgrimage to the seventh day.

So the sabbath is both a doctrine and an experience. It illuminates all the aspects of Christian faith, and it brings our essential identity as a human beings into focus. The sabbath also gives us a unique experience of the reign of God. It acknowledges his sovereignty over our lives and celebrates his accomplishments. The sabbath enables us to appreciate the marvelous gift of God's presence, and in doing so, it takes us to the heart of Christianity.

STUDY HELPS

Questions for review

1. What biblical evidence supports the Christian observance of the sabbath?

2. What makes the weekly sabbath unique among Old Testament commands and practices?

3. How did Christians come to worship on the first day of the week, rather than the seventh?

4. According to SDA theology, what is the eschatological significance of sabbath and Sunday observance?

5. What does the sabbath contribute to our understanding of God, man, creation, salvation, and last things?

6. What are the basic principles of effective sabbath observance?

Questions for discussion

1. To what extent does a rewarding sabbath experience depend on observing a specific day? Can a sincere Sunday-keeper worship as effectively as a sabbath-keeper?

2. Should the Seventh-day Adventist Church establish denominational standards for sabbath observance? Should church members in

different cultures decide how they can best keep the sabbath? Or should the matter be left entirely up to the individual?

3. Traditionally, devout Jews refuse to fast on the sabbath because they feel an obligation to make it a day of joy. What can we do to make the sabbath a positive experience, and not merely avoid "breaking" it?

4. Ellen White recommends spending part of sabbath in a natural setting in order to appreciate God's creative power more fully. What can people unable to leave cities or suburbs on sabbath do to achieve this purpose?

5. Several years ago a prominent evangelical Christian suggested making Saturday a legal holiday in the United States. He argued that the country needs a national day of rest and making it Saturday would avoid offending sabbath-keepers such as Jews and Seventh-day Adventists. How should Seventh-day Adventists react to such a proposal?

6. How is sabbath keeping an application of the Protestant principle of *sola Scriptura*—taking the Bible alone as the final rule of Christian faith and practice?

7. Seventh-day Adventists sometimes describe sabbath observance as the last great test human beings will face. How does it resemble the first test human beings faced in the Garden of Eden? Is it possible that some issue other than the sabbath will be decisive at the end of human history?

Suggestions for Bible study

1. The weekly sabbath was one of a number of days that the Hebrew people were commanded to observe. Study those mentioned in the following passages: Leviticus 23; Isaiah 1:13–14; Ezekiel 45:17; Hosea 2:11. What were they and what did their observance involve? How is the weekly sabbath similar to and different from other religious days?

2. Many people believe that three passages in Paul's writings indicate that Christians have no obligation to observe the sabbath. Carefully examine Romans 14:5–6; Galatians 4:8–11; and especially Colossians 2:14–17. You may also want to consult Bible commentaries on these verses. What is at stake in Paul's comments—sabbath keeping as such, or a particular kind of sabbath keeping?

3. Another New Testament passage mentioning the sabbath is Hebrews 4:3–10. Do these verses support Christian sabbath observance? Why or why not?

4. Study the various "sabbath miracles" of Jesus: (1) Mark 1:23–28 (cf. Luke 4:33–37); (2) Mark 1:30, 31 (cf. Matthew 8:14–17; Luke 4:38, 39); (3) John 5:1–16; (4) Mark 3:1–6 (Matthew 12:9–14; Luke 6:6–11); (5) John 9:1–41; (6) Luke 13:10–17; (7) Luke 14:1–6. What do these miracles tell us about both meaning and observance of the sabbath?

5. The themes of creation and salvation are closely related in the Bible. In fact, certain biblical scholars see a striking parallel between creation week and "Passion Week"—the last week of Jesus' earthly ministry. Compare Genesis 1 with the closing chapters of the four Gospels. Do you find any similarities? How do they illuminate the meaning of the sabbath?

6. Several biblical passages speak of God's people as receiving a "mark" or "seal": Ezekiel 9:4, 6; Revelation 7:3; 14:1, 9–11. According to these verses, what is the purpose of the seal and who receives it? What reasons are there for identifying the seal of God as the sabbath?

SUGGESTIONS FOR FURTHER READING

From Adventist writers

Ellen G. White discusses the sabbath in many different passages. She deals with the origin and significance of the sabbath and the origin and significance of Sunday observance in *Patriarchs and Prophets,* pp. 331–342, and *The Great Controversy,* pp. 433–460. She explores the meaning of the sabbath in the ministry of Jesus in *Desire of Ages,* pp. 281–289, and she makes a number of suggestions for effective sabbath keeping in *Testimonies for the Church,* vol. 6, pp. 349–368.

Besides Ellen White, of course, many Adventists have written on the sabbath. A complete listing of their books and articles would no doubt fill a book of its own. The following suggestions focus on some of the more recent publications.

For someone just beginning to think about the sabbath in theological terms, Fritz Guy's series of articles, "The Meaning of the Sabbath" (*Insight,* February 5, 12, 19, 1974), will be very helpful. Another readable work is John C. Brunt's discussion of Jesus' sabbath miracles, *A Day for Healing: The Meaning of Jesus' Sabbath Miracles* (Washington, D.C.: Review and Herald Publishing Association, 1981).

Perhaps the most comprehensive study of the sabbath by Adventist scholars is the symposium volume, *The Sabbath in Scripture and History,* ed. Kenneth A. Strand (Washington, D.C.: Review and Herald Publishing Association, 1982). Its first two sections discuss the sabbath and Sunday in the biblical period and in Christian church history. Its final section is devoted to "sabbath theology."

Niels-Erik Andreasen examines the biblical sabbath in two books: *The Old Testament Sabbath: A Tradition-Historical Investigation* (Chico, Calif.: Scholars Press, 1972); and *Rest and Redemption: A Study of the Biblical Sabbath* (Berrien Springs, Mich.: Andrews University Press, 1978). In a third work, *The Christian Use of Time* (Nashville, Tenn.: Abingdon, 1978), Andreasen explores the significance a weekly day of rest can have in the Christian life. General readers will find this discussion particularly interesting.

The transition from sabbath to Sunday observance by Christians has always fascinated Seventh-day Adventists. Samuele Bacchiocchi presents a scholarly examination of the phenomenon in *From Sabbath to Sunday: A Historical Investigation of the Rise of Sunday Observance in Early Christianity* (Rome: The Pontifical Gregorian University Press, 1977). The same author has also formulated a theology of the sabbath: *Divine Rest for Human Restlessness: A Theological Study of the Good News of the Sabbath for Today* (Berrien Springs, Mich.: Samuele Bacchiocchi, 1980).

Other contributions to a theology of the sabbath include the first part of Sakae Kubo, *God Meets Man: A Theology of the Sabbath and Second Coming* (Nashville, Tenn: Southern Publishing Association, 1978), and a special issue of *Spectrum* (vol. 9, no. 1), devoted entirely to the topic of the sabbath, entitled "Festival of the Sabbath." Besides offering a number of stimulating theological articles by Adventist authors, it also explores the sabbath in Christian art. One of the most helpful items in this issue is a selected bibliography with annotations on "Theology of the Sabbath." For students interested in pursuing Adventist work in this area, this bibliography is a good place to start.

From other writers

The sabbath may be one of the few theological topics on which Adventists have written about as much as anyone else. But there are some treatments of the subject by other writers that are immensely valuable, and a couple of them have exerted influence on Adventist thought in this area.

One is Abraham Joshua Heschel, *The Sabbath: Its Meaning for Modern Man* (New York: The Noonday Press, 1975). This meditation by a well-known Jewish rabbi will move anyone who has the slightest religious sensitivity. It is an excellent book for someone who wants to know how rewarding a sabbath experience can be.

Karl Barth discusses the sabbath in two passages of his great work, *Church Dogmatics,* ed. G. W. Bromiley and T. F. Torrance (Edinburgh: T & T Clark): vol. 3, bk. 1 (1958), pp. 98–99, 213–228, and vol. 3, bk. 4 (1961), pp. 47–72. Barth is always challenging, but his work is richly rewarding for the determined reader.

INDEX OF
BIBLICAL REFERENCES

INDEX OF
PERSONS

INDEX OF
SUBJECTS